THE STRUGGLE FOR
THE FALKLAND ISLANDS

THE FALKLAND ISLANDS

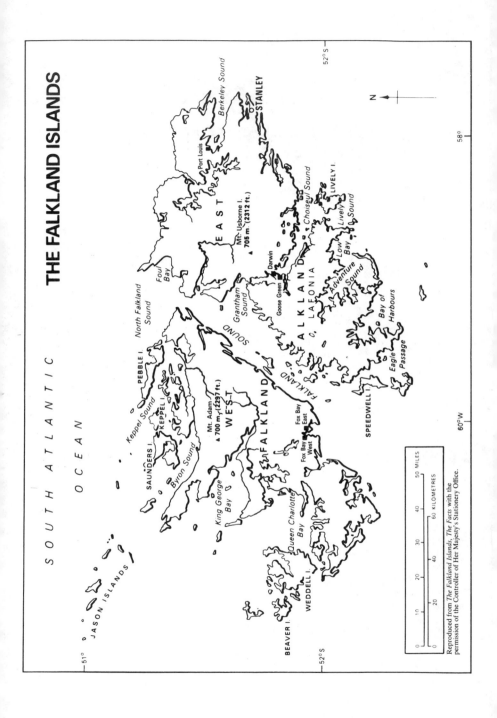

THE STRUGGLE

FOR THE

FALKLAND ISLANDS

A STUDY IN LEGAL AND DIPLOMATIC HISTORY

JULIUS GOEBEL

WITH A PREFACE AND AN INTRODUCTION BY
J. C. J. METFORD

YALE UNIVERSITY PRESS
NEW HAVEN AND LONDON

The publishers are grateful to the Royal Institute for International Affairs for permission to reproduce the article 'Falklands or Malvinas? The Background to the Dispute' by J. C. J. Metford which first appeared in *International Affairs*, July 1968, vol 44, no 3.

Printed in Great Britain by Hazell Watson & Viney Ltd, Aylesbury, Bucks

ISBN 0-300-02943-8 (cloth)
     0-300-02944-6 (paper)

CONTENTS

PREFACE
by J. C. J. Metford

IN 1951, when the voice of General Juan Domingo Perón, president
and 'democratic Caesar' of the Republic of Argentina, was at its most
strident, there was much to astonish a visitor to Buenos Aires. Streets
named *Defensa* ('Defence') and *Reconquista* ('Reconquest') recalled
the so-called 'English Invasions' of 1806–7 when Sir Horne Popham
carried off the Spanish royal gold in an unauthorised expedition,
leaving Sir David Baird to face the consequences, and the ill-fated
General John Whitelocke to surrender after failing in a government-
approved attempt to establish Britain on the River Plate. These events
are scarcely ever mentioned in English history books, but they loom
large in the minds of the people of Argentina.

The 1950s were a period of great outbursts of nationalistic and
xenophobic enthusiasm. Festooning the streets were banners proclaim-
ing, 'The Malvinas are ours'. At huge rallies in Luna Park stadium
members of the Peronista party and their supporters, after they had
exhausted shouts of 'Perón! Perón! Perón!', launched into, 'Englishmen! Give us back the Malvinas!' The intensity of feeling on this
issue could not be doubted. It united all Argentinians, *descamisados*
('shirtless ones') of the poverty-stricken suburbs, members of the
small urban middle class, even the beleaguered landowners who had
most to fear from the confiscatory policies of the new régime.

At school, children were taught that the English had deprived their
nation of lands which were rightfully theirs. Textbooks, atlases and
stamps showed a conglomeration of islands, constituting in all an area
about the size of Wales, as belonging to Argentina. In addition, the
Falkland Island Dependencies, South Georgia, the South Sandwich
Islands, and the Shag and Clarke Rocks to which there could be no
conceivable Argentinian claim, except that they were administered
from Port Stanley, were coloured as national territory. For good
measure, British Antarctic Territory was also included.

Two generations of Argentinians, like their predecessors, have thus
been conditioned to an axiomatic irredentism which no factual
discussion can remove. That is the reason why a brutal, dictatorial
military régime which has tortured and suppressed its opponents,
intellectuals and workers alike, was able to count on the wholehearted
support of the populace when it launched the invasion of the Falklands
and South Georgia in April 1982. Even such a prestigious and
respected figure as Señor Adolfo Pérez Esquivel, winner of the 1980
Nobel peace prize, himself opposed to the Military Junta and not
condoning the use of force, proclaimed that, like the rest of his fellow-

countrymen he supported their claims, 'for historic, legal and geographical reasons'. He added that 'the status of the islands represents a relic of colonialism in the context of Latin America'. (*The Times*, London, 19 May, 1982.)

That even responsible persons should be so emotional over such an issue; that a whole nation should be prepared to damage itself economically at a time when it could least afford it; that it could contemplate with equanimity the sacrifice of thousands of its men for some bleak, windswept islands suitable for penguins, sheep and those who can face a toilsome existence is difficult to understand. Thirty years ago I was similarly perplexed that such a fuss was being made over what seemed to an outsider to be a relatively unimportant issue when what really mattered then (as now) were the almost insoluble problems arising from the need to transform an agrarian, feudalistic society into a modern, industrial nation through much-needed measures for social reform and improvements in conditions for the mass of the people. Above all, a sensible expenditure of national resources would be the exploitation of the potential mineral wealth of Patagonia rather than the pursuit of claims to a territory which had been under continuous British administration for more than a hundred years, constituting thereby a more than presumptive title.

To assess the justification for Argentina's emotive attitude was difficult. The only substantial work in English was the book here reprinted. It is an impressive examination of the material available at that date for the early history of the dispute. Although additions are now necessary, particularly for the later nineteenth and twentieth centuries, it remains essential reading. Access to archival material in the U.S.A. and Britain (despite the fact that many crucial files in the Public Record Office, London are 'closed' and thus unavailable to researchers) now makes possible a more detailed assessment of events and diplomatic exchanges, but Dr Goebel's work is still of considerable worth.

In an attempt to supplement Dr Goebel's researches and to discover what really happened in the 1930s, I undertook an examination of documents in the Public Record Office, London, and the mass of largely repetitive and assertive material emanating from Buenos Aires. Some of my conclusions were incorporated in the brief article here reprinted as an introduction.

Dr Goebel's book must be read in the context of the sentiments prevailing at the time when it was written. It was a period when isolationism in the U.S.A. was at its most vociferous, and nowhere more so than in the Law School of Yale University. Revulsion from the enormous casualties suffered in the 1914–18 war, the rise of pacifism and disillusionment with Europe, all contributed to the belief that the Americas should entrench themselves behind the barrier of the Atlantic Ocean and never again become involved in a European war. Colonialism was thought to be the root-cause of European rivalries and one way to protect the New World would be to neutralise existing British, French and Dutch possessions there. Presumably this was the subconscious motive for Dr Goebel's researches, but it must be acknowledged that he approached the question of the sovereignty of the Falkland Islands with commendable scholarly integrity.

Many questions remain unanswered. No substantive archival material has yet been adduced to prove the existence of the 'secret agreement' to which Dr Goebel devotes much attention. He should also have explained why, after persistently refusing to recognise Argentinian rights (to avoid claims for removing Argentinian settlers from the Falklands in 1831), the U.S.A. became more sympathetic when it became necessary to placate Latin American nations so that they would align themselves with her particular policies. He could also have recounted Argentinian protests on every possible occasion, whether over the issue of stamps or questions of citizenship, and detailed British replies, but this would have made his book at least twice the present size.

The tragedy of the present situation is that Argentina has created a myth which no rational or legal argument can destroy. From the 1880s onwards, every document which might support Argentina's case has been carefully collated and published in 'white and blue books' (the national colours), historians have written vast tomes, politicians have whipped up mass hysteria. The result is that every Argentinian is convinced of the justice of their cause and is prepared to die for it, without asking whether the end result would be worth the sacrifices which they would be called upon to make. For them ultimate sovereignty is a matter of national honour and no arbitrator will convince them that they should accept less, even if it means becoming a colonial power over fewer than two thousand people, over three hundred miles from their shores, who wish for nothing more than to continue their peaceful lives as British subjects.

There is also another dimension to the problem which Latin American and other nations should not overlook. Whatever their possible wealth in oil (yet to be proved), fisheries, and natural products still to be exploited, the Falkland Islands hold the key to the Straits of Magellan and South Georgia to the Antarctic. Whoever holds them will control the development of that area for the rest of this century.

May 1982

INTRODUCTION
by J. C. J. Metford

FALKLANDS OR MALVINAS? THE BACKGROUND TO THE DISPUTE

'A LAND without form or expression', wrote Viscount Bryce when he visited the Falkland Islands in the early years of this century. Never had he seen 'any inhabited spot that seemed so entirely desolate and solitary'. It is an ironical comment on the conduct of international affairs that the question of sovereignty over such an unprepossessing part of the world should once have brought Britain, France and Spain to the brink of war. It is equally incredible that, for over a century and a half, the disputed possession of the islands should have embittered relations between Britain and Argentina, two nations which, traditionally, and for the most cogent of economic reasons, should be firm friends.

During the 1950s, when General Perón was in power, slogans on banners and buildings stridently demanding: 'Englishmen, give us back the Malvinas!' were accepted as part of the *peronista* technique of bidding for popular support by playing upon the xenophobic passions of the masses. Nevertheless, years after Perón was driven into ignominious exile, the same slogans reappear with monotonous frequency and the demand for the 'return' of the Falklands is as insistent as ever, as the recent history of the dispute will show.

On December 16, 1965, yielding to unremitting Argentine lobbying, the Twentieth General Assembly of the United Nations adopted Resolution 2065 which invited the United Kingdom and Argentina to enter into discussions which would lead to a peaceful solution of the differences between them. Success in obtaining such international recognition of the dispute encouraged renewed activity in Buenos Aires. In January 1966, the Argentine Government created the *Instituto y Museo Nacional de las Islas Malvinas y Adyacencias* (Falkland Islands and Dependencies Institute and National Museum) to be housed in a building under the control of the Ministry of Foreign Affairs. The object of the Institute was 'to stimulate the national conscience' to demand the return of the Islands to Argentina, and to collect and disseminate information about this question. Arrangements were made for the establishment of a specialist library, and for propaganda talks and films throughout the nation. At the same time, advantage was taken of the visit of Mr. Michael Stewart, in his first period of office as British Foreign Secretary, once more to press the Argentine claim. Then, in February 1966, influential Argentines reactivated their Committee for the Recovery of the Falklands (*Junta de Recuperación de las Malvinas*), with the object of stimulating their Government 'to seek a rapid solution of this long-standing dispute'. Later, Sir George Bolton, Chairman of the Bank of London & South America, conscious of the damage which was being done to Anglo-Argentine trade relations, urged that the 'running sore' should be excised by the establishment of a condominium.

These developments attracted little attention in the United Kingdom, but the comic-opera attempt on September 28, 1966, by 20 young Argentine extremists belonging to the *Movimiento Nueva Argentina* (The New Argentina Movement) to stage *Operación Condor*, a 'symbolic' seizure of the islands, made the British public generally aware of the existence of the dispute. This episode may have been no more than a publicity stunt, organised by an illustrated magazine, which was reported to have put a special supplement on the Malvinas on the news stands in Buenos Aires within a few hours of the receipt of the news of the 'invasion'. The 'invasion' was said to have angered President Onganía, and to have been condemned by responsible opinion in Argentina as making the country appear ridiculous in the eyes of the world, but there is no doubt that the gesture was acclaimed by a large section of the populace. The 'invaders' became national heroes overnight. They were praised by the 62 pro-Perón trade unions, and the *Confederación General del Trabajo* (The General Confederation of Labour) threatened a 24-hour general strike if the extremists were punished for their patriotic action. President Onganía skilfully avoided trouble by having the 'invaders' removed from the Falklands, not to Buenos Aires where they would have been fêted, but to Ushuaia on the grounds that their offence had been committed within the jurisdiction of the Governor of Tierra del Fuego.

Something of the Argentine President's displeasure over this episode may have been due to the fact that talks then being conducted with the British Government offered the distinct possibility that Argentina's ambitions might at last be fulfilled. The substance of these negotiations may be inferred from the fact that early in 1968 Sir Cosmo Haskard, the Governor of the Falkland Islands, returned to his post after talks in London and reported to his Executive Council certain matters which they were sworn to secrecy not to reveal. Nevertheless, the Unofficial Members of the Council appear to have been so alarmed by the episode that, on February 27, they addressed an open letter to Parliament warning members that negotiations were in progress which could result in the handing-over of the islands to Argentina. They pointed out that the 2,000-odd islanders had never been consulted regarding their future and reiterated in bold type that they did '*NOT want to become Argentines*'.

Their appeal to fair play and to the right of self-determination may have had the effect of delaying an announcement which the Government was about to make regarding their future. Mr. George Brown's resignation may also have saved them momentarily. In any case, it fell ironically to Mr. Stewart, as almost his first act following his reincarnation as Secretary of State for Foreign Affairs, to face persistent questioning in the House of Commons about negotiations which probably began during his first term of office. Having previously given a pledge that nothing would be done to change the status of the islands without the consent of the inhabitants, he could scarcely do other than reiterate what he had said in Buenos Aires in 1966.[1]

For the moment, therefore, the Falkland Islanders are appeased but not wholly reassured. Lord Chalfont's ' philosophising ' in the House of Lords over the power of the United Nations made them suspect that a deal with Argentina was still a possibility.[2] As the persistent questions in the House of Commons revealed, many Members of Parliament shared the islanders' anxieties.

The British public is somewhat bewildered by the situation. In the past, while momentarily irritated (or slightly amused) by such episodes as the shooting-up of the British Embassy in Buenos Aires when the Duke of Edinburgh was staying there, the burning of Union Jacks in the streets and the sacking of the British Consulate in Rosario, they have felt no animosity against Argentina. Recently, however, their mood has changed and there are signs that, as in the case of Gibraltar, they are not disposed to hand over to an alien Power people who want to remain British. Nevertheless, accustomed to the erroneous charge that Britain spent most of the 19th century acquiring territory to which she had no right, and ignorant of the historical facts, the public wonders secretly whether there is some foundation for the Argentine claim. They have not been helped by successive British governments who have

---

[1] ' In our experience, no good is served by keeping unwilling subjects under one's flag, but when the inhabitants' wishes are clear, as in this case they are clear, then the wishes of the Falkland Islanders are more important than those of either the Government of the United Kingdom or that of Argentina.' *The Times*, January 14, 1966.

[2] ' Confirming that negotiations with the Argentine Government over the future of the Falkland Islands are continuing, Lord Chalfont, Minister of State, Foreign Office, caused a minor storm in the House of Lords yesterday by apparently suggesting that the views of United Nations might come before those of the islanders.'

Lord Conesford asked : ' " What right, if any, has the United Nations to interfere with our sovereignty over the Falkland Islands? " Lord Chalfont replied : " The very fact of membership of the United Nations implies that countries that belong to it derogate a certain amount of sovereignty to it." Later he said his remark was " philosophical ".' *The Times*, March 14, 1968.

consistently taken Lord Palmerston's view that there is nothing to discuss and have consequently refrained from publicising the British case.

On the other hand, the people of Argentina have been subjected over the years to such a barrage of propaganda, and to the publication of so many one-sided books and articles, that they regard as axiomatic the statement that the islands really belong to their nation and were filched from them by Great Britain.

What follows in the present article is therefore intended as a contribution to Anglo-Argentine understanding. Perhaps a statement of the chief arguments adduced by Argentina will make the British aware of the reasons why Argentines are so emotional about the question of sovereignty. It may also reveal to Argentines that there is also something to be said for Great Britain's present attitude.

*   *   *

It is essential at the outset to make clear what is in dispute. Argentina's maximum claim is to the Falkland Islands and the Dependencies. The Dependencies consist of South Georgia, the South Sandwich islands, the South Orkneys, the South Shetlands, the Graham Land peninsula and various barren Antarctic islands; they were brought under the administration of the Governor of Port Stanley, in the Falklands, in 1908. However, by the Antarctic Treaty of 1959, it was agreed to hold in abeyance all territorial claims in the area where there was international co-operation for scientific purposes. This means that, for the time being, Argentina will not press her claims to the South Orkneys, on the grounds that she has maintained a meteorological station on one of the islands, nor to Graham Land, on the principle of continental projection, nor to the other islands because they are dependencies of the Falklands, which she maintains are hers by right. The nub of the present question is therefore the status of the Falkland Islands.

These islands form an archipelago of about 200 small and two large islands enclosed within a rectangle of 120 by 60 miles and lying some 300 miles off Patagonia and 250 miles from the entrance to the Magellan Straits. When Charles Darwin visited the region in H.M.S. *Beagle* in 1834, he estimated that the total surface area of the islands was about half the size of Ireland, but the area of Northern Ireland alone would probably now be considered as nearer the mark. The two largest islands in the group, on which the history of the archipelago centres, are East Falkland, with an area of 2,500 square miles, where once stood Port Louis, or Puerta de la Soledad, now the seat of the capital, Port Stanley, and West Falkland (also called Gran Malvina). It is not certain why these islands became known in England as the Falklands, but the designation may be an extension of Falkland Sound, the name given to the strait between the East and West islands by Captain John Strong in the *Welfare* in 1690, probably in honour of Anthony Cary, third Viscount Falkland, then a Commissioner of the Admiralty and later First Lord. Las Malvinas, the name by which the archipelago is known in Argentina, is the hispanisation of the French name Les Malouines, recalling the intrepid Breton sailors from St. Malo who fished and hunted seals in those waters in the early 18th century.

East Falkland was first colonised as a consequence of the French hope of finding on the west coast of America compensation for their loss of Canada. In 1764, Antoine Louis de Bougainville, who had served in Quebec under Montcalm, was given permission by the Duc de Choiseul, Louis XV's Minister, to settle men and women from Acadia (Nova Scotia) and St. Malo on that island, so that it could serve as a staging post for the French penetration of the Pacific. Bougainville built a fort called Port Louis in honour both of his name-saint and his king, and laid the foundations of a French settlement. This caused consternation in Madrid because the Spaniards claimed dominion over all South America, except for the parts occupied by the Portuguese. Charles III therefore protested to his partner in the Bourbon Family Compact, and eventually a compromise was reached whereby Bougainville withdrew his colony but received a large sum by way of compensation. A Spanish governor took over from him, and Port Louis became known as Puerto de la Soledad.

Meanwhile, the British had been active in West Falkland. On January 23, 1765, Commodore John Byron, grandfather of the poet, obeying instructions to find a good harbour which could be a base for further surveys, went ashore on Saunders Island and took possession of it and all the neighbouring islands in the name of George III. He called the anchorage Port Egmont, in honour of the Earl of Egmont, then First Lord of the Admiralty, and left his subordinate, Captain Macbride, to reconnoitre the area. Macbride found Bougainville's settlement, told the settlers to depart because the islands belonged to Britain, and went back home to report. Within a year he was back in Port Egmont with some 100 settlers, but, in 1769, the Spaniards, having got rid of the French, resolved to remove the British and warned them to leave. As no notice was taken of their warning, the Spanish intendant in Buenos Aires sent a force of 1,400 soldiers to expel the settlers. Out-numbered, the small British garrison was obliged to capitulate and the Spanish occupied Port Egmont on June 10, 1770.

This insult to the British flag brought Britain, France and Spain to the point of war. Spain tried to calm the British by saying that the Governor of Buenos Aires had acted on his own initiative. Britain demanded that the governor's action should be disavowed and the settlement at Port Egmont restored. The diplomatic battle lasted until

January 22, 1771, when, the French having made it clear that they were in no position to go to war, and the Duc de Choiseul having been dismissed by King Louis, Spain agreed 'to deliver up . . . the port and fort called Egmont'. It was formally handed over on September 16, 1771, to Captain Scott of the frigate *Juno*. However, the cost of keeping the settlement was disproportionate to its value, and in 1774, as part of a general retrenchment, the naval garrison was withdrawn. A plaque was left reiterating British rights and concluding: 'In witness whereof this plate is set up, and his Britannic Majesty's colours left flying as a mark of possession'.

The Spaniards left West Falkland alone, and concentrated their activities on Puerto de la Soledad, which was used as a prison settlement. Governors were appointed, subservient to the Viceroy at Buenos Aires, until the Napoleonic invasion of Spain and the imprisonment in France of the Spanish royal family broke the links between the Spanish Crown and the Spanish possessions overseas. On May 25, 1810, the people of Buenos Aires set up the 'Provisional Governing Junta of the Provinces of the Río de la Plata', ostensibly to administer the area until Ferdinand VII should regain the throne of Spain. Early in 1811, Xavier Elío, Viceroy of La Plata, who refused to recognise the Junta, and regarded himself as the sole remaining representative of royal authority, agreed that the Governor of Montevideo should withdraw what was left of the Spanish garrison on the Falklands. The islands were thus uninhabited for many years, although they were visited at will by foreign whalers and vessels of many nationalities. From then onwards Spain took no further interest in the islands.

Much of the Argentine case for sovereignty rests on her claim that she inherited the rights which Spain abandoned. These rights in turn are held to be based on the papal grant of 1493, the Treaty of Tordesillas of 1494, and on discovery, and occupation. It is therefore necessary to examine briefly each of these points.

The papal bulls *Inter Caetera* of 1493, issued by Alexander VI, a Spaniard notoriously beholden to Ferdinand and Isabella, granted Spain all territory in the Indies to the west, and Portugal all territory to the east, of a line drawn from Pole to Pole 100 leagues west of the Azores and Cape Verde Islands. This arrangement was subsequently modified by the Treaty of Tordesillas of 1494, between Spain and Portugal, by which the demarcation line was set 370 leagues west of the Cape Verde Islands. The intention of these decisions, which were not acceptable to other European monarchs, was to avoid war between Spain and Portugal by defining spheres for discovery and colonisation; but the treaty was broken decades later when the Portuguese extended their settlements in Brazil to the west and south-west. In effect, therefore, Spain's claim to the exclusive possession of most of America was acknowledged only in so far as she could maintain it by force. In the centuries which followed, her supremacy was challenged many times. By the end of the colonial period the English, French and Dutch had established themselves in lands which Spain claimed as hers but from which she was powerless to expel the so-called intruders.

It is equally difficult to make a case for Spain on the grounds of discovery. An accurate answer to the question ' who first sighted the Falklands? ' is unlikely ever to be forthcoming. When evidence adduced from accounts of early voyages is submitted in support of one explorer as against another, it is always qualified by expressions of probability or possibility. Undoubtedly, Amerigo Vespucci, on his third voyage along the coast of South America, or Magellan on his way to the straits that bear his name, or Sir Francis Drake on his way round Cape Horn, or Hawkins when he found his ' Maiden-land ', *could* have caught a glimpse of the islands, but there is no certain proof that they, or the other candidates for the honour, ever did so. Scholars will continue to exercise their ingenuity to explain ambiguous marks on charts and maps, or to expound tantalising sentences in log-books and journals, but it is unlikely that anything positive will result from their efforts. Even in the 19th century, with improved navigational aids, mariners found it difficult to make a landfall on the Falklands, and, before then, ship after ship must have sailed quite near the archipelago without being aware of the existence of the islands.

If the balance of probabilities is to be struck, then there is much to commend Dr. Samuel Johnson's view that John Davis, commander of the *Desire*, a vessel in Cavendish's squadron, sighted some of the islands in the group on August 14, 1592. Another good candidate is Sebald van Weerdt. In January 1600, in command of the *Geloof*, he emerged from the Straits of Magellan on his return journey to Rotterdam and sighted three small islands, inhabited only by penguins and not marked on any map. The Dutch called these islands the Sebaldes and later identified them with islands in the West Falklands group. The name ' Sebaldes ' covers the archipelago on maps of the 17th and 18th centuries, and it was the name used by Bougainville in his initial proposals to colonise them. However, mere discovery without settlement has little bearing on the present question of sovereignty. This was admitted by Manuel Moreno, the Argentine Minister in London, who acknowledged to Palmerston in 1833 that ' to establish a right to dominion on the fortuitous act of discovery, or on a momentary possession, is not sufficient: it must be formal or tranquil settlement, which includes habitation and culture '.

No one would contest Bougainville's claim to be the first founder of a settlement on East Falkland at Port Louis, nor Spain's to have acquired his title by purchase. It is likewise accepted that the British were the first to settle on West Falkland, at Port Egmont. The agents of both parties proclaimed their rights over the rest of the territory, but the actual decision as to which claim was valid was a matter of diplomatic bargaining between Madrid and London, with the French intervening to help out the Spaniards.

When Captain Macbride was instructed to make a settlement at East Falkland, he was told to warn off settlers of any other nation whom he might encounter, but to refer the question of sovereignty to London. The subsequent forcible occupation of Macbride's settlement at Port Egmont by the governor of Buenos Aires obliged the Spaniards to choose between war and restitution and, unable to count on the support of France, they chose the latter course. Prince de Masserano, the Spanish Ambassador in London, stated in his declaration to Lord Rochford in 1771 that the restoration of the fort and port ' cannot, nor ought, any wise to affect the question of the prior rights of sovereignty '. This sentence was pointedly ignored in Lord Rochford's counter-declaration which spoke only of the Spanish disavowal of the Buenos Aires expedition against Port Egmont and the restoration of ' all things . . . to the precise situation in which they stood before the 10th of June 1770 '.

Spain's action in restoring the *status quo* has much embarrassed successive generations of proponents of the Argentine case. They have sought to explain it away by saying that Spain agreed to the compromise in order to avoid war, and because there was a secret agreement that, once honour was satisfied, the British would withdraw from Port Egmont, after a suitably discreet interval. However, no document embodying such an agreement has come to light to sub-stantiate this assertion. When, in 1833, Manuel Moreno, the Argentine representative in London, raised this point as part of his protest against the British reoccupation of the islands, Lord Palmerston immediately ordered a search through all the official correspondence of the period and was able to assure Moreno that there was no allusion in the cor-respondence between London and H.M. Ambassador in Madrid to any such undertaking. The Argentine evidence is drawn from Spanish and French dispatches, and proves no more than that Masserano was under the impression that the British would withdraw once they had received satisfaction. There was certainly no formal agreement in writing signed by both parties.

What seems to have happened is the following. During the weeks of negotiations following the expulsion of the British from Port Egmont, there were various suggestions as to what could be done to restore good relations between Britain and Spain. Spain twice raised the pos-sibility of evacuation by both sides, but linked this suggestion to other conditions which the British could not accept. At one point in the exchanges, Lord North, speaking unofficially, as he was at pains to point out, because it was not his department, hinted to one of the staff of the French embassy that Britain really did not want to remain in the Falklands and would leave if honour were satisfied. This conversation was naturally reported to Masserano, and by him to Madrid, but he could not obtain official confirmation from the British Government. Weeks later, when Charles III realised that he would have to go to war without his French ally if he did not come to terms, Masserano was instructed to accept the British demands in the knowledge (presumably based on the French embassy report) that the British would later leave the Falklands. After the agreement to restore the settlement had been fulfilled, Masserano asked the British when they were going to leave, but was told that no promise to this effect had been made. Eventually, of course, the British did go, but for reasons of economy, not because of any secret promise, and they left their flag flying and a plaque asserting their rights.

This act may have been 'perfidious Albion's' way of getting the best of both worlds. At the time of the negotiations, in order to avoid war, it may have suited a weak British ministry to let Masserano delude himself as to British intentions. Certainly the storm which raged in Parliament when it became known that the question of sovereignty had not been settled, made the government fully aware that they could not hope to survive public wrath if they abandoned Port Egmont. By leaving in 1774, for reasons of economy, the British kept their honour unstained, but made it clear where they stood on the matter of sovereignty.

However, the argument about the 'secret promise' is academic in both the practical and the figurative sense of the word. Spain abandoned the islands in 1811, and, although the Cortes at Cadiz expressed their intention of reoccupying them when the situation was more propitious, this moment never arrived. For almost 10 years the islands were *res nullius*, used by sealers and whalers but under no visible authority.

*   *   *

Spain never reasserted her rights in the Falklands, nor, more particularly, to East Falkland which she had acquired by purchase from Bougainville. That these rights passed to Argentina is a matter of assertion by Argentines rather than of direct transfer by Spain. In 1816, a majority of the provinces in what was formerly the Spanish Viceroyalty of La Plata declared themselves independent as the United Provinces of La Plata. The government of Buenos Aires, as the former seat of the Viceroy, assumed the lead in foreign affairs and in 1820 sent Captain Jewitt, an American in their service, to take possession of the Falklands. He ran up the flag of the new republic on the site of Puerto de la Soledad and returned to Buenos Aires. His action was without any noticeable effect on the masters of vessels in the vicinity who continued to fish and to slaughter wild cattle as they were accustomed to do. (It must be remembered that, at that period, the United Provinces had been recognised only by the U.S.A. but that other nations with interests in South America did not officially accept their independent existence. Britain did not grant recognition until 1825.) However, in 1824, Louis Vernet, who had settled in Buenos Aires, obtained a grant of land in East Falkland. His attempts to found a colony failed, largely, Vernet claimed, because foreign vessels would not respect the exclusive rights to cattle and fisheries granted him by the Buenos Aires Government. To give himself an appearance of authority, because Buenos Aires was powerless to help him, Vernet obtained in 1828 from the Government of the United Provinces of La Plata a grant of full sovereignty over East Falkland and Staten Land and, in 1829, the title of Military and Political Governor of the Falkland Islands.

Britain immediately made it clear to the Argentines that they had acted without taking into account British rights in the islands. The naval force, it was pointed out, had been withdrawn from Port Egmont in 1774 for reasons of economy, but sovereignty had not been abandoned and it was open to the British to return when they judged the moment appropriate. They had contested the Spanish claim to sovereignty and were certainly not prepared (as Palmerston put it in 1834) to permit ' any other state to exercise a right as derived from Spain which Great Britain had denied to Spain itself '.

The fact is that the United Provinces' proclamation of their ' right ' to succeed to Spanish possessions in their area was no more than a statement of intention. How much they could actually acquire depended, not on formal cession by Spain, but on how far they could prevent Spain from re-establishing her authority in a given area. For many years after the defeat of their armies in America, the Spaniards still hoped that they might one day win back their lost territories. When, finally, Spain agreed to recognise the independence of Argentina in 1859, it was Argentina without the Falklands, with no explicit transfer of any rights which Spain may have held over the archipelago. As Britain was mediator between the newly constituted nation and the former mother country, it would have been most unlikely that she would have permitted any such transfer or allowed into the treaty of recognition anything which could be interpreted as a challenge to British sovereignty in the islands.

A corollary to Argentina's claim to have succeeded to Spanish rights in the Falklands is her appeal to the principle of *uti possidetis.*

This was an arrangement adopted by the emergent Spanish American republics in the absence of any formal transfer of territories by the Spanish Crown. It meant that each of the new South American nations should be deemed to have succeeded to the lands attached to the former Spanish authorities in their areas at the 'critical date' of 1810 (or 1821 in the case of Central America)—*uti possidetis, ita possideatis,* 'as you possess, so you may possess'. As the Falklands were administered by the Governor of Buenos Aires in the last decades of Spanish colonial rule, it was claimed that they should pass into the control of the United Provinces of La Plata, later the Argentine Republic.

This argument obscures a number of facts. *Uti possidetis juris* was a rough and ready agreement between the new Latin American states to establish their respective territorial limits. (It led to many controversies and conflicts between the new nations, some of which persist.) As a principle, it could be applied only to a dispute between Latin American nations. For example, it could be invoked if Uruguay claimed the Falklands on the grounds that, at the 'critical date', the islands were, in fact, administered from Montevideo, and it was the Governor of Montevideo who withdrew the garrison and settlers. Whether it is applicable in a dispute with a non-Spanish American nation is open to doubt. In any case, *uti possidetis* was not formally adopted until the Congress of Lima in 1848, by which time the Falklands had again been under British control for a number of years.

*　　　*　　　*

The man who did most to assist Argentina's claim to the Falklands, or at least, to East Falkland, was Louis Vernet. As has been noted above, Daniel Jewitt's unsubstantiated proclamation of the sovereignty of the United Provinces in 1820 was not taken seriously by the subjects of any other nation. Vernet managed to establish a settlement on East Falkland, which may be said to have lasted from 1826 to 1831, and was able to obtain in 1829 the title of military and political governor of the islands, although there were formal British protests. Vernet was first and foremost a business man. The Buenos Aires Government owed his wife's family £20,000. He estimated that the right to the wild cattle, seals and fisheries in and around East Falkland would enable him to recoup the debt, and that the sale of provisions to the ships which put in at his settlement at Puerto de la Soledad would bring him a reasonable profit, as, indeed, proved to be the case.

It was a pity that this active and enterprising business man should have committed the cardinal blunder of trying to enforce his authority as reputed governor on American sailors who regularly fished in waters which he considered to be exclusively his. In July 1831, having acquired, as military governor, a small force of soldiers from Buenos Aires, he seized three United States vessels. One escaped, one was allowed to fish on condition that Vernet was given a share of the profits, and the third, with Vernet on board, proceeded to Buenos Aires so that the master could stand trial for illegal fishing.

Unfortunately for Vernet, United States affairs in Buenos Aires were in the hands of George W. Slacum, the consul, who was angered by the sight of a United States vessel under arrest by the forces of a government for which he appears to have had scant respect. Also unfortunate for Vernet was the appearance in the River Plate of U.S.S. *Lexington.* After hearing Slacum's complaint, her captain, Commander Silas Duncan, sailed to Puerto de la Soledad, arrested six Argentines, destroyed the battery and armaments and declared the islands free of all government. He justified his action on the grounds that Buenos Aires had no right to the islands and that, in interfering with United States ships on their lawful occasions Vernet had acted as a pirate and could therefore be treated as such in accordance with international law. President Jackson approved of Duncan's action and the islands became once more *res nullius.*

It is not relevant at this point to pursue the protracted controversy between Argentina and the United States which was the result of Captain Duncan's swift and brutal act of retribution. Diplomatic relations between the two countries were suspended for 11 years and the question of reparations was kept alive by Argentina for the rest of the century. What is of interest, however, is the fact that, at that period, the United States did not take seriously the Buenos Aires claim to the islands. In his famous message to Congress in December 1823, President Monroe had warned European Powers that they should no longer think of establishing colonies in the western hemisphere. Nevertheless, the United States did not protest when the British reoccupied the islands in 1833. The United Kingdom was regarded as continuing the 18th-century settlement. The Falklands were thus classed with the existing possessions of European Powers in America which, as Monroe had stated, were accepted by the United States. In the latter half of the 19th century, U.S. consular practice also showed acceptance of British sovereignty, and in 1902 the State Department included the Falklands in its list of British possessions.

As far as Vernet was concerned, Captain Duncan's actions put an end to any pretensions which he may have had to continue as an officer of the Buenos Aires Government. He resigned as governor, because he was no longer convinced of the justice of the Buenos Aires claim. Indeed, even as early as 1829, he had told Woodbine Parish, the British Consul-General in Buenos Aires, that he would like the British Government to take his settlement under their protection. He later stated that when he was assured that the British had not made a secret agreement with Spain to withdraw from West Falkland, he had realised that Buenos Aires had no claim to the islands. He therefore directed his efforts for many years after these events to securing compensation from Great Britain for the wild cattle and the property at Puerto de la Soledad which he said were his.

*   *   *

Much is made in successive presentations of the Argentine case of the next episode in the history of the islands: the supposed fact that Great Britain ' brutally ' and ' forcefully ' expelled the Argentine garrison in 1833. The record is not nearly so dramatic. After the commander of the *Lexington* had declared, in December 1831, the Falklands ' free of all government ', they remained without any visible authority. However, in September 1832, the Buenos Aires Government appointed, in place of Vernet, an interim commandant, Juan Mestivier. The British representative immediately lodged a protest, but Mestivier sailed on the *Sarandi* at the end of the year to take charge of a penal settlement at San Carlos, his Government's reserve on East Falkland. There was a mutiny, led by a sergeant of the garrison, and Mestivier was murdered. At this juncture, on January 11, 1833, H.M. sloop *Clio* arrived at Puerto de la Soledad when Pinedo, the commander of the *Sarandi* and 25 soldiers were attempting to re-establish order. The so called ' brutal ' eviction is laconically recorded in Captain Onslow's log:

> Tuesday 1 Jany. 1833.
> P.M. Mod. with rain 12.20 shortened sails and came to Port Louis (Soledad), Berkeley Sound . . . found here a Buenos Ayrean flag flying on shore. 2.30 out boats. 3 furled sails. 5.30 Moored ship . . .
> Wednesday Jany. 2. Moored at Port Louis
> A.M. Mod. cloudy . . . loosed sails and landed a party of marines and seamen and hoisted the Union Jack and hauled down the Buenos Ayrean flag and sent it on board the schooner to the Commandante. Sailmaker repairing the Main top Gallant sails. . . .

In the interval between these two entries, Onslow had ' civilly ' (his report) told Pinedo that he had come ' to exercise the right of sovereignty ' on the islands and asked him to haul down his flag on shore. Pinedo protested, but said that if the Buenos Aires flag were allowed to fly until January 5, he would leave with his soldiers and anyone else who wished to go. When Onslow proved adamant, Pinedo agreed to embark his soldiers, but he left his flag flying on shore. This was why Onslow sent it to him by one of the *Clio's* officers. Pinedo sailed on January 4 and was later punished by the Buenos Aires Government for failing to offer any resistance.

The British therefore reasserted their rights in the Falklands without a shot being fired. They could justify their action on three grounds: they were continuing the jurisdiction which they had exercised in the 18th century; they had never recognised any rights of the Buenos Aires Government in the islands and had protested against Vernet's and Mestivier's appointments. In any case, Spain's withdrawal from the islands in 1810, and the American destruction of Vernet's settlement in 1831, had made the islands *res nullius*, under the control of no visible authority, and thus open to occupation by any Power which could maintain itself on them.

*   *   *

Since these events in 1833, the Falkland Islands have been in the possession of the United Kingdom. The hoisting of the flag in Port Egmont and Puerto de la Soledad in January 1833 was followed a year later by the installation of a British governor. Since then, British administration has been continuous and, as it has been unbroken for over a hundred years, there is no doubt as to the international legality of the British title. To do justice to the Argentine case, however, it is necessary to mention at this point one other episode in 1833 which has been made much of by certain Argentine apologists: the supposed guerrilla activity of patriotic Argentines against the occupying British.

When Pinedo withdrew at Onslow's request, he appointed as governor, Juan Simón, headman of the *gauchos* who had remained on the island after the destruction of Vernet's settlement. This appointment had no validity, but the *gauchos*, and William Dickson, who had been Vernet's storekeeper, together with two former ship's masters, Matthew Brisbane and William Lowe, decided to carry on with Vernet's plans for a trading settlement. On August 26, 1833, three *gauchos*, one of whom was a certain Antonio Rivero, in company with five of the former convicts from Mestivier's prison settlement, killed Brisbane, murdered Juan Simón, brutally despatched a German and a Spanish settler, stole all they could and fled into the interior. Those settlers who escaped, including a woman and three children, took refuge on a small island where they endured great hardship until January 1834, when H.M.S. *Challenger* arrived with the new governor, Lieutenant Henry Smith. As soon as he had repaired the settlement, Smith, with a party of six Royal Marines, hunted down the murderers. One of the *gauchos* was killed by his fellows, another, Luna, turned King's evidence, and Antonio Rivero was sent to prison in England but later was returned to the River Plate.

A few years ago, there was set up in Buenos Aires a *Comisión Pro Monumento a Rivero*, a committee to erect a monument to Antonio

Rivero. According to the broadcast given in January 1967 by the committee's Vice-President, the murder of Brisbane and others was a patriotic revolt against the British invader, a deliberate guerrilla war undertaken so that the Argentine flag would once more fly over Puerto de la Soledad. The committee therefore advocated the erection of a statue to Antonio Rivero at Río Gallegos, the nearest point in Argentina to the Falklands, until such time as it can be transported to Puerto de la Soledad when it is once more the capital of the 'Islas Malvinas argentinas'.

Unfortunately, the truth is not in the least heroic. There was no British 'occupying force' on the island; the murderers did not hoist the flag of the United Provinces when they killed Brisbane; and the motive for their action was that Brisbane was paying them in worthless paper money, previously printed by Vernet, instead of in dollars.

* * *

From the foregoing it is evident that Argentina's 'historic' claim to the Falkland Islands is, to say the least, open to considerable doubt. It was not taken seriously by any nation at the time when it was first advanced, and it could not be maintained later against the United States or the United Kingdom. However, in addition to their appeal to history, Argentine apologists adduce three other arguments which must now be examined.

The first asserts that the islands belong to Argentina because they are geologically part of Patagonia. Only geologists can say whether this statement is well-founded, but scientific opinion does seem to have changed since the theory was first put forward in the 19th century. Fossil remains and the theory of continental drift suggest that the islands have an affinity with South Africa rather than South America. In any case, this point would be worth considering only if the islands were res nullius at the present time, and this is clearly not the case.

The second argument is based on geographical propinquity and, again, it would be relevant only if the islands were uninhabited, or not under continuous administration by some Power. As the main islands are beyond the 100-fathom line, they cannot be said to be on the continental shelf. Their position 300 miles away from the nearest Argentine territory scarcely makes their inhabitants near neighbours of the Patagonians. On this basis, Chile could make an equally good claim to possession, on the grounds of the propinquity of the Falklands to Chilean territory in the Straits of Magellan.

In this connection, it should be recalled that when the United Kingdom reoccupied the Falklands, Argentina had not incorporated Patagonia, partly because possession of that area had long been the subject of dispute with Chile. It was not until 1884, after the United

Kingdom had administered the islands for close on half a century, that the Argentine Government reopened the question of sovereignty, using propinquity as the excuse. The Argentine Foreign Minister, Dr. Ortiz, told Edmund Monson, the British Minister in Buenos Aires, that 'now that the country was consolidated and rounding off its territory' the Falklands should be handed over 'by reason of their geographical position'. The British representative reported to Earl Granville: 'In the interests of civilisation they [the Argentines] may have been justified in dividing with Chile the unexplored Pampas, hitherto only populated by nomad Indians. The pretext does not serve with regard to the Falklands which have by English occupation been converted into a peaceable and prosperous settlement.' This statement is still valid.

The third argument which Argentines frequently put forward is that there are no Falkland Islanders, only colonists, and colonialism is incompatible with the American ideal. This overlooks two facts: 80 per cent. of the present population is native born and some descendants of the very first settlers still live there. Moreover, successive American Presidents have not regarded British sovereignty as contravening the famous Monroe anti-colonial Doctrine.

*   *   *

On the basis of history, or equity, or international law, therefore, it would appear that Argentina would experience some difficulty in obtaining a settlement satisfactory to her national pride. Politically, because of the present international situation, she is in a much stronger position. Although the Uruguayan delegate to the Organisation of American States, remembering Argentina's retention of the Island of Martín García, in the River Plate, must listen with some scepticism to certain passages in the Argentine case, most Latin American states are convinced of the rightness of her cause. Guatemala, with claims on British Honduras, is an active ally and Venezuela, because of the Guyana border question, an interested observer of the progress of the Malvinas dispute. Argentina can therefore count on the unanimous support of the Latin American members of the Organisation of American States should the dispute ever be referred to that regional organisation.

Similarly, Argentina can also count on support in the United Nations of the Afro-Asian group, naturally predisposed in principle to rally to the cry of 'anti-colonialism'. This accounts for her success in 1965 in obtaining official recognition of the existence of the dispute, and the passage of the resolution urging Anglo-Argentine discussions on the matter. As the United Nations is notorious for its ability to overlook the provisions of its charter when such a course is politically expedient, the Falkland Islanders, like the Gibraltarians, are unlikely in the present circumstances to obtain much satisfaction from an appeal to the principle of self-determination.

The United States is also likely to favour a solution satisfactory to Argentina. As the *Lexington* incident is now forgotten, there is no need for her to question Argentina's original claim to the islands. Hemispheric solidarity also predisposes her to support an American state, especially where such action would, at no cost to herself, give her prestige a much-needed boost in the Organisation of American States. Most important of all, the U.S.A. desires a prolonged period of stability in Argentina. Although initially censuring the military uprising of June 1966, the United States Government seems now to have come round to the view that General Onganía, an anti-Communist, and demonstrably able to control the *peronista* trade unions, offers the best hope for settled government. If he secured the Malvinas for Argentina, his prestige would be so high that the continuity of his régime for many years would be virtually assured.

Finally, Argentina's best ally at the present time may well be, paradoxically, British officialdom. The Falklands were acquired at a time when a base near the Straits of Magellan was essential for naval control of the Pacific coast of South America and the South Atlantic. In two world wars the facilities at Port Stanley were vital for the defeat of German raiders and naval units. Strategically, they are now no longer important, even if giant tankers were to find it cheaper to avoid the Panama Canal by going round Cape Horn, or if that canal were ever put out of action. To the realistic official mind, therefore, the islands are scarcely worth retaining, especially in view of the damaging effect of the dispute on Anglo-Argentine commercial relations. The signs are that this line of thought may have prevailed in recent discussions. The two governments may have been very near agreement on the terms of the transfer of sovereignty when pressure of British opinion made it inexpedient, for the moment, to make a public statement to that effect. It should be noted, however, that the seemingly categorical replies given to questions in the House of Commons leave open the possibility of a change of status at some future date, when it can be shown to be in the best interests of the inhabitants.

Whether the Falklanders will be allowed to say that they approve of such benevolence, or whether it will be imposed on them, remains to be seen. They themselves know exactly where they stand. Rather than accept Argentine rule, for which they have no respect, they will leave the islands from which, against considerable odds, they and their predecessors have contrived for over 130 years to extract a livelihood.

*   *   *

The present position of the dispute may therefore be summed up as follows:

(1) The Falklands are now of scant economic or strategic importance. There are no known minerals, no oil deposits, and the wool-clip, since the failure to establish a refrigeration plant for the export of frozen mutton, is the only source of wealth. The soil is unfertile, the climate inhospitable, and only tough and resourceful people like the present inhabitants can stand the isolation. A population of around 2,000 is about the maximum that could be supported, even with such adjuncts as a missile or satellite tracking-station, or a naval base, or a centre for Antarctic exploration.

(2) Argentina's claim is founded on emotion and recurrent irredentist fever. She has no need for more territory and has far more attractive lands than the Malvinas to develop. It is also doubtful whether her cattle-and-grain-minded farmers would ever take kindly to sheep. Nevertheless, their almost mystical sense of *nuestra tierra*, their irradicable belief that there is a wrong to be righted, their impression derived from their publicists that the islands are an earthly paradise, compel the Argentines to be unyielding in their attempts to secure the transfer of sovereignty. Certainly any politician in difficulties has only to raise the cry of *Las Malvinas son nuestras* and he will have the whole nation behind him.

(3) Britain would like to dispossess herself of the last remnants of an imperial past, especially when they are of no economic benefit, but she has an inescapable moral commitment to the Falkland Islanders who have no wish to be other than British.

In these circumstances, it is difficult to see an immediate solution to the dispute. Some comment on it has used the argument that the islanders' future is bound up with that of her neighbours. It is always assumed that these are Argentines. However, although the islanders, in the past, contributed to the development of the Patagonian region, they also have links with sheep farming in the Chilean Punta Arenas region. Although Montevideo is 1000 miles away, they also have associations with Uruguay, which is their normal point of contact with the outside world. Either of these countries would appeal more to the Falklanders than Argentina, a country which has always made life difficult for them by imposing trade controls, non-recognition of passports, alleged obligation to military service, restrictions on postal services and similar constant irritants. In a sensible world, successive Argentine governments would have wooed the islanders, encouraged them to use the port of Buenos Aires instead of forcing them to use Montevideo, and attempted to convince them that they would be better off under Argentine administration! The fact remains, nevertheless, that the islanders have no wish to be other than British, and a plebiscite (which the Argentines say they would not recognise) would give a complete confirmation of this attitude.

There seems to be only one helpful suggestion which can be voiced at this juncture. Many young islanders are emigrating to New Zealand where their expertise with sheep is appreciated, their English tongue preserved and their devotion to free institutions safeguarded. It would not cost a phenomenal sum to offer all the island families generous resettlement grants there (or in Wales, or the Scottish islands and highlands from which many of their ancestors came). If the majority accepted, the Falklands could then be offered for hard cash to Argentina, Chile or Uruguay, or to any interested bidder, provided the Monroe Doctrine were not violated. Unless some action such as this is taken, Britain must retain sovereignty until the inhabitants agree to a transfer. If their present mood is maintained, such an event is unlikely to happen in this generation.

July 1968

FOREWORD

THE discovery of the new world at the end of the fifteenth century marked the beginning of an epoch in the history of international law. The foundations of this system had been laid during the middle ages by the feudal states of the time, but the sphere of its operations was vastly increased during the period of colonial expansion and many new matters were found to be susceptible of legal regulation. In this development of the law Spain from the very first took the lead, and her efforts to submit to international rules the many economic and political problems arising out of colonial competition did not abate until her great empire had fallen into pieces about her.

This view of Spain's rôle in international politics is one not usually advanced; nor is the idea that international law was a force of importance in the relations of European states during the seventeenth and eighteenth centuries by any means prevalent. The political historian tells us of an ever-decaying Spain embroiled for over two centuries in endless disputes, in which her policy was restrained not by law but only by expediency. The historian of international law is prone to envisage the development of his subject during this era as wholly guided by the jurist and publicist. But these views are both distortions. The truth of the matter is that modern international law was forged in the fires of the economic and political struggles over colonial possessions and the control of the seas, and due to the initiative of Spain was a real and vital force in European affairs from the beginning of the sixteenth century onward.

The present volume deals primarily with a famous controversy the ghost of which has even to this day not been laid. The account is based upon manuscript material heretofore never used and places the merits of the dispute in a new light. The issues originally involved in the controversy

were of such far-reaching historical importance, the current
view of the period, as we have stated, is so inaccurate, that it
has been deemed necessary to reconstruct in certain details
the system of international law as it was actually practiced
during the seventeenth and eighteenth centuries. It has
been, in the nature of things, impossible to reconstruct this
system in its entirety, for the field is vast and involves a
new interpretation of history. In respect, however, of the
doctrine that the mere discovery of a new land can give
rights of sovereignty the results of this survey are presented in some detail. The author believes he has demonstrated beyond a doubt that this theory is baseless in law
and in fact, and entirely at variance with the principles of
Roman law upon which, through the efforts of Spain, the
international law relating to the acquisition of sovereignty
was founded. The author trusts that these results will once
and for all put an end to the frivolous and uncritical acceptance by law writers of the idea that discovery can give any
shadow of right, and that they will move historians to abandon the fantastic picture of Spain seeking to exclude the
rest of Europe from the new world by setting up merely a
right by discovery to regions which she did not in fact control.

The author is under great obligations to his friends. He
desires particularly to express his gratitude to the President of the Hispanic Society of America for his encouragement and aid, and to Professor William R. Shepherd, Dr.
E. L. Stevenson and the Honorable John Bassett Moore for
their many helpful suggestions. The author's thanks are
further extended to the Trustees of Columbia University,
who appointed him a travelling fellow in the years 1915 and
1916 and thus made it possible for him to examine sources
otherwise inaccessible; to Mr. Roger Howson, Librarian of
Columbia University, Dr. Mariano Alcocer of the Archivo
General de Simancas, and to Dr. Miguel Gomez-Campillo,
of the Archivo Nacional at Madrid, for aid in securing

manuscripts. To the generosity of Miss May L. Godfrey of Grand Rapids, Michigan, the author is indebted for the purchase of important documents, and for this he is most grateful. Lieutenant Roger Brooks, U.S.N., very kindly read Chapter I and made many suggestions regarding the problems of navigation there discussed. Finally, the author desires to express his appreciation of the interest of his friend Dr. Edwin M. Borchard, and of the patience and care with which the manuscript was read and criticised by his father, Professor Julius Goebel, and by his wife, Dr. Dorothy Burne Goebel.

JULIUS GOEBEL, JR.

New York City,
June 16, 1926.

CHAPTER I

THE DISCOVERY OF THE FALKLAND ISLANDS

"I TARRY in this unhappy desert, suffering everything for love of God." Thus wrote the pious priest, Fr. Sebastian Villanueva, in the year 1767 from the newly settled Spanish colony on the East Falkland Island. Not a tree, not a shrub, was there to remind him of the more gentle lands which he had quit; the incessant gales of wind and the monotonous tossing of the sea served only to heighten the barren cruelty of the soil on which he lived. Little wonder that these islands should have been the last of the great discoveries in the West to be settled by Europeans, and that only the love for one's country or one's God could persuade men to remain in the face of such an unfriendly nature. Undoubtedly the rigors of the South Atlantic climate had much to do in postponing the exploration and charting of the Patagonian coast and its environs. The tale of early discoveries in these regions was one of hardship, shipwreck and suffering; none but the more intrepid navigators who sought a direct passage westward to the rich lands of the East ventured southward, and they, indeed, lingered no longer than they were obliged to do. All of these factors explain the singular sparsity of records that have been left us. Nations were interested in the New World primarily for material gain, and hence, although we have a wealth of documents relating to the development of the lands to the north, our accounts of these economically less productive territories are few. It was only later, when the devastating wars of the seventeenth and eighteenth centuries had stripped France of her colonies, and had threatened the control of Spain over her own possessions that the importance of protecting trade routes by all possible means led to an appreciation of the strategic importance of the South Atlantic regions. Then it was that chancelleries made hasty excursions into the records of the early voyagers in search of evidence to support their claims to sovereignty, and the shadowy and incomplete accounts of the resultant state papers have been the chief reliance of historians from those times forth.

The mystery that surrounds the discovery of the Falkland Islands is one of the most striking examples of what has just been said. Navigators of four different nations have been credited with having first sighted these islands; the claims of all of them have been subjected to the casual scrutiny of statesmen and to the more dispassionate investigation of historians; but to this day there has been no careful examination of the records, no sifting of the proof, no trustworthy exposition of the relative merits of the conflicting claims. And this is all the more surprising when we consider the fact that, upon more than one occasion when the title to the islands was under discussion, the right to occupy and possess was grounded upon the allegation of discovery.

The fact has already been alluded to that the records of the early voyages into the South Atlantic are exceedingly meagre; and those that we still possess are often sketchy and inaccurate. Both of these circumstances have contributed largely to misunderstanding and controversy. Writers have been influenced by certain preconceptions, or they have felt the always latent and hardly suppressed emotion of national pride. Many of them have neglected to make use of material which, though not in the nature of direct proof, has an important inferential bearing upon the question with which they deal. Still others ignore the most elementary premises of seamanship and oceanography, and consequently arrive at conclusions that are unlikely to bear scientific scrutiny. The problem of the discovery of the Falklands is, therefore, approached by the present writer with a due appreciation of the difficulties and dangers that beset it.

The first navigator to voyage into the lower South Atlantic was Amerigo Vespucci. In the letter to Piero Francesco Soderini,[1] recounting the vicissitudes of his third voyage, he states that, having journeyed along the South American coast some 500 leagues, 150 leagues west from Cape St. Augustine and 600 leagues to the southwest,[2] it was decided that they should leave the coast and "be off to encounter the sea in some other direction." Accordingly, they commenced sailing on a southeasterly course. He goes on to say:[3]

And we sailed on this course until we found ourselves at such an altitude that the South Pole had an elevation of full 53 degrees above our horizon and we no longer saw the stars of either the Ursa major or the Ursa minor. And we were already distant from the harbor whence we set forth full 500 leagues on a south-eastern course; and this was the third [day] of April. And on this day there began so violent a sea-tempest that it made us lower sail altogether; and we ran on with bare mast in a violent wind which came from the south-west bringing with it huge seas, and the wind was very violent. Such was the tempest that the whole fleet stood in much fear. The nights were very long; for we had a night on the seventh day of April which was of 15 hours; because the sun was at the end of Aries, and in this region it was Winter as your Magnificence may well be aware. And while we were going along in this tempest, on the seventh day of April we sighted new land, about 20 leagues of which we skirted; and we found it all barren coast; and we saw in it neither harbor nor inhabitants. I believe this was

[1] The *Vespucci Reprints*, texts and translations, issued by the McCormick fund of Princeton University were used. The translation of the Soderini letter by Professor G. T. Northup contains what purports to be the first critical examination of the extant Vespucci texts and consequently throws much light on the controversies that have arisen over places and dates, not to speak of the influence that various careless translations had upon the cartographers.

[2] Varnhagen places this place of departure somewhat east of the Rio de la Plata; cf. the chart in his *Amerigo Vespucci* (1865).

[3] Northup, *The Soderini Letter Translation*, p. 39 (*Vespucci Reprints, Texts and Studies*, IV).

because the cold was so great that nobody in the fleet could endure it. So seeing ourselves in such peril and in such a tempest, that scarcely could we see one ship from the other on account of the high seas which were running and the excessive thickness of the weather, we arranged with the admiral to signal the fleet to put about, and that we should leave the land and take our course toward Portugal.[4]

What was this new, barren and uninhabited land that Vespucci claims to have sighted? It is, of course, impossible to answer this query with any degree of scientific accuracy, although it seems obvious enough when we consider the fact that the Falkland Islands lie between 51° and 53° south latitude,[5] and are southeast of the point at which Vespucci left the mainland. It was the view of Bougainville,[6] who planted the first colony on the Falklands, that Vespucci sighted these islands, and one would seem to violate no canon of common sense in accepting this conclusion.

But the simplicity of this conclusion has by no means satisfied the geographers, primarily because they claim that the intrinsic evidence in Vespucci's account negatives any such result. Humboldt[7] was the first of the modern writers to raise a doubt regarding the earlier view. The conclusion of Bougainville is rejected as "not even possible," and the other conjectures of earlier geographers suffer the same fate. Humboldt concludes his note with the philosophic statement that in "the history of geography as in other

---

[4] In the letter to Lorenzo di Medici (*Mundus Novus,* translated by G. T. Northup, *Vespucci Reprints, Texts and Studies,* 1916), p. 4, Vespucci states, "We advanced to within seventeen and a half degrees of the Antarctic circle. . . ." This would have put them north of 50° south latitude.

[5] Between 57° and 62° west longitude.

[6] Bougainville, *Voyage autour du Monde* (1771), p. 47; Navarrete, *Colección de los Viages* (1829), vol. 3, p. 278 n., suggests that Vespucci had sighted the group Tristan de Cunha, or the Island Diego Ramirez (*sic*).

[7] Humboldt, *Examen Critique de l'Histoire de la Géographie* (1839), vol. 5. Humboldt questions the correctness of Navarrete's suggestion.

places, it is prudent not to wish to explain everything.'' Unfortunately, however, Humboldt was not satisfied with this philosophic reflection, for later in the same volume[8] he hazards the suggestion that, if it was not an accumulation of icebergs, it was the east Patagonian coast that was sighted. Humboldt arrives at this conclusion by a reference to the Medici letter,[9] where Vespucci states that he has been considering a fourth voyage, ''that I may apply myself to the discovery of new regions to the South along the eastern side following the wind-route called Africus.''

With all due respect to Humboldt, it is submitted that these grounds are far too frail upon which to support any satisfactory conclusion. Vespucci might well have had in mind a return to the Brazilian coasts from which he departed when he set his course to the southeast. Earlier in the Medici letter Vespucci speaks of having sailed along the South American coast ''until we passed the tropic of Capricorn and found the Antarctic pole fifty degrees higher than that horizon. We advanced to within seventeen and a half degrees of the Antarctic circle. . . .''[10] Certainly the reader, ignorant of the Soderini letter, would be inclined to assume that Vespucci had continually followed the coast. As a matter of fact, the two accounts are by no means reconcilable in all details, and it is not of much avail to attempt to say which account is the more correct.

After Humboldt, Varnhagen's opinion on the subject of the third voyage is worthy of serious consideration, largely because of his profound studies in the life of Vespucci.[11]

---

[8] *Ibid.*, p. 116, ''. . . après avoir quitté le littoral de Brésil, serait revenue sans le savoir, poussée par les courans ou les vents vers le Nouveau Continent, c'est à dire vers la côte orientale patagonique.'' As we shall presently see, neither the currents nor the prevailing winds would have favored such a result, unless Vespucci had hugged the coast.

[9] *The Mundus Novus in Translation*, p. 13.

[10] *Ibid.*, p. 4.

[11] *Cf.* especially Varnhagen, *Amerigo Vespucci* (1865); *Nouvelles Récherches sur les derniers Voyages du Navigateur Florentin* (1869).

Varnhagen's guess—and this it may properly be called—is that the land sighted on April 7 was South Georgia.[12] His conclusion is based upon the fact that if on April 3 Vespucci's vessel was in latitude 52° sailing on a southeast course, a strong four days' wind would have driven him to latitude 54° by the seventh of April. The Georgian coasts, he adds, extend some thirty-one leagues when approached from the direction in which Vespucci said he was sailing, and their aspect and climate coincide exactly with the account of the great navigator.

The evidence that Varnhagen cites in support of his view is not at all convincing.[13] As far as the appearance and climate of South Georgia are concerned, what he says is equally applicable to the Falklands. He relies, furthermore, upon the correctness of Vespucci's statement of the number of leagues sailed from a purely hypothetical locality on the South American coast in a straight and unvarying southeasterly course. One who has dealt with the early accounts of voyagers and explorers to any extent soon learns that estimates of distances are to be treated only as estimates, and that a conclusion in no case can be posited on such highly questionable evidence. Furthermore, the statement of Vespucci that, upon leaving the coast, a southeasterly course was set, by no means can be accepted as conclusive for the whole period they were at sea until land was again sighted. Even had Vespucci, as Humboldt surmises, sailed along the Patagonian coast, his course would of necessity have been primarily a southeasterly one to avoid being wrecked on the shores.[14]

[12] *Amerigo Vespucci,* p. 111.

[13] Varnhagen relies in his notes upon the account of Cook, who visited South Georgia in 1775.

[14] Groussac, *Les Iles Malouines* (1910), p. 462, leans to the Humboldt theory on the ground that the purpose of the expedition was to find a southwestern passage. He makes a further suggestion that the word in the text *libeccio* be changed to *scilocco* in order to explain how Vespucci, in

One other fact needs to be taken into consideration and that is the effect of the ocean currents in this region. Assuming that Vespucci left the southern coast of Brazil, yet, unless he remained within reasonably close proximity to the shores, the tendency of the Brazil current would have been to drive him eastward into the centre of the South Atlantic.[15] Particularly after passing the fortieth parallel, where the Falkland current meets the Brazil current, only by skirting the shore would he have had the advantage of the Brazil current as far south as he states he sailed, and thus have avoided the northeasterly swing of the Falkland current. These factors, moreover, seem to have some bearing upon the return voyage. If Varnhagen's surmise regarding South Georgia is true, it is difficult to see how Vespucci, sailing in the west wind drift, should on his return to Europe have made his first landfall at Sierra Leone. On the other hand, if he actually reached the vicinity of the Falkland Islands, the current would have favored a course such as he presumably followed, and would have rendered his landfall at Sierra Leone almost inevitable.[16]

From what has been said, it will have been observed that one cannot determine with any degree of scientific accuracy

spite of the wind which he said prevailed, reached the Patagonian coast. From the philological point of view such a change is preposterous.

[15] *Cf.* Krümmel, *Handbuch der Ozeanographie* (1911), vol. 2, pp. 312, 604; Schott, *Geographie des Atlantischen Ozeans* (1912), p. 142 *et seq.*, Tafel xvi, p. 223. The earlier edition of the *Handbuch der Ozeanographie* of Boguslawski and Krümmel (1887) deals with this question at vol. 2, p. 438.

[16] Vespucci writes: "And we sailed on this course until we found ourselves at such an altitude that the South Pole had an elevation of full 52 degrees above our horizon and we no longer saw the stars of either the Ursa Minor or Ursa Major." *The Soderini Letter*, p. 39. Groussac, *op. cit.*, p. 460, tries to use this to prove Vespucci was not as far south as he pretended. It seems more probable that the reference to the stars was merely intended as a rhetorical figure to emphasize how far south Vespucci had travelled.

the identity of the lands sighted by Vespucci. The evidence, such as it is, points, in the writer's opinion, more to the Falklands or to the Patagonian coast than to any other locality, but a conclusion of this sort can scarcely be said to be incontrovertible.

In one important respect the account of Vespucci's third voyage had a pronounced influence upon subsequent discovery. This was in its relation to contemporary cosmography; for not only did the discoveries of the time have a revolutionary effect upon map making, but the maps themselves had much to do in shaping the course of navigators. These maps are, therefore, an indispensable supplement to the accounts of exploration.[17]

The caution of the early cosmographers is illustrated by the fact that in none of the earliest extant maps[18] which record the discoveries of Vespucci's third voyage is there any attempt to depict the lands that lay in 52° south latitude. This is true of the Cantino (1502)[19] and the Canerio

[17] Harrisse, *The Discovery of North America* (1892), gives a list of these maps at p. 365 *et seq.* There is also a list in Nordenskiöld, *Periplus* (1897), p. 177 *et seq. Cf.* also Ruge, *Die Entwickelung der Kartographie von Amerika bis 1570* (1892), p. 33 *et seq.;* Lowery, *A Descriptive List of Maps of the Spanish Possessions* (Phillips ed., 1912), p. 1 *et seq.*

[18] The earliest extant maps of the period are those of Juan de la Cosa and the Pesaro map, both *circa* 1500. The former may be found in Rio Branco, *Atlas Annexe au 1er Memoire présenté par les États Unis de Brésil . . .* (1900), Plate I, an atlas prepared for the arbitration of the Brazil-French Guiana boundary dispute and cited hereafter as Rio Branco, *Atlas.* This map is also annexed in volume 5 of Humboldt, *Examen Critique.* The Pesaro map has been photographed by Dr. E. L. Stevenson and hangs on the walls of the American Geographic Society. It has not as yet been edited and circulated. Another early map, the so-called King chart, is to be found in Nordenskiöld, *Periplus,* plate XLV. Kretschmer, *Die Entdeckung Amerikas, Atlas* (1892), has many early maps beautifully reproduced. *Cf.* also Kunstmann, *Die Entdeckung Amerikas, Atlas* (1859), and the reproductions on small scale in Ruge, *op. cit.*

[19] Stevenson, *Maps Illustrating Early Discovery and Exploration in America, 1502-1530* (1906), no. 1, Cantino map (hereafter cited as Stevenson, *Maps*).

(1502)[20] maps, which we may call the type-maps of the period. For some years to come the maps that were subsequently drawn show the most faithful adherence to the Canerio[21] type, and this may explain why, until the appearance of Schöner's first globe, there is no land on the maps[22] that in any way suggests that Vespucci ever sailed further south than 32° south latitude.[23]

The Schöner globe of 1515[24] appears to be the first attempt on the part of cosmographers to depict the lands below 52° south latitude. Schöner divides his South American

[20] Stevenson, *Marine World Chart of Nicolo de Canerio Januensis* (1908), text and map.

[21] For this early period, in addition to the maps mentioned in the text, the following were also examined: Munich-Portuguese, 1503 (?), in Stevenson, *Maps*, no. 2; Pilestrina, 1503, *ibid.*, no. 3; Ruysch, 1503, in Nordenskiöld, *Facsimile Atlas* (1887), plate XXXII; Waldseemüller, 1506, in Fischer and v. Wieser, *Die Weltkarten Waldseemüllers* (1903), and also in the *Cosmographiæ Introductio of Martin Waldseemüller* (*sic*) (United States Catholic Historical Society, *Monographs*, IV, 1907), of the same authors; globe attributed to Waldseemüller, 1509, in Stevenson, *Terrestial and Celestial Globes* (1921), vol. I, fig. 32; Lenox Globe, 1510, *ibid.*, fig. 35; Jagellonic Globe, 1510, *ibid.*, fig. 37; Glareanus, 1510, a map of the Waldseemüller type in Nordenskiöld, *Periplus*, fig. 82; Ptolemy (Silvani ed., 1511) in Nordenskiöld, *Facsimile Atlas*, plate XXXIII; Ptolemy (Stobnicza ed., 1512), *ibid.*, plate XXXIV; Ptolemy (Argentinæ, 1513), *ibid.*, plate XXXV and XXVI; Boulengier Gores, 1514, *ibid.*, plate XXXVII; Gregorius Reisch (Strassburg, 1515), *ibid.*, plate XXXVIII.

[22] On the Ruysch map mentioned in the preceding note is the following legend printed below the Rio de Cananor: "*Naute Lusitani partem hanc terre huius observarunt et usque ad elevationem poli antarctici 50 graduum pervenerunt nondum tamen ad eius finem austrinum.*"

[23] The Cantino map differs from the Canerio in this important respect, that the southernmost point of South America depicted runs off in a southeasterly direction. This may have been suggested by Vespucci's account, as the map shows evidence of the results of his third voyage and it may indicate the southeasterly course set by Vespucci.

[24] On this see especially v. Wieser, *Die Magelhâesstrasse* (1881), and the reproductions of the Schöner globes at the end of the volume. *Cf.* also Stevenson, *Terrestial and Celestial Globes*, vol. I, figs. 43, 44, and Coote, *Johann Schöner* (1888).

continent into a northern half which he calls *America* and
which resembles the Canerio delineation, and a southern
half which is called *Brasilie Regio*. At about 45° a strait
separates the two halves. The eastern shore of the *Brasilie
Regio* falls away rapidly in a southeasterly direction and at
52° describes a great bay. The importance of this globe has
hitherto seemed to lie primarily in the fact that it shows a
southern passage into the Pacific. To the writer, however,
the significance of an attempt to depict Vespucci's landfall
is of greater interest. Von Wieser, in his able disquisition
on the Schöner globes, has discussed at some length the
sources of Schöner's knowledge, and has come to the conclusion that the southern continent—the *Brasilie Regio*—
was an attempt to depict the region mentioned by Vespucci.[25]

After a comprehensive examination of many maps and
globes of the period, the writer is of the opinion that for
nearly a hundred years the charting of the region south of
52° was determined by the current notion of geographers
that an austral continent was seen by Vespucci and by the
consequent adoption of this view in the Schöner globe.[26]
It is the acceptance of such an idea in the contemporary
maps that makes it difficult for the modern investigator to

---

[25] v. Wieser, *Die Magelhâesstrasse*, p. 62. He cites Enciso, *Suma de
Geografia* (1519), as referring to the same matter, and of importance for
the 1520 globe of Schöner. The passage reads as cited: "*Este cabo de buena
esperança tiene al oeste a la tierra que llaman austral. ay desdel cabo de
buena esperança hasta a la tierra austral quatrocientas y cincuenta leguas
esta en xlii grados esta tierra austral esta del cabo de sant agostin seyci-
entas leguas hasta santagostin al sueste, quarta al sur desta tierra no se
sabe mas de quanto la han vista desde los navios, porques no han descen-
dido enella.*"

[26] v. Wieser also shows that the African lines of the *Brasilie Regio* of
Schöner's globe were determined by another work used by this great geographer. This was the *Zeytung auss Presillig Landt*. In that work language
was used which moved Schöner to fashion his austral continent after the
general appearance of North Africa.

deal with the voyagers' accounts and the maps until the voyage of Drake. It is by no means incomprehensible that, even if a voyager had sighted the Falklands, he might have believed them to be a part of a great austral continent, particularly if his charts bore out such a view; and this was actually the case where we have accounts of voyages in the Tierra del Fuego region. This circumstance is a very striking illustration of how the maps influence the voyagers' views of what they discovered and how, as we shall presently see, the maps themselves simply added confirmation to what was already known when the cosmographers came to interpret new material.[27]

It has seemed proper to give a detailed account of the current view regarding the New World south of the Tropic of Capricorn largely to explain why the epoch-making discovery by Magellan of the strait that bears his name did not sweep away the fictions that had grown up about the third voyage of Vespucci. The explorations of Magellan, it is true, made possible the charting of the whole Patagonian coast, but they did not settle the geography of Tierra del Fuego, nor of the Falklands, nor of the so-called Terra Australis. Here was land on which the geographers could still let their imaginations play.

[27] The Schöner globe of 1520 follows the general outlines of the globe of 1515. Even his globe of 1533, after the voyage of Magellan, continues to depict the great *terra australis*. v. Wieser, *op. cit.*

The maps up to the time of Magellan's voyage that resemble Schöner's globe are the Juan Vespucci map of 1533, in Nordenskiöld, *Periplus,* plate XLVII; the Green Globe, 1515, Stevenson, *Terrestial and Celestial Globes,* vol. I, fig. 38. The maps that follow the older type maps are the Waldseemüller map of 1516, Fischer and v. Wieser, *op. cit.;* Boulengier globe gores of 1518, Stevenson, *Terrestial and Celestial Globes,* vol. I, fig. 40; Lichtenstein globe gores, 1518, *ibid.,* fig. 39; Maiollo map, 1519, Stevenson, *Maps,* No. 4; Kunstmann, *op. cit.,* plate V; Rio Branco, *Atlas,* plate 1a (the latter work dates this map 1515); Munich-Portuguese map, 1519, Stevenson, *Maps;* Kunstmann, *op. cit.,* plate IV; Apianus, 1520, Nordenskiöld, *Facsimile Atlas,* plate XXXVIII; Ptolemy (Frisius ed., 1522); Nordenskiöld, *Facsimile Atlas,* plate XXXIX.

For our own purpose the voyage of Magellan was productive of certain reported discoveries off the east coast of Patagonia that in some respects are as enigmatical as those narrated by Vespucci, and that in other respects are more closely linked to the discovery of the Falklands than is the Vespuccian story.

Magellan[28] sailed from Sevilla on August 10, 1519. He arrived in the region with which we are concerned in the first month of the following year. Having passed the Rio de la Plata, the expedition sailed some distance and found two islands, which they named the Islas de los Patos, on which they found "geese" and "sea-wolves." Pigafetta, an Italian who accompanied Magellan, writes about this as follows:[29]

Then proceeding on the same course toward the Antarctic Pole coasting along the land we came to anchor at two islands full of geese and sea-wolves. . . . Leaving that place we finally reached 49 and one-half degrees toward the Antarctic Pole. As it was Winter the ships entered safe port to winter.[30]

The so-called Islas de los Patos, as we shall see presently,

[28] The writer has used Navarrete, *Colección de los Viages y Descubrimientos de los Españoles*, vol. IV; Pigafetta, *Magellan's Voyage Around the World* (Robertson ed., 1906), 3 vols.; Lord Stanley of Alderly, *The First Voyage Round the World of Magellan* (Hakluyt Society, No. 52); Pastells and Bayle, *El Descubrimiento del Estrecho de Magallanes* (1920), 2 vols.; Herrera, *Historia General de los Hechos de los Castellanos* (1730 ed.); Medina, *El Descubrimiento del Océano Pacífico* (1920), vol. 3; Kohl, *Geschichte der Entdeckungsreisen und Schiffahrten zur Magellans Strasse* (1877); v. Wieser, *Die Karten von Amerika in dem Islario General des Alonso de Santa Cruz* (1908).

[29] Pigafetta, *op. cit.*, vol. I, pp. 46-49.

[30] The Puerto San Julian. The bay where the expedition encountered the storms was called in early maps the Baja de los Trabajos. It has been identified by Kohl (*Zeitschrift für Erdkunde*, vol. XI, p. 362) with Desvelos Bay. Robertson thinks it is Puerto Deseado, *q. v., op. cit.*, note 85. Herrera, *op. cit.*, dec. 11, lib. IX, c. XI, XII, deals with these incidents in some detail; Medina leans heavily upon him for his account.

figured prominently on maps and were soon identified by map makers with the so-called Sanson group which we are about to discuss. The islands in question were probably the Seal Island, at the northeastern point of the rocky entrance to the Puerto Deseado, or Penguin Island, off the northeastern point of Sea Bear Bay eleven miles southeastward of Point Desire.[31] In the maps of the period, however, the islands are placed at some distance from the shore. This, however, does not seem to the writer to be in any way determinative of the locality visited by Magellan, however much it may have contributed to the confusion surrounding the early geography of the region.

Mention has already been made of the Sanson Islands. They appeared in the maps in 48° and 49° south latitude, shortly after the full account was obtained of the Magellan voyage, and probably after the famous junta of geographers that met at Badajoz in 1524, the direct result of whose labors we have so unfortunately lost. Neither Pigafetta's account nor Alvo's log book of the voyage make any mention of islands lying off the Puerto San Julian; nor is there mention of any such discovery in the account of Herrera. Kohl[32] has made concerning this group several ingenious but unsupported conjectures, some of which later discoveries of old maps rendered nugatory.[33] It was not until the publication of Santa Cruz' *Islario*[34] some years ago that the mystery of the name at least was finally solved.

Santa Cruz was the *cosmógrafo mayor* of Charles V in 1540. The *Islario* was probably composed in 1540-1541 and

[31] United States Navy, Hydrographic Office No. 173, *The South American Pilot* (hereafter so cited), vol. 2, pp. 91-93; charts nos. 617 and 3909.

[32] Kohl, *Die Beiden Ältesten Generalkarten von Amerika* (1860), p. 156.

[33] He suggests that Schöner's *Insule 7 delle pucelle* in 36° south latitude may have been these islands. In the Waldseemüller map of 1507 these islands figure off the coast of Africa topped by a Portuguese flag.

[34] v. Wieser, *Die Karten von Amerika in dem Islario General des Alonso de Santa Cruz* (1908).

is, in every sense of the word, an official work. Santa Cruz, describing the voyage, says, after mentioning the stay in the San Julian Bay, that, "leaving this Bay, some Islands were discovered East thereof at a distance of some 18 leagues which they called *Yslas de Sanson y de Patos,* because they found there many very fat penguins, so fat that they were scarcely able to walk, and only half feathered,"[35] the latter fact reminding the sailors of the Biblical hero.

The origin of the name and the fact of discovery must be regarded as definitely settled largely because the account was written, only two decades after the discovery, by an official who was in a position to have all the details, written as well as verbal, a fact which renders the testimony of Santa Cruz in the present instance as reliable and direct as that of any immediately contemporary account. But it is far from clearing up the mystery. A careful scrutiny of present-day charts of the region[36] fails to reveal any island within the distance stated. Indeed, one is confronted with a complication in respect to the identity of the islands that is as difficult of solution as the identity of the land sighted by Vespucci.

The fact has already been mentioned that, in these early accounts, the statements as to distance are generally untrustworthy. At the same time it should be noted that the eighteen-league distance mentioned almost precludes the suggestion that the nearest of the Falkland group, some seventy-five leagues away, may have been discovered. We know that while wintering in Puerto San Julian, Magellan dispatched one of his vessels, the *Sant Iago* under Serrano,

---

[35] The passage (*ibid.,* p. 58) is as follows: *Y de aqui tomaron su demanda por la costa adelante haviendo allegado y descubierto unas yslas que estan al oriente de puerto de San Julian por diez y ocho leguas que pusieron nomber yslas de Sanson y de Patos porque en ellas hallaron muchas y muy gordos que casi no podian andar y medio pelados to los de los quales llevaron muchos para su viaje.*

[36] United States Navy, Hydrographic Office, Charts no. 617, no. 1515.

to explore the coast, and that this vessel, after discovering the Bay of Santa Cruz, was wrecked on the coasts. It is entirely possible that on this, or on one of the reconnoitering expeditions[37] that Magellan sent out, the Falklands, or at least the outlying Jason Islands of the Falkland group, may have been found, a landfall that the prevailing southwesterly to northwesterly winds in this region may, to some extent, have facilitated.[38] We are obliged, however, to satisfy ourselves with a mere conjecture.[39]

In mentioning the Islas de los Patos it was stated that subsequent cartographers paid but little attention to the probable actual situation of these islands in relation to the coast. This is true, of course, in the same degree in regard to the charting of the Islas de Sanson. The earliest extant map showing the Strait of Magellan is the so-called Turin-Spanish map of 1523.[40] Dr. Stevenson has suggested that it incorporates information brought back by El Cano in 1522. In any event, it shows no islands off the coast of Patagonia and is exceedingly meagre as to detail in these re-

[37] Herrera, *loc. cit.*

[38] *The South American Pilot*, vol. 2, p. 91.

[39] Groussac, *op. cit.*, p. 462, gives the Magellan voyage but scant consideration and makes no mention of the great cartographical significance of the voyage along the east coast of Patagonia.

[40] Stevenson, *Maps*, no. 6.

The origin of this name not appearing in any of the works that had currency in these times, it remained a considerable mystery and may explain the reason why it was so frequently given in an abbreviated or corrupt form. It appears sometimes as Ascension, and hence the assumption arose that Sanson, the original form, was a corruption of Asençao. This is not only philologically absurd, but it also shows a lamentable ignorance of the rough humor of seamen. The tendency of the voyagers in Magellan's expedition to "see big" was the foundation of one of the amusing legends of contemporary exploration. For decades after Magellan's visit to Patagonia navigators were wont to confirm the reports of giants in these regions. The Samson-like penguins are a fitting counterpiece to the Patagonian giants. Doubtless the bracing air of America was responsible for this larger vision.

gions. The Sabiati map,[41] on the other hand, which Harrisse dates 1525 and Uzielli 1527, shows a group of islands off the Bahia de los Trabajos, but gives no name. The islands appear as the Yslas de los Patos and the Yslas de Sanson for the first time in the Weimar-Spanish map of 1527.[42] Thereafter, the bulk of the maps of the period, with but few exceptions, at least where they are of purely Spanish origin, do not fail to depict this group of islands.[43] They are a geographical fixture for the next decades.

Following the Magellan voyage there were four expeditions sent to the strait, of which the most famous were those of Loaysa and Alcazaba, and, of the most importance for our purpose, the expedition sent out by the Bishop of Plasencia in 1539. In none of the preceding expeditions is

[41] *Ibid.*, no. 7.

[42] *Ibid.*, no. 9; *cf.* also Stevenson, *Early Spanish Cartography of the New World*, p. 13.

[43] The Wolfenbuettel-Spanish map, 1525-1530, Stevenson, *Maps*, no. 8; also in Stevenson, *Early Spanish Cartography;* Maiollo, 1527, Stevenson, *Maps*, no. 10; Rio Branco, *Atlas*, plate 3, where the islands are shown, but not named; Weimar-Ribero, 1529, Stevenson, *Maps*, no. 11; Verrazano, 1529, *ibid.*, no. 12. The map in Peter Martyr, *Historia de L'Indie Occidentali*, 1534; Nordenskiöld, *Facsimile Atlas*, fig. 67, shows the islands without name; so, too, the map in Ptolemy (Basel ed., 1540), Nordenskiöld, *Facsimile Atlas*, fig. 73.

Other maps appearing prior to the world map of Santa Cruz that show no trace of the islands are the Thorne map, 1527, Nordenskiöld, *Facsimile Atlas*, plate XLI; the Gilt Globe, 1528, Harrisse, *Discovery of North America*, plate XXI; the Nancy Globe, 1530, Stevenson, *Terrestial and Celestial Globes*, vol. I, fig. 50b; the Bailly Globe, 1530, *ibid.*, fig. 52; Apianus, 1530, Nordenskiöld, *Periplus*, plate XLIV; Orentius Finæus, 1531, Nordenskiöld, *Facsimile Atlas*, plate XLI; Grynæus, 1532, *ibid.*, plate XLII; Vadianus, 1534 (Epitome trium terræ partium), *ibid.*, fig. 66; Paris Wooden Globe, 1535, Harrisse, *op. cit.*, plate XXII; Mercator, Cordiform Map, 1538, Nordenskiöld, *Facsimile Atlas*, fig. 54; Anonymous Globe Gores, 1540, Stevenson, *Terrestial and Celestial Globes*, vol. I, fig. 44a; Ulpius Globe, 1541, *ibid.*, fig. 58; Mercator, 1541, *ibid.*, fig. 61.

The maps of Battista Agnese, Nordenskiöld, *Periplus*, plate XXIV, date between 1536 and 1556 and show the Islas de Sanson.

there the least evidence of the sighting of islands that correspond with the Islas de los Patos or the Islas de Sanson.[44] Nor, indeed, is there evidence of anyone else ever having seen them in these years until the expedition of which we are about to speak.

The armada of the Bishop of Plasencia[44] was under the command of his relative, Francisco Camargo,[45] and had, as its purpose, the colonization of the strait region.[46] The expedition left the port of Sevilla in August, 1539, and on the twelfth of January, 1540, it crossed the Sarmiento Banks

[44] *Cf.* Pastells and Bayle, *op. cit.*, vol. 1, pp. 139, 163; Sir Clements Markham, *Early Spanish Voyages to the Strait of Magellan* (Hakluyt Society, *Works*, 2d series, no. 28, 1911).

[45] The first reprint of the fragment of a log kept by one of the vessels of the expedition, which is our chief source of information regarding the voyage, was made by Torres de Mendoza, *Colección de Documentos Inéditos en los Archivos de Indias,* vol. 5, p. 551. It was taken from the *Colección* of Múñoz. Mendoza stated that there were two copies extant, one of an early date and the other of 1570, both badly written. The log was again reprinted in the *Anuario Hidrográfico de la Marina de Chile* (1879), vol. 5, p. 449. Markham, *op. cit.,* p. 159 *et seq.,* published a translation with the notes of the Chilean edition, a fact that reflects none too glowingly on the scientific circumspection of the editor, as shall be presently demonstrated. Herrera, *op. cit.,* dec. VII, lib. I, c. viii, follows the account of the log very faithfully and adds details not therein set forth as to the subsequent fate of Camargo, the leader of the expedition. v. Wieser's reprint of the *Islario of Santa Cruz,* p. 58, has further confirmatory evidence of the account here relied upon. Pastells and Bayle, *op. cit.,* vol. 1, p. 177 *et seq.,* gives a calendar of documents in the Spanish archives relating to the expedition. Some of these documents are textually reproduced in Medina, *Colección de Documentos Inéditos,* vol. 3, p. 360 *et seq.* The log is likewise reprinted in this latter work, p. 407.

[46] Medina, *Colección de Documentos Inéditos,* vol. 3, p. 360, royal cédula of November 6, 1536. There seems to be some doubt as to Camargo's given name. In Herrera it appears as Alonso. Medina and Pastells and Bayle, on the basis of more recent research, give it as Francisco.

Markham, *op. cit.,* p. 159, states that the object of the expedition was to open up communication with the ports of Chile and Peru by sea. He gets this from Herrera, but makes no mention of the fact. The documents support what is stated in the text.

and presently anchored near Cape Virgins at the entrance
of the Strait of Magellan. Having been driven off by storms
the armada finally entered the strait on January 20. Two
days later the flagship of the fleet was wrecked in the entrance of the strait.[47] The captain general with his crew was
rescued and he proceeded on his way to Peru. The third
vessel, of whose log alone we still possess a fragment,
turned back and was driven by a gale to Cape Virgins. Here
she was forced to anchor, unable to rejoin the captain general. On January 31 the wind blew so violently from the
south southeast that the anchor cable parted and the ship
made sail. Some hours later the ship was so close to land
that they were about to cut away the masts and then "it
pleased God to moderate the weather."[48]

The log goes on to say:[49]

On the fourth of the said month and year[50] in the morning we
sighted land, which seemed to us to be some eight or nine islands,
that were on the chart and because we were already caught between
lands for we had land to the north northeast on the port side, and
land stood out likewise to the south. And as it seemed so to us, to
me and all the others that we were among the said islands, we kept
on running, it seeming to me that among [these islands], as the
chart showed, there were channels through which we might pass,
for each island was set down on the chart by itself all clear and with
no shoals. And proceeding thus, at noon, we observed the land to be
one stretch [of territory] into which ran great bays with some very
high mountains, in the manner of islands,[51] and we then tried the

---

[47] The *Anuario Hidrográfico* and Markham both state that this was the
northeast end of the first narrows. In the Mendoza reprint (p. 566) it
states, "*es perdío la nao capitana a la salida deste estrecho.*" The Markham
translation has touched up the original in many spots.

[48] Markham translates: "it pleased God to send fair weather." This
would indicate that the wind had shifted, an assumption we have no right
to make.

[49] Mendoza, *op. cit.*, p. 566.

[50] Error in the MS. The writer means, of course, February 4.

[51] Markham translates: "At noon we observed a great bay with lofty

other tack to see if we could double the land which we saw to the northwest. We worked the sail all that day until nightfall without being able to round it, and night coming we tacked toward the south to see if we could pass on the other course; in that night the weather freshened so that in the passage we could show no sail.

In the Chilean reprint[52] of this account it is suggested that the landfall on the fourth of February was the Bay of San Sebastian; and this view is reiterated by Sir Clements R. Markham. It is the writer's view that such a conclusion is utterly untenable.

On January 31 the ship, which for want of her real name we shall call the *Incognita,* is in a bad storm with wind south-southeast. The storm abates, but there is no notice of a change of wind. For this season of the year and at the present time southeasterly gales appear to be infrequent, and the general tendency is for them to haul around to the south as the gale increases. The prevailing winds are westerly. We are justified in assuming that in the present case the easing of the storm resulted in a swing to the south.[53] It was probably impossible in those days to sail much closer to the wind than six points,[54] and as a landward tack would have brought disaster the vessel must have been sailing due east as long as the south-southwest wind continued, and generally on a more southeasterly course if the wind hauled to the south, a fact that is confirmed by the four days' navigation without a landfall. Moreover, the ship could have stood off from the coast not many miles before it would

mountains at a distance like islands." The Spanish text is: *"y nos ansi yendo á horas de medio dia, vimos ser toda la tierra una solamente, que metia, adentro grandes ensenadas con unas montanas muy alteras á manera de islas. . . ."*

[52] *Anuario Hidrográfico de la Marina de Chile,* vol. 5, p. 449.

[53] *The South American Pilot,* vol. 2, pp. 27, 29 *et seq.,* 187.

[54] There may be some question as to whether this is correct. The writer has the authority of Commander Chambers, R.N. (*Geographic Journal,* vol. 17, p. 420).

have encountered the Cape Horn current moving northeastward slowly but diligently, between one and two knots an hour.[55]

The notion that a landfall was made at San Sebastian Bay, as the Chilean editors and Markham suggest, is preposterous. In the first place, if the vessel had been sailing on a southerly course it is difficult to understand how land could have been sighted on the port hand to the northeast. Moreover, the description in the log hardly tallies with the appearance of the San Sebastian Bay. According to the *South American Pilot*,[56] from Cape Espiritu Santo to Nombre Head the land is several hundred feet high and from Nombre Head to Cape San Sebastian the land is so low that it cannot be seen from a vessel's deck until within the horizon. The land only commences to rise inshore of the Cape San Sebastian. The modern charts[57] and the *Pilot* show no indication of the Bay of San Sebastian in any way resembling the description of the log of the *Incognita*. Furthermore, it may be added that in a stiff gale, even beating against the wind, a ship would make more than the thirty miles from Espiritu Santo to the Bay of San Sebastian in four or five days.

The statement in the log that the charts showed islands is difficult to explain. The only chart of these regions that is left us is the Pigafetta map of the strait.[58] This map shows some islands in the entrance of the strait, but nowhere near the coast are there any other islands. On the basis of our present cartographical resources we may surmise that the log refers to the Sanson Islands, that had been appearing on maps for the past twelve years. There is no record of surveys having been made south of the Cape Espiritu

[55] *The South American Pilot,* vol. 2, p. 25; Krümmel, *op. cit.,* vol. 2, pp. 608, 713; Schott, *op. cit.,* p. 142.

[56] *The South American Pilot,* vol. 2, pp. 308-309.

[57] United States Navy, Hydrographic Office, chart no. 453.

[58] Pigafetta, *Magellan's Voyage Around the World,* vol. 1, p. 82.

Santo. Indeed, men rounding Cape Virgins were glad to proceed at once into the strait. It seems probable, therefore, that the captain of the *Incognita* believed he was among the Sanson Islands.

The log goes on to say that the next day, *i.e.*, the fifth, another point appeared which they thought they could double, and they actually succeeded when they sighted more land to the southeast. In the midst of this they saw a great bay with mountains on either side, and these still seemed like islands because there were great arms of the sea running between one mountain and the other. On the afternoon of this day the master thought he saw a channel opening to the south.[59] Later they made sail, standing off and on until they found themselves "surrounded by land which continued to the South." This range of mountains they found ran east and west taking a turn to northwest and southeast. There were many streams and arms of the sea running into the land, but these they could not enter as the wind blew steadily across the top of the land.[60] Finally, toward the northeast, a small inlet was found where they stayed eight days, and they called this port the Puerto de las Zorras because of the many foxes they found there.[61] The account continues:

And this land seems to me to be a point of the mainland, that is to say, the land which lies to the south when one enters the Strait, and it seems thus because the land which proceeds from this point runs to the west and this point is east and west with the mouth of the Strait.[62] And we found at this point of land many shrubs, and

[59] Markham, *op. cit.*, says this was the Le Maire Channel.

[60] Markham, *op. cit.*, translates this: "the wind was always blowing from the mountains."

[61] Markham states, "these data show that the position was on the south side of Tierra del Fuego."

[62] Markham cites the editor of the *Anuario de Hidrográfico de Chile* as fixing this in the Beagle Channel. Modern photographs of the Beagle Channel, as well as the early descriptions of it, disclose the fact that the scenery there is very beautiful and that the shores are heavily wooded. These facts are hard to reconcile with the statements in the log.

wood which had been burned and hence it seems that all the wood that comes out of the Strait reaches this bay, for while we were here, there was washed up one of the scuttles (*escutrucle*) of the ship *Capitana* (*i.e.*, the flagship) which we had lost in the Strait and other things also.

All this country is bare with not a bit of woods, very windy and very cold because eight months in the year it snows and the prevailing winds are southwest, west and northwest, for very rarely are there other winds. In all this land there are many fowls (*patos*), both from the land and the sea, and so too, many sea lions with hides 36 feet long and on the land there is a great deal of cedar wood. All about the coast there are many small islands, a fact it is well to know. The land where we lost the *berzos* (anchors) is an island and in the bay there are many [islands] and consequently many shoals, and everywhere many arms of the sea which run far into the land. And here the Summer is no longer than four months, January, February, March and April, and in May Winter commences and it snows a great deal until the end of December.

In this land there is much game, fowl, foxes and sea lions, and here we were for six months and afterwards took in water and wood and prepared our ship to return to Spain.

The *Incognita* left the Puerto de las Zorras on November 24, sailing up a gulf, but the weather getting bad they put into a bay to the south that was landlocked and where there were no foxes, according to which they assumed it to be an island. On a cape of the island they found much wood and a piece of new board which they believed came from the strait. This port, says the log, is a good place to winter for a vessel that "wants to make the Straits by secure land and there are no Indians."

It was not until the third of December, 1540, that the voyage to Spain was resumed. With fine weather and a south and southwest wind they sailed free, doubling the island where they had first sought to anchor. The wind changed to southwest and they ran with this two days seeking the mainland to the north. On the fifth the sun was taken in 49° 20′, and on the thirtieth they had reached the mouth of the La Plata.[63]

It is extraordinary that geographers and historians have been satisfied with the careless editing of the Chilean reprint and the English translation of this log. An indication of the scientific value of this work has been given in respect to the landfall made on February 4. This was stated to have been the Bay of San Scbastian; a day later these geographical prestidigitators have put the vessel in the Le Maire Strait, and the day after it is snugly berthed in the Beagle Channel. Every canon of oceanography and seamanship rebels against such conclusions. A small vessel with scarcely the sailing capacity of a schooner travels thirty miles in four days and then suddenly accomplishes two hundred the next day and a good hundred on the following, the previous sailing record, according to the log, being usually about some sixty miles a day.

The writer, having examined the data with some care, has come to the conclusion that the land discovered by the *Incognita* was the Falkland group, and that any other conclusion is excluded by the peculiar climatic and oceanic conditions of this region, and by the details of the voyage given in the log.

We have already dealt with the effect of the wind on the probable course of the *Incognita* after she was driven out of the strait, and have pointed out that as long as the wind was south-southeast or south the necessity of maintaining an easterly course rendered impossible an attempt to skirt the coast. It seems, further, that the experience on the thirty-first of January, when the wind drove the *Incognita* so close to shore that the crew were on the point of cutting away the masts, must have demonstrated to the master the dangers of trying to sail on that tack. It has also been stated that the *Incognita* was making up to this time about a sixty mile a day average. If we assume that this was her speed

[63] There is no record of when the vessel reached Spain.

the first four days of February, it was quite possible for her
to have negotiated the distance between Cape Virgins and
the outlying islands of the Falkland group—some 265 miles
—within this length of time.

Turning to the external appearance of the lands explored
by the *Incognita,* there can be no question that they resemble the Falklands more than the Fuegian coasts. A glance
at the map reveals the fact that here are the great bays and
estuaries, the countless small islands, the mountains from
which the winds never cease to blow.[64] In all probability the
land first approached was the West Falkland Island, and
here they wintered. The place where the second stop was
made was probably on the East Falkland or off it, for the
log speaks of a gulf (*i.e.,* the Falkland Sound) being between the second island visited and the Strait of Magellan.
What is said about the mountains likewise serves to confirm
this view. The maps reveal that on the West Falkland Island, the conformation of the southern extremity is such as
to make the mountains along the shore give the appearance
of a range running east and west. The range on the extremity between King George Bay and Byron Sound runs
northwest and southeast. The ranges on the Falkland
Sound run northeast and southwest. On the East Falkland
these characteristics are somewhat less pronounced, but in
a general way the hills run east and west except along the
Sound where they run northeast and southwest.

There are other details that add weight to the view expressed. The desert and bare aspect of the land are characteristic of the Falklands rather than of southern Tierra del
Fuego, for the former were and are now totally without indigenous arboreal vegetation. The earliest colonizer, Bougainville,[65] reported this fact, and it was likewise observed

[64] United States Navy, Hydrographic Office, charts nos. 2451, 2452.
These charts contain elevations of the coast at various points of the com-
pass and show several places that may have been visited by the *Incognita.*
[65] Bougainville, *Voyage autour du Monde,* p. 54.

by Darwin.[66] Bougainville also speaks of the presence of the foxes—the *canis falklandicus,* a strange hybrid of fox and wolf that was finally extirpated some fifty years ago.[67]

One statement in the log which is by far the most puzzling is that relating to the finding of a part of the *capitana* that was wrecked in the strait. This bit of data may have moved previous annotators of the log to place the regions visited in Tierra del Fuego. Such a conclusion, however, is difficult to reconcile with certain simple oceanographic facts that seem to the writer to admit of only one explanation.

As far as can be ascertained there is no current in the Magellan Strait other than the tidal currents.[68] The latter, however, seem to have some bearing on our problem. In this region the tidal stream appears to originate in the Pacific tide which sweeps around the southern end of the Tierra del Fuego, and which passes with some velocity through the Le Maire Strait and moves north and northwest up the eastern coast of Tierra del Fuego until it reaches the southern end of Sarmiento Bank off the strait where it divides, one part entering the strait, the other continuing northward up the coast. The ebb current coming out of the strait is met and turned to the southward by the tidal current sweeping down the coast and across the entrance in the same direction. This causes, of course, a very strong set of the ebb to the southward.[69]

[66] Darwin, *Journal of Researches into the Natural History and Geology, etc.* (1890), p. 49.

[67] Skottsberg, *The Wilds of Patagonia* (1911), p. 13. Skottsberg's account is valuable as it is the record of a Swedish scientific expedition. The account of the climate accords with what is said in *The South American Pilot,* vol. 2, p. 24, where it is stated that frosts and snow in summer are not uncommon.

[68] Mühry, *Die Frage einer Meeresströmung in der Magellanes Strasse* (Petermann's *Mittheilungen,* vol. 16, p. 112).

[69] *The South American Pilot,* vol. 2, pp. 193-194. Krümmel, *Handbuch der Ozeanographie,* vol. 2, p. 312. Harris, *Manual of Tides* (U.S. Coast and Geodetic Survey, *Report* [1906], appendix 6), p. 361.

With this division of the northward bound flood and the southeasterly sweep of the ebb, it is not difficult to understand that wreckage would be carried out of the strait in a southeasterly direction for some distance, for the speed of the flood tide is considerable and it produces a correlative velocity in the ebb stream. It is, of course, easy to overestimate the effect of this temporary current upon drifting wreckage. Clearly with prevailing westerly winds, and at the time of which we are writing, of a south-southeast wind, it is not likely that the driftwood would be carried very far to the south. Moreover, another element of great importance enters into consideration. This is the Cape Horn Stream.[70] This current is the southern branch of the South Pacific Westwind Drift. It runs along the western coast of Patagonia and has an easterly and northeasterly direction. At Staten Island it has a decided northerly trend. A branch of the current pushes through the Le Maire Strait at a speed of some twenty miles a day and flows toward the Falkland Islands, where it becomes merged with the Falkland Stream. Darwin[71] relates that canoes of the Fuegians had been found stranded on the Falklands and the eminent oceanographer Krümmel states that driftwood from Tierra del Fuego is frequently washed up there. The general direction and tendency of the current have been fixed, furthermore, by observations of the course of icebergs coming from the Antarctic regions.[72] Finally, mention may be made of extensive experiments carried on between the years 1900 and 1904 with floating bottles.[73] One of the bottles set in the waters off the West Fuegian coast was found on the East Falkland Island.

[70] On this *cf.* especially Krümmel, *op. cit.,* p. 713.

[71] Darwin, *op. cit.,* p. 50.

[72] Krümmel, *op. cit.,* vol. II, fig. 172, and pp. 608-609.

[73] Krümmel, *Flaschenposten* (*Meereskunde,* vol. 2), p. 30. Schott, *Die Flaschenposten der deutschen Seewarte* (*Aus dem Archiv der deutschen Seewarte,* 1897, no. 2), pp. 19 and 22.

From what has been said it will have been observed that under no conceivable circumstance could driftage from the entrance to the strait have been lodged on the southern coast of Tierra del Fuego, and consequently, if we are to believe the statements in the log of the *Incognita,* that such driftage was found, the interpretation of the Chilean reprint and of Sir Clements R. Markham that the vessel was on the south Fuegian coasts is not entitled to serious consideration. On the other hand, unless the wreckage had drifted far enough in a southeasterly direction, it could scarcely have come into contact with the Falkland Stream and have been washed up on the Falkland Islands.

In his study of the Falkland Stream, Klaehn[74] has found that the northward flowing waters of the Falkland Stream pressed between the main waters of the Brazil Stream and the weaker coastal waters, both proceeding southward. These weaker coastal waters presently were rotated and deflected into the northward flowing Falkland Stream. It has been found, on the basis of some 16,665 observations over a period of ten years, that the waters in the strait region along the eastern coast of Tierra del Fuego have a similar tendency to run south for a short distance and then swing into the northward flowing Cape Horn Stream. Without stretching the facts beyond a reasonable application in

[74] Klaehn, *Über die Meeresströmungen zwischen Kap Horn und der La Plata Mündung* (*Annalen der Hydrographie,* 1911), pp. 654, 656, figs. 34, 38. *Cf.* also Krümmel, *Bemerkungen über die Meeresströmungen und Temperatur des Falklandsee* (*Aus dem Archiv der deutschen Seewarte,* 1882 no. 2), pp. 16, 18. Also, Krümmel, *Aequatorialische Meeresströmungen in dem Atlantischen Ozean* (1876). *Cf.* also the articles in *Aus dem Archiv der deutschen Seewarte,* vol. 5 (1882), no. 2; *Annalen der Hydrographie,* 1883, p. 453; *Zeitschrift für Wissenschaftliche Geographie,* vol. 4 (1883), p. 209. Earlier works are Rennell, *Investigation of the Currents of the Atlantic Ocean* (1832); Maury, *Physical Geography of the Sea* (1855). The recent German works in view of the exhaustive character of the researches in this region appear everywhere to be accepted as authoritative.

the present case, it seems correct to assert that the wreckage of the *capitana* was washed upon the Falkland Islands.

There are but two more matters mentioned in the log that point to a likelihood of the Falklands having been visited by the *Incognita*. The first of these is the statement that no Indians were found in the lands by the voyagers. On the Falklands there were no aborigines. The first inhabitants were the French settlers more than two hundred years later. Both Patagonia and Tierra del Fuego, on the other hand, were inhabited, and in this relation one need examine only the Pigafetta account for the former land, and for the latter the account of the brothers Nodal, who in 1618-19[75] made the first extensive survey of the eastern and southern Fuegian coast. The story of the Nodal voyage contains a wealth of detail, all of which is far different from the essential facts of the log of the *Incognita,* and as the data of the Nodals is confirmed by modern exploration any assumption that the *Incognita* visited the Fuegian coasts is precluded. Finally, it may be pointed out that after leaving the islands on December 3, the *Incognita* sailed for two days, when her latitude was taken at 49° 20'. Assuming that they started from somewhere on the Falkland Islands the distance covered in these two days as disclosed by this latitude is in accord with the previous sailing rate.

One of the most extraordinary and inexplicable facts in the log is the utter failure to relate at any time between January, 1540, and December 5, 1541, the position by latitude of the voyagers; indeed, it seems almost inconceivable that this was not done. Equally strange is the apparent abandonment of any attempt to rejoin Camargo and the rest of the expedition. One is led to wonder whether the master of the vessel was not contemplating a defection, after the manner of Estevan Gomez' desertion of the Magellan expedition. This latter question we can, of course, not

[75] In Markham, *Early Voyages to the Strait of Magellan,* p. 194.

answer, but in respect to the question of latitude we have a secondary source of information which adds great weight to the conclusions hereinbefore stated. This is the map of the strait region in the *Islario* of Santa Cruz.[76]

The important official position of Santa Cruz at this time (1541) has been mentioned. According to Navarrete,[77] one of the objects of the expedition sent out by the Bishop of Plasencia was the testing of a certain newly devised scheme of Santa Cruz for determining longitude, a matter of great uncertainty in these days. Indeed, Santa Cruz himself hoped to have accompanied the armada, but was retained by Charles V for the reason that the emperor enjoyed the lectures of his cosmographer too much to dispense with his presence at court. It was natural, therefore, that Santa Cruz should have felt an intense interest in Camargo's undertaking and that any references to the success of the expedition are entitled to particular consideration. Moreover, the *Islario* was in all probability completed shortly after the return of the *Incognita* from the newly discovered islands, and we can well imagine the eagerness with which Santa Cruz must have interviewed the officers and crew of the ship and have incorporated in his text the verbal as well as the written accounts of the discoveries.

The last map in the *Islario* is an attempt to depict the strait region on the basis of the latest and most comprehensive data. It represents the strait itself in much greater detail than had theretofore been the case, for, as the text of the *Islario* discloses, the Camargo expedition had made extensive surveys in the shores of the strait and on the west coast of Tierra del Fuego and of Chile. These surveys were undoubtedly made by the men who had continued through the strait on their way to Peru. We know that

[76] v. Wieser, *Die Karten von Amerika, etc.,* reprints the text of the *Islario* in so far as it relates to America.

[77] Navarrete, *Opúsculos,* vol. 2, p. 69.

Camargo[78] reached this region and enough time had elapsed for the news to have reached Spain. As for the region with which we are more directly concerned, it is depicted as a promontory of a southern mainland off which lie two small islands. These islands are situated some sixty leagues east of and parallel to the Strait of Magellan in the same latitude. The intervening southern mainland is shown as a stretch of territory scalloped with numerous bays and no islands, much in the same manner as the Terra Australis in Schöner's globes. In the text Santa Cruz states:

Beyond the cape of the Straits the coast turns to the southeast forming a great bay for almost forty leagues. And from there the bay turns to run northeast for fifty leagues to a cape which adjoins a bay called de las Islas (of the Islands) which is between two capes and off which are two little islands. All of this coast which as we have said was also discovered by the armada of the Bishop of Plasencia is full of great and small bays. The aforementioned cape is sixty leagues east northeast of the mouth of the strait. Beyond this cape and the Bay of the Islands the coast runs to the southeast.[79]

The map and description of Santa Cruz are not easily to be reconciled with the actual geography of this region. Furthermore, Santa Cruz fails to remark upon the fact that the Camargo expedition was dispersed and he renders the account of the various discoveries as if they had been made jointly by all the vessels, whereas we know that the *Incognita* never rejoined the captain general and that Camargo proceeded upon his voyage to Peru. Those accounts of the armada that are left us, therefore, show that the discoveries incorporated by Santa Cruz in his map were the result of two distinct operations and that Camargo himself in all probability did not visit the eastern coast of Tierra del Fuego.

By far the most puzzling feature of the Santa Cruz map

[78] Herrera, *op. cit.*, dec. I, lib. 7, c. 8.
[79] v. Wieser, *Die Karten von Amerika, etc.*, p. 58.

is the depiction of the coastal line south of the entrance to the strait to the Bahia de las Yslas. There is nothing in the log of the *Incognita* to indicate that any land was sighted before the landfall of February 4, and thereafter the vessel merely threaded its way about the island-like group then found, within what appear to have been spatially narrow confines. Santa Cruz' own account of these regions excludes any inference that the shores of Tierra del Fuego were coasted continuously to the Bahia de las Yslas for the latter are said by him to be situated east-northeast of the strait. What is likely, therefore, is that the intervening stretch of coast is pure fiction inserted under the influence of the Schöner geographical notions and for which Santa Cruz found support in the surmise of the log-keeper that the islands were a part of the mainland. The latter, it is true, believed them to be south of the strait, a view which the intrinsic evidence in the log negatives, but for which Santa Cruz made allowance by depicting a continuous coast line running first southeast and then northeast; and herein were the fictions of Schöner's first globe perpetuated for years to come.

Contemporary cosmography rapidly accepted the findings of Santa Cruz, for they were embodied in his world map[80] and the political association of Germany and Spain at this time facilitated the absorption of the Spanish maps by the German map makers.[81] The French maps, histori-

[80] Dahlgren, *Map of the World by the Spanish Cosmographer Alonso de Santa Cruz, 1542* (1892).

[81] The important map attributed to Sebastian Cabot, 1544, Rio Branco, *Atlas,* plate 6; a large, but not yet edited photograph, made by Dr. E. L. Stevenson, of which a copy hangs on the walls of the American Geographic Society; in the Ptolemy of Venice, 1548, islands in the position of the Islas de Sanson are depicted but without name, Nordenskiöld, *Facsimile Atlas,* fig. 45; the Apianus-Frisius of 1551, Nordenskiöld, *Facsimile Atlas,* fig. 44, is a copy of the Santa Cruz model; Anonymous of 1554, Nordenskiöld, *Periplus,* fig. 146, is on the Santa Cruz model but without the Sanson Islands; in Rio Branco, *Atlas,* plate 10a, this map is

cally less important, do not show the same tendency to copy from Santa Cruz: indeed, the Ribero influence so patent in attributed to Jacques Gastaldo. The Antonius Florianus globe gores have no Sanson Islands, but the *terra australis* is of the Santa Cruz type, *cf.* Stevenson, *Terrestial and Celestial Globes,* vol. I, fig. 66. The Paulo di Forlani map from Lafreri's Atlas, 1556-1572, Nordenskiöld, *Facsimile Atlas,* fig. 80, has the Patos Islands and the Santa Cruz *terra australis.* Diego Homem's maps of 1558, Rio Branco, *Atlas,* plates 11 and 12; and of 1568, Rio Branco, *Atlas,* plate 17a, and the map of Bartolome Velken, 1561, are modelled closely after Santa Cruz; Johannes Honterus' map in *De Cosmografiæ Rudimentis,* 1561, leaves out the Sanson Islands, but has the Santa Cruz type *terra australis.* The same is true of Ramusio (1566 ed.), Nordenskiöld, *Periplus,* fig. 76. The Gastaldi map of 1562, Nordenskiöld, *Periplus,* fig. 77, and the Diego Gutierrez of 1562, Rio Branco, *Atlas,* plate 7, are faithful adherents of Santa Cruz. The cordiform map of Orontius Finæus (1566) shows the islands without name and has a Santa Cruz type southern continent. The Ortelius Maps (1570-1587) show the greatest variety of data. Two of them are reproduced in Rio Branco, *Atlas,* plates 20 and 21. In the former islands at 48° are shown, but without name; in the latter no islands at all are to be seen. The Ortelius of 1587, Rio Branco, *Atlas,* plate 31, shows no islands, whereas plate 32 shows the islands under the name Isla d'Ascençion. In all cases the southern continent shows the Santa Cruz influence. The Vaz Dourado Map, 1571, in Kunstmann, *op. cit.,* plate VIII, the Thevet Map, 1575, Rio Branco, *Atlas,* plate 23, and the Giovanni Mazza, 1584, *ibid.,* plate 29, are all of the Santa Cruz school. The Belleforest, 1575, Rio Branco, *Atlas,* plate 24, and the Martines, 1582, *ibid.,* plate 27, have the *terra australis* of Santa Cruz, but although they depict the islands the latter are without name. The Mercator of 1587 is of the Santa Cruz type, but there are no islands off the Patagonian coast, Nordenskiöld, *Facsimile Atlas,* fig. 47, Rio Branco, *Atlas,* plate 33. The de Bry map of 1592 is of the same variety, Rio Branco, *Atlas,* plate 34. Peter Plancius, 1592, calls the group I. de Acenca, Rio Branco, *Atlas,* plate 37. The Cornelius de Judæis maps of 1593 in the one case shows no islands at all, Rio Branco, *Atlas,* plate 35, Nordenskiöld, *Facsimile Atlas,* fig. 84; in the other, the I. de Acenca are shown. By this time the metamorphosis in the name of Sanson seems to have been complete, for in 1596 de Bry shows them under the name of Acenca, Rio Branco, *Atlas,* plate 41, and in the Langeren map of the same year they are called Aceçam, Rio Branco, *Atlas,* plate 41. The Michael Mercator map of 1593 gives them no name at all, Rio Branco, *Atlas,* plate 39. Jodocus Hondius, despite his connections with the Mercator family,

the drawings of this region by the *Cosmógrafo mayor* is nearly imperceptible in the Desliens charts.[82]

Not all the Spanish or German maps were drawn from the Santa Cruz model.[83] The depiction of the strait region in older maps is frequently repeated, but on most of the maps of this period we find the Sanson Islands. Indeed, so fixed was the belief that these islands existed that it is not until the seventeenth century,[84] and then only on a few maps, that we find the group encircled with the dotted line denoting a doubt as to their existence. The infrequency of the visits to these regions certainly contributed to this. Following the voyage of Camargo and his armada nearly forty years elapsed before the Spanish government again sent out an expedition. It is true that an extensive survey was made of the western coast of Tierra del Fuego by Juan Ladrillero,[85] but this was under the auspices of the Peru-

shows no islands off the Patagonian coast in his map of 1597, and this despite the further fact that he must have known of Davis' alleged discoveries, Rio Branco, *Atlas*, plate 43.

Matthias Quaden, 1598, calls the islands Isla d'Ascencion, and J. B. Vrient, 1599, modifies the name to Asença, Rio Branco, *Atlas*, plate 48. Both of these maps follow Santa Cruz' delineation of the *terra australis*. This is also true of the Ptolemy of 1598, but no Sanson Islands are depicted there, Nordenskiöld, *Periplus*, fig. 79.

[82] Nicolas Desliens, 1541, Rio Branco, *Atlas*, plate 5; Pierre Descelliers, 1546, Nordenskiöld, *Periplus*, plate LI; Rio Branco, *Atlas*, plate 9; Mongenet gores, 1552, Stevenson, *Terrestial and Celestial Globes*, vol. I, fig. 63. Darinel, Le Sphère des Deux Mondes, Nordenskiöld, *Periplus*, fig. 75, shows the Sanson group.

[83] Freire, 1546, *Kohl Collection*, no. 394, Library of Congress; Nicolas Vallard, 1547, *Kohl Collection*, no. 447, Library of Congress; Calapoda, 1552, Nordenskiöld, *Periplus*, plate XXVI; Girava, 1556, Nordenskiöld, *Facsimile Atlas*, plate XLV; Langenes, 1548, Rio Branco, *Atlas*, plate 43b; Herrera, 1601, Nordenskiöld, *Periplus*, fig. 93; Crescentio, *Nautica mediterranea*, 1601, map of the Magellan Strait, Nordenskiöld, *Periplus*, fig. 27.

[84] Pastells and Bayle, *op. cit.*, vol. I, p. 303.

[85] The Hondius Mercator, 1606, Rio Branco, *Atlas*, plate 53. Van Langeren, 1630, Rio Branco, *Atlas*, plate 61b; de Jongh, 1640, Rio Branco,

vian viceroy and Ladrillero did not sail beyond the Atlantic entrance to the strait. Not until the exploits of British navigators in these waters had awakened in the Spanish an understanding of the importance of controlling the southern passage to the Pacific were fleets again fitted out to perfect and strengthen the Spanish hegemony.

Of the British navigators the geographer owes to Sir Francis Drake[86] a debt considerably greater than to almost any of his contemporaries. His exploit in sailing around the Horn definitely exploded the notion that the Strait of Magellan separated the South American mainland from an austral continent. The Spanish might mutter their dark epithet, *"el corsario,"* against him, but Drake nevertheless aided them both directly and indirectly in their task of mapping the New World.

Drake's discoveries south of 52° south latitude appear first to have been incorporated into the map of Hakluyt of 1587;[87] and although the Santa Cruz delineation of the South Atlantic regions persisted for some time, the series of voyages initiated by Drake in this part of the world brought to light data which fixed the cartographical notions both of the strait region and of Tierra del Fuego. The Falkland Islands, however, still remained something of a geographical mystery, but the alleged British discoveries during the latter years of the sixteenth century formed the basis of their later claims to the Falklands.

The first of these discoveries is said to have been made

Atlas, plate 65. It will be observed that these are maps of Dutchmen. No doubt the announcement by Sebald de Weert of his discovery may have had something to do with this skepticism.

[86] Vaux, *The World Encompassed by Sir Francis Drake* (Hakluyt Society, *Works,* no. 54); Nuttall, *New Light on Drake* (Hakluyt Society, *Works,* series 2, no. 34, 1914). In the latter work is a map drawn of the straits region and indicates that no islands were sighted until Drake reached the group which he named after his sovereign.

[87] This map is in the Hakluyt edition of Peter Martyr's *Decades,* and is reproduced in Nordenskiöld, *Facsimile Atlas,* fig. 82.

by John Davis.[88] Davis was in command of the *Desire*, one
of the vessels of the second expedition of Thomas Cavendish, which sailed from Plymouth on August 26, 1591. According to the account of Cavendish's own historian, he was
treacherously deserted by Davis off Puerto Deseado.[89]
Davis' historian, on the other hand, one John Jane, set
forth in his account of the incident what purported to be a
statement signed by the whole crew of the *Desire*, tending
to show that, far from failing to keep a rendezvous with
Cavendish, they lost sight of the latter in a fog on May 21,
1592, and being unable to locate him, after a lengthy period
of waiting and search they proceeded on their way to the
south.[90]

Having stopped at Penguin Island on August 7, they set
their course for the Strait of Magellan, where Jane says
they hoped to find Cavendish. He goes on to relate:[91]

The ninth wee had a sore storme, so that wee were constrained to
hull, for our sailes were not to indure any force. The 14 wee were
driven in among certain Isles never before discovered by any
knowen relation lying fiftie leagues or better from the shoare East
and northerly from The Streights: in which place unlesse it had
pleased God of his wonderfull mercie to have ceased the winde wee
must of necessitie have perished. But the winde shifting to the East
wee directed our course for the Streights, and the 18 of August
wee fell with the Cape in a very thick fogge and the same night
wee anckered ten leagues within the Cape. The 19th day wee passed
the first and the second Streights.

Close upon the heels of Davis came the celebrated navigator, Richard Hawkins.[92] Hawkins, unlike some of his con-

---

[88] A. H. Markham, *Voyages and Works of John Davis* (Hakluyt Society, *Works*, no. 59, 1880), p. 93.

[89] Purchas, *His Pilgrimes* (1904 ed.), vol. 16, p. 146.

[90] *Voyages and Works of John Davis*, p. 107.

[91] *Ibid.*, p. 108.

[92] *Observations of Sir Richard Hawkins, Knight, in his Voyage into the
South Sea* (Hakluyt Society, *Works*, no. 1, 1848).

temporaries, was fortunate in pursuing his way under a commission from the queen. His voyage, as he says, was undertaken for the purpose of discoveries in the East by way of the Strait of Magellan. Setting sail from England on June 12, 1593, Hawkins reached the Patagonian coast early in the following year. His account of what is generally supposed to have been the discovery of the Falklands is as follows:[93]

The second of February, about nine of the clock in the morning we discryed land, which bare south-west of us, which wee looked for not so timely; and comming neerer and neerer unto it, by the lying, wee could not conjecture what land it should be; for wee were next of anything in forty-eight degrees, and no platt nor seacard which we had made mention of any land which lay in that manner, neere about that height; in fine, wee brought our lar-bord tacke aboord, and stood to the north-east-wardes all that day and night, and the winde continuing westerly and a fayre gale, wee continued our course alongst the coast the day and night following. In which time wee made accompt we discovered well neere threescore leagues of the coast. It is bold and made small shew of dangers.

The land is goodly champion country, and peopled; we saw many fires, but could not come to speake with the people; for the time of yeare was farre spent, to shoot the Straites, and the want of our pynace disabled us for finding a port or roade; not being discretion with a ship of charge, and in an unknowne coast to come neere the shore before it was sounded; which were causes, together with change of winde (good for us to passe the Straite), that hindered the further discovery of this lande, with its secrets: this I have sorrowed for many times since, for that it had likelihood to be an excellent country. It hath great rivers of fresh waters; for the out-shoot of them colours the sea in many places as we ran alongst it. It is not mountaynous, but much of the disposition of England, and as temperate. The things we noted principally on the coast are these following; the westermost poynt of the land, with which we first fell, is the end of the land to the west-wardes, as we found afterwards. If a man bring the poynt south-west, it riseth in three

[93] *Ibid.,* p. 106.

mounts, or round hillockes: bringing it more westerly, they shoot themselves all into one; and bringing it easterly, it riseth in two hillocks. This we call poynt Tremountaine. Some twelve or foure-teene leagues from this poynt to the east-wardes, fayre by the shore, lyeth a low flat iland of some two leagues long; we named it Fayre Iland; for it was all over as greene and smooth as any meddow in the spring of the yeare.

Some three or foure leagues easterly from this iland, is a goodly opening, as of a great river or an arme of the sea with a goodly low countrie adjacent. And eight or tenne leagues from this open-ing, some three leagues from the shore lyeth a bigge rocke, which at the first wee had thought to be a shippe under all her sayles; but after, as we came neere, it discovered it selfe to be a rocke, which we called *Condite-head;* for that howsoever a man cometh with it, it is like to the condite heads about the cittie of London.

All this coast so farre as wee discovered, lyeth next of anything east and by north, and west and by south. The land for that it was discovered in the raigne of Queene Elizabeth, my soveraigne lady and mistres, and a maiden Queene, and at my cost and adventure, in a perpetuall memory of her chastitie, and remembrance of my endeavours, I gave it the name of HAWKINS *maiden-land.*

Before a man fall with this land, some twentie or thirtie leagues, he shall meete with bedds of oreweed driving to and fro in that sea, with white flowers growing upon them, and sometimes farther off; which is a good show and signe that land is neere, whereof the westermost part lyeth some threescore leagues from the neerest land of America.

To the accounts of both Davis and Hawkins the same critical tests may be applied, albeit in the case of the latter we have considerably more data to deal with to form a basis of judgment. With one exception[94] there has been a lament-able failure to treat these two accounts with any degree of scientific skepticism. This is probably due to the fact that the British writers who have concerned themselves most with their two compatriots have instinctively accorded them

[94] Commander Chambers, R.N., in *Geographic Journal,* vol. 17, p. 414, *Can 'Hawkins' Maiden Land' be Identified as the Falklands Islands?*

a greater deference than they would feel toward alien navigators. Nevertheless, in view of the slight and rather inaccurate data given by Davis and Hawkins, there is very little reason for being dogmatic in the claim that one of the two discovered the Falklands.

As far as the location of the islands is concerned, Davis gives no latitudinal bearings whatever, although he states that they lie some fifty leagues from the Strait of Magellan. Hawkins, on the other hand, states that at the time he sighted the islands they were "next of anything in forty-eight degrees." This information is unfortunately of no particular aid, as the Falklands lie between latitude 51° and 53° south. In view of the fact that Hawkins is generally correct in his statements of position we cannot dispose of the matter by saying that in this instance he probably was mistaken. The account of Davis' voyage, by the same token, deserves no more credence than the relation of Vespucci's third voyage, for in addition to the fact that Jane's journal is replete with inaccuracies, the statements relative to the discovery are scarcely more definite than those of Vespucci. To the stories of the two Englishmen, therefore, greater weight may be attached to that of Hawkins.

Some years ago Commander Chambers, R.N., published a careful analysis of the Hawkins account. On the basis of extensive first-hand knowledge of these coasts Commander Chambers came to the conclusion that Hawkins was probably off the Patagonian coast in the region south of Puerto Deseado. Commander Chambers stated his reason for this to be that if Hawkins approached the Falklands from the north none of his data excepting that relative to Cape Tremountaine—which might be Pebble Island—coincides with the topography of the Falkland coast, whereas it does coincide with the aspect of the Patagonian coast. There is no discolored water about the Falklands, and there are no rivers running into the sea; neither is the coast a "goodly low countrie," as Hawkins calls it, for the mountains rise to a height of 2,000 feet. Moreover, there are no threescore leagues of coast available for exploration, but at the most some thirty leagues. Finally, it should be pointed out that the islands were uninhabited and the possibility of observing fires was, therefore, remote.

In the notes is reprinted verbatim the text of Commander Chambers' conclusions.[95] He hazards the opinion that Haw-

[95] *Ibid.*, p. 421. "The question now naturally presents itself, if not the Falkland Islands, where was the land which Hawkins undoubtedly saw? It is natural to turn to the map of the coast and next in anything 48, let us see what we find. Curiously enough, in lat. 47 5 S., lies a point—Cape Tres Puntas—which at once attracts attention by reason of its name, not less than its marked and salient position on the coast, for it is the commencement of an outlying flange which runs, not in truth east by north, but north and by east and is rather over three score miles, (not leagues) in extent. In the centre of this piece of coast, and just 14 leagues from Cape Tres Puntas, is the Desire River. Sir Richard's least estimate of the distance between the goodly river and the cape of three hillocks is 15 leagues, and the tides are strong on the coast. This coincidence is sufficient to attract attention at once.

"Nearly 8 leagues from the Desire River lies the Serius or Eddystone rock, which agrees almost exactly with Sir Richard's estimate. This rock as its name would seem to indicate, was at one time of considerable height, and was marked as such in the old charts; it is now supposed to have become worn away by the action of the sea, and is a rock awash. Some authorities state that it is the same as the Bellaco reef, but this is doubtful; either position would agree as to distance from shore, and the Bellaco resembles a ship under sail. But if the Bellaco be taken to be the Condite Rock, some little adjusting of the distance run must be made to agree with the larger estimate of 10 leagues. Its actual distance is 17 from the Desire River; but, as I have before stated, Sir Robert [*sic*] was not great upon dead reckoning, and the currents are strong in that part up to 3 knots an hour being experienced.

"The coast in all this district is low and undulating, much what Sir Richard, who was more familiar with the south coast of England than the sterner northern parts of the British Islands, would consider 'of the disposition of England.' The weather is far milder than in the Falklands, and at that time it must have been well peopled by a race who delighted to raise signal smokes to attract the attention of passing vessels.

"The question now arises where is Fayre island to be found? It cer-

kins, being out of his reckoning, thought when he first sighted land (Cape Tres Puntas on the mainland, according to Commander Chambers) that it was hitherto unexplored territory; that later Hawkins realized his error but that he kept his own counsel. Hawkins and his crew were later cap-

tainly requires some stretching to believe that Sorell ledge, which occupies the position indicated with reference to the Desire river, can have been diminished by the erosion of the sea to this extent, though the changes which have taken place on this part of the coast are undoubtedly considerable—vide recent surveys of Port S. Julian as compared with those of Nasoa. It is, of course, also possible that the so-called island, the ship not being very near, and telescopes not yet discovered, may have been merely a strip of greensward upon the coast itself. There is no such strip on the west coast of the Falklands. As for Cape Tres Puntas, the Sailing Directions thus describe it: 'Is the termination of a long range of tableland trending north and south; . . . the cape shows three distinct upright heads of a light earthy coloured cliff.' There would probably be plenty of discoloured water about also kelp in the vicinity. One argument more before I come to my summing up. If this coast be followed for a distance of three score leagues, and then course be set for the straits, the remaining distance will be just as estimated by Hawkins—another three score leagues, or 180 miles."

Commander Chambers states that the weak point in his analysis is that it would be necessary were Hawkins in this neighborhood to "bring the ship to the wind upon the starboard tack (or right hand) instead of the 'larborde'; and secondly the direction of the coast is W. by E. and not E. by W." He explains this by the fact that Sir Richard wrote without papers and from memory many years later.

It should be stated that Commander Chambers has pointed out that in years of experience in these regions he never saw discolored water about the Falklands, and that there is no possible island on these coasts meeting the description of Fayre Island. Commander Chambers also states that he believes if Hawkins had been in the Falklands he would certainly have spoken less kindly of the weather than he did. Finally he points out the strange circumstance that if the *Daintee* had followed the course to the strait that Hawkins says he set it would have been impossible for him not to have seen the Jason Islands. *Cf.* further *The South American Pilot*, vol. 2, p. 88 *et seq.* Nuño da Silva's log book in Nuttall, *op. cit.*, p. 280, has the entry for May 17, 1578, "On the same course along the coast and we sighted a great rock six leagues out at sea in 48½."

tured by the Spanish, and although the crew returned to England, Hawkins himself was long a prisoner in Spain. He wrote his "Observations" some twenty-five years after the event and probably without many of his ship's papers. This fact alone may offer an adequate explanation of some of the statements in his account of the voyage.

Jane's account of Davis' voyage appeared in 1600; the Hawkins "Observations" some eighteen years later. In view of the vagueness of detail in Jane's account already mentioned and the glaring improbability of certain statements made by him in other relations, such as the length of time taken to pass through the strait, it may be that Jane appropriated the verbal accounts of Hawkins' voyage, undoubtedly well known to all seafaring men in England, for the glory and honor of his own captain, particularly as Davis' defection of Cavendish must have been regarded as somewhat unsavory. On the other hand, it may well be that the reverse was the case and that Hawkins appropriated the discovery of Davis. This latter view has been advanced by one writer,[96] but it deserves little consideration. A far more plausible explanation of these alleged discoveries yet remains.

We have already seen that the Spanish maps for over sixty-five years had almost without exception not failed to include the Islas de Sanson, or as they were later called, Ascension, off the Patagonian coasts in 48° south latitude. Unquestionably some of these maps were in English possession, and although Hakluyt's map in his edition of Peter Martyr did not include these islands, the current editions of Ortelius showed them sometimes with a name and sometimes without. The comprehensive *Index Geographicus* of Robert Hues in his treatise *De Globis* proves that the British navigators were generally familiar with contemporary car-

[96] Groussac, *op. cit.*, p. 474, thinks that Hawkins may simply have stolen Davis' story. It does not occur to him that if we are to indulge in such sinister suggestions it may have been just as well the other way about.

tography. It seems, therefore, almost impossible that such able navigators as Davis and Hawkins were not well informed about these charts.[97] In any event, what could be more likely than, knowing of this group of islands at about 48°, both navigators should have believed themselves to be among them, or if they did not actually see the islands that they believed they saw them, knowing that they were supposed to be there? During his long stay in Spain Hawkins must certainly have seen Spanish charts and as it was at this period when doubts as to the existence of the Islas de Sanson first arose, it would be scarcely human if, having seen land in these regions, he failed to assume the credit for discovering the islands as far as his countrymen were concerned, particularly as the Spanish seemed to doubt their existence.

Whatever view of these discoveries we take, there seems little excuse for accepting without challenge the statement that the Falklands were discovered either by Hawkins or Davis on the basis of data by no means more detailed or convincing than the accounts of the Spaniards that we have already examined. Certainly the English cartographers of the period took no immediate notice of the claims of either Hawkins or Davis, for we find no record of them in the contemporary maps. The great map published in the 1600 edition of Hakluyt and attributed to Wright and to Molyneux,

[97] Kohl, *Descriptive Catalogue of those Maps and Works relating to America that are Mentioned in Volume III of Hakluyt's Great Work* (1857). In Peter Martyr, *Decades* (Lok trans.), sixth chapter, seventh decade, it is stated that Magellan saw many islands, but that his mind was so greedily set upon the Moluccas that he had no eyes for any other islands. Consequently other expeditions had the task of discovering more about these islands. This work was known in England many years before the Davis expedition. It is not surprising that men should be thinking that they were finding these islands which Magellan was too busy to investigate. It may also be stated that the idea of unknown islands seems for centuries to have worked peculiar fascination upon the minds of men. *Cf.* Babcock, *Legendary Islands of the Atlantic* (1921).

depicts the Sanson group close to the Patagonian coast and calls it by this name. Undoubtedly the map makers were satisfied that whatever Davis saw it must have been the same land that the Spanish claimed decades before to have discovered.[98]

It has been stated that the English voyages to the Strait of Magellan gave a great impulse to certain attempts on the part of the Spanish to occupy and consolidate their discoveries in this region. These attempts were the result of the brave and indomitable spirit of Pedro Sarmiento de Gamboa.[99] Sarmiento had made a comprehensive survey of the strait in 1579-1580, and in 1581, largely in consequence of

[98] The so-called Hakluyt map of 1599, Nordenskiöld, *Facsimile Atlas*, plate L, Rio Branco, *Atlas*, plates 49 and 49a. In view of the fact that no islands are discernible in the 1587 map in Hakluyt's edition of Peter Martyr, it may be that he intended these islands to represent the country discovered by Davis. There is, of course, no evidence of Hawkins' alleged discovery.

There is nothing to indicate a knowledge of the Davis report in the van Sype map corrected by Drake and preserved in the Hispanic Society at New York City. It is reproduced in Nuttall, *op. cit.*, at p. lvi.

In this connection mention should be made of the Hondius maps. Hondius, though a Dutchman, learned his profession in England and resided there a number of years. His maps are silent of any knowledge of Davis' reputed discovery. The map of 1595, reproduced in Hakluyt Society, *Works*, no. 16, shows no islands off Patagonia. His edition of Mercator of 1602 has an island off Patagonia south of 50° south latitude, Rio Branco, *Atlas*, plate 51. Another map from the same work gives this island the name *Ascension, ibid.*, plate 52. In the 1600 edition of Mercator it is called *Acencam*. The map of 1611, which is Hondius' supreme achievement, shows no islands whatever; *cf. Map of the World by Jodocus Hondius, 1611*, text and map (Stevenson and Fischer eds., 1907). But see the inset showing an elevation of the Sebald Islands in the map of the Magellan Straits in the Mercator-Hondius atlas of 1606.

[99] Pedro Sarmiento de Gamboa, *Viaje al Estrecho de Magallanes* (Yriarte ed., 1768). The account of his attempt to found a colony in the Strait region is in Torres de Mendoza, *op. cit.*, vol. 5. These works are both translated in Markham, *Narratives of the Voyage of Pedro Sarmiento de Gamboa* (Hakluyt Society, *Works*, no. 91, 1895). *Cf.* also the documents in Pastells and Bayle, *op. cit.*, vol. 2, p. 11 *et seq.*, p. 73 *et seq.*

his representations, a large expedition was fitted out under the command of Flores de Valdes to colonize the strait region. Sarmiento was commissioned governor of this colony. The expedition and the colony were doomed to a most miserable and heartrending end, and its brave and self-sacrificing governor was eventually to be captured by the English. What is especially noteworthy in the present connection is that Sarmiento made two voyages to the strait and three unsuccessful attempts to reach his colony. On none of these occasions did he come within sight of the Falklands. Not many years after the failure of Sarmiento's expedition, the spread of Spanish power was severely checked by the defeat of the Great Armada, and by the rapid rise of the Dutch as a seafaring power. Just as the increased commercial activity of England was initiated by the spectacular feats of Cavendish and Drake, so in Holland the expeditions of Mahu, Cordes, and Weert, and of Spilberg ushered in an energetic movement to obtain possessions overseas. The first of these Dutch expeditions is of direct concern to ourselves.

On June 27, 1598, there sailed from Rotterdam five vessels under the command of Jacob Mahu.[100] By April of the following year the ships were halfway through Magellan's Strait, when they encountered in the Long Reach Channel the most devastating storms. The passage of the strait was at length effected, but in the Pacific the weather became so unendurably bad that the five ships agreed to separate. The *Geloof,* under the command of Sebald de Weert, proceeded to return to Holland. On January 16, 1600, the *Geloof* ran out of the strait into the Atlantic. The account of the voyage rendered by the ship's surgeon goes on to say:[101]

[100] De Bry, *Americæ Nona Pars* (Frankfurt, 1602). Bernard Jansz, *Relatio Historica.* On de Weert *cf.* Wieder (ed.), *De Reis van Mahu en de Cordes door de Straat van Magalhães naar Zuid-Amerika en Japan* (1923), vol. 1, p. 91. This volume has Jansz' account in Dutch.

[101] De Bry, *op. cit.,* p. 52.

On the 24th day about dawn, three little islands were sighted, hitherto neither noted nor drawn on any map. These were given the new name *Sebaldes*. These islands are distant from the continent sixty leagues toward the east and southeast in 50° 40′ latitude. In the same place they found an extraordinary number of penguins which, if they had not lost their skiff, they could with difficulty have passed by.

On the 26th day with a N.N.E. wind blowing they sailed beyond these islands and they ran on the same course until the thirtieth day.

The landfall of de Weert was in all probability the Jason Islands lying northwest of the West Falkland Island. The Jasons actually lie between 51° and 51° 50′. The bearing given by de Weert's chronicler is sufficiently accurate for us to regard the notice of the landfall as correct, although in view of the conflicting reports of prior discovery we cannot with justice call de Weert the discoverer of the group. The statement as to the number of leagues the islands lie from the continent is incorrect, but as we have already seen these estimates are rarely reliable. It is curious that having just proceeded out of the strait the islands should have been spoken of as lying south and southeast of the continent, for one would normally expect a statement of position with reference to the place last visited.

With de Weert's account we can regard the first phase of the history of the Falklands as having come to a close. These islands were at last definitely fixed on the charts, for we find that the Dutch cartographers[102] accepted the facts as related by de Weert and on their maps the Sebald Islands gradually replace the Sanson group of the Spaniards.

[102] This was particularly true of de Weert's treatment of the Strait of Magellan. *Cf.* the map in De Bry, *op. cit.*, at the end of the Jansz account. Hondius is believed to have used de Weert's map as the basis for his own delineation of the Strait in Purchas, *op. cit.*, vol. 14, p. 544. *Cf.* also Laet, *Novus Orbis* (1633), p. 509, and the Blaeu map of 1640, where a particular acknowledgement is made to de Weert. *Cf.* also Wieder, *op. cit.*, vol. 2 (1924).

Indeed, in such high esteem did the Dutch hold de Weert's geographical data that any other result was excluded.[103] Moreover, the expedition of Le Maire and Schouten[104] which sailed from Holland in 1614 reported having sighted the Sebaldes, and thus any lingering doubts as to the correctness of de Weert's account were dissipated. None of the navigators related tales of the beauty and wealth of the islands such as would lure on adventurous and romantic souls to a closer examination of these windswept roosts of the penguin; and decades were to pass before men were to set foot upon their shores.

[103] Cf. the map in Laet, *Nieuwe Wereldt* (1624), p. 391. The map in Speed, *A Prospect of the Most Famous Parts of the World* (1631), also shows the Sebald Islands, and hence it would appear that the alleged Davis and Hawkins discoveries were not regarded with the same respect as those of de Weert. This was probably due to the fact that the Le Maire and Schouten expedition, which reported the very important discovery of the Strait of Le Maire as well as Staten Land, also sighted the Sebald Islands and reported them by name. Cf. Barlaeus, *Descriptio Indiæ*, where the Le Maire journey is set forth and the map of their journey is reproduced, fol. 67. De Bry, *op. cit.* (1619), fol. 67. The Noort map in his *Description du Pénible Voyage* (1602) shows no islands off Patagonia. Noort met de Weert shortly before the latter discovered the Sebald group.

[104] Barlaeus, *op. cit.* De Bry, *op. cit.*

Through the courtesy of Dr. Rosenbach the writer was privileged to examine certain *portolani* in the Phillips' Collection. No. 8275, map 1, shows four unnamed islands off the Bahia de los Trabajos; map no. 2 shows six Islas de los patos. No. 22796 shows the Sanson group. No. 16365, a map of the straits, likewise shows islands in the position of the Sansons. It has the "c. de l'isoloti" of Santa Cruz. No. 24051, nos. 5 and 6, presumably Agneses of 1553, show six islands, and the islas de Sanson, respectively.

CHAPTER II

DISCOVERY AND OCCUPATION IN INTERNATIONAL LAW

MAN can find no new field of activity into which the cold relentless figure of the law does not follow him. Before the discovery of America European nations gave little thought to the international problems of colonies and control of the seas, partly because there was at first little or no competition between them, and partly because the notion of owning colonies was not conceived until the discoveries in Africa a few decades before Columbus' initial voyage took place. The method by which sovereign rights over the newly discovered regions could be acquired was a matter which concerned the Spanish from the very first, because they had at hand a great maritime rival, and, unless war was to ensue, some peaceful method of settling conflicting claims had to be found. Was it enough that a nation could claim that its navigators had made the first discoveries? Was it enough to plant the royal ensign on territory, and then sail away, leaving the land actually to be occupied at a later date? Was it necessary, to secure sovereignty, at once to plant a colony on the territory claimed? All of these problems were attacked by the Spanish and Portuguese courts immediately upon the return of Columbus. The answer to them worked out in the early days of exploration profoundly affected the subsequent claims of title to the Falklands, and for this reason it is necessary for us to examine in detail the rules governing discovery and occupation.

The discoveries of Columbus mark the commencement of a commercial and economic policy of European states that was chiefly the result of the ruling theories of mercantilism. From the political point of view these new policies attempted to carry over to the relations of the mother state with its colonies the same restrictive and cohesive form of economic machinery that obtained within the territorial boundaries of the state itself. As a system the commercial development of the state which had colonies was favored, and it was intended to exclude from the benefits of colonial possessions states which had no colonies. Indeed, in its earliest and most extreme form this system resulted in restricting among a few powers the dominion over colonies, and as a necessary part of the scheme the claim to exclusive jurisdiction over the seas was advanced.

We cannot concern ourselves here too minutely with the earlier phases of the extraordinary assertions made by Portugal and Spain, and later by other nations, to a legal dominion over the high seas. At the outset of both Portuguese and Spanish expansion overseas, claims of this sort were advanced as a means of justifying their attempts to absorb the newly discovered worlds, and these claims enjoyed a fiercely contested existence as an integral part of this policy. But it was not long before it became apparent that claims to exclusive dominion derived their validity not from the books, but from the fact of their successful enforcement, and hence the notion of the closed sea (*mare clausum*) presently was restricted to narrower fields of political use, and finally was definitely rejected.

When the claims to an exclusive dominion over the seas (*dominium maris*) were first asserted, the European world still lay under the spell of ecclesiastical sanctions, albeit somewhat restlessly, that had characterized international politics during the middle ages. It was, furthermore, at the time when the revival of interest in the Roman law had cast in some places a few last drops of oil upon the feebly flickering flame of universal monarchy. The glossators and commentators on the Roman law had, it is true, busied themselves with demolishing the arguments inherent in the Roman law in favor of a system of universal sovereignty, and yet the *Corpus iuris civilis* was peculiarly pertinent on all

matters in which exclusive imperial control could be asserted. Moreover, this was before the time when the Roman
law had been adapted to the new science of international
law, and before any unanimity had been found among jurists as to the extent to which this adaptation was sound and
pertinent in international affairs.

The Spanish claims to an exclusive jurisdiction over the
seas had their origin in the bulls of Pope Alexander VI of
1493, by which the line of demarcation was drawn delimit-
ing the Spanish and Portuguese spheres of colonization and
right.[1] These bulls were the most celebrated in a series of
similar measures by which the papal power confirmed the
claims to exclusive right made by the Portuguese monarchs
for the preceding discoveries of the fifteenth century. At
the time, the legal validity of these letters patent, as we may
well designate them, seems to have been unquestioned. The
power of the pope to issue them is supposed to have rested
in the last instance upon the so-called Donation of Constantine, which was alleged to have conveyed to Pope Sylvester
and his successors the title, among other lands, to the islands of the world.[2] The implications of this alleged gift
were elaborated by St. Augustine into the accepted doctrine
of the church that the whole world was the property of God
in which mankind had only a usufructuary interest. Accordingly the pope, as the vicegerent of God on earth, had
the power of disposition over the unoccupied lands of the
earth. The power of the pope was also justified in his right

---

[1] Nys, *La Ligne de Démarcation d'Alexandre VI* (*Revue de Droit Inter-
national et de la Legislation Comparée,* vol. 27, p. 474); Harrisse, *The
Diplomatic History of America* (1897); Bourne, *Essays in Historical
Criticism* (1901); Dawson, *Lines of Demarcation of Pope Alexander VI*
(*Transactions of the Royal Society of Canada,* 2d series (1899), vol. 5,
p. 467); Gellman, *Die Völkerrechtliche Okkupation* (*Zeitschrift für das
Privat und Öffentliche Recht* (1915), vol. 41, p. 641; Pastor, *Geschichte
der Päpste* (1899), vol. 3, p. 517.

[2] On this *cf.* Coleman, *Constantine the Great and Christianity* (1914),
p. 175 *et seq.;* Fournier, *Etudes sur les fausses Décrétales* (1907).

and duty to effect the conversion of the heathen, a matter of which we shall treat later in connection with the jurisdiction over new-found lands.

It is familiar learning that the supposititious Donation of Constantine was the object of attack during the latter middle ages, in so far as it formed the basis of papal claims of hegemony over the temporal princes of Europe. In respect to the unoccupied lands, however, it seems to have been regarded as possessing some validity. This was due not only to the attitude of the law writers,[3] but also to an early precedent which was treated with some respect. John of Salisbury, in his *Metalogicus,*[4] states that Henry II obtained from Pope Hadrian a grant of Ireland at the time that he was about to conquer that land. The authenticity of the bull *Laudabiliter,*[5] which is the chief remaining evidence of this assertion, has been questioned, but the fact remains that English authorities claimed this papal patent as the basic legal justification of their sovereignty over Ireland.

The bulls granted by the popes appear to have been animated by the purpose of spreading the Christian faith in the world, and their practical effect was to add color of right to the mere naked fact of possession of hitherto unoccupied territory. In other words, at a time when there were no recognized rules of law to govern discovery and occupation, papal permission supplied a sanction that was in general respected by all states. It was in this manner that the Portuguese consolidated their claims to the African coasts. The first of these bulls was one issued by Nicholas V

---

[3] Gellman, *op. cit.,* p. 465, states that the great Italian jurist, Bartolus, in his *Tractatus de Insula* (*Opera Omnia,* Venice, 1595, vol. 10), supports the pope's right to make grants of newly discovered territory. This is a misstatement of Bartolus' view. The latter uses language which excludes such a sweeping conclusion.

[4] John of Salisbury, *Opera Omnia* (*Patrologiæ Latinæ* (1855), vol. 199, p. 825). *Cf.* Eggers, *Die Urkunde Papst Hadrians IV* (in *Historische Studien,* no. 151, 1922).

[5] Rymer, *Fœdera,* vol. 1, p. 5.

on June 18, 1452,[6] by which Afonso V of Portugal was authorized to attack and subjugate all countries of infidels, and it appears to have applied generally to non-Christian countries. Two years later, on January 8, 1454,[7] another bull of Nicholas V granted to the same sovereign all the regions discovered, and in future to be discovered, south of Cape Bojador and Cape Non toward Guinea, and all those regions on the south coast and on the east *"usque ad Indos."* Finally, on September 12, 1484, Innocent VIII confirmed the previous bulls in similar language, by which the Portuguese claim to the vast area of Africa and the intervening lands to India was apparently fixed.

The bull of 1452 is phrased in the most general terms of a broad grant of sovereignty and makes no specific mention of the sea, although it itemizes cities, towns, provinces, etc., in a manner indicating an intention to convey dominion only over lands. On the other hand, Pope Nicholas V's pronouncement of 1454 is specific in relation to the control of the seas, for not only are the latter specified in terms in the grant, but other states are warned from them in the most solemn language.[8]

The fiat of the pope was no mere idle phrase. It was

[6] Latin text in Raynaldus, *Annales Ecclesiastici* (1752), vol. 9, p. 600.

[7] Latin text in Gaude, *Bullarum diplomatum et privilegiorum sanctorum romanorum pontificum* (1860), vol. 5, p. 110. Translated in Davenport, *European Treaties bearing on the History of the United States* (1917), p. 20. This latter work is most useful and excellent; the research is thorough and enlightening.

[8] ". . . *ad obviandum præmissis, ac pro suorum iuris et possessionis, conservatione, sub certis tunc expressis gravissimis pœnis prohibuerint et generaliter statuerint quod nullus nisi cum suis nautis ac navibus et certi tributi, solutione obtentaque prius desuper expressa at eodem rege vel infante licentia ad dictæ provinci ac navigare aut in earum portibus contractare, seu in mari piscari presumeret."* Cf. also the bull, *Inter Cætera*, of Calixtus III, of March 13, 1456, Davenport, *op. cit.*, p. 17; and *Æterni Regis* of June 21, 1481, *ibid.*, p. 49. Harrisse mentions a bull of September 12, 1484, but none of the collections available to the author contain it. Cf. Harrisse, *op. cit.*, p. 8.

accepted as a mandate, binding upon all the monarchs of Christendom, and there is no more cogent proof of this fact than the warning conveyed to Columbus by the Spanish monarchs, when he set out upon his journey, that he should stay away from the forbidden territory.[9] It is proper to remark, however, that there was a specific recognition by Spain of the Portuguese rights in Article 8 of the Treaty of Alcaçovas of 1479, by which the Spanish crown bound itself to observe the sovereignty granted to Portugal in not permitting expeditions to proceed into these seas for the purpose of discovery or commerce, except as licensed by the Portuguese.[10] Obviously, however, a grant in such all-embracing terms as these two bulls of Nicholas V was possible only so long as cartographical knowledge was restricted in its scope, and so long as relatively few persons knew what was being granted, and had no interest in an attempt to poach upon the rights of the grantee. Such a state of affairs existed only for a short period.

Upon the return of Columbus from his first voyage, and as a result of the immediate and energetic action of Ferdinand and Isabella, the famous bulls of Alexander VI were issued on May 3 and 4, 1493.[11] We are concerned here only with the bearing of these documents upon the claims of the Spanish to an exclusive right of occupancy and control over the region assigned to them. These regions were fixed as lying west of a line one hundred leagues west of the islands "commonly called de los Azores y Cabo Vierde" and running from pole to pole. The grant embraced all islands and *terra firma,* discovered and to be discovered, with all their "domains, cities, strongholds, places, cities, rights and jurisdictions and appurtenances" and conveyed "full and free power, authority and jurisdiction of every kind." Furthermore, all persons of whatever estate were warned, under

[9] Herrera, *Decadas,* Dec. II, lib. II, cap. IV, p. 40.
[10] Davenport, *op. cit.,* p. 36.
[11] Gaude, *op. cit.,* vol. 5, p. 361 et seq.; Davenport, *op. cit.,* p. 56 *et seq.*

pain of excommunication, from coming into these regions, except they be so licensed by the grantees, all previous grants of the pope to the contrary notwithstanding.

It will be observed that this grant, although not specifically mentioning the sea, contains a clear implication of dominion over it in the provision excluding other sovereigns from access to it. And this seems to have been the understanding of the Spanish rulers. Navarrete[12] gives the text of a royal *cédula* of May 28, 1493, in which it is stated, ''It is our will that you be admiral of the said Ocean sea which is ours and which commences at a band or line which we have had marked, etc.'' The same theory must have obtained in Portugal, for there was an immediate initiation of negotiations to determine the difficulties that might arise from a conflict in the rights granted to Portugal and Spain, respectively, and in the interim the King of Portugal held in port the fleet which he had fitted out to pursue discoveries in the New World.[13] This conflict of jurisdiction appeared to be inevitable, in view of the fact that on September 26, 1493, the bull *Dudum Sequidem*[14] was issued by Alexander VI, in which the rights conveyed by the earlier bulls were extended to embrace the territories that might be in the route of navigation toward the west or south, whether ''in western parts or in the regions south and east of India.''

The Treaty of Tordesillas, June 3, 1494,[15] which fixed the rights of the two powers, altered the demarcation of Pope Alexander VI by moving the line 270 leagues farther west than the boundary laid down in the bull of May 4. It was expressly provided in this treaty that each power pledged itself that henceforward neither would dispatch ships into

---

[12] Navarrete, *Colección de los Viajes y Descubrimientos* (1825), vol. 2, at p. 60.

[13] Harrisse, *The Diplomatic History of America*, p. 59 et seq.

[14] Davenport, *op. cit.*, p. 80.

[15] Martens, *Recueil des Traités* (Supplement), vol. 1, p. 372; Davenport, *op. cit.*, p. 86.

the regions assigned to the other for the purpose of discovery or of trade, or conquest. Moreover, in view of the fact that ships of Spain would have to cross the seas on the Portuguese side of the line, the right of crossing these seas was granted, and any discoveries that might be made in these waters were to belong to the king of Portugal and were to be surrendered to him.

The circumstance that this treaty effected a change in the substance of what had been granted by the pope does not appear to alter the fact that at the time the treaty was negotiated the grants were regarded as the real source of the rights of the parties. That twelve years were to elapse before the treaty was confirmed by Julius II with the bull *Ea Quae*[16] does not seem in any way inconsistent with this view. Indeed, as has already been pointed out, not only previous precedent but certain law writers supported the view that in newly discovered lands investiture by the pope was necessary to the exercise of sovereignty. This was certainly true with reference to claims of dominion over the sea. As we shall presently see in regard to the lands with which these documents dealt, the Holy See may have postulated its grant upon possession; but such a postulate was, in the case of the sea, an impossibility. In this relation the Roman law doctrine that the sea was common to all gave way to the mediæval notion that the pope had the inherent power to convey rights over things which were not otherwise subject to the ordinary modes of acquiring property. In such a manner, therefore, did the moribund doctrines of the mediæval church reach out into the modern age to precipitate a conflict that was to last for centuries.

There seems to be no doubt but that the arrangements concluded at Tordesillas were regarded by the two parties as definitely determining their mutual rights. The extent to which these rights were accepted by other powers is very

---

[16] Davenport, *op. cit.*, p. 108. Also in da Silva, *Corpo Diplomatico Portuguez*, vol. 1, p. 91.

problematic. At this time the relations between England and Spain were of a most cordial nature, for negotiations were on foot over the marriage of the Infanta Catherine with Prince Arthur. Moreover, the fact that Henry VII was finally induced to enter the so-called Holy League in 1495 seems to have been due chiefly to the efforts of Ferdinand. Another circumstance which is of importance in this connection is that the maritime strength of England was at a low ebb and the interest in exploration was consequently not enthusiastic.[17]

Whether or not the voyage of John Cabot precipitated any conflict over the dominion claimed by Spain it is impossible to say. The Spanish ambassador at London, Don Diego de Puebla, seems to have been more devoted to his physical comfort and the business of extracting largesses from Henry than to his sovereign's interest. It may be, too, as Harrisse[18] suggests, that the stories of icy wastes and polar bears brought back by Cabot not being calculated to stimulate further exploration, the incident was permitted to pass unchallenged. In any event, the Cabot voyage was reported to Ferdinand and Isabella in a dispatch which is unfortunately lost. In the reply of these sovereigns they state:[19] "But we believe that this undertaking was thrown in the way of the King of England by the King of France, with the premeditated intention of distracting him from his other business. Take care that the King of England be not deceived in this or in any other matter. The French will try as hard as they can to lead him into such undertakings, but they are very uncertain enterprises, and must not be gone into at present. Besides they cannot be executed without

[17] On these relations *cf.* Schacht, *Englische Handelspolitik gegen Ausgang des Mittelalters* (1881), vol. 1, p. 268 *et seq.;* Williamson, *Maritime Enterprise 1485-1558, passim.*

[18] Harrisse, *The Diplomatic History of America,* p. 48.

[19] *Calendar of State Papers, Spanish* (Bergenroth ed., 1862), vol. I, p. 89. Hereafter cited as Bergenroth.

prejudice to us and to the King of Portugal.'' Again, in 1498, in a dispatch from Pedro de Ayala (of July 25, 1498)[20] the Spanish monarchs were informed of a design to make explorations in Brazil in derogation of the Spanish king's right, but there is no notice of any protest against the voyage.[21] The political situation in Europe may have been the cause for this, although there is some reason to suppose that, in the following year, the treaty concluded between Spain and England conferred the right of trafficking in the regions claimed by Spain overseas. The fourth article of this treaty provided:[22] ''The subjects of either of the allies are at liberty to travel and carry on commerce, or other business in the dominions of the other ally. Neither general nor special passports are required. They shall be treated like the native born subjects of the country in which they are staying.''[23]

At the time when this treaty was signed, Spain had but a single colony in the New World, and hence an extension of commercial privileges was by no means an extraordinary concession. But if by ''other business'' is meant exploration and discovery, the rights conceded were unprecedented. Such a concession seems unlikely, for the language of the agreement hardly conveys the idea that such rights were bargained away.

The treaty of 1499 marked the end of a hard-fought struggle on the part of the Spanish to secure a commercial foothold in England. At the same time, due to the maritime superiority of the Spanish, the English commerce with Spain was practically wiped out, and a new commercial war seems to have been averted only by the political exigencies of the time. This result was, however, merely temporary,

[20] *Ibid.,* p. 176.
[21] Williamson, *op. cit.,* p. 79, reads into the negotiations things which the records do not support.
[22] Bergenroth, *op. cit.,* p. 210.
[23] Ratifications including Portugal, *ibid.,* nos. 251, 252, 261.

due to the policy of both countries to establish an independent and superior merchant marine; and despite the more or less solemn treaty pledges, the actual working of the relationships between the merchants of the two countries was a thing of difficulty and despair.[24]

In 1501 there was issued to a group of English and Portuguese merchants a royal patent[25] giving authority to explore countries hitherto unknown, which, if found, were to be taken possession of and occupied. Moreover, the Portuguese members of the company were to be naturalized and given most of the rights of Englishmen. One of these Portuguese had been given a patent in 1499 by his sovereign, King Manuel, authorizing him to make voyages in the northwest, and another patent was issued him in 1508.[26] The sagacity of this move on the part of the English is characteristic of their genius for trade. A business organization operating under the patents of two monarchs was in a peculiarly favorable position in those days of frequent reprisals; but of even greater significance to our purpose is the implied admission of the rights of the Portuguese subjects under the papal patents and the treaty with Spain. Henry VII,[27] unwilling to involve his political relationships with disputes over commercial matters, adopted a form of association that placed the enterprise under the ægis of Portuguese protection, and thus removed any possibility of conflict with Spain at a moment when the long-negotiated marriage of Catherine of Aragon was about to reach a satisfactory conclusion. This aspect of the matter is confirmed by the fact that the company appears to have operated in

[24] Schanz, op. cit., p. 275.

[25] Biddle, A Memoir of Sebastian Cabot, p. 306, gives the text. Cf. also Williamson, op. cit., p. 104.

[26] Harrisse, Evolution Cartographique de Terre Neuve, p. 41.

[27] Busch, England unter den Tudors (1892), vol. 1, p. 153 et seq.; p. 367.

the *Terra Corterealis*[28] (Labrador), which the Portuguese had somewhat carelessly, albeit designedly, it would seem, placed upon their maps as falling within their side of the line of demarcation. Moreover, the patent issued by Henry VII to the reorganized enterprise in 1502 contains an express recognition of the rights of the sovereigns of Portugal and Spain.[29] After conferring the authority to take possession, subject and govern newly found lands, the charter stated: "Provided always, that in no manner shall they enter upon or hinder (*impediant*) those countries, nations, regions or provinces, heathen or infidel, which have previously been found by the subjects of our most dear brother and cousin the King of Portugal, or of any other prince, friend, or neighbor of ourselves, and which already are in the possession of the said princes." The patent provided further, as had its predecessor, that in the lands settled by the patentees the right was conferred upon them to oust any intruders, even if the latter should be the subjects of a friendly or allied power.[30]

The form of this patent is exceedingly interesting because of the qualified acknowledgment of the rights of Portugal and other states in the newly discovered lands, and particularly because the navigators were warned away from lands discovered and already *in the possession* of other princes. The provision giving a right to oust intruders is a most cogent proof that the English king recognized possession as the only true source of right; the importance of this notion we shall presently discuss in detail.

From these facts it seems fair to assume that Henry VII regarded the claims of the Spanish and Portuguese to certain exclusive rights in the new continent as defensible only

[28] Williamson, *op. cit.*, p. 105 *et seq. Cf.* also Harrisse, *John and Sebastian Cabot* (1896), p. 145.

[29] Rymer, *Fœdera,* vol. 13, p. 37. Dated December 9, 1502.

[30] Biddle, *loc. cit.* Also in Hakluyt Society, *Works,* vol. 7, introduction (Jones ed.).

in so far as these claims were supported by actual possession. He was, however, too shrewd a politician to proceed into the open with any such doctrine, and it was unquestionably because he recognized the fact that the papal bulls gave to Spain and Portugal a political, if not a legal, claim of some merit that he adopted the clever device of carrying on the English colonial projects in association with Portuguese nationals. The usefulness of such a device lay, not only in the fact that it served as a cloak for territorial designs, but also in the fact that with respect to the sea, the legal status of which was far from settled, the papal patents had conveyed something more than a mere color of right.

The existing European view of the sea was very complicated.[31] The ancient Roman law[32] idea had been that the sea was common to all and was not capable of ownership. As a matter of fact, the Romans had exercised a practically undisputed imperium over the seas after the defeat of the

[31] The writer has consulted the following works: Nau, *Grundsaetze des Völkerseerechts* (1802); Azuni, *Maritime Law* (New York, 1806 ed.), vol. I; Fulton, *The Sovereignty of the Sea* (1911); Niewind, *Der Kampf um die Freiheit der Meere* (1919); With, *Die Entwickelung des Theorie der Meeres Freiheit* (1913); Loccenius, *De Jure Maritimo* (1652); Solorozano, *Politica Indiana* (1776); Selden, *Mare Clausum* (1636); Grotius, *Mare Liberum* (1773); Nuger, *Les droits de l'Etat sur la Mer Territoriale* (1887); Prida, *Estúdios de Derecho Internacional* (1901), p. 141; Tellegen, *Disputatio de Jure in Mare* (1847); Cauchy, *Le Droit Maritime International* (1862); Reddie, *Researches in Maritime International Law* (1844); Steir-Somlo, *Die Freiheit der Meere* (1917); Schücking, *Das Küstenmeer im Internationalen Recht* (1897). The whole subject is one that still awaits a thorough and comprehensive scientific study. The recent work of Potter, *Freedom of the Seas* (1923), in no way achieves this. Potter's discussion of the mediæval views fails to mention the *De Insula* of Bartolus, perhaps the most important juristic utterance regarding territorial waters to the time of Bynkershoek. Such statements as appear on p. 51, that Vasquez "goes mainly on Digest XLI," are the sort of thing that scarcely merit the term scholarship.

[32] Pernice, *Die Sogenannten res communes omnium* (*Festgabe für Heinrich Dernburg*, 1900), p. 125 et seq., Inst. 2, 1, 1; D. 47, 10, l. 13, § 7; D. 43, 8, l. 3, § 1; D. 8, 4, l. 13; D. 8, 4, l. 13; D. 14, 2, l. 9; D. 1, 8, l. 2, 1.

Carthaginians, and the rule of law contained in the dictum
of Emperor Antoninus to the effect that he was lord of the
earth, but the law was the lord of the sea,[33] was rather a
rule of private than of public law. With the growth of the
separate European states after the disintegration of the
Roman Empire the control of the seas became a matter of
concern to all.[34] There were many reasons why the private
law of the Romans appeared to have no application to the
attempts of certain states to exercise jurisdiction over particular seas. Indeed, it seems questionable whether there
was any attempt to extend the Roman private law principles to the situation on the Mediterranean and the North
Sea much before the extraordinary development in the public law of Europe that commenced with the thirteenth century. The reasons for this were partly the primitive state
of navigation, and partly the fact that the areas over which
control was asserted were very narrow. But even more fundamental to the whole matter was the fact that generally
wherever a claim to control of the seas was asserted it appears to have been based primarily upon the fact that the
states making such assertions undertook to keep the regions
free from pirates, and consequently the claim had a real
basis in fact. This circumstance, together with the spatially
narrow limits on which this jurisdiction was supposed to
operate, leads one to the conclusion that these claims were
nothing more than attempts to extend territorial jurisdiction. They were in no sense general claims of dominion over
the seas, such as were asserted later by Spain and Portugal
after the issuance of the papal bulls.

That these claims to control over portions of the sea were
really attempts to extend territorial jurisdiction appears
from the Venetian claims to jurisdiction over the Adriatic,

[33] D. 14, 2, 1. 9.

[34] Nau, *op. cit.*, p. 21; Tellegen, *op. cit.*, p. 7. Nau regards the discovery
of America as marking the beginning of positive maritime law.

the Genoese claims over the Ligurian Sea,[35] and the English claims over the Channel and other adjacent seas.[36] The English had support for their point of view chiefly in their own law; but the claims of Venice and Genoa were supported by the Roman lawyers, and as the Roman law system enjoyed widespread acceptance, their rights rested upon a legal basis that more closely approximated an international law sanction than did local statutes. Thus the statement of Bartolus[37] to the effect that a state possessed jurisdiction over the seas for one hundred miles from the shore, or two days' journey, was regarded as an ample justification of the rules for which both Venice and Genoa contended, particularly as later jurists were inclined to follow in his footsteps. Among these were no lesser lights than Baldus[38] and, much later, Jean Bodin.[39]

The idea of a control over certain specified regions of the sea was by no means a new one in 1493. But it had, in all preceding cases, a certain well-defined and recognized justification which the Spanish claim, based upon a pure donation, could not have. We shall see that the papal grants in respect to the lands in the New World, due to the right of the Holy See to have the heathen converted, had a basis in canon law which in turn had an implied recognition in secular jurisprudence. This was not true as far as the ocean was concerned. Here the pope rested upon the frail staff of Constantine's donation of the world to him, and consequently it was, in the eyes of the Roman law, no more than the donation of something over which he had no right of disposal.

[35] Tellegen, *op. cit.*, p. 10.

[36] Fulton, *op. cit.*, Introduction.

[37] Bartolus, *De Insula* (*Opera Omnia*, vol. X).

[38] Tellegen, *op. cit.*, p. 14.

[39] Bodin, *Les six livres de la Republique* (1599), l. 1, chap. X, p. 246. In the original Latin Bodin states the distance to be sixty leagues, and cites a decision reported in Cacheran, *Decisiones,* which in turn relies on Bartolus. The distance is corrected in the French edition. *Cf.* Tellegen, *op. cit.*, p. 15.

The inherent weakness of the legal position of the Spanish and Portuguese was disclosed by the contempt in which their claims were held once the Protestant revolt had gained substantial headway. Had they, as had the Venetians, been able to support their claims by adequate maritime force, there might, in the final analysis, have been some basis in fact for their assertion of right.

What contributed greatly to the flouting of Spanish jurisdiction over the seas was the extension to foreigners of rights to trade in the Indies. Once this concession was made, the desire to embark independently on colonial adventures was bound to follow. Thus the commercial treaties with England before the Spanish colonial system tightened up gave Englishmen so-called freedom of commerce in Spanish dominions, which because its exact terms had never been defined was sufficiently valuable to move the English, in 1604,[40] to refuse to relinquish the right of trading in these regions. Similarly, the French claimed the right to trade in the New World,[41] and they went even so far as to refuse to be excluded, in 1555, from any regions not in the actual possession of Spain.

The culmination of the whole dispute was reached in the reign of Elizabeth. French corsairs[42] and English freebooters like Hawkins and Drake had scoured the seas over which Spain claimed dominion, and had made very effective mock of this pretended jurisdiction. For a short time during the reign of Mary, Philip II, her husband, had succeeded in securing a royal prohibition of any legitimate ventures in the forbidden seas,[43] and for this reason, among others, the nominal piracy of foreign nations flourished. Not until Elizabeth's time, however, had these piratical voyages at-

[40] Davenport, *op. cit.*, p. 246.

[41] *Ibid.*, p. 220.

[42] La Roncière, *Histoire de la Marine Française* (1899-1920), vol. 3, p. 579.

[43] Williamson, *op. cit.*, p. 287 *et seq.*

tained a sufficient glory to warrant a royal assumption of responsibility for them. Drake's voyage around the world, however, was the signal in 1580 for a bitter complaint from Mendoza, the Spanish ambassador, to which Elizabeth replied in her famous words,[44] that

she would not persuade herself that [the Indies] are the rightful property of Spanish donation of the Pope of Rome in whom she acknowledged no prerogative in matters of this kind, much less authority to bind Princes who owe him no obedience, or to make that New World as it were a fief for the Spaniard and clothe him with possession: and that only on the ground that the Spaniards have touched here and there, have erected shelters, have given names to a river or promontory: acts which cannot confer property. So that this donation of *res alienæ* which by law (*ex jure*) is void, and this imaginary proprietorship, ought not to hinder other princes from carrying on commerce in these regions and from establishing colonies where Spaniards are not residing, without the least violation of the law of nations, since without possession prescription is of no avail (*haud valeat*), nor yet from freely navigating that vast ocean since the use of the sea and air is common to all men; further that no right to the ocean can inure to any people or individual since neither nature nor any reason of public use permits occupation of the ocean.

It may be that Elizabeth's Protestantism, more than anything else, led her to accept this view. But it was not until the defeat of the Great Armada that the Spanish claims were effectively disposed of for all practical purposes, and although mutterings of their rights continued even as late as the beginning of the Virginia colony, the Spanish thereafter retreated from their first line of legal defense to the surer ground of the rights conferred by prior occupation in the New World or by treaty. On this latter count, their claim that the seas, and particularly the Pacific and the Gulf of Mexico, were a part of their dominions, continued as late,

[44] Camden, *Annales Rerum Anglicæ et Hiberniæ* (1717), vol. 2, pp. 359-360.

at least in the latter case, as the American Revolution.[45] All expeditions, therefore, in these waters they regarded as piratical, and as their colonies spread and their commercial relations became more and more exclusive, by the assertion of the principle of territorial waters to the distance of one hundred miles from the shore, they were able to stand on legal ground more firm and more capable of effective enforcement.[46]

When the first discoveries were made in the New World there were no principles of law universally recognized as governing the manner and effectiveness of the acquisition of territory which can truly be denominated principles of international law. The reasons for this are obvious—the western world was completely occupied by Christian peoples, or at least by peoples who were able to defend their rights, and hence there could be no original acquisition of sovereignty. It was to be had only by derivation, either by enfeoffment, by cession or by conquest. Indeed, the whole feudal system was built up on the theory that all the known property of the world was vested in an overlord, and that the dominion over it was exercised by him either mediately or immediately. We have already observed how this view had been developed with some precision by the church. The pretensions of the latter to a universal overlordship had been resisted as far as Europe was concerned by the temporal rulers, and we may regard as the last stand of the ecclesiastical theory the effort to invest Spain and Portugal with specific rights in respect of the territories discovered by them. An accompaniment of this struggle was the effort of the European monarchs to free themselves from all implications of suzerainty arising from the notion of

[45] Jay to President of Congress, October 3, 1781 (Wharton, *Diplomatic Correspondence of the American Revolution,* vol. 4, p. 738), sets forth the Spanish claims to exclusive jurisdiction over the Gulf of Mexico.

[46] The doctrine of territorial waters will be discussed further in subsequent chapters.

universal monarchy inherent in the Holy Roman Empire, and in the principles of Roman law which were then regarded as the primary legal authority for this view.[47] This victory was accomplished from the formal juristic point of view when Bartolus first announced the view that not all corporate bodies acknowledged a superior as a matter of law. Henceforward the legal independence of states, which was to be the basis of the modern international society, was assured; at the same time feudal society, which was theoretically based upon a single supreme overlord, was doomed to be discarded.

Legal victories, however, by no means denoted the acceptance of these views in matter of fact. The view of Bartolus served primarily as a bludgeon in international relations in matters involving incursions of either the pope or the emperor into the independence of the other rulers. It was not a theory that furthered either the development of strongly centralized national states, or the modern notion of sovereignty as a conception disassociated from the actual tenure over land.[48] In other words, in respect to the territory of the state, the mediæval view which confounded dominion with *imperium* and treated sovereignty as a sort of property right was still prevalent.

The importance of this view of sovereignty which treated as an absolute private right what is at present regarded as merely political control (*imperium*) exercised by the state is chiefly in regard to the acceptance of the principle of oc-

[47] This question the writer has discussed at length in his *Equality of States* (1923).

[48] Heimburger, *Der Erwerb der Gebietshoheit* (1888), p. 11 *et seq.* It will be observed that the writer takes issue with Heimburger in many respects. The latter's theories have been largely relied upon by other writers on occupation. The works on international occupation consulted include: Nuger, *op. cit.;* Salomon, *L'occupation des Territoires sans Maître* (1889); Tartarin, *Traité de l'occupation* (1873); Deherpe, *Essai sur le Développement de l'Occupation* (1903); Gellman, *op. cit.;* Adam, *Die Völkerrechtliche Okkupation* (1891), in *Archiv für Öffentliches Recht,* vol. 6, p. 193.

cupation in international law. And the fact that it persisted throughout the period of exploration and settlement, modified only by the notion that the property right was in the monarch and a usufruct only in the subject, will explain why what were originally rules of private law regulating property rights should emerge as doctrines of public law. Obviously if the monarch, as the personal embodiment of the state, was vested with the whole range of property rights connected with the territory over which he ruled, the acquisition of these rights was governed by principles of private law, and the public rights that were incidentally acquired were a necessary implication from the circumstances. At the same time it may be said that these rules of Roman law governing occupation, although primarily understood as rules of private law, nevertheless were by no means originally devoid of certain public law application.[49] This was not clearly understood or expressed when the rules were first put into practice in the sixteenth century. At least modern writers have been prone to regard the whole process as being essentially a private law matter, and as having been approached as such.[50] A sounder view, and one which seems to be a more close approximation to what really took place, is to regard the process as the application of rules of private law by monarchs in whose minds the feudal ideas of property were uppermost and whose conception of public rights was conditioned primarily by this latter fact.

Whether the rights to newly discovered lands were acquired as the result of public or private law is of juristic importance primarily because of the nature and content of these rights. But the determination of this question does not

---

[49] Täubler, *Imperium Romanum* (1913), p. 14; Mommsen, *Das Staatsrecht des Römischen Reichs* (3d ed.), III, p. 716 *et seq.* On the territory of Rome, p. 824 *et seq.*, Mommsen, III, p. 828, asserts that the state can acquire by occupation.

[50] *Cf.* especially Salomon, *op. cit.*, p. 16.

alter the fact that the Roman law rules, as they were then understood, were applied in a fairly thoroughgoing manner. Before passing to a consideration of these rules it is necessary to speak of the most recent view of state and territory, for this phase of the question is generally treated as being of great consequence, because those international law writers who regard the relation of the state to its territory as a real (*i.e.*, a property) right have assumed that the analogy between states and individuals is a perfect one.[51] It is true that they generally refer to territorial sovereignty as *imperium,* and yet very generally the discussion of this subject is framed about conceptions of property rights in the sense of *dominium* (private law title).[52] The word *imperium,* however, conveys simply the idea of the power to command, and, as Jellinek has aptly pointed out, only human beings can be commanded. Accordingly, the power of the state over its territory is exercised only through its citizens to the extent that they can be commanded. In other words, the state acquires and exercises a right or interest in territory only through the acts of its citizens. The direct exercise of rights over territory would be ownership. Such the state does not have, unless in a purely private law capacity, the same as an individual citizen. We are driven thus to the conclusion that at international law the state's relationship to its territory is purely an indirect one, resulting from the fact that it is owned or controlled by its citizens.

The importance of this for the law of occupation is obvious. The legal effect of the occupation of territory not under the control of another state is that the *dominium* is acquired by the individuals, and that the *imperium* is ac-

---

[51] Thus Calvo, *Le Droit International Théorique et Pratique* (1887), vol. 1, p. 382; Pradier-Fodéré, *Traité de Droit International Public* (1885), vol. 2, p. 127; River, *Principes de Droit des Gens* (1896), p. 288 *et seq.*

[52] Jellinek, *Das Recht des Modernen Staates* (1913), p. 386.

quired by the state solely by virtue of the legal relation of the individuals to the state.

This idea seems to have been the theory of the Romans. It is most concisely expressed in the maxim of Seneca, *"omnia rex imperio possidet, singuli dominio."*[53] The Roman law, however, had not developed the modern conception of sovereignty. The distinction between the group as a collection of persons and as a unit was unknown.[54] The individual, therefore, in the international relations with other states, was one of the group making up the state. When the state acted it was the act of every individual member of the group. This relationship is shown in the way in which the property of the state was treated. The *res publicæ* were the property of the state, and by this was meant the property of the group. It was, therefore, not subject to the rules of the private law (*ius privatum*), but of the public law (*ius publicum*), and the acquisition of such property was clearly not governed by principles of private law. In other words, the modern notion did not obtain that the state, in its relation to property, has a direct interest only at private law, and its public law relation to property is indirect throughout its relation to its citizens.[55] This much, however, was true, that what the individual might acquire of things the property of no one (*res nullius*) by way of occupation was subject to the political control of the state through the control over the individual, but this property was not public property (*res publica*) in which the whole body of citizens had an interest.

We have thus far dealt only with the relation of the Roman state and the individual to property within the state's territory. When we come to examine the international rela-

[53] *De Beneficiis,* lib. VII, c. V.

[54] Gierke, *Die Staats und Korporationslehre des Alterthums und des Mittelalters* (1881), p. 53.

[55] Rabel, *Grundzüge des Römischen Privatrechts* (in Kohler, *Enzyklopädie der Rechtswissenschaft,* 1914), vol. 1, p. 428.

tions of Rome, we find a situation that more closely approximates the problem with which we are dealing. A feature of the early Roman expansion was the so-called "dedition" treaties.[56] These were treaties with a non-Roman people by which the latter were incorporated into the Roman state. Dedition was not cession, for it involved the complete legal destruction of the one contractant, and to this extent most closely resembled the acquisition of territory by conquest. As a result of these treaties no new law of possession is created, but the basis of an act of possession, and the new property relations were consummated by an act of occupation. It is upon this latter act that the transfer of sovereign and possessory right passed to the Romans. From the strict legal point of view, the process of dedition and occupation was generally a simultaneous process.[57]

Occupation by the state in a manner closely analogous to that just outlined was the so-called wartime occupation (*occupatio bellica*). This was occupation of hostile property by the state in a just war (*indictum bellum*). It is important to observe that the occupant was the state and not the soldier, and consequently the property occupied became, upon such occupation, *res publicæ populi Romani*.[58] The right to the property was unencumbered and was, as in the case of all *res publicæ*, public property as distinguished from *res privata*. The so-called *dominium* exercised by the state over the *res publicæ* is treated by some writers as being a private law ownership.[59] Other writers, with whom better opinion sides, assert that this control was in the nature of *imperium*, yet the *res publicæ* were subject to a public law of prop-

[56] Täubler, *op. cit.*, p. 14 *et seq.*

[57] *Ibid.*, p. 15.

[58] D. 49, 15, 1. 20, § 21.

[59] Dernburg, *System des Römischen Rechts* (8th ed.), vol. I, p. 59, sec. 3. *Cf.* also Windscheid, *Pandekten* (8th ed.), vol. 1, § 146, sec. 4; Dernburg, *Entwickelung und Begriff des Juristischen Besitzes des Röm. Rechts* (1883), p. 5.

erty analogous to the private law.[60] In any event, it appears that in such property individuals only had a use; in other words, both *imperium* and *dominium* were in the Roman people, but the *dominium utile* was in the individual.[61]

This theory of the relationship of state to territory is almost the exact counterpart of the view that obtained during the period of exploration and discovery.[62] It should be added that the *occupatio bellica* was regarded in Roman law as extinguishing all preëxisting rights.[63] The state could accordingly dispose of the property as it might see fit to private individuals. Such title as the latter might acquire would necessarily be derivative.

Turning to occupation as a conception of Roman private law, it may be said that in the law of the time of the Digest *occupatio* was the means by which an individual acquired ownership in an object which previously had no owner (*res nullius*).[64] It was the method of original acquisition as distinguished from derivative acquisition of title,[65] and being regarded by the Roman jurists as a principle of natural law,[66] it was believed to reach back into the remotest antiquity, antedating formal law.[67] In other words, the idea of occupation was as old as human reason itself and was the

[60] Jhering, *Geist des Römischen Rechts* (5th ed.), vol. 3, p. 361, esp. note 476; also his *Zweck im Recht* (2d ed.), vol. 1, p. 466. *Cf.* also Eisele; *Über das Rechtsverhaltniss der Res Publicæ* (1873), *passim*.

[61] Gaius, *Inst.*, II, 6, 7: "Sed Provinciali placet plerisque solum religionis non fieri quia in eo solo. Dominium populi Romani est vel Cæsario nos autem possessionem tantum vel usumfructum habere videmur."

[62] Heimburger, *loc. cit.*

[63] Glück-Czylharz, *Ausführliche Erläuterung der Pandekten nach Hellfeld ein Commentar,* Ser. Bks. 41-42 (*de adq. rer. dom.*), p. 169. Hereafter cited Czylharz.

[64] Gaius, *Inst.*, II, 66.

[65] Czylharz, *op. cit.*, p. 27; Dernburg, *op. cit.*, vol. I, p. 342 *et seq.*

[66] *Inst.*, II, 1, 11, 12.

[67] D. 41, 2, l. 1, § 1: "Dominiumque verum ex naturali possessione coepisse Nerva filius ait, eiusque rei vestigium remanere de his quæ terra mari cæloque capiuntur. . . . ."

basis consequently of custom that expressed a certain universal human experience.[68] The ready application by states of these principles for the regulation of the international status of newly discovered territory is itself testimony of the fundamental nature of these principles.

With reference to the objects to which title by occupation might be acquired, it may be stated that all things without owners and which were capable of being owned were proper objects.[69] Occupation, consequently, was not applicable to things which were already owned, to the things outside of trade (*res extra commercium*),[70] the *res sacræ, et religiosæ*, and, as we have seen, in particular to the things common to all (*res omnium communes*), such as the air, the sea, and freely flowing waters.[71] But parts of the latter two, in so far as they were separable and were actually taken into possession, were regarded as proper objects of occupation. In respect to the sea, in addition to the waters thereof, the most important examples given by the jurists of a *res nullius* were the islands that might arise therein, the so-called *insula nata*,[72] the products of the sea, the bottom of the sea, and the coast which reached to the highest floodmark. Of things regarded as *res nullius* we may mention, in addition to the things taken from the sea and the air, a further class, the wild animals, for it is in regard to these that English law has closely followed the rules of the Roman. Finally may be mentioned the enemy property (*res hostiles*), which were those things belonging to the enemy that at the outbreak of war were within the confines of the state.[73] The rules of occupation were extended to this class of things,

[68] Leist, *Natur des Eigentums,* p. 73; Maine, *Ancient Law* (3d Am. ed.), p. 243.

[69] D. 41, 1, l. 3.

[70] Gaius, II, 4, 5.

[71] D. 41, 2, l. 2, § 1.

[72] *Inst.,* II, 1, 22; D. 41, 1, l. 7, 3.

[73] D. 41, 1, l. 51, 1.

not because of the law of war (*ius belli*), as in the case of
the *occupatio bellica,* which as we have seen was a distinct
legal conception, but because of the completely extra-legal
position of the enemy by virtue of which his property was
regarded as being without ownership. Accordingly, one occupying such things had an original title, and not a derivative title through the state, as in the case of things taken
iure belli. Such a view was the logical result of a system
which was regarded as exclusive.

The means by which occupation was effected was by the
taking possession of the *res nullius.*[74] Possession, in turn,
meant not alone the material apprehension of the thing, but
the accompanying intention, to hold it *pro suo* or for another.[75] If this intention existed, it was necessary that it
should contemplate an exclusive control for an indefinite
period.[76]

Of equal importance in the process was the act—the taking possession—and this must be some physical act, for no
mere declaration was sufficient; and this act in relation to
unoccupied land had to be one of economic significance. The
mere casual presence upon the land was not sufficient; it
was necessary to take possession, entering upon the land,
and such entry was regarded, because of the notion of
physical control which it conveyed, to be sufficient to affect
land in the immediate vicinity.[77]

The leading modern commentator on Digest 41, *de acq.
rer. dom.,* has remarked that the rules in respect to realty
apply *a fortiori* to islands arising in the sea,[78] as well as to
those newly discovered and unoccupied. In respect to these,
the mere *intrare,* or casual entry, no more than declarations

[74] D. 41, 2, l. 3, 2.

[75] Voet, *Commentaria* ad D. 41, 1, 2; D. 41, 1, l. 5, 1; l. 4, 1; l. 5, 6.

[76] Czylharz, *op. cit.,* p. 173; Pininski, *Der Thatbestand des Sachbesitz-
erwerbs* (1885), p. 130.

[77] D. 50, l. 6, l. 115.

[78] Czylharz, *op. cit.,* p. 188.

from shipboard could effect a legal occupation. Accordingly, the mere finding of a thing, or knowing its whereabouts, was not a sufficient physical act to effect possession.[79] The Roman law ignored this element, for *dominium* was acquired only by natural possession in the manner described.[80] Where an island is occupied by the agents of the state, an *imperium* is certainly established in law, and the matter of *dominium* is a question of fact. An occupation by an individual is regarded by Czylharz as merely a *de facto* possession,[81] as ownership presumes a legal order which is lacking in an unoccupied region. To this it may be observed that the individual is never divested of his national character (except in the rare instances where he is *staatenlos*) and hence the legal order of his sovereign accompanies him, and by virtue of this personal control the acquisition of *dominium* and *imperium* may be effectuated simultaneously.[82]

To sum up, it may be said that occupation in private law is the acquisition in fact, and not the mere casual exercise of power over a thing, for the latter is no more than a precedent step to the completed act, and is consequently without enduring legal significance.[83]

Before proceeding to the discussion of the application of these principles to the new situation that arose upon the discovery of America, it is necessary to advert to the discussions that took place in the mediæval jurisprudence with reference to the title to islands. The word island as a technical term for new and uninhabited land was suggested by references in both the Digest and Institutes to islands arising in the sea (*insula nata*). Indeed, it was for a long period

[79] Voet, *op. cit.*, ad D. 41, 1, l. 9.

[80] D. 41, 2, l. 3, 3; l. 1, 1.

[81] Czylharz, *op. cit.*, p. 189.

[82] Of course, the occupation is legally effective *pro tanto* as it is in fact accomplished. It cannot be effected by any mere visual survey. *Cf.* Pininski, *op. cit.*, p. 194.

[83] Czylharz, *op. cit.*, p. 194.

the usual expression for newly discovered land, not only in the law but in the current literature. The supposed existence of legendary islands in the Atlantic also served to perpetuate the currency of this term.

The leading treatise on the subject to which reference has already been made is the *Tractatus de Insula* (fourteenth century) of Bartolus, and in this work the latter laid down rules which profoundly influenced the development of international law.[84] The treatise was based upon the passage from the Institutes:[85] ''An island which rises, in the sea, which rarely happens, may be occupied as it is held to be *nullius.*'' Having defined an island, and what is meant by a rare happening, Bartolus goes on to say that by occupation of an island is meant the entering upon it and occupying the whole, although it is not necessary to go over the whole of the island; it is sufficient if the act is done in accordance with rules of possession of realty spoken of above.[86] Occupation is, therefore, effected by natural reason (*naturalis ratio*), and it could take place only by one subject to the jurisdiction of someone, in order that crimes which might be there committed could be punished, and that the law could be laid down to those who might inhabit the island. One having jurisdiction over the territory adjacent to the sea, says Bartolus, has jurisdiction over the sea for one hundred miles, notwithstanding the fact that the sea is common to all, and it follows from this that jurisdiction over the islands within such waters is properly vested in the nearest

[84] Bartolus, *Opera Omnia* (1596), vol. X, p. 137. The treatise is printed as a separate disquisition. It is really a part of his *Tyberiadis* in the same volume and references are often made to the latter treatise. Fulton, *op. cit.*, p. 539, to the writer's mind commits a serious blunder by treating Bartolus' headnote as if it were a part of the text.

[85] *Inst.*, II, 1, 22; Gaius, II, 72.

[86] D. 41, 2, l. 3, 1. The whole theory of contiguity and hinterland in its early phases rested on an interpretation of this statement of the Digest. Pernice, *op. cit.*, p. 144, gives examples of extension of jurisdiction over the coastal waters.

state.[87] For two days' journey, says Bartolus, is what the law regards as sufficiently near on land, and one hundred miles at sea is less than two days' journey.[88]

An island upon the high seas, if near an island enjoying the territorial propinquity described above, will be regarded as appertaining to the mainland to which the latter island is subject, as, says Bartolus, the island of Sardinia is near the island of Corsica which is in turn near to Italy. If, however, the island is neither near the shore nor near an island which has the proper territorial propinquity, then it is within the jurisdiction of no one unless it be the emperor, who is the lord of all.[89] Such an island may be occupied in such a way as to acquire *dominium;* but if in absence of the sovereign's order an individual assumes magisterial powers he will incur certain penalties by Roman civil law.[90] By law of nations (*inter gentes*) sovereignty will be obtained. The question, however, arises whether such islands can be occupied if they are already inhabited ''as sometimes happens,'' and sometimes when a special concession is made by pope or a prince or someone else having jurisdiction.

Bartolus' references indicate that in this relation he has in mind territory in the hands of heretics or infidels and his chief concern is over the acquisition of rights where there are several occupiers. Thus, he says, where an occupation is for a joint purpose, all occupy jointly. He then speaks of occupations for private use by reason of private law; then of occupations for private use but by reason of public law, and such occupations, says he, are open to all if the land is

[87] Citing D. 50, 16; l. 99, 1.

[88] D. 39, 2, l. 4, 9.

[89] D. 14, 2, l. 9.

[90] D. 48, 3, l. 4, is his reliance for this statement. It illustrates how Bartolus treated the Roman law *jurisdictio* as at least analogous to the powers of sovereignty exercised by feudal lords. *Cf.* also his *Tractatus de Jurisdictione,* § 34 in *Opera Omnia,* vol. X; Bartholomæus Caepolla, *Tractatus de Servitutibus Rusticorum Prædiorum* (1555 ed.), c. 26, § 16.

res nullius.[91] As far as concerns the right of occupation for public defense (*vindictam*) (which is proper chiefly for public benefit), the decision regarding the acquisition of rights while matters are still in a state of preparation is left to the feudal superior. Where a man once enters with his army for the purpose of occupation, Bartolus states that no one else can legally occupy the territory, for it is acquired by him who enters with the army. Where, however, such a person enters with a small force for the mere purpose of incursion, there is neither a taking nor occupation sufficient to acquire title.[92] The occupying force must be measured according to the exigencies of the situation. Bartolus states that a (feudal) superior may give the right of occupation, as has frequently been done by the pope. In such an event, if the one to whom the right is given fails to occupy, or if having an army he is able to do so but fails for some good reason to occupy, he loses his right. In the case where he has not the

[91] He refers to his comment on D. 43, 12, 1. 2, and also D. 30, 1, 1. 33. By *Decr. Greg. IX*, lib. V, tit. vii, c. 13, § 3, the pope claimed the right to give a power to occupy lands where the ruler refused to root out heresy and to recognize the ecclesiastical authority. At the same time the emperor asserted the same right by virtue of a constitution of Frederick II, of 1220, which was incorporated in the *Libri Feudorum*. By banning such a recalcitrant ruler the feudal rights necessarily reverted to the emperor. *Cf. Libri Feudorum*, lib. V, tit. 17, c. 5, 6, 7, 8, in *Corpus Juris Civilis* (Gothofredus ed., Antwerp, 1726), vol. 2. Also in *Monumenta Historica Germaniæ*, Legum, sectio IV, vol. 2, p. 106 (*Constitutiones*). On this see further, *Jahrbücher der Deutschen Geschichte*—Winkelmann, *Kaiser Friedrich II* (1889), vol. 1, p. 113; Ficker, *Die Gesetzliche Einführung der Todesstrafe für Ketzer* (in *Mitteilungen des Instituts für Österreichische Geschichtsforschung*, 1880), vol. 1, p. 192.

[92] Citing D. 45, 1, 1. 137, 3. It will be noted that Bartolus is here drawing no distinctions between peaceful *occupatio* and *occupatio bellica*. His concern is primarily with regard to the fixing of conflicting public rights of competitive parties. Obviously the mere granting of a concession to occupy does not fix these. This passage may help to understand why later Spain armed with a papal concession, nevertheless, undertook to satisfy the requirements of the law relating to occupation. On this passage see further Gryphiander, *Tractatus de Insulis* (1623), c. 22.

right to occupy, but the territory itself is granted, this can be done if the grantor is not subject to the law. If, however, the concession is made by one subject to law (a lesser feudal superior), then the land must have been his, for if the territory never was in the control of the one giving the right, but in the hands of the enemy, then it cannot be granted.

Where one is on territory with an army and it appears to be occupied, the question arises whether the right to it at once is fixed. This depends upon the facts. If the occupier holds some chief place which he is able to retain, then he may be said to have established his right. But if he is not able to hold what he is upon, and there is opposition to him, then he cannot be said to occupy it.[93]

It will be observed that in his brief analysis Bartolus combines in an ingenious fashion the Roman law and the current view of the feudal law. But what is of even greater importance is the fact that he does not apparently distinguish as sharply as did the Romans the *occupatio bellica* and the *occupatio* of private law. Indeed, it is clear that what he effected was a fusion of the two doctrines by which an occupation of an island not only fixed public rights, but private rights as well. This was possible largely because the development of feudal law had emphasized the personal relation between the individual and the sovereign, and there

[93] Speaking of the concession of territory as against the concession of the *right to occupy* Bartolus is thinking in terms of feudal legal theory. When he speaks of a person not subject to law, he means either emperor or the pope, for he sees no restriction on any grant made by such persons. The writer is inclined to think Bartolus means only the emperor, for elsewhere in the treatise he speaks of the emperor as the lord of all. A person subject to law is presumably one who stands in feudal relationships to a superior for his granting power is limited to what he has or at one time held. On Bartolus' view of imperial power *cf.* Woolf, *Bartolus of Sassoferrato* (1913), c. 2; on the Donation of Constantine, p. 94 *et seq. Cf.* also Figgis, in the *Transactions of the Royal Historical Society,* vol. 19 (1905), p. 147.

was a closer approach to what we have indicated is the modern view of the relation of the state to its territory. The old Roman law idea of the social ownership of property had given way to the individualistic notions of the feudal system. At the same time, the idea of jurisdiction in the north of Italy was gradually developing into the modern notion of sovereignty which gives to the state an interest in the property of its citizens by virtue of the individual's political and legal relation. The importance of this will presently appear in greater detail when we examine the application made of these principles to the discovery of America.

The statement of Bartolus that the emperor, being the lord of the earth, has dominion over all islands requires some explanation. Bartolus elsewhere expressed the view that the emperor was the lord of the universe, and that persons denying this were heretics.[94] On the other hand, as we have seen, he also first elaborated the idea that there were corporate bodies which did not recognize a superior, and this suggestion formed the basis of a legal discussion reaching through centuries culminating in the conception of the territorial independence of states. Unquestionably, Bartolus, in drawing this distinction, had nothing more in mind than the assertion of the independence of the Italian city states; we can, therefore, regard his statement concerning the jurisdiction over islands in the high seas as the accepted doctrine.

Another point of considerable importance is the fact that Bartolus does not appear to have regarded the pope as having exclusive jurisdiction over these islands. He says, indeed, that grants have been made by the pope, but he nowhere intimates that this is more than fact, and his previous statement regarding the rights of the emperor indicates that such acts on the part of the pope were devoid of par-

[94] *Tractatus Represalliarum; cf.* also his comment ad D. 48, 1, l. 7, 14; D. 49, 15, l. 24, no. 3; C. 10, 10, l. 1, no. 11; D. 26, 1, l. 26. Generally on this *cf.* the writer's *Equality of States,* p. 60.

ticular legal meaning. It is inconceivable that to Bartolus can be ascribed any views supporting the right of the pope to make the grants of undiscovered territory.[95]

The doctrines of the *Tractatus de Insula* were received by later writers and passed over into the accepted body of Roman law. It is, therefore, proper to assume that they were well known to the Holy See at the time when the bull *Inter Cætera* was issued in 1493, although these views were in direct contradiction of the theories of the papal writers regarding the jurisdiction conferred by the Donation of Constantine, already spoken of in connection with the jurisdiction over the sea. This was, however, not alone the ground upon which the pope claimed the right to issue patents covering discoveries in Africa and America. The bulls of Alexander VI laid emphasis upon the fact that the Spanish sovereigns were to undertake the conversion of the inhabitants of the newly discovered lands, and in fact some writers have gone so far as to see in this the consideration for the grant of the pope. Although this latter view is patently absurd, as no consideration would be required in return for such a grant, the charge upon Ferdinand and Isabella to undertake the conversion of the natives was the real legal justification of the pope's grant.

One of the chief powers of the pope, as the head of Christendom, has been the propagation of the Christian faith.[96] Moreover, by virtue of his primacy and his independence of any external control in the administration of church affairs, he has on various occasions exercised, for what he has conceived as the good of the Church, the most far-going rights in the form of a canon of belief or morals, not only over princes, but over territories and peoples. This principle is nowhere more concisely expressed than in the bull *Pastor Æternus,* issued by Pius IX on July 18, 1870.[97] In the fourth

[95] *Cf.* footnote 3, *supra.*
[96] Sägmuller, *Kirchenrecht* (1914), vol. I, p. 101 *et seq.;* also p. 384.
[97] *Collectio Lacensis,* 485.

section it is stated that it is "a canon of belief revealed by
God: that the Roman Pontiff when he speaks *ex cathedra,*
that is to say, when, apostolic authority defines the doctrine regarding faith and morals to be held by the universal
church in the exercise of his office as shepherd and teacher
of all Christians, such doctrine, because of the divine aid
promised to him in the person of Saint Peter, possesses
that infallibility with which the divine Redeemer desired
his church to be endowed in defining a doctrine with regard
to faith or morals; and that for this cause such definitions
of the Roman Pontiff are irreformable in themselves and
not because of the consent of the church."

The pope speaks *ex cathedra,*[98] therefore, when he deter-
mines a teaching which affects the faith or morals, and in so
speaking he is acting as a shepherd and teacher of all Christians, and he alone has the power of determining the limits
of what he can say. The doctrine of the infallibility of the
pope, which is indicated or implied in a long series of bulls,
is an additional fortification of the power itself.[99]

The eminent canon lawyer, Schulte, has analyzed the
papal pronouncements which fall under various categories
of this power of *ex cathedra* utterances.[100] These include the
assertions of control over temporal matters, and in particular the right to grant and withhold temporal power. The
bulls of Nicholas V granting the Portuguese the rights in
Africa, Schulte bases upon the assertion of papal right to
send to non-Catholic peoples and countries Catholic governors who had the right to enslave the population if necessary for conversion. This power is clearly set forth in the
grant contained in the bull *Romanus Pontifex,* already mentioned, and is repeated in the bull *Imper Non* of January 9,

[98] Schulte, *Die Macht der Römischen Päpste* (1871), p. 20. Of course
the words *ex cathedra* have here a technical legal meaning describing this
peculiar sort of spiritual sovereignty in the pope.

[99] Sägmuller, *op. cit.,* vol. 1, p. 387.

[100] Schulte, *op. cit.,* p. 43.

1454, and was confirmed in the other bulls mentioned in this connection.[101]

The bull *Inter Cætera* of May 4, 1493, is regarded by Schulte as a similar exercise of power. The grants conferred by it are expressly made "of our own accord . . . of our own unmixed liberality, and certain knowledge, and out of our apostolic plenitude of power by the authority of Almighty God conferred upon us in blessed Peter and of the vicarship of Jesus Christ which we hold on this earth. . . ." Obviously, a document which refers in this wise to the source of right has force and validity only to the extent that its sanction, the canon law and the spiritual supremacy of its author, are recognized. In its language it refers neither to the Roman law nor to the spurious Donation of Constantine for its validity, although the doctrine which had been evolved from the latter was undoubtedly a circumstance of some political importance. The Spanish themselves regarded the bull *Inter Cætera* as resting primarily upon the jurisdiction of the pope over the unbelievers,[102] and consequently the missionary activities in the Indies were pursued with the greatest vigor.[103] It is easy to understand, therefore, how zealously the Spaniards upheld the right of the pope to speak *ex cathedra* in this wise, particularly as the title of "Catholic Monarch" was conferred upon Ferdinand shortly after the issuance of the bull.

An interesting contemporary source of information regarding the legal justification of the bull *Inter Cætera* has recently been found in the shape of a broadside copy of the bull[104] with a headnote referring to two sections in the *Cor-*

[101] Solorzano, *Política Indiana* (1776), lib. I, c. 10 and 11, has a lengthy discussion of this point of view.

[102] *Ibid.*, lib. I, c. 11, no. 6.

[103] Pastor, *Geschichte der Päpste,* vol. 3, p. 486 *et seq.* Ehrle, *Die Päpstliche Abtheilung in der Weltausstellung (Stimmen aus Maria Laach,* vol. 46, p. 389).

[104] The reference is to an advertisement in catalogue VIII of Paul

pus Juris Canonici. The headnote is as follows: "Copia de la bula del decreto y concessi(on que) hizo el papa / Alexandro sexto al Rey y a la Reyna nuestros señores de las Ind(ias) conforme al capitu. / Per venerabilem rationibus / qui filii sint legitimi / y al cap. (. . . ?) n. xxiij. q. iiij."[105]

The section first referred to is from a decretal of Gregory IX and asserts a general jurisdiction of the pope over regions without the papal patrimony on the basis of Deuteronomy 17: 8-13. The passage from the Scriptures asserts that in cases too hard for ordinary judgment reference is to be made to "the priests, the Levites and the judge" at a place chosen by God. This jurisdiction, the decretal reasons, is exercised now by the pope. Presumably the right to the New World was regarded as a case which ordinary men had not the capacity to judge.

The second passage is difficult to locate, due to the mutilation and inaccuracy of the reference, but from its form it obviously indicates a section in the *Corpus Juris Canonici* and presumably in the *decretum* of Gratian, for there alone is the law cast in the form of *questio* and *causa.* The "n" is obviously a misprint for "c." If this assumption is correct the passage is from Questio IV, Causa xxiii. The chapter reference is almost impossible to select and the various glosses give no clue.[106] Questio IV deals in general with the attitude of the church toward the wicked and here-

Gottschalk, of Berlin, issued in 1925. The headnote cited is printed in the catalogue. Unfortunately the author was unable to examine the document itself.

[105] Gottschalk conjectures the broadside was printed at Valencia or Alcala de Henares in 1511, and leaves open the question whether it is an earlier or the same edition as the copies in the John Carter Brown Library and the Library of Congress. The Brown copy, however, has no headnote, a fact of which apparently Gottschalk did not know or take notice.

[106] The writer has examined various editions of the *Corpus Juris Canonici,* both contemporary and subsequent, all of which purport to have complete collections of glosses. Nor was he able to find a clue in any collateral sources.

tics, as well as its duties respecting their conversion. It contains some fifty-four chapters, any number of which might be apposite.[107] The important point is that emphasis is placed upon the duty of conversion as the legal justification of the bull, and that a contemporary source confirms the theories outlined above.

The bull *Inter Cætera* relied for its most potent sanction upon the threat of excommunication, *late sententiæ,* of any persons who might, without license from the Portuguese or Spanish monarchs, enter the regions granted by the bull. This threat, however, had scarcely the same potency that it had conveyed in the Middle Ages, and the Spanish monarchs, therefore, buttressed their claims, as we shall see, by meeting the requirements of the Roman law as it was then understood, with regard to the acquisition of territory. The bull itself contained an admission of the effectiveness of these principles. In granting the rights to the territory discovered or to be discovered, they were given

with the proviso, however, that none of the islands and mainlands found and to be found, discovered and to be discovered, beyond that said line towards the west and south, be in the actual possession of any Christian King or prince up to the birthday of our Lord Jesus Christ just past from which the present year one thousand four hundred and ninety-three begins. And we make, appoint you and your heirs and successors lords of them with full and free power and authority and jurisdiction of every kind; with this proviso, however, that by this our gift grant and assignment no right acquired by any Christian prince, who may be in actual possession of said islands and mainlands prior to the said birthday of our Lord Jesus Christ is hereby to be understood to be withdrawn or taken away.[108]

[107] It might be c. 38 (Heretici ad salutem etiam inuiti sunt trahendi) or c. 41 (A regibus terræ contra inimicos suos ecclesia auxilium petat) which was intended. *Cf.* also *Decr. Greg. IX.,* lib. V, tit. vii, c. 13, § 3, *Si vero dominus temporalis.*

[108] Davenport, *op. cit.,* p. 71 *et seq.* The bull *Inter Cætera* of May 4, 1493.

The recognition of the effect of possession in fixing the rights of monarchs is in itself a confirmation of the validity of the canon law upon which the bull was based, and of the view that the primary purpose of the latter was to provide for the Christianization of the heathen living in these new lands.[109] If the theory of the pope's action was that in him was vested the supreme control over monarchs and nations, there could be no reason why he would hesitate to disturb the bona fide possessor if he so desired, as he had done in previous centuries under a claim of temporal hegemony. The authority to carry out a missionary purpose, however, was the true legal import of the pope's action, and the control over the lands must be regarded as an incident to this primary purpose. This is without doubt the only legal interpretation of the documents which in any way conforms with the theories of the Roman law or of the canon law.

The legal quality of the act of the pope by no means limited its political significance. Indeed, the political purposes which the grant was made to serve almost immediately tended to give the matter a pseudolegal significance that in no way coincided with the original purposes of the grant. In other words, the bull *Inter Cætera,* instead of being construed as a charge to convert the heathen, was treated as a grant of territory.

Neither Spain nor Portugal was interested exclusively in the Christianization of the vast numbers of aboriginal American heathen. But they did have a most active interest in the development of their commerce and colonial holdings. The papal bull, supplemented by the Treaty of Tordesillas had the same international effect as any regional understanding would have between two powers—such as an agreement respecting spheres of influence—with this difference, that the threat of excommunication from the spiritual head of Christendom insured an observance of this under-

[109] Gellman, *op. cit.,* does not understand or evaluate correctly the importance of the papal grant and its true legal sanction.

standing by third powers, which might otherwise not have been the case in a two-party treaty.

It is clear that the papal grant could have effect in fixing the rights of all nations to the New World only so long as Spain and Portugal were regarded as his sole missionary agents. How long the sanctity of such a purpose could impress European monarchs, or how much they were deceived by such a diaphanous covering for the imperialistic designs of the two states, is clear from the subsequent events. No one desired to get into difficulties with the Holy See, but no one was going to be restrained from trying his hand in the new and adventurous game in which Columbus had led the way. The device of Henry VII already spoken of shows how astutely a formal respect was paid to the legal rights of his allies and of the pope, and how inevitably the shadowy rights conceded by the papacy were to fall before the exigencies of the practical politics of the period. On the other hand, the earlier patent granted to Cabot, it is true, discloses little deference for the legal authority of either the pope or his beneficiaries, for Cabot was authorized "to subdue, occupy and possess" such regions as he might find.[110] There is some reason to suspect, as we have seen, that the Cabot voyage drew protest from Spain, and this may account for the form taken by the next adventure of the English. In any event we have noted how, in the second charter given by Henry to the merchant adventurers, the patentees were warned to respect the rights of the bona fide possessors.

Henry VII's action was quite in accordance with the theory of English law which developed elaborate rules to protect the possessor against other parties.[111] Indeed, in the whole common law there is no conception more fundamental

---

[110] Rymer, *op. cit.*, vol. XII, p. 695.

[111] Pollock and Maitland, *History of English Law* (2d ed.), vol. 1, p. 146; vol. 2, p. 1 *et seq.* The ensuing discussion is based on the common law as it existed at the time of the discovery of America.

than that of seisin, and yet, as has already been stated, the
available land of England being subject to the system of
tenure, there was therefore no room for the development in
the courts of the Roman law doctrine of occupation. It is
true that Bracton reproducing the Institutes speaks of the
insula nata, but he knows no other vacant land and hence
has no correlative theory of occupation.[112] Pollock and
Maitland, in their *History of English Law,* mention the fact
that in later law the case where a tenant for life gives land
to another *pour autre vie,* the latter dying and the life estate having been conveyed, the land becomes subject to occupation by anyone who chooses, before the termination of
the grantor's life estate.[113] This, however, was by no means
the acquisition of a *dominium* in the sense in which the Romans used the doctrine of occupation, and we are therefore
justified in saying that to the common law the doctrine of
occupation as a means of acquiring title to land was wholly
strange.

The emphasis upon possession in the English law indicates that the English king would be disposed to regard as
resting on a firm legal basis claims which were based upon
de facto possession[114] rather than upon vague assertions of
proprietary rights that rested ultimately upon a sanction
emanating from an authority preëminently spiritual, particularly when such sanction could be withdrawn, as the bull
Præcelsæ Devotions of June 14, 1514, had shown.[115] At the
same time the common law certainly discreted no rules
which would support the acquisition of title by discovery;
and although this latter doctrine of discovery has, as we

---

[112] Bracton, *De Legibus et Consuetudinibus Angliæ* (Twiss ed.), fol.
8 b, 9 b; Maitland, *Bracton and Azo* (1895), p. 98 *et seq.;* Britton (Nich-
ols ed.), lib. 2, c. 2, § 3, 4. Esp. § 5 for *insula nata. Post,* note 116.

[113] Pollock and Maitland, *op. cit.,* vol. 2, p. 80.

[114] Harrisse, *The Diplomatic History of America,* p. 47 *et seq.,* makes
a great point of the homage rendered the pope by Henry VII. He exag-
gerates the legal aspect of what was purely diplomatic.

[115] Davenport, *op. cit.,* p. 113.

shall presently see, been put forward from time to time by the English crown, it neither has nor deserves support in the English law, and it was never anything more than a fugitive political argument advanced by a chancellery that was unable to find adequate support in accepted international custom.[116]

It has been deemed necessary to make this rather lengthy analysis of Roman, canon, feudal and common law for the purpose of distinguishing the various factors which determined the principle that received international recognition in the regulation of the acquisition of sovereignty over newly discovered lands. Unquestionably the attitude of a state toward any new rule of international law is conditioned very largely by the extent to which such a rule is analogous to a similar doctrine of the municipal law of such a state. What attitude the jurists may take is a matter that does not concern us particularly, for the determination of rules of international law is usually made without much reference to the creative imagination of the lawyers, except

---

[116] The passages in Bracton cited in note 112, deal almost exclusively with wild animals. Here the Roman law rules of occupation were in a general way received in the English law. Bracton, however (f. 8 b), states: "The dominion over things by natural right or by law of nations is acquired in various ways. In the first place through the occupation of those things which belong to no one, and which now belong to the King by civil right, and are not common as of olden time." What ensues is certainly not occupation in the Roman law sense, for everything already has an owner if the king has this civil law right. This idea is later on repeated (f. 9) where he says that a species of occupation takes place in respect to the sea and seashore, etc., and that the same rule applies to islands which arise in the sea and in similar cases and to things left derelict unless there is a custom to the contrary in favor of the public treasury ("propter fisci privilegium"). This reservation in favor of the king was of considerable importance in later discussions when the question of colonizing the newly discovered lands arose. In fact it was in complete accord with the development in the courts of the king's prerogative rights in respect of the lands outside England. *Cf.* Callis, *Readings on the Statute of Sewers* (2d ed., 1685), c. 44 *et seq.*; Comyns' *Digest* (1762-1767), tit. *prærogative*.

in so far as they may have a hand in dealing with the settlement of a particular problem where the rule is applied. With these considerations in mind, we can proceed to discover how the new international situation precipitated by Columbus' discovery was dealt with by the European states as a matter of law.

The *capitulación*, or charter of the Spanish monarchs to Columbus,[117] as well as the patent of privileges and prerogatives which was issued to him before his first journey to the West, are instructive as a mirror of how the Spanish crown expected to gain title to the possible discoveries Columbus might make. These documents both speak of the discovery and acquisition (*ganar*) of new islands and lands, and also of their conquest. Columbus was acting as the mandatory of the monarchs, a fact clearly shown by his appointment as "our Governor," and by the provision that in the treasures he was to find he was given only a tenth interest, the remainder accruing to the crown. The *capitulación* and the patent both antedating the papal bulls of 1493 are a better index of the current conception of the acquisition of territory as a matter of law, than the patents or grants later issued.

The fact has been mentioned that feudal legal theory contemplated no original acquisition of property. The doctrines of the Roman law, however, which we have already examined, were well known in Spain,[118] and the work of Bartolus, in particular, was held in the highest esteem by both the Spaniards and the Portuguese.[119] No more direct proof of the influence of the Roman law upon Spanish jurisprudence exists than is to be found in the famous code of Alphonso

---

[117] Navarrete, *op. cit.*, vol. 2, p. 7, p. 9.

[118] Branchitsch, *Geschichte des Spanischen Rechts* (1852), p. 81, 86; Savigny, *Geschichte des Römischen Rechts im Mittelalter* (2d ed.), vol. 2, p. 81.

[119] Duck, *De Authoritate Juris Civilis Romanum* (1653), l. 2, c. 6, no. 29; Savigny, *Geschichte des Römischen Rechts*, vol. 6, p. 154.

the Wise (*c.* 1265) known as the *Siete Partidas.* Formulat-
ing the rule for the acquisition of title over islands, the code
states :[120] ''Pocas vegadas acaesce que se fagan islas nueva-
mente en la mar, pero si acaesciese que se ficiesi hi alguna
isla de nuevo suya decimos que debe seer de aquel que la
poblare primeramente. Mas aquel ó aquellos que la poblaren
deben obedescer al señor en suyo señorio es aquel logardo
paresció tal isla.''[121] This passage is of significance largely
because of the Spanish rendition of the Latin *occupare.* The
use of the word *poblar* (populate) is conclusive proof that,
as far as Spanish law was concerned, occupation was syn-
onymous with colonization, and that there were no implications concealed in the word that would support theories that
mere discovery would give title. In view of these facts we are
justified in assuming that when the *capitulación* speaks of
acquiring (*ganar*)[122] territory it is using the Roman law
vernacular. A different conclusion seems out of the question, for there was known no other means of acquisition of
res nullius, as the islands were, except as laid down in the
Roman law. The Columbus patent also uses the word *conquer.* The results of such a process were for both Roman
law and feudal law the same; the monarch in whose name
the conquest was effected became owner of the conquered
land, and consequently it was subject in his hands to such
disposition as he might see fit to make.[123]

Both the acquisition of territory by occupation and its
conquest required continuous and uncontested possession.

[120] *Las Siete Partidas* (Lopez de Vargas ed., 1847), Part III, tit. 28,
ley. 29.

[121] *Ibid.,* Part IV, tit. 21, ley. 8, and note, for the attitude toward the
infidels and the legal consequence of conquest. On the *Espéculo* of Alfonso
cf. Barrio, *Historia General del Derecho Español,* vol. 3, p. 166, 169, especially as to occupation.

[122] The translation given in the text was confirmed by several Spanish
scholars.

[123] Waitz, *Deutsche Verfassungsgeschichte,* vol. 8, p. 254; Schroeder,
Lehrbuch der deutschen Rechtsgeschichte (6th ed.), p. 208, 579.

It followed, therefore, that as a matter of law, no right to the newly found lands could be maintained in the absence of the necessary physical acts, which the law would regard as sufficient. Columbus, obviously for the purpose of protecting the rights of his sovereigns, accordingly left a number of his followers on the island of Hispaniola, consequently establishing, as well as circumstances permitted, the sovereignty of Spain.

After the issuance of the bulls of 1493, the legal situation becomes somewhat complicated by reason of the claim to exclusive dominion in the regions demarcated and assigned to Spain. As against the rest of the world the rights of Spain were presumptively fixed. Intruders were at least warned off, and the Spanish crown could ostensibly go about the business of discovery without the necessity in every case of taking and holding possession. This assumed security is reflected in the patents and grants thereafter issued. They fall roughly into two classes, those which merely grant a right to make discoveries, and those designed to effect a colonization of the lands found. These patents and grants are accordingly without great international law significance, being primarily instruments of domestic policy, the international rights having been determined by the bulls and the Treaty of Tordesillas. It was not until the great conflict with Portugal over the Moluccas that recourse was had to a law without the purview of papal granting power.

The second patent to Columbus of May 23, 1493,[124] which may or may not have been issued before knowledge of the papal bulls had reached Spain, speaks of the purpose of mastering and holding (*señorear y poseer*) the islands and *terra firma* already taken possession of in the name of the Spanish monarchs, and of discovering other islands, and gives the authority to outfit a new expedition. On the same day a further patent was issued forbidding all access to the

[124] Navarrete, *op. cit.*, vol. 2, p. 48.

lands discovered except by license of the crown.[125] It is, therefore, clear that the Spanish monarchs regarded all rights and titles to the new lands as vested in themselves, and any individual who sought to acquire rights could only secure them through the crown. In other words, the individual could secure only a derivative title.

The instructions issued to Columbus on May 29, 1493, show the great change of heart with which the bulls of the same month had animated the Spanish monarchs, for at the very outset they lay upon the admiral the charge of converting the Indians to the Christian faith. This document, however, like many other licenses to make discoveries that followed, presumes the acquisition of sovereignty in these regions.[126] Thus, the license granted June 5, 1500, to Rodrigo Bastidas to make discoveries warns the licensee to respect the rights of Columbus, of previous licensees and of the king of Portugal. It merely gives the power to make discoveries and says nothing of taking possession. Similarly worded is a *capitulación* with Alonzo Pélez de Mendoza of June 20, 1500.[127] On the other hand, the patent given to Alonzo de Hojeda of June 8, 1501,[128] contains the following instruction:

That you go and follow that coast which you have discovered which extends east and west as it appears, because it goes towards that part where it has been reported that the English are making discoveries, and that you set up marks with the arms of their Majesties or with other signs that may be understood, such as may seem fitting to you, so that it may be known that you have discovered that land in order that you may stop discoveries of the English in that direction.

This document may seem on first impression a claim to right by discovery. But such a view is wholly untenable, for

[125] *Ibid.,* p. 5.
[126] *Ibid.,* p. 244.
[127] *Ibid.,* p. 247.
[128] *Ibid.,* vol. 3, p. 85.

the direction to Hojeda to erect signs was simply a device to show to the world at a time when most of the known maps were in the hands of the Spanish and Portuguese that the regions discovered were in the area assigned by the pope and were *terra prohibita* as far as other states were concerned.

The grants and patents for the colonization of the New World indicate that they were issued to perfect the taking of possession that was a part of the process of discovery.[129] Undoubtedly, at this time, the mere formality of taking possession in the regions assigned by the pope had a certain legal significance. But this was more from the point of view of private law than of public law. The discoverers, as a rule, were given a right or interest in the regions found, and the formal taking of possession was largely important in fixing their rights. It was an act totally without international importance as long as the papal demarcation was respected.

As far as the right by conquest was concerned, the grants immediately subsequent to that of Columbus disclose that this was not contemplated any longer as a means of acquiring rights. It is true that the commission to Christianize the Indians contained an implication that measures of violence might justifiably be used in attaining this object. This was

---

[129] Thus the cédula to Francisco de Garay (1521), Navarrete, *op. cit.*, vol. 3, p. 147; the título to Davila (1513) and instruction given him. *Cf.* also the letter of Balboa to the king, *ibid.*, p. 258. The cédula of April 13, 1513, giving to the colonizers of Cuba the same privileges as those of the island of Hispaniola, speaks of the *"descubierto e poblado,"* conquest apparently being regarded as an entirely different legal act (*Colección de Documentos Inéditos Relativas á las Antiguas Posesiones Españolas de Ultramar*, ser. 2, vol. 1, p. 37). *Cf.* also the cédula of February 28, 1515, approving the acts of D. Diego Velazguez in the *pacification* and *colonization* of the island (*ibid.*, p. 56). On the other hand, the cédula of Nov. 7, 1518, giving rights of making discoveries to the inhabitants of Fernandina speaks of conquest and bringing under the sovereignty and service of the crown (*ibid.*, p. 81).

looked upon by the Dominican Franciscus de Victoria as the chief justification of the action.[130] The Spanish government, however, seems to have thought otherwise, for after the initial enslavement of certain Indians by Columbus, the crown ordered the return of the Indian slaves except only those taken in open war.[131] Moreover, in the instructions given to Ovando,[132] when he was sent to the New World in 1501, the charge was laid upon him to treat the Indians with especial tenderness. The policy of the division of labor or *repartimiento,* however, inevitably worked unspeakable hardships upon the natives. The ostensible course of Ferdinand and Isabella was laid down in the orders of October 30, 1503,[133] and December 20, 1503.[134] In the former decree relating to cannibals the officers of the crown were warned against the use of force on the Indians, except in case of their rebellion. The Indians, in the second document, were specifically declared to be free, but Ovando was given the right to compel them to work.

The superficial aspect of this policy was an attempt to conciliate the natives that was to be in accord with the mandate imposed upon Spain by the pope. As a matter of fact, the actual working of the system was a reign of terror for the Indians, more in accordance with a policy of conquest and consolidation than peaceful settlement and colonial development. A reflex of the policy outlined in the decree of October 30, 1503, is to be found in the instructions given to Magellan May 8, 1519.[135] These instructions are drawn up on the theory that Magellan was going, not as a conqueror, but as an explorer, and he was particularly warned to make

[130] Victoria, *Relectiones Morales* (*De Indis*), Rel. II (Nys, ed.).

[131] Herrero, *Décadas,* Dec. 1, lib. 4, c. 7; Navarrete, *op. cit.,* vol. 2, p. 246.

[132] Torres de Mendoza, *Colección de Documentos Inéditos,* vol. 30, p. 113.

[133] Navarrete, *op. cit.,* vol. 2, p. 414.

[134] *Ibid.,* p. 298.

[135] *Ibid.,* vol. 4, p. 130.

treaties with the chieftains of the Spice Islands. He was further ordered that Moros on the Spanish side of the line of demarcation were to be treated well, but Moros on the other side might be seized in just war (*buena guerra*). Similarly the instructions given to Cortes by Velasquez, October 23, 1518,[136] prior to the invasion of Mexico, stressed the importance of kind treatment to the aborigines, a fact that the nature and armament of the expedition itself belied. The commission to Pizarro, on the other hand,[137] speaks of conquest, as does the *cédula* giving Camargo the governorship of Patagonia.[138]

It is, of course, virtually impossible to state with any degree of certainty the relative importance of conquest as the basis of Spain's claim to *imperium* over the New World. As a matter of law, the basis of her right, briefly summarized, may be said to have been the papal bulls, plus occupation or conquest. Of these three elements occupation may be said to have been the most important from the standpoint of international law. And by occupation is not meant the mere formal act, such as is suggested in Hojeda's patent. The significance of this was purely feudal; it was the formal entry of the common law—the seisin without which a title was invalid in feudal law. But the seisin, of course, had significance only as an act where a derivative title was conferred. It had no importance as a means of original acquisition of title.[139] Certainly, therefore, in international relations where various states might claim as original occupiers, a temporary entry was a mere formality and was inapplicable to a situation which called for continuous and uninterrupted

[136] *Apuntes sobre la Historia del Nuevo Mundo* (1843), no. 93.

[137] Vicuña, *Estudio Histórico sobre el Descubrimiento y Conquista de la Patagonia y de la Tierra del Fuego* (1903), Apéndice, no. 1; Prescott, *The Conquest of Peru* (1847), vol. 2, p. 490.

[138] Vicuña, *op. cit.*, p. 252.

[139] On the notion of seisin *cf.* Maitland, *The Seisin of Chattels*, in *Law Quarterly Review*, vol. 1, p. 324; Ames, *Lectures in Legal History* (1913), p. 173.

exercise of control over the land. The formal taking of possession, therefore, was an attempt to apply a feudal custom to effect a result that would be internationally recognized. The attempt failed because the rules that creep into international law must bear an obvious relation to fact, the law being intolerant of theories that have no relation to realities.

The bearing of what has just been said is forcibly illustrated by the second great conflict that arose over the New World, namely, the sovereignty over the Moluccas. This question was brought to an issue by the successful circumnavigation of the globe, for both Spain and Portugal claimed that the islands fell within the region assigned to them by the pope. Obedient to the instructions that had been issued to the Magellan expedition, treaties had been concluded with the Moluccan chiefs by which the latter had declared themselves to be the vassals of Spain, possession was taken, and according to the Spanish king held continuously.[140]

The Portuguese, on the other hand, based their claim on prior discovery, and fortified their rights by reference to the bull *Præcelsæ Devotionis* of Leo X, of November 3, 1514,[141] by which their rights under preceding bulls were extended, as they claimed, to the east.

The instructions issued by Charles V[142] to his ambassadors contained a most clear-cut statement of the law as it was then conceived, and it had probably never been more forcibly set forth. After cautioning his ambassadors to proceed in a manner calculated to secure a settlement, and after discussing the project of sending an expedition to survey the region, the king, in support of his right to send an expedition to the islands, went on to say:

[140] Navarrete, *op. cit.*, vol. 4, pp. 295-298.

[141] Davenport, *op. cit.*, p. 113.

[142] Navarrete, *op. cit.*, vol. 4, p. 301; Blair and Robertson, *The Philippine Islands* (1903-1909), vol. 1, p. 139 *et seq.*

He [the King of Portugal] is aware that I am received and obeyed as King and lord of those Malucco Islands and that those who, until the present held possession of these regions have rendered me obedience as King and rightful seignior, and have been in my name, appointed as my governors and lieutenants over the said regions. He knows too that my subjects, with much of the merchandise carried by my fleet, are at the present time in these regions. For these reasons it is not reasonable to ask that I discontinue my possession of these districts during the time of determining the demarcation especially since the most Serene King has never held possession past or present, of any of the said Malucco Islands, or of any others discovered by me up to the present; nor has his fleet touched at or anchored therein.[143]

A further instruction to his Ambassador Juan de Zúñiga of December 18, 1523, is even more to the point:[144]

And, in proof thereof (to continue the above), our present possession, which had been public and without any opposition by the said most serene King of Portugal, was sufficient. And this possession of ours has been continued with his knowledge, sufferance, and good grace, and had been likewise known and suffered by the Most Serene King Don Manuel, his father. . . .

It could not be denied that Malucco had been found and taken possession of first by us, a fact supposed and proved by our peaceful and uninterrupted possession of it until now; and the contrary not being proved legally, our intention in the past and present is inferred and based upon this possession. . . .

Furthermore it was declared in our behalf, that, although Malucco had been discovered by ships of the King of Portugal—a thing by no means evident—it could not, on this account, be made to appear evident, or be said that Malucco had been found by him. Neither was the priority of time, on which he based his claims, proved, nor that it was discovered by his ships; for it was evident, that to find required possession, and that which was not taken or

---

[143] Navarrete, *op. cit.*, vol. 4, p. 303; Blair and Robertson, *op. cit.*, p. 142.

[144] Navarrete, *op. cit.*, p. 312 *et seq.;* Blair and Robertson, *op. cit.*, p. 145 *et seq.*

possessed could not be said to be found, although seen or discovered. . . .

From the above it followed clearly that the finding of which the said treaty speaks, must be understood and is understood effectually. It is expedient to know, by taking and possessing it, that which is found; and consequently the Most Serene King of Portugal, nor his ships, can in no manner be spoken of as having found Malucco at any time, since he did not take possession of it at all, nor holds it now, nor has it in his possession in order that he may surrender it according to the stipulations of the said treaty.

And by this same reasoning it appeared that Malucco was found by us and by our ships, since possession of it was taken and made in our name, holding it and possessing it, as now we hold and possess it, and having power to surrender it, if supplication is made to us. . . .

Furthermore the right of our ownership and possession was evident because of our just occupation. At least it could not be denied that we had based our intention on customary law, according to which newly-found islands and mainlands, belong to and remain his who occupied and took possession of them first, especially if taken possession of under the apostolic authority, to which—or according to the opinion of others, to the Emperor—it is only conceded to give this power. Since we, the said authorities, possessed these lands more completely than any other, and since the fact of our occupation and possession was quite evident, it followed clearly and conclusively that we ought to be protected in our rule and possession, and that whenever anyone should desire anything from us, he must sue us for it; and in such suit must be the occasion for examining the virtue and strength of the titles, the priority, and the authority of the occupation alleged by each party to the suit.

The Treaty of Vitoria of February 19, 1524,[145] resulted from the negotiations between Spain and Portugal. By this treaty a conference was to be held between Badajoz and Elvas, pending which no expedition for trade was to be sent to the Moluccas by either side. Delegates at the conference were to determine the demarcation, and in particular three

[145] Davenport, *op. cit.*, p. 121; Navarrete, *op. cit.*, vol. 4, p. 320.

lawyers appointed by each side were to inquire into and determine the possession of the Moluccas; ''and in case the question of ownership and demarcation is determined, then that of possession shall be understood to be decided and absorbed.'' This latter rule was laid down by virtue of the Treaty of Tordesillas, which gave the *right* of possession to the sovereign in the region assigned to him. The treaty goes on to say:

> If only the question of possession is determined by the said lawyers, without their being able to determine that of ownership as aforesaid, then what still remains to be determined of the said ownership, and likewise of the possession of the said Molucca shall, in accordance with the terms of the treaty, remain in the same condition as before this present compact.[146]

It is clear from the treaty that the rights to the Moluccas were governed by two facts: first, the *right* to possession under the Treaty of Tordesillas, and second, the question of possession as a matter of international law. The treaty intended that if the line of demarcation were fixed, as it had not been, the question of the right to possession would automatically be determined. The lawyers, however, would have the second alternative of deciding the question of possession alone, which would leave the matter of ownership as it stood prior to the treaty, *i.e.*, that the rules of law outside the treaty would apply.

The arbitration of Badajoz was not a success.[147] At the first meetings the attorneys wrangled interminably as to who should appear as plaintiff, a matter of importance, as it involved a *prima facie* presumption in favor of the pos-

---

[146] Dr. Davenport has apparently adopted the Blair and Robertson translation of the treaty (*op. cit.,* vol. I, p. 160). There are renderings in this translation with which a lawyer must take issue: thus, the translation "treaty" for *capitulación* (sec. 2). Obviously the word "charter" is the nearest approach to what is meant.

[147] The documents are in Navarrete, *op. cit.,* vol. 4, p. 333 *et seq.;* Blair and Robertson, *op. cit.,* vol. 1, p. 165 *et seq.*

session of the defendant. The meagre minutes of the conference preserved by Múñoz show a long and stormy discussion of the question of possession in which the opinions of
Bartolus and Baldus played a rôle. But no conclusion can
be drawn as to what was actually laid down by each side as
law, beyond what we know of the Spanish view as stated in
the instruction to Zúñiga. As both sides wished to be in *loco
defendentis* the conference failed on the case of possession,
and on the question of demarcation there was such wide
divergence of view as to the place from which the measure-
ments should begin and how they should be made, that it
was impossible to reach a conclusion.

It is not proposed to carry the discussion of this particular cause through the unratified treaty of 1526,[148] and the
two treaties of Saragossa[149] by which Charles V eventually
mortgaged to Portugal his claim to the Moluccas. The incident has been mentioned in such detail primarily because it
has such great significance in the development of international law. By laying down the rules of occupation as understood in the Roman law as the criteria of determining sovereign rights, the whole question of acquisition of new lands
was removed from the limbo of semi-ecclesiastical politics
onto a firm juristic basis. Writers like Victoria[150] might
claim that Spain was relying upon mere discovery for her
title to these new regions, but state acts such as the foregoing are better proof of the law than the cerebrations of
the jurists and the theologians, particularly when the law
is in a formative state.

Not alone by Spain was the principle of possession recognized as determinative of right. The first patents issued by
the English crown were likewise insistent on this point, and
in view of the fact that the English stood without the benefits of the papal grants, and in view of what has been said

---

[148] Davenport, *op. cit.*, p. 132.
[149] *Ibid.*, p. 149.
[150] Victoria, *op. cit.*, Rel. II, no. 7; a view which he rejects.

about the principles of common law, this acceptance of the Roman law doctrine by the English crown is of particular importance.

In the first patent given to John Cabot, issued under circumstances similar to those existing at the time of Columbus' first voyage, we find language strikingly like that in the patent of Columbus.[151] Cabot is given authority to seek out, discover and find new islands and lands, and to conquer, occupy and possess them. The second patent of 1498[152] makes no mention of these powers—indeed, it is little more in substance than a *laissez passer*. The next patent issued by Henry in 1501 has already been mentioned. The Anglo-Portuguese company was authorized to enter into, take possession and conquer the regions assigned them, with the power to resist and throw out invaders, even if they were subjects of friends or allies. This provision was repeated in the second patent issued to the company, but, as we have seen, there was an express recognition of the rights of others previously in possession.

The favorable commercial treaties with Spain and Portugal[153] and the lucrative carrying trade which the English pursued with the latter state had the tendency to divert the energies of the merchant marine into the channels of European trade. Henry VIII renewed in 1515 the treaty with Spain[154] providing for freedom of commerce, and this provision, though not interpreted in any broad sense, apparently had the advantage of permitting the English to establish factories in the Indies.[155] The measures[156] of Philip and Mary, already mentioned in connection with the freedom of

[151] Rymer, *op. cit.*, vol. 12, p. 595.

[152] Harrisse, *John and Sebastian Cabot*, p. 393.

[153] Shillington and Chapman, *Commercial Relations of England and Portugal*, p. 193.

[154] Rymer, *op. cit.*, vol. 13, p. 520.

[155] Williamson, *op. cit.*, p. 225 *et seq.*

[156] *Ibid.*, p. 240 *et seq.*; Harrisse, *Discovery of North America*, p. 46 *et seq.*; Schanz, *op. cit.*, p. 319 *et seq.*

the seas, also show clearly how maritime enterprise in this direction was allowed to languish.[157]

As far as can be ascertained, there were no further patents issued for exploration or settlement in the New World by the Tudor kings prior to the time of Elizabeth, and it is therefore not possible to determine through the medium of acts of the government whether there was any substantial change in the attitude of the English crown. In the intervening period, however, we do know that at least one other country, France,[158] took the view, in an oral agreement regarding the trade and exploration of the Indies, that the fact of possession was the solitary ground for exclusion from these regions; in other words, that the foundation of international right was possession.

In the reign of Elizabeth, on June 11, 1578, letters patent were issued to Sir Humphrey Gilbert,[159] licensing him to discover and view countries "not actually possessed of any Christian prince or people . . . the same to have, hold, occupie and enjoy to him," with a power to expel any invaders. In the same form was the charter to Sir Walter Raleigh of 1584.[160] The warning against the occupation of territory in the actual possession of a Christian prince was likewise repeated in the first two Virginia patents.[161]

It is difficult to escape the conclusion that these facts pre-

[157] Of course the great development of the European carrying trade had a healthy effect upon the growth of the English shipping, without which the extensions of maritime power in Elizabeth's time would have been impossible.

[158] Davenport, *op. cit.*, p. 220. This question does not seem to have arisen with regard to the settlements in Canada. *Cf.* the patent to Cartier (1500), Hazard, *Historical Collections* (1792), vol. 1, p. 19, in which the territory is spoken of as in the possession of the Indians, and the patent to De Monts (1603), *ibid.*, p. 45.

[159] Shafter, *Sir Humphrey Gilberte* (Prince Soc., *Publications*, p. 95); Hazard, *op. cit.*, vol. 1, p. 24.

[160] Hazard, *op. cit.*, vol. 1, p. 33.

[161] Hening, *Virginia Statutes*, vol. 1, p. 57, p. 80.

sent. The English crown, far from asserting a right to territory by discovery, seems to have laid great stress upon the
fact of possession. This is evidenced not alone by the provision requiring the possessions of other princes to be respected, but by the fact that the patentees were themselves
authorized to colonize. The language used in the Gilbert
and Raleigh patents regarding discovery is by no means an
assertion of the basis of the right of discovery, as some
writers have thought; it merely has reference to the power
to choose a locality at which to plant the settlement.[162]

One thing which seems to have given credence to the view
that the English relied upon discovery as the basis of their
rights in America is the frequent reference to voyages,
mostly mythical, the purport of which was largely to the
effect that the queen, by reason of a long series of voyages
of discovery, had as good title to the New World as other
sovereigns, if not a better.[163] This is evident in Hakluyt's
Discourse Concerning Western Planting[164] (1584) and in
what he has to say in his dedication of the *Divers Voyages
Touching the Discovery of America*.[165] Elizabeth herself,
however, as we have seen in the reply to the Spaniard, Mendoza, refused to recognize rights not based on possession.

The works of contemporary English writers on geography smack too obviously of propaganda to be of great value
in fixing the English view of the law.[166] A safer index is to
be found in the law writers, so far as they deal with the
question. We have already observed how the common law
had left no place for the development of a principle of occupation that in any way resembled the Roman law. The rules

[162] Hinsdale, *The Right of Discovery* (*Ohio Archæological and Historical Quarterly,* vol. 2, p. 351).

[163] *Cf.* the map of Atlantis in vol. 8 of the Glasgow edition of Hakluyt.

[164] In the Maine Historical Society, *Collections* (1877), 2d ser., vol. 2.

[165] Hakluyt Society, *Works,* no. 7 (1850), p. 17.

[166] Mr. Cheyney's article on *International Law under Queen Elizabeth*
(*English Historical Review,* vol. 20, p. 659) furnishes no information on
this subject.

of the latter, it is true, were applied with some modification to the acquisition of dominion over wild animals, but only in the case stated of an open tenancy did the law treat the one first making entry as an occupant on land.[167] But according to Coke the occupant must claim a *que estate* and aver the life of a *cestui que vie*. In other words, the right he had was, from the procedural point of view, derivative.

Both Littleton and Coke, however, know of occupation in time of war,[168] but what they have in mind seems to be a disseisin in the homeland that is effected by reason of the fact that the courts do not function. However this may be, what Coke has to say about occupation is interesting. "Occupation," says he, "is a word of art, and signifieth a putting out of a man's freehold in time of war." It is proper only in this sense but *"occupare* is sometimes taken to conquer." This last statement seems to be of particular significance because of the development by Coke of a doctrine that was of consequence to the English view of their colonies.

A few years before Coke wrote, there appeared the first Latin edition of Cowell's *Institutes of the Laws of England*.[169] Cowell sought to blend the Roman and the common law. It is, therefore, not surprising that we find him repeating the passage regarding the islands rising in the sea belonging to the occupier.[170] But what is of even greater importance is what he says regarding occupation generally. "Dominion or propriety in things, by the laws of nature and nations," he writes, "was first created by occupation and possession of those things which did not belong to any person. Occupation includes fishing, hunting, fowling, en-

---

[167] Coke, *On Littleton* (1817), 41 b.

[168] *Ibid.*, 249 b.

[169] Cowell, *Institutes of the Laws of England* (1651). This is the first English edition. On Cowell, *cf.* Hicks, *Men and Books Famous in the Law* (1921), p. 28.

[170] Cowell, *op. cit.*, c. 23, giving the reference to Bracton already examined.

closing, seising. The Law of Nations puts the property of things thus gotten into the person who hath possession, but ours does not."[171]

Many years were to elapse before the English common law was to approach the solution suggested by Cowell. In 1598, it had been decided in a case involving rights in the Isle of Man[172] which were in dispute, that this territory, not being a part of England, the king might grant commission under the great seal to seise lands into the king's hand, and this being done and return made of record, it was brought into the king's seisin and possession. Coke[173] seems to have regarded the Act of Parliament declaring the island conquered territory to be the reason for this. The opinion itself leans to the view that the fact that the lands were out of England and the king claimed them was sufficient. In any event, this appears to have been the theory by which the control over extra-English lands was gained, a conclusion which the patents already spoken of confirm.

Coke's views of the question were destined to receive classic expression in an opinion that excited enough admiration to be embodied in Wingfield's Maxims.[174] In Calvin's Case, he laid down the rule that all infidels were perpetual enemies, for, said he, "the law presumes they will not be converted, that being *remota potentia.*" Between them and Christians there are perpetual hostilities. Accordingly,

---

[171] *Ibid.,* c. 12. This section is of great importance because it showed the way for the adoption of rules of occupation by a reference to the law of nature, a conception with which the British judges were already familiar.

[172] 2 *And.* 116. On this question *cf.* also McIlwaine, *The American Revolution* (1923), p. 82 *et seq.,* dealing with the constitutional problem. *Cf.* also re Wales in 3 *Keble* 401, Craw v. Ramsey, *Vaugh* 279; and the argument in Dutton v. Howell (1693), *Show. H. L.* 31, 32, where the familiarity with the literature of international law and the applicability of its theories to the problem before the English courts is well illustrated.

[173] Coke, *Institutes,* vol. 4, p. 283; Calvin's Case, 17 *Coke* 77.

[174] 17 *Coke* 77; Wingfield, *Maxims* (1658), no. 7, p. 10.

when an infidel country is conquered, there being no established law among infidels which a Christian people can recognize, the rules laid down by the king apply. The view here stated was reiterated in *East India Co. v. Sandys* (1685),[175] where it was argued that infidels were looked upon as enemies not in a spiritual sense alone but in a temporal sense "and were so to be treated and are so accounted in law."

The high point reached in the development of this view seems to have been in the case of *Smith v. Brown,*[176] where Holt, C. J., stated that as soon as a negro came into England he was free. He went on to say: "You should have averred in the declaration that the sale was in Virginia and by the laws of that country negroes are saleable, for the laws of England do not extend to Virginia, being a conquered country their law is what the King pleases."

It is not to be assumed that the extraordinary doctrine of these cases represented the view of the English crown of its rights as far as other nations were concerned. Like the Spaniards, they might claim dominion by conquest, but their international rights were based upon occupation if for no other reason than that, the heathen being common enemies, a conquest of territory from them would not necessarily be a good title in international law.

The insular imperviousness of the common law to change was at length doomed in the reign of Charles II, when, in the case of *Geary v. Bancroft,* it was said by way of dictum:[177] "The law of occupancy is founded upon the Law of

---

[175] 1 *Skinner* 165. This was the idea put forth by counsel.

[176] 2 *Salk* 666.

[177] 1 *Sid* 347. This was a case of "general occupancy" arising in England (*cf.* note 167), and the court was endeavoring to show that the situation was governed by rules analogous to those obtaining in the case of original acquisition of territory in a new country. The significance of the analogy lies in the fact that these latter rules were apparently well known to the court and are spoken of as if they had received judicial recognition. Of this no earlier evidence can be found, but later Geary v. Bancroft is treated as if it were authority for these rules whereas they are really dicta.

Nature, viz., *quod terra manens vacua, occupanti concedi-tur.* So as upon the coming of the inhabitants to a new coun-try—he that first enters upon such part and manures it, gains the property . . . so that it is the actual possession and manurance of the land which was the first cause of oc-cupancy and consequently is only to be gained by actual entry." In the case of *Blancard v. Galdy*[178] the plaintiff at-tempted to carry the principle further arguing that the property in the soil was gained by the possessor; the gov-ernment and dominion belonged to the crown,[179] and hence

The court in this case also refers to the custom of Cornwall and the Stan-naries. In the Stannaries peculiar rules derived from the Roman law were applied by the special courts there and had reference chiefly to the acquisi-tion of mining rights. These customs were not strictly part of the common law but they are worthy of mention because being in a sense an indigenous development, their existence must have facilitated the acceptance of the international law rules by the common law courts in the matter of occu-pation. On the Stanneries, *cf.* Holdsworth, *History of English Law* (1922), vol. I, p. 153 *et seq.;* Lewis, G. R., *The Stannaries* (1908).

[178] *Comber* 228; 4 *Mod.* 222; 2 *Salk* 412. The opinion of the court here, plus the dictum, marks the beginning of the integration of the two currents of opinion, that which treated America as conquered country, and that which leaned toward the Roman law idea. The process is completed in the case cited in note 179. It should further be observed that in Blancard v. Galdy, the court is using *found* in the sense of *occupied.* This seems a fair deduction from the elaboration of the dictum by the Privy Council, which goes on the principle that the law follows the person, and from the argu-ments of counsel. In any event while in neither instance the courts are lay-ing down the rules of occupation, such are assumed in order that the conclusion can be reached that English law is applicable *ab instante occu-pationis.*

[179] In 2 *Peer Williams* 75 is a memorandum giving the purport of this opinion by the Privy Council as follows: "1. Where a new and uninhabited country is found by English subjects, such new country is governed by the laws of England, the laws following the person. After settlement Acts of Parliament made in England will not bind unless the foreign plantation is named. 2. Where the King conquers a country, a right and property in its people is acquired. In consequence of which he may impose such Laws as he pleases. 3. Until the conqueror gives such laws the Laws of the con-quered country hold place unless these are contrary to English religion or

English law obtains. The court held that in case of conquest the conqueror's law obtained only when established. It further stated, by way of dictum, that in the case of an uninhabited country newly found out by Englishmen, English law applied. A later Privy Council decision indicates that by "found out" was understood "occupation."[179]

These rules seem to have been no more than a belated acceptance by the courts of what was already well recognized by the English crown in its foreign relations. The common lawyers were wrestling with the solution of a problem for which their materials were entirely inadequate. The limitation of the common law was never more strikingly illustrated than the cumbersome way in which this problem was confronted and met. In the end recourse was had to the law of nature, or the law of nations, which was in this instance nothing more than the principles of the Roman law that we have examined. At the same time the writers on the common law as well as on the Roman law were clearly bothered by the question of the true nature of the title to the new lands. Victoria in Spain, believing the inhabitants of America to have some claim to the land, as human beings, could not conscientiously treat the territory as *res nullius,* and he had recourse to conquest as the real foundation of Spanish rights. Coke, familiar as he was with Bracton's pallid repetition of the passages of the Institutes, could not see over the wall which surrounded the garden of his legal ideas, and because he regarded all property rights as derivative, he too resorted to the same solution of the problem. Of the two writers, however, separated by a century, the warmer human sympathy flowed in the veins of the Spaniard. The final view of international law was to be a theory more in accordance with the facts, and one which ultimately resulted in less violence to the aborigines.

Happily for the English colonial development the crown

malicious in se or are silent in which event the Laws of the conquering country prevail" (1722).

itself felt none of the same strictures in dealing with the international aspects of the new undertaking. The initial problem of a colonial policy had been met by Elizabeth in her flat declaration to the Spanish ambassador, Mendoza, that the seas were free to all. Thus, as far as access to the uncolonized regions was concerned, the English very justly refused to be bound by the Spanish claims of exclusive dominion over the seas, and the claims of the latter to the lands that lay beyond the Atlantic were weakened *pro tanto* when the first bulwark of their claims was overthrown.

The modest beginnings of the English colonial system, and the fact that the realm was rent by great internal strife shortly after this beginning was made, account for the relatively insignificant rôle played by England in the establishment of rules governing the acquisition of sovereignty over new lands. When we consider the theories of the common law courts, these facts move us to no great feeling of regret. Whether or not the English court was cognizant of the discussion at Badajoz and what seems, as we have shown, to have been the prevailing view on the Continent, it is impossible to say. Nevertheless, at the very inception of the Virginia enterprise, the official attitude of the English court was in accordance with these views.

Mr. Alexander Brown, in that excellent work, *The Genesis of the United States,*[180] has printed the translation of innumerable dispatches that passed between the Spanish court and Don Pedro de Zúñiga, the Spanish ambassador at London. The latter appears to have followed the progress of the Virginia project with the keenest interest and with an extraordinary intelligence service.[181] Zúñiga, filled with righteous indignation at the violation of his master's rights, seems to have regarded the enterprise as intended to establish a base for piratical descents upon the Spanish colonies. His mind was no doubt filled with grim recollections

---

[180] Brown, *The Genesis of the United States* (1897), vols. 1 and 2.
[181] The first dispatch is dated March 16, 1606, *ibid.,* vol. 1, p. 45.

of Elizabethan days, and he accordingly urged counter-measures with much fervor. His representations by no means fell upon deaf ears,[182] and yet the Spanish court, despite the action of the Council of State favoring active intervention, was strangely supine. The attitude of King Philip III is expressed in a note[183] of June 12, 1607, where he bases the right of Spain to Virginia upon the principle of contiguity. But, throughout the letter, the king's concern is primarily a reflection of Zúñiga's forebodings of piracy,[184] and also a fear of religious infection by the English. Zúñiga was further charged to interview King James on the subject.

The interview recounted by Zúñiga in a dispatch of October 8, 1607, throws light upon James I's methods of diplomacy.[185] He told Zúñiga he did not know particularly what was going on, and he did not know that Philip had a right to the navigation to Virginia, for the Spanish colonies were far away, and he had stipulated in the treaty of 1604 not to go near the Indies, but this place (*i.e.,* Virginia) was not mentioned. It seemed to him, further, if Spanish subjects discovered new lands, his own people might do likewise. Zúñiga then said that it was a condition of the treaty that they should not go near the Indies. James replied that if his people went there, he would not complain if they were punished. This did not satisfy Zúñiga, who urged James to take measures himself. The later promised to do so. The result of this promise was characteristic of James. The Earl of Salisbury[186] told Zúñiga that the king had decided if the English went where they had no business to go, they should be punished, and it seemed to him they might not go to Virginia. Therefore he would not be offended if these men were

[182] *Ibid.,* vol. 1, pp. 100, 125.
[183] *Ibid.,* vol. 1, p. 102.
[184] *Ibid.,* vol. 1, p. 118.
[185] *Ibid.,* vol. 1, p. 120.
[186] *Ibid.,* vol. 1, p. 123.

punished, but he did not wish to take measures himself, as this would be an acknowledgment of Philip as lord of the Indies.

The treaty of 1604,[187] to which reference was made and which ended the long war with Spain, had extended trading rights to the English subjects in places where they had traded "before the war." This concession, which was regarded by the English as including the Indies,[188] was made only after the English delegates had attempted to secure rights of access except in such places where the Spanish were actually planted. The way was, therefore, left open to future dispute.

The English view of the treaty was clearly set forth in a speech of the Earl of Salisbury of June 15, 1607, at a conference of the Commons and Lords.[189] He said: "Such was his Majesty's magnanimity in the debate and conclusion of the last treaty as he would never condescend to any article importing the exclusion of his subjects from that trade [*i.e.*, with the Indies] as a prince that would not acknowledge that any such right could grow to the crown of Spain by the donative of the Pope whose authority he disclaimeth; or by the title of a dispersed and punctual occupation of certain territories in the name of the rest; but stood firm to reserve that point. . . ." The speaker then went on to speak of Virginia as a place where the Spanish had neither people nor possession.[190]

The efforts to oppose the Virginia colony were fruitless, despite the talk of preparation to destroy it in Philip III's notes to his ambassadors, and finally on May 23, 1613,[191] the

---

[187] Davenport, *op. cit.*, p. 246.

[188] *Ibid.*, p. 249.

[189] Bacon, *Works* (1740), vol. 4, pp. 253-254.

[190] Brown, *op. cit.*, vol. 2, p. 669, reproduces a document on the extent and limits of Spanish possessions. This was, says he, rough notes for a reply to the Spanish claims to America. The paper is drawn up on the theory of possession giving right.

[191] *Ibid.*, p. 631.

king stated that nothing would be done, as there was no immediate cause of apprehension. The fact that an exchange
of prisoners taken by the Virginia colonists with some
which the Spanish held was arranged, indicates official
countenance of the colony. Some months later (November
3, 1613)[192] the English ambassador at Madrid, Digby, reported to Sir Dudley Carleton, English ambassador to Venice, the purport of an interview with the Spanish secretary
of state, in the course of which the latter complained of
English colonies as a violation of Spanish rights, based
upon the fact that Spaniards had long fished in the northern
seas and the fact that their dominion had been unchallenged. To this Digby replied that the Spanish had only recently come into these regions and that

I could no way yield unto him that eyther Virginia or ye Ber-
mudos were parts of the conquest of Castile, but that the[re we]
. . . [were] [our]selves the first Possidents. . . . Soe that I supposed what is sayd of the whale-fishing was to bee debated and disputed in the same nature the Indies were which the crown of Castile
without controversie discovered and possessed. And that then hee
would see that his Majestie [meaning James I] only followed theire
owne foot steppes. . . . And that I conceaved the same reason of
being the first Possident was equallie to holde in both.[193]

In a later dispute with Spain on another question in 1621,
the English viewpoint on the rights over the new territories
was expressed in the House of Commons by Sir Edwin
Sandys, who requested that the king's right to the Amazon
lands be considered, "that Plantation there being first made
by his [King James'] subjects about twelve years since."
He then denied the validity of Alexander VI's bull to give
title and added that "if the King will not take on him the

---

[192] *Ibid.*, p. 668.

[193] Beer, *The Origins of the British Colonial System* (1908), pp. 18-19,
states that James I at first evaded the issue in the dispute with Spain, but
that "ultimately he assumed full responsibility." For this statement he
offers no direct proof.

Sovereignty of that Country and Territory, yet, it being a vast Country, it is by the Law of Nations and Nature the Occupiers, for in such Cases *Seges est Occupantis,* it is a good Title and Claim."[194] In the same year, Sir Dudley Carter was instructed to use similar language in protesting the projected Dutch colony at Manhattan. The instruction reads: "You should represent these things unto the States Generall in his Ma[ts] name (who *iure primæ occupationis* hath a good and sufficient title to those parts) and require of them that as well those shipps as their further prosecution of the plantation may be presently stayed."[195]

There can be no question that, whatever the views of the common law courts were, the official attitude of the English crown was no different from that of the other European states which sought to break the Spanish-Portuguese colonial monopoly, and which the two latter countries applied in disputes between themselves. The current view is concisely, albeit somewhat bitterly, expressed by Bacon in his argument of Calvin's case when he says: "And if King Henry VII had accepted the offer of Christopher Columbus whereby the crown of England had obtained the Indies by conquest or occupation, all the Indies had been naturalized. . . ."[196] Well into the opening years of the seventeenth century, therefore, there was no pretension that discovery could be the source of title; indeed, the lesser maritime powers, by the assertion of a principle of this sort, would have rigorously excluded themselves from the benefits of colonial expansion.

The practice of the European powers regarding occupa-

---

[194] *Proceedings and Debates of the House of Commons in 1620 and 1621* (Tyrwhitt ed.), p. 250.

[195] Brodhead, *History of New York* (1874), vol. 1, p. 140; *Documents Relative to the Colonial History of New York* (1853), vol. 3, pp. 6-8. On New York as a conquered country *cf.* Campbell v. Hall, 1 *Cowp.* 204 (1774).

[196] Bacon, *Works* (1740), vol. 4, p. 197.

tion being in this state at the opening of the century, it is proper to turn once more to an examination of the opinions of jurists. The most widely known Spanish contribution on the subject has been mentioned. This was the *Relectio de Indis* of Victoria. The latter, as we have seen, expressly rejected the view that discovery could give any sort of title, and this assertion, together with the robust manner in which he combated the claim of a title through the papal bulls, furnished ammunition for a much greater man in his attack upon the Portuguese monopoly in the East Indies— the *Mare Liberum,* written by Hugo Grotius, defending Dutch rights to traffic in these regions, that at the time represented the attitude of all the lesser maritime powers.

The *Mare Liberum* was first published in 1608 and was written in the idiom of Roman private law. It illustrates in a very clear manner how cunningly Grotius applied the tenets of the old *ius gentium* to the new situation of a number of independent states governed in their relations to each other by many ancient precedents which were not yet embodied into any recognized system of jurisprudence.[197] Applying the Roman concepts of property to the relation of a state to its domain, Grotius starts out by saying that the Portuguese are not lords (*domini*) of the East Indies because no one is lord of anything which he himself or someone in his name has not possessed. The islands, he claims, were *sui juris* and the circumstances showed that the Portuguese went here not as conquerors but as foreigners. Their claim to dominion was not sufficient because possession is a prerequisite, and having a thing is different from having a right to acquire it.[198]

[197] Grotius, *Mare Liberum* (1773). The Magoffin translation (1915) is unfortunately not always an exact rendition of the meaning of the text, particularly when legal terms are involved. It is, of course, no easy matter to determine in what sense Grotius uses such words as *dominium,* but one is safer in assuming the conventional Roman law meaning.

[198] *Mare Liberum, c.* 2.

By discovery no right was obtained by the Portuguese because ''to discover a thing is not only to seize it (*usurpare*) with the eyes but to take real possession of it. The grammarians accordingly use discover (*invenire*) and occupy (*occupare*) as having the same meaning. Natural reason, the precise words of the law, and the interpretation of scholars all show clearly that discovery suffices to give a title of lordship only when it is accompanied by possession.'' This rule applied both to movables and to immovables that are marked off and guarded.

Grotius proceeds to dispose of the claim that the Indies were *res nullius,* and he then demolishes with true Protestant fervor the claim to right emanating from the papal bulls.[199] Proceeding to examine the claim that occupation could have been effected with reference to the sea, he states that possession of immovables required the erection of buildings (*instructio*) or fencing in (*limitatio*). Territories (*i.e.,* in sense of the public domain) were constituted through occupation by a people just as private property arises out of occupation by individuals; and he goes on to say that ownership can only arise out of physical possession, and unless boundaries can be shown, either natural or artificial, no title can be set up; otherwise the earth would long ago have been divided.

The work of Grotius was well known in England, and the use to which he put the Roman law must have found readier acceptance in view of the writings of Cowell, and the esteem in which Bracton was held. Indeed, the conception of a law of nations, sometimes used synonymously with the law of nature, was not unfamiliar to Coke, and we find reference to it in the argument of Bacon of the case of the post-nati (Calvin's Case)[200] that leads one to the conclusion that what-

---

[199] *Cf. ibid.,* c. 5. Whatever by occupation can become private property can also become public property, that is, the property of the people.

[200] Bacon, *Works* (1740), vol. IV, pp. 189, 200. Also in his *Observations upon a Libel, ibid.,* p. 342.

ever hold the antiquated English common law system may have had upon the determination of individual rights in the kingdom, men were ready to accept the broader principles of the *ius gentium* in the determination of matters outside the purview of English jurisprudence. The lack of a precise distinction between a law of nations and the law of nature, the latter a most familiar refuge of the English judge, undoubtedly assisted in this process of fertilization of the insular mind.

It was natural that the distinctions drawn in the *Mare Liberum* should have found repetition in Grotius' epoch-making *De Jure Belli ac Pacis* (1625),[201] but the latter work really goes further than the *Mare Liberum* in defining an international law of occupation. This advance was affected primarily by a distinction between lordship (*imperium*) and ownership (*dominium*). "In things properly no one's," says Grotius, "two things are occupable, the lordship and the ownership in so far as it is distinguished from lordship."[202] There are two matters commonly regarded as subject to *imperium;* first, persons, which matter alone sometimes suffices, as in the case of an army of men, women and children seeking new settlements, and secondarily, a place which is called territory. Hence although lordship and ownership are usually acquired by one act, they are distinct concepts. As to what may be occupied, Grotius enumerates places hitherto uncultivated (having *terra firma* in mind), uninhabited islands, wild beasts, fishes, birds.[203]

Occupation as a legal act is not described in the detail that distinguishes *Mare Liberum,* but the inference is clear that Grotius regarded the Roman law rules as applicable. The most important modification of the Roman law effected

---

[201] Grotius, *De Jure Belli ac Pacis* (Whewell ed.). The writer has not followed the Whewell translation in cases where he disagrees with the rendition.

[202] *Ibid.,* lib. II, III, iv, 1.

[203] *Ibid.,* lib. II, II, iv.

by Grotius to meet the conditions of acquisition by the state, seems to be in the following passage :[204]

At the same time this should be noted, sometimes the first acquisition by a people or by the head of a people is made in such a manner that not only the imperium, which includes the *ius eminens* of which we have spoken, but that also the full private ownership (*dominium*) was acquired at first for the people generally or its head. And then the property was distributed particularly to each private individual, so that the ownership of the latter depended upon the prior ownership, if not in the same way as the right of the vassal upon that of the seignior, or the right of a tenant upon that of a proprietor, nevertheless in some other mode of tenure.[205]

When we compare that statement with what has been said about the Roman concept of the interest of the state in the acquisition of property, it will be observed that under the influence of feudal ideas Grotius was able to lay down a rule of ownership in individuals in cases where the original acquisition had been made by the state; and such a rule was certainly in accordance with the practice of the European monarchs in issuing patents to settlers in the New World. The idea of a real right of the sovereign in the territory of his domain had not yet been supplanted by the modern theory, and hence the unrestricted use of Roman law rules of property, subject only to the modification mentioned above, could persist in international relations.[206]

The course of legal development outlined in this chapter has demonstrated how little Grotius' views had to do with the evolution of international practice in regard to the acquisition of sovereignty over newly discovered territory.

[204] Compare this with Bartolus' treatment of the same problem.

[205] *Ibid.*, lib. II, III, xix, 2.

[206] Grotius also repeats the ideas of Victoria regarding discovery as follows: "It is no less unjust to claim lands on the ground of having discovered them when they are occupied by another even though the possessors be bad men, with wrong notions of God, and dull intellects. For those lands only can be discovered which belong to nobody." Lib. II, XXII, ix.

Nor were these views of overwhelming importance in the field of jurisprudence, for neither the *Mare Liberum* nor the *De Jure Belli* were accounted by contemporaries as having the authoritative quality which is at present attributed to them. One reason for this lack of reverence was the fact that prior to the publication of the *De Jure Belli*, a German jurist, Johann Gryphiander, had composed (1623) a *Tractatus de Insulis*,[207] which dealt exhaustively with the problem of occupation and in which the learning was the equal of Grotius' productions. If we can judge from the extent to which it was cited there can be no question but that it was long the leading work on the subject.

Gryphiander has a great deal to say about discovery in relation to the acquisition of rights over territory.[208] To him the word imports not merely the casual finding of land; it is the finding plus the actual effective occupation. There are, says Gryphiander, three requisites for acquiring title by discovery. First, there must be the intent to acquire for oneself (*animus sibi habendi*); second, the corporal apprehension of the island (*corporalis apprehensio*);[209] third, the object discovered must be *nullius*, otherwise no rights are acquired.

Owing to the great currency of Gryphiander's work we may assume that the term discovery in the legal literature of the seventeenth century was a word of art having a much broader connotation than the merely physical fact of finding. Indeed, it is difficult to see how *inventio* (discovery), as Gryphiander uses it, differs from the *occupatio* of other writers, and one is led to conjecture that it was chiefly the passion of the seventeenth century jurist for classification which induced him to devote a chapter to acquisition by this

[207] Gryphiander, *Tractatus de Insulis*. Gryphiander's real name was Griepenkerl. *Cf. Allgemeine Deutsche Biographie,* vol. 10, p. 73.

[208] *Ibid.,* c. 19.

[209] Gryphiander points out that *invenire* denotes "entering upon," a combination of *in* and *venire*.

mode. A careful examination of the *Tractatus de Insulis,* however, discloses some proof of the fact that Gryphiander, far from attempting to state a new doctrine inconsistent with the notions of occupation then practiced by states, was merely developing a terminology for international law which would serve to distinguish the new public law of occupation from the private law on the subject.

In a chapter dealing with *apprehensio*[210] (in the sense of occupation) the second requisite in his law of discovery is developed at length, and it is absolutely patent that the author is not speaking of discovery in the sense in which it was later used by the English (*i.e.,* that the mere casual finding of new land gave an inchoate title to it). His views are nothing more or less than a restatement of the Roman law in terms of the modern conditions. *Apprehensio* is used for peaceful occupation in distinction from wartime occupation discussed above as *occupatio bellica.* As everything which Gryphiander has to say is along conventional lines it is not necessary to repeat his statements.

In one important particular Gryphiander makes a contribution to the theory of acquiring sovereignty.[211] He recognizes the distinction between *dominium* and *imperium,* but he solves the problem of the acquisition of public right through individuals in a clearer and more deft fashion than Grotius. Where, says Gryphiander, there is no private ownership (*dominium*) there is no territory and consequently no *jurisdictio* (exercise of public right). But so much as the individuals possess in private right so much is encompassed in the *imperium* of the prince, and, indeed, more, because his rights of jurisdiction embrace more than does mere private *dominium* including among other things the sea and the shore.[212]

---

[210] Gryphiander, *op. cit.,* c. 21.

[211] *Loc. cit.,* par. 80-81.

[212] There is considerable discussion at various places in the work on the extent to which islands lying off the continent are properly a part of the

Gryphiander proceeds to elaborate his idea, showing clearly that what he has in mind is that the control of the sovereign over his individual subject is the element which perfects his public right at the moment that the individual acquires his private right. This is entirely in line with the modern view and for that reason is worthy of remark.

No one examining this treatise can fail to be struck with the sanity and scholarly spirit which pervade it. Far from being tainted with any vice of propagandism which distinguished so much of the writing on international relations during this period, it preserves an aloofness which gives it added weight. Thus in relation of the claims of Spain to the New World the author remarks that although any rights claimed through the papal bulls are to be branded as without legal foundation, the Spanish have perfected their claims by occupation and it is on this ground that they must rest.[213] What a welter of controversial writing would the world have been spared had men but heeded the simple explanation of this forgotten scholar!

continent in the sense that the continent being under occupation the islands though not themselves occupied are subject to the sovereign's jurisdiction. Gryphiander is inclined to the view that in certain circumstances they are. *Ibid.*, par. 84 and 94-96.

[213] *Ibid.*, c. 24, par. 54-66. It should be noted that Gryphiander points out that a title can come from but one source and hence the Spanish claim to the Indies must rest either on the pope's bull or on occupation. *Ibid.*, c. 24.

CHAPTER III

THE PUBLIC LAW OF EUROPE AND THE OLD COLONIAL SYSTEM

THE Falkland Islands did not become a major problem of diplomacy until the middle of the eighteenth century, yet the contest between England and Spain for the sovereignty over this group was but a single phase of a much greater struggle which had been going on in European politics since the destruction of Philip II's Great Armada in 1588. It is consequently necessary to review in some detail the several elements in the relations between Spain and England that furnish the background for the incidents which introduced the Falklands into the stormy seas of world politics.

It is of course a truism to characterize Anglo-Spanish relations during the seventeenth and eighteenth centuries as a struggle for the economic control of the western hemisphere. The diplomatic negotiations, the wars and to some extent the commercial gambits of this great contest are all generally known. On the other hand, the rôle of international law in the history of these two centuries is almost totally forgotten; and yet the offensives and defenses were not all purely of a military or political nature. The short periods of peace which ensued between the almost incessant warfare were all characterized by deliberate attempts on the part of states to govern their relations by law, and, curiously enough, the breaking of the peace was almost invariably occasioned by some torrid discussion over the meaning or application of these principles of law. This paradox that law bred war was due in part to the disappearance of international arbitration as a mode of settling international disputes, and in part to the uncertainty as to what the principles of law really were. The law was in the making and the sword was often used as proof of right as well as of might.

The development of international law, during these years, in relation to colonial problems followed in the main two lines. On the one hand, special rules were developed to cover specific situations of fact such as the occupation of new territory just discussed; on the other hand, it was sought by general treaty provisions to give an international legal sanction to the colonial systems of the various European states. The rules developed in the manner first spoken of remained imbedded in the general body of international law. The treaty provisions, attempting as they did to regulate legally matters of pure political action, enjoyed only a transitory existence and eventually disappeared with the systems to which they sought to give legal validity. The impulse to secure international recognition and status for domestic colonial policies was a phase of the movement which crystallized in the form of the so-called "public law" of Europe.[1] Every treaty which fixed a *status quo* in the political life of Europe from the Peace of Westphalia (1648) onward was a contribution to the public law of Europe. This law included such things as territorial settlements, marriage arrangements between sovereigns, successions and the whole mass of matters which today are looked upon as falling primarily in the sphere of political action. In the seventeenth century the public law of Europe was, as has been said, extended to colonial questions, and although at the present time these rules would not be regarded as rules of international law, during the century and a half preceding the French Revolution they were generally treated as having legal validity equal to the rules governing matters about which today there is no doubt as to the regulation by

---

[1] There is no systematic treatise on this which explains how the "public law" of Europe differed from the international law of today. *Cf.*, however, Mably, *Le Droit Public de l'Europe* (1748), 2 vols.; Abreu, *Derecho Público de la Europa* (1746), 2 vols.

law. Thus, in addition to the law of occupation which was to govern the acquisition of sovereignty over the Falklands, the law set up by such instruments as the American Treaty (1670) and the Treaties of Utrecht (1713) was an element of greatest moment; for in colonial questions the law of occupation applied only if there was no infraction of these general international obligations.

To understand how the European colonial systems were eventually regulated by treaty it is necessary to explain the nature of these systems as well as the legal implications arising out of the treaties. We have already seen how Spain, immediately after the return of Columbus from his first voyage, had sought to assure to herself an exclusive right to the new lands by securing a papal patent, and how with the advance of the Protestant revolution the non-observance of this fiat progressively destroyed any legal force it may at first have had. The Portuguese claims having been effectively regulated, Spain next devoted herself to a policy of extensive colonization, spreading her settlements over so wide an area that she could rely upon the application of rules of occupation agreed on with Portugal to exclude claims of sovereignty from all other sources,[2] particularly as the colonial activities of other states were at first almost negligible. In only one other way besides colonization could a second-rate maritime power acquire a share in the benefits of the riches of America—this was by direct commercial relations with the colonies. Partly because the crown had a personal pecuniary interest in the colonies, and partly because it was desired to reserve the benefits of the latter to Spanish subjects, an elaborate system of rules[3] was put into effect which restricted the trade to Spanish subjects or per-

[2] This is well illustrated by the steps later taken to settle Patagonia. *Cf.* chapter 9.

[3] On this see Solórzano, *op. cit., passim;* Veitia Linaje, *Norte de la Contratación* (1672); Haring, *Trade and Navigation between Spain and the Indies* (1918).

sons domiciled in Spain,[4] and which limited navigation to the colonies to Spanish ships.[5] The theory was that no alien could have access to or profit from the colonies.[6]

This system, of which we can give only a bare outline, could have vitality only so long as there was no strong maritime power to dispute it, and so long as Spain could exercise an effective police over colonial waters. In a very real manner it premised and sought to effectuate a closed sea in the same manner as Alexander VI's famous bulls. Thus Spain sought to guarantee, by indirection, observance of that which she had not been able to secure directly.

The existing commercial treaties of Spain with other powers were of consequence in this relation. It is of course impossible to examine these in detail. We may cite, however, the treaty relations with England as an example of what happened. We have noted the commercial treaty,[7] concluded in 1499 between Henry VII and Ferdinand, provided for the right of the English to traffic in all the dominions of Spain. As has been remarked, it is extremely doubtful whether this was intended to cover Spanish lands overseas, as the colonization of these had only begun. The evidence reviewed in the last chapter points to the contrary. In the succeeding treaties[8] the privilege was renewed, but as the colonial system was in full operation by 1540[9] the implication is fair that only trade with Spain in Europe was

---

[4] Atuñez, *Memorias Históricas* (1797), p. 268. The instructions to Ovando of September 17, 1501, mentioned previously, are the earliest indication of this policy.

[5] *Recopilación de Leyes de los Reynos de las Indias* (1774), lib. 9, tit. 30, fol. 51. (Hereafter cited *Recopilación*.)

[6] *Ibid.*, lib. 9, sit. 26, fol. 1.

[7] Rymer, *Fœdera*, vol. 12, p. 741.

[8] Treaty of June 5, 1507, in Rymer, *op. cit.*, vol. 13, p. 167; Treaty of June 19, 1519, *ibid.*, p. 520; of April 11, 1520, *ibid.*, p. 714; of August 5, 1529, Dumont, *Corps Universel Diplomatique*, vol. 4, pt. 2, p. 42; of December 3, 1543, *ibid.*, p. 252.

[9] Haring, *op. cit.*, p. 101.

intended. Nevertheless, the British appear to have done some direct trading with the Indies and to have laid the foundations for future claims.

While Spain thus endeavored to secure sole enjoyment of the western hemisphere by colonizing as extensively as possible, and by refusing other states access to the unsettled shores, English maritime power increased. During Elizabeth's reign, as we have seen, the closed sea theory of Spain was challenged both in word and in deed, and so effectively that when the war came to an end with the accession of James I, the Spaniards sought to secure a definition of the situation by treaty.

At this moment England had no American colonies. She was, therefore, bent upon clinging to such rights as she had enjoyed by use and to assure freedom of navigation and commerce with the Spanish Indies as far as this was possible. In the succeeding years this object was never lost sight of, and even after she had acquired colonies in North America and the West Indies, England sought both by commerce and by plantation to break Spain's monopoly in the Caribbean and the South Atlantic. In this contest, which waxed fiercer as Spanish power waned, the whole resources of English politics and trade were concentrated on the object of striking a breach in South America which would give her not only the political but the economic control of the western hemisphere. The attempt on the Falklands occurred in the final stages of the struggle, and here the whole defensory apparatus of law which Spain had built up was put to the test.

In the discussions with England preceding the conclusion of the treaty of 1604 it was obvious from the first that some sort of compromise would have to be reached.[10] The English had been very implicitly instructed[11] not to surrender the rights previously acquired and to resist to the uttermost

[10] Cf. Hist. MSS. Comm., *Eighth Report*, pt. I, p. 95 *et seq.*
[11] Text in Davenport, *op. cit.*, p. 247, note 4.

the Spanish pretensions of excluding other nations from the unsettled regions. This position was, of course, actively contested by the Spanish plenipotentiaries, and after a good deal of debate the article agreed upon permitted trade "where commerce existed before the war agreeably and in accordance with the use and observance of old alliances and treaties before the war."[12] In other words, the previous practice was made the guide, and as no one knew what the precise limits of this practice were the door to unending dispute was left open. This article was renewed in the Treaty of Madrid of 1630.[13]

The purpose of this clause was twofold; on the one hand, it was to guarantee such rights of trade as had been acquired; on the other, it was supposed by the English to give a right of access to unsettled shores. We have already considered its operation with respect to the Virginia colony. The Spanish made no sharp protest in this case for the reason that there was no ground upon which they could possibly claim possession themselves. The case was otherwise with the enterprises of Raleigh and others to effect a settlement in Guiana.[14] Here the Spanish crown not only had a settlement, but being sovereign over the Portuguese it was able to lay claim under the rights of the latter to Brazil. The protests of the Spanish ambassador, Count Gondomar, against the Raleigh expedition,[15] on the ground that Spain had antecedent possession, were heeded, and in 1620,[16] when the Amazon Company sought to resume the task ended by Raleigh's execution, the English government, acting upon the Spanish complaint, undertook to punish the promoters of the project.[17]

[12] *Ibid.,* p. 256.
[13] *Ibid.,* p. 308.
[14] Williamson, *English Colonies in Guiana* (1923).
[15] *Ibid.,* p. 74.
[16] *Ibid.,* p. 83.
[17] *Ibid.,* p. 107 *et seq.,* for other expeditions.

The English were not the only power to challenge the Spanish claims. The French, as we have already seen, and then the Dutch embarked upon overseas adventures which challenged the colonial hegemony of Spain both in America and in the East Indies. As the Dutch wars entered their final phase the question of peace was complicated by the status of the trade and settlements which had sprung up during the war. These colonies were looked upon by Spain as threatening to her colonial system equally whether they were the result of conquest or settlement. The Truce of Antwerp of 1609[18] had conceded to the Dutch the right to trade in Spain and in places where Spanish allies were allowed to trade; outside of these places there could be no trade in places possessed by Spain except by royal permission. In places not so held the Dutch might trade with permission of the natives.

The question of colonial trade was thus for a second time left in conveniently vague form, and the question of right to occupy territory was undecided, although the implication was clear that no obstacle stood in the way,—that is to say, by admitting the right of the Dutch to trade without license in unoccupied places the right to settle was unquestionably included. The Dutch made the most of this, but their aggressiveness made the question of the Indies trade an increasingly greater obstacle to peace.

In the negotiations at Münster from 1646 to 1648[19] this question was the most bitterly contested point. In the end the Spanish took the bull by the horns and adopted the principle of *uti possidetis*[20]—*i.e.*, actual possession was to govern the right of sovereignty. The fifth article of the treaty

[18] Davenport, *op. cit.*, p. 258 *et seq.*

[19] *Ibid.*, p. 353 *et seq.*

[20] On this *cf.* especially J. B. Moore, *Memorandum on Uti Possidetis* (1911), *passim.*

provided for the possession by Spain and the Dutch of such[21]

lordships, cities, castles, fortresses, commerce and countries in the East and West Indies as also in Brazil and on the coasts of Asia, Africa, and America respectively as the said Lords, the King and the States respectively hold and possess, and in this comprehending particularly the places and forts which the Portuguese have taken from the Lords the States and occupied since the year 1641; comprising also the places (*lieux et places*) which the said Lords, the States may conquer and possess hereafter without infraction of the present treaty.

The sixth article provided that as respected the West Indies the subjects of each state were to refrain from traffic and navigation in "all the harbors, localities, and places" provided with fortifications or posts and "all others possessed by the one or the other party." The places held by the States General, the treaty further provided, should include the places which the Portuguese had occupied "out of the hands of the States and have been in possession of ever since the year 1641, as also all the other places which they possess at present as long as they remain in the hands of the said Portuguese. . . ."

The joker in this article was that the parties were mutually excluded from "all other places" possessed by the other. In view of the antecedent negotiations, and particularly the Spanish claims of possession to the large stretches of uninhabited lands lying between their scattered settlements, it was undoubtedly intended to limit the Dutch to what they actually held and to exclude them not only from trade in the Spanish ports but from access to the wild shores where they might found settlements or at least do business with natives. The most that was conceded was a free hand to plague the Portuguese in Brazil.[22]

[21] Davenport, *op. cit.*, p. 363.
[22] On the meaning of this provision *cf.* Burr, *Report as to the Meaning*

The result of this treaty was, first, to give a definite international legal status to the Spanish and Dutch colonial systems. The prohibition on trading was absolute in so far as inhabited places were concerned—by implication it applied to the uninhabited regions which were flanked by Spanish establishments. In the second place, by accepting as a principle of international settlement the theory of *uti possidetis,* the rule of possession hitherto applied received important collateral support. The result of this was to weaken *pro tanto* the Spanish claims of monopoly over the available lands in the western hemisphere, wherever a legal title by conquest or peaceful settlement could be shown. This latter method of acquiring title Spain sought to limit by restricting access to the shores. In other words, *the agreement not to trade with the Spanish Indies was to operate so as to make not only the littoral but the high seas off the Spanish possessions closed seas.* For the next one hundred and fifty years the diplomacy of Spain was devoted to enforcing this notion. That it was to be strenuously combated is obvious, yet Spain by sacrificing to her enemies the actual conquests made by them was, nevertheless, able to have this principle reasserted in every pacification up to the French Revolution. During the piping times of peace, therefore, it was legally impossible to acquire colonies in the Spanish sphere of influence, and the maritime states at first contented themselves with carrying on a lively contraband trade with Spanish colonies. Later, when the Spanish power waned, these states became bolder and sought to occupy the

of *Articles V and VI of the Treaty of Münster,* in United States Commission on Boundary between Venezuela and British Guiana, *Report and Papers* (1896-1897), vol. I, p. 71 *et seq. Cf.* also British Guiana Boundary, Arbitration with the U.S. of Venezuela, *The British Counter Case* (1898), p. 46 *et seq.* Prof. Burr shows that Spain clearly did not concede to the Dutch the right to acquire land from the natives.

Of course these provisions were ineffective to stop contraband trade—it continued without abatement.

territory itself. The Falkland incident falls in this latter period.

Twenty years after the Treaty of Münster the Spanish secured from England a recognition of the principles accepted by the Dutch. This was the Treaty of Madrid of July 8/18, 1670,[23] known as the American Treaty, made in amplification of the Treaty of Madrid of May 23, 1667,[24] which had ended the many years' war with England. The American Treaty may be regarded as the chief instrument regulating the colonial question prior to the Peace of Utrecht, and has a direct bearing upon both English colonization and navigation in the South Atlantic shortly subsequent to the conclusion of the treaty. The preceding treaty of 1667 had recognized the English right to her possessions in America, but trade with the Spanish colonies was restored to the vague *status quo*.[25] The state of peace which the treaty was supposed to introduce prevailed, however, only in Europe and left the situation in the colonies unaffected. The activities of the freebooters, who were the chief agencies of English aggression in the New World, continued without abatement.[26] The second Peace of Madrid was accordingly signed for the purpose of settling all the disputes between the two countries and to bring actual peace in the overseas possessions of the two countries.[27]

Article VII of this second agreement provided in part as follows:[28]

Moreover, 'tis agreed, that the most Serene King of Great Britain, his Heirs and successors, shall have, hold, keep and always possess, in full right of sovereignty, Signiory, Possession, and Propriety,

[23] *A General Collection of Treatys,* vol. I, p. 162.

[24] Berard, *Recueil des Traités* (1700), vol. 4, p. 193 b.

[25] *Cf.* Art. IV.

[26] Beer, *The Old Colonial System* (1912), vol. 2, p. 59 *et seq.*

[27] Some data on the conclusion of the treaty is to be found among the documents contained in Godolphin, *Hispania Illustrata* (1703).

[28] *A General Collection of Treatys,* vol. 1, p. 162.

all the Lands, Countrys, Islands, Colonys and other places, be they what they will, lying and situate in the *West Indies* or in any part of *America* which the said King of Great Britain and his subjects now hold and possess; insomuch that they neither can nor ought hereafter to be contested or call'd in question for them upon any account or under any pretense whatever.

The eighth article prohibited any navigation or traffic by either party in the East Indian possessions of the other. The tenth and eleventh articles, based upon the prohibition of access to ports made provision for the treatment of vessels entering under duress. The fifteenth article provided:

This present treaty shall no way derogate from any preeminence, right, or Seigniory which either the one or the other of the Allys have in the seas, straits, or fresh waters of *America;* and they shall have and retain the same as full and ample a manner, as of right they ought to belong to them; and 'tis always to be understood that the freedom of Navigation ought by no manner of means to be interrupted, when there is nothing committed contrary to the true sense and meaning of these Articles.

This provision was an additional safeguard of the provisions of the earlier treaty, that had simply granted the same liberty of commerce previously enjoyed which, as we have seen, was probably *nil* as far as the Indies were concerned. In other words, it sought in a roundabout manner to affirm the existing exclusive character of the trade with the Indies and the unapproachability of the Spanish dominion as a matter of law. The freedom of navigation spoken of in the fifteenth article was something different from what its name indicates; it was in reality restriction of navigation. That this was so is borne out by the proceedings in the West Indies immediately after the signing of the treaty.

The arts of peace which the treaty introduced were as profitable to England as the arts of war which preceded it. The war in America, just ended, had been carried on most successfully by privateers operating under commissions from the English crown. These warriors were recruited from a class of men usually in desperate straits either as to fortune or honor, so that the sort of warfare practiced by them was both adventurous and profitable in a high degree. The signing of the peace in 1670 was of no greater concern to them than had been the peace of 1667. They continued to plunder the Spaniards with equal gusto and with increasing ferocity. The termination of the war had *ipso facto* made void the royal commissions. The English government, desiring to secure a semblance of permanent pacification in the Americas, sent repeated notices to its representatives to put a stop to this continual preying upon Spanish commerce, but without avail.[29] The raids upon Spanish towns and ships continued, acts of unexampled violence and horror succeeded one another; the Spanish government retaliated with measures of stern cruelty, but without immediate success. The English buccaneers, as they are still picturesquely styled with pleasant euphemism, continued to outrage everyone, including eventually their own countrymen.

It was not alone through the illegal warfare of these pirates that the English persisted in their challenge of the colonial empire of the Spanish. Already at this early date an interest was disclosed in the dye industry. Equally daring though less bloodthirsty adventurers undertook to enter into the Spanish possessions for the purpose of cutting logwood, a proceeding that was not only not authorized by the treaty, but was in direct contravention of its terms. It was sought by pursuing this action in the more or less uninhabited places of Spanish America to establish the basis of a right to possession under the treaty itself. The Spanish, however, protested the procedure, and even the English ambassador at Madrid warned his government against supporting its subjects in their designs.[30] The correspondence

---

[29] *Calendar of State Papers (Colonial,* 1669-1674), 103, 573, 578, 516.

[30] Beer, *op. cit.,* vol. 2, p. 65 *et seq.; Colonial Calendar* (1669-1674), p. 357. Beer suggests that as the cargoes of logwood were not contraband the

discloses the fact that the principle of *uti possidetis* expressed in the treaty of 1670 was applicable to the *status quo* at the time of the conclusion of the agreement, and was, of course, not prospective. Furthermore, although the treaty merely contained a recognition of English territorial rights, read in the light of the antecedent compact of 1667 and the established restrictions on navigation it was likewise an implied recognition of the Spanish possessions, and an implied guarantee on the part of England not to interfere with them.[31]

The most spectacular undertaking in the course of these post-bellum depredations upon Spanish colonies was the capture of Panama by Morgan and his buccaneers. This event was important in relation to our own subject because it opened up to the pirates of the West Indies a new sphere of activity. The ease with which this great centre of Spanish trade on the Pacific had fallen and the vastness of the booty suggested to the fertile imaginations of these empire-builders the glowing prospect of unlimited and lucrative business in the South Sea.[32] It was in pursuance of this dream, already carried out by others, that an expedition was organized which again brought the English into the environs of the Falklands.

This expedition was organized by various buccaneers in

Spanish were not justified in seizing them. This is patently absurd. The wood was taken in contravention of the treaty and was consequently subject to recaption as any stolen property would be. In 1662, by statute 13 and 14 *Chas.* II, c. 11, § 36, two earlier statutes, 23 Eliz., c. 9 and 39 Eliz., c. 11, were repealed. These early statutes had forbidden the use of logwood and had made it forfeit. The government complicity in the logwood cutting is thus established.

[31] *Cf.* Godolphin to Charles II, July 19/29, 1670, in *Downshire Papers*, vol. 1, p. 4, Hist. MSS. Comm. (1924); on the logwood cutting, Godolphin to Arlington, May 10/20, 1672, in Hist. MSS. Comm., *Tenth Report*, p. 200.

[32] Burney, *A Chronological History of the Voyages and Discoveries in the South Sea* (1816), vol. 4, p. 69.

Virginia following a successful season in the Caribbean.[33] It was under the command of one Captain John Cook, and it set sail from Accomac on the Chesapeake in August, 1683. Two of the leaders of the voyage, Ambrose Cowley and William Dampier, have left accounts of their peregrinations and it is from these sources that we obtain our chief accounts of its achievements. Of these two men, Dampier was by all odds the more extraordinary. He was what might be called a "good" pirate, for not only did he have his moments of apostasy, but he likewise was an indefatigable collector of botanical and zoölogical specimens with which he improved his shining hours, contributing substantially to contemporary science if not to the uplift of his companions.

The earlier part of the voyage was for its kind relatively law-abiding. Except for an unfortunate Dutchman and a Dane no vessels were captured or plundered. The latter ship, however, being superior to the *Revenge* in which the pirates had set out, was chosen to be the craft to round the Horn. The buccaneers burnt their old vessel and, rechristening their prize *The Batchelors' Delight,* reëmbarked for the South Sea.

It was in January, 1684, that the great discovery of the voyage was made. This was the famous Pepys Island. Cowley states in his journal[34] that while in the latitude 47° 40' they spied an island to the west of them, covered with woods, with a harbor big enough for five hundred sail of shipping. Cowley believed the island to be one of Sebald de Weert's and although he sailed along the shore he was unable to land as the crew told him they had not come out to make discoveries.

Burney states that William Hacke, the editor of Cowley's

[33] *Ibid.,* p. 134 *et seq.;* Dampier, *Voyages* (Masefield ed., 1906), vol. 1, *passim.* Masefield's introduction and notes are a delightful companion-piece to Dampier's travels. The Cowley journal is reproduced in part by Burney from the MS.

[34] Cited by Burney, *op. cit.,* vol. 4, p. 137.

journal, dropped the 40' of latitude and the conjecture that
the island was one of the Sebaldes, and then proceeded to
name the island Pepys Island in honor of the then secretary of the admiralty.[35] This bit of editing was the cause of
much later perplexity. For more than a hundred years to
come, navigators sought this fabled island, and it was not
until very late that it was dropped from the charts.[36]

Dampier makes no mention of Pepys Island in his journal. He states:[37] "January 8th we made the Sibbel de
Wards which are three islands lying the latitude 51 d, 25 m
South and longitude West from the Lizard in England by
my account 57 d, 28 m. The variation here we found to be
13d, 10 m." Dampier goes on to say that he thought they
might get water here before proceeding to Juan Fernandez,
and thus hinder the design of going through the strait instead of around the Horn. However, finding neither anchorage nor water, they proceeded on their way to the strait.[38]

The visit of Dampier and his associates to the Sebald
Islands was purely fortuitous and apparently attracted no
great notice, but the news of a large harbor on Pepys Island reported by Cowley was too important a bit of intelligence to be completely overlooked. This alleged discovery
was not published widely, as Cowley's account of the voyage
remained in manuscript. Nevertheless, as has been intimated, mariners seem generally to have known of it, and the
vision of a harbor holding five hundred sail was later to
animate the British admiralty to set on foot a project for
a naval establishment in these regions. At this time, however, under the treaties of 1667 and 1670 such an undertak-

[35] *Ibid.*

[36] *Cf.* chart in text.

[37] Dampier, *op. cit.,* vol. 1, p. 108.

[38] Dampier describes the islands as follows: "They are three rocky barren Islands without any tree, only some Dildo Bushes growing on them.
And I do believe there is no water on any one of them for there is no appearance of any water."

ing was not to be considered. The depredations of the buccaneers, the activities of the log-cutters and the smuggling of traders were all individual efforts which the English government could disavow, and which involved no formal breach of existing obligations. On the other hand, an official enterprise such as the occupation of Pepys Island involved consequences that the government was not at the time prepared to shoulder.

Not long after the visit of *The Batchelors' Delight* to the Sebaldes, a more comprehensive survey of the Falklands was made, and the group received the name which they were destined henceforward to bear. This was done in 1690 by Captain John Strong.[39]

The immediate occasion of Strong's visit to the South Atlantic was the situation in Europe, which found both England and Spain fighting as allies against France. It does not appear either from the treaty of alliance[40] or from contemporary negotiations that the commercial restrictions of either country had been in any wise relaxed to favor indiscriminate commercial intercourse.[41] On the contrary, the restrictions probably were rigidly enforced. Nevertheless, fighting in a common cause undoubtedly resulted in the waiving of conventional rules as far as shelter and aid to privateers and public armed vessels were concerned. Thus, although England might decline to relax her navigation laws to permit Spain to import negroes from the West Indies,[42] she would not hesitate to harbor Spanish war vessels, or come to the aid of Spain's treasure fleet when the French had severely harried it.

Taking advantage of this situation, several English merchants joined for the equipping of a ship to trade with Spanish settlements and to fish up treasure from certain

[39] Burney, *op. cit.*, vol. 4, p. 330.
[40] Dumont, *Corps Universel Diplomatique,* vol. 7, pt. 2, p. 267.
[41] Guttridge, *The Colonial Policy of William III* (1922), p. 150 *et seq.*
[42] *Colonial Calendar* (1687-1692), 369.

wrecks on the Pacific coast. The admiralty appears to have issued a privateers' commission for a cruise against the French, and it was under color of this document that the *Welfare,* Strong commanding, sailed from the Downs on October 12, 1689.

When off the Patagonian coast the westerly winds were so persistent that Strong was unable to put in at Puerto Deseado as he had intended, and January 27, 1690, found him off the Falklands.[43] Apparently the *Welfare* approached the islands from the north, because the journal speaks of seeing a large land along which they steered east by north and at six the next morning they stood into a sound which Strong gave the name of Falkland Sound, from which the name of the whole group was later derived.

Strong does not appear to have made a very thoroughgoing investigation of the sound. He reported good harbors and a heavy growth of kelp. Except for the favorable notice regarding water and game there was nothing in his account particularly calculated to encourage interest in the region visited. Strong himself identified the islands with Hawkins' alleged discovery, for he refers to them in his journal as *Hawkins Land.*[44]

[43] Burney, *op. cit.,* p. 330. "Monday the 27th we saw the land. When within three or four leagues we had 36 fathoms. It is a large land and with East and West nearest. There are several Keys [small islands] that lye along the shore. We sent our boat to one, and she brought on board abundance of penguins and other fowls and seals. We steered along the shore E. to N. and at eight at night we saw the land run Eastward as far as we could discern. Latitude 51° 3′ S. Tuesday the 28th: This morning at four o'clock we saw a rock that lyeth from the main Island four or five leagues. It makes like a sail. At six we stood into a *Sound* that lies about 20 leagues from the Westernmost land we had seen. The sound lyeth South and North nearest. There is 24 fathoms depth at the entrance which is four leagues wide. We came to an anchor six or seven leagues within in 14 fathoms water. Here are many good harbors. We found fresh water in plenty and killed abundance of geese and ducks as for wood there is none."

[44] The name was probably given in honor of Anthony, Viscount Falkland (1659-1694), who was at the time a Commissioner of Admiralty and

The visit of Strong was the first landing of Englishmen on the Falklands. It was of no conceivable legal consequence, for it involved neither a mere formal taking possession of the islands, nor an occupation. Inasmuch as the voyage was undertaken with the intention of violating the treaty between England and Spain and the Spanish rules of trade, and was so treated by the Spaniards,[45] it can scarcely be said that as against Spain any acts of Captain Strong had the effect either of establishing or perfecting any claim of the English to the Islands.

How rigidly the Spanish interpreted the existing conventional and legal restrictions has been seen in regard to the logwood cutting activities in Yucatan. It was further exemplified after the Treaty of Ryswick (1697) in regard to the settlements of the Scotch on the Isthmus of Panama. In this case the Spanish protested the settlement, although it had been made far from territory already occupied, and the English government, admitting the justice of the Spanish contentions, declined to support or assist the Scotch colonists.[46] It is true, of course, that a clearer violation of Spanish right existed in this instance where a settlement was attempted on mainland previously taken possession of than would be the case in occupying an outlying island far beyond the territorial waters. At the same time, the Treaty of

later First Lord. *Cf.* Gibbs and Doubleday, *The Complete Peerage* (1921), pp. 241-242; Hervey, *Naval History of Great Britain* (1779), vol. 4, p. 427. Writers have hitherto incorrectly stated that the name given was after Falkland Castle in the county of Fife, Scotland. The name of the sound was later applied to the group, for what reason no one knows. In the eighteenth century, the West Falkland Island was generally referred to as Falkland's Island to distinguish it from the East Falkland which was known by the Spanish or French name. For the French nomenclature *cf.* note 78.

[45] This is shown by what took place off the coast of Chile when Strong reached these regions. The Spanish treated Strong as if he were an enemy.

[46] *Cf.* Guttridge, *op. cit.,* p. 170; Burney, *op. cit.,* p. 359; *Colonial Calendar* (1699), 456, 434 (ii), *passim.*

Madrid unquestionably sanctioned a sort of *mare clausum* as far as the Spanish coasts are concerned. Any approach to these coasts raised a presumption of illegal intent and for this reason the Spanish stubbornly persisted in arresting all ships found in regions peopled exclusively by Spaniards. In this way, therefore, a *de facto* control of the seas was maintained, of which, in view of their own support to the buccaneers, the English could not well complain.

There can be no doubt but that this policy was practically carried out with considerable success by Spain up to the War of the Spanish Succession. At the same time, the closing years of the seventeenth century found the Spanish monarchy in a most parlous state, a condition which was reflected in the colonial administration, and particularly in the colonial trade. The melancholy condition into which the Spanish government had sunk is to be seen in the treaties of partition of the Spanish during wars entered into by Louis XIV with his royal *confrères*. But this was merely a flourish compared with the damage inflicted less patently by the putting into operation of other designs of the European states upon Spanish commerce, by which indirectly the Spanish domain was to be disrupted. Just as the treaties of partition reflected the decay of the Spanish political structure, so the incursions on the Spanish trade reflected the weakness and unsoundness of the Spanish theories of colonial administration. The interest of the home government appears to have been directed chiefly toward obtaining treasure only in its most negotiable form. The colonies themselves were poorly supplied from the homeland, and the uncertainties of traffic created by the almost incessant wars in which Spain was involved further served to whet the appetites of the overseas establishments for contraband trade. Accordingly, the alien traders conferred not only an immediate benefit upon the colonial merchants by furnishing at a lower price articles of necessity, but they likewise opened a market for local products unhampered by tariffs which otherwise were difficult to evade.[47]

The interest of Spain in immediately negotiable values was enhanced by the fact that wars were costly and required treasure for speedy disbursement rather than the slower returns through the sale of goods. The system of tariffs, it is true, was an important source of income, but these tariffs in turn had the effect of discouraging legitimate trade, and other forms of direct taxation were not in use in such a manner as to bring liquid assets into the hands of the state at short notice.[48]

The most valuable of the commercial assets appertaining to the Spanish colonial system was the negro slave trade. This trade was preëminently adaptable to the exigencies of Spanish finance, in that it lent itself to monopolistic organization, and, being susceptible of high returns, it could be farmed out in such a manner as to be exceedingly lucrative to the crown. At the time about which we are writing the Spanish government, being in severe financial straits,[49] succumbed to the representations made to it by the Portuguese and assigned the assiento—as the slave trade was called—to the Company de Cacheu.[50] The offer of purchase made by the latter was the sum of two hundred thousand pesetas, and, in view of the amount, the Spanish government required no bond or sureties, as had hitherto been the case.[51]

---

[47] Scelle, *La Traite Négrière* (1906), vol. 2, p. xiv; *cf.* Alcedo y Herrera, *Las Piraterías en la America Española* (Zaragoza ed., 1883), p. 202; *cf.* also Salcedo, *Tratado Iurídico-Político del Contrabando* (1654), on Spanish countermeasures.

[48] Haring, *op. cit.*, p. 59.

[49] La Fuente, *História de España,* vol. 12, c. 10.

[50] In 1696, Scelle, *op. cit.,* vol. 2, p. 36.

[51] Summarized in *ibid.*, vol. 2, p. 47 *et seq.* Before this concession, which was quasi-public in nature, the assiento had been distinctly subject to Spanish administrative regulation and law. Hence, although the assientists had been usually alien individuals, the control was much more rigid than

The liberal terms of the grant to this Portuguese company marks an epoch not only in Spanish colonial history but in that of Europe, for it opened up not merely the slave trade to the concessionaires but by indirection the general trade with the Indies. Once the ships of a foreign state were permitted access to Spanish colonial ports on authorized business, the whole structure of the colonial system, the whole network of treaties and statutes of exclusion, was doomed to destruction, simply for the reason that human nature and particularly merchants' avarice would lead the beneficiaries of the contract to deal in things other than those stipulated in the bond, and the sailors and traders once having been admitted, the way would be opened to those of other nations. These dangers had, to a certain extent existed in the previous contracts with alien individuals, but they became a real menace in this instance, partly because the assientist was a company, partly because of the terms of the assiento, and partly because of the fact that the Portuguese crown was financially interested in the company, thus lending to the enterprise a quasi-public character.

It is interesting to note that not only were the Portuguese bidders for the assiento, but the Dutch and the English as well. Indeed, the latter offered the sum of 200,000 crowns,[52] but in view of their naval power, and their aggressive commercial policy, the Spanish government ignored their overtures. This action, however, appears not to have dampened English ardor; in fact, the real pivot of the subsequent political transactions between the European governments was the struggle to secure control of the assiento. We are not concerned with earlier phases of this contest, nor, indeed, with the question itself beyond its immediate

was possible with a company, particularly as the Portuguese government had taken a hand in these negotiations.

[52] Scelle, *op. cit.*, vol. 2, p. 39.

bearing upon the development of the public law and particularly the colonization of the Falklands.

The second step in the opening of the Indies to foreign trade was the transfer of the assiento to France. This came about as a result of the succession to the Spanish crown of Philip V, the grandson of Louis XIV, and the defection of Portugal from the alliance with Spain. The Spanish alliance[53] had been one of the early acts of Louis XIV in assuming a paternal direction of the Spanish government,[54] and as it was accompanied by an agreement between the two crowns regarding the assiento, by which the latter question was given an international legal status, there seemed reason to believe that there would be no necessity for delivering Spanish colonial trade into the hands of a more powerful maritime state. This solution of the question, however, was destined to be of brief duration, for the Portuguese king, protesting that France had not fulfilled the promises[55] made to him, joined the alliance against Spain and France[56] and in the same year (1703) entered into the treaty of commerce with England that has gone down in history as the Methuen Treaty.[57]

The French had long been engaged in the contraband trade both with Spain and her colonies. The chief centre of this activity in France had been the port of St.-Malo, where privateers were fitted out to scour the seven seas for Spanish prizes. Moreover, their commerce with Africa was in a flourishing state, and the basis existed for a successful prosecution of the slave trade.[58] Louis XIV appears to have cherished deeply laid schemes for the winning of a part of the Spanish colonies, for during the war between France

[53] Cantillo, *Tratados*, p. 7.

[54] Baudrillart, *Philippe V et la Cour de France*, vol. 1, p. 57 *et seq.*

[55] Scelle, *op. cit.*, vol. 2, p. 104.

[56] Dumont, *op. cit.*, vol. 8, pt. 1, p. 127.

[57] Jenckinson, *Collection of Treaties*, vol. 4, p. 334.

[58] Scelle, *op. cit.*, vol. 2, p. 115.

and Spain in 1691 he considered among other things the conquest of the La Plata region in order to open Buenos Aires to the St.-Malo sailors.[59] This design he later disclaimed, stating that he merely desired to facilitate the commerce of his subjects. If we bear in mind the fact that this region exercised a particular attraction to the St.-Malo men as an *entrepôt* for contraband, we can understand the reasons for the later contests to secure a foothold in this locality.

The negotiation of the assiento agreement with France is an exceedingly interesting commentary upon the intimacy of the relation between Louis XIV and Philip V.[60] The agreement was signed August 27, 1701, and conveyed to the *Companie Royal de Guinée*,[61] the monopoly of the slave trade for a period of twelve years. In return the company agreed to furnish the negroes to both the island and mainland possessions of Spain so far as necessary for the cultivation of the plantations. The Spanish and French kings each had a quarter interest in the enterprise.

It is beyond our purpose to dwell either upon the details of the friction which, despite formal agreements, came to exist between the two allies, or upon the disastrous course of the war. The relations between Spain and France during the contest for the Spanish succession illustrate what the Conde de Aranda had in mind when he remarked that the Spanish and French were like oil and water; they could mix only under conditions of violent turmoil and when this ceased the French, being more oleagenous, would rise to the top. This was the unconscious fear of the Spanish nobles. They appear to have been well aware of the effect upon their political and economic structure of the concession of the assiento to France. Indeed, the operations of the com-

[59] *Ibid.*, vol. 2, p. 112.

[60] *Ibid.*, vol. 2, p. 122 *et seq.*, for negotiations.

[61] Bonnassieux, *Les Grandes Compagnies de Commerce* (1892), p. 385.

pany met with relentless opposition in the colonies,[62] and the efforts of Louis XIV to lighten the deadweight of the Spanish alliance by the acquisition of direct economic and territorial advantages for France was sullenly resented by the Spanish officials. Louis apparently recognized that the Indies were the vital nerve of the Spanish state, and he sought in every way to revivify the fast decaying economic organism. At the same time he realized the necessity of a vigorous defense of the Spanish possessions in the war then being waged, if any ultimate advantage was to be gained from the alliance. To this end he urged upon Philip V a recognition of the legality of French establishments on the Mississippi,[63] and the temporary cession of Pensacola for purposes of defense. To this the Spanish replied by questioning the French rights in Cayenne and by brandishing once again the bull of Alexander VI. It is interesting and important that to these pretensions Louis XIV replied by a reference to the rule of international law that sovereignty was acquired by effective occupation and that his colonies in Cayenne, New France and the Mississippi were occupied by all the recognized modes.[64]

In relation to our own inquiry the alliance affected the course of things in the Americas in more than one important respect. Orders were sent to the Spanish governors in America to open all ports to French war vessels and supply ships,[65] and although Louis prohibited his officers from engaging in any and all commerce,[66] the Spanish rightly regarded this as a mere pretext to cover evasions of their laws. Indeed, considering the fact that maritime warfare was largely carried on at this time by privateers, who were in the business of making war primarily for their own profit

[62] Scelle, *op. cit.*, vol. 2, p. 145.
[63] *Ibid.*, p. 153.
[64] *Ibid.*, p. 154.
[65] *Ibid.*, p. 152.
[66] *Ibid.*

and not for the pleasure of fighting, the Spanish attitude was not unreasonable. The order to open the colonial ports was far in advance of anything theretofore done to aid an ally in time of war; it had not been done for England in the antecedent war, and it shook to the very foundations the system of a colonial *mare clausum,* which, as we have seen, was then an accepted doctrine of public law sanctioned by practice and treaty alike.

During the long wars between France and Spain that had preceded the Bourbon alliance, the monopoly of the South Atlantic had been seriously threatened by the French traders. In 1664 the *Companie des Indes Orientales*[67] had been chartered with the privilege of operating in the Pacific and along the region of the Strait of Magellan. Subsequently, in 1698, owing to the non-user of the latter part of this privilege, a new company, the *Companie de la Mer du Sud,*[68] was chartered for the purpose of trading from Cape San Antonio to the Straits of Magellan and Le Maire and the places washed by the Pacific. Previously, and later pursuant to this royal privilege, the St.-Malo sailors and traders had frequented these regions in great numbers. In fact, there was substantially an official recognition by France of their contraband trade. It was not until the conclusion of the assiento agreement in 1701 that Spanish protests were finally heeded and the *Compagnie de la Mer du Sud* was wound up.[69] It is interesting to note that the first voyage undertaken by the *Compagnie de la Mer du Sud* was under the command of de Beauchesne Gouin, who explored the

[67] Bonnassieux, *op. cit.,* p. 264.

[68] *Ibid.,* p. 385

[69] *Ibid.,* p. 386. *Cf.* also Pommepy, *Les Compagnies Privilégiées de Commerce de 1715 à 1717* (1922), p. 7. Both writers speak of the *Compagnie de l'Assiento* as an amalgamation of the *Compagnie de Guinée* and the *Compagnie de la Mer du Sud.* Scelle, *op. cit.,* p. 167, whose study is well fortified with documents, denies this. The writer has accepted Scelle's view.

Patagonian region and added somewhat to current knowledge regarding the Falklands group.[70]

The French government's efforts to curb the activities of the Malouin sailors were not successful and the commerce with Peru and Chile continued via the Strait of Magellan. Indirectly by the revenues which it produced it enabled the Bourbons to carry on the war for a longer period than would otherwise have been possible. Indeed, it was not until 1716 that a more or less effectual brake was put on these activities by an edict of the regent prohibiting this commerce under pain of death.[71] The Spanish crown itself, on the other hand, contributed to the breakdown of the system of closed seas by farming out certain privileges to French privateers in exchange for gold.[72]

The voyage of Beauchesne Gouin has already been mentioned.[73] He sailed from St.-Malo in December, 1698, and passed through the Strait of Magellan, going as far west as the Galapagos Islands. On the return journey, in 1701, Beauchesne took the route around the Horn. January 19, an "unknown" island was found in latitude 52° 50′ south, and distant some sixty leagues east of Tierra del Fuego. This island was called *Ile Beauchesne*. It was described as being five or six leagues in circumference, and a day's sailing from the Sebald Islands. It is interesting that Beauchesne's alleged discovery was marked by de Lisle as a single island.[74] In later charts, however, it appears as two islands, probably due to the fact that Frézier's map so depicted them.[75]

[70] Dahlgren, *Les Relations Commerciales et Maritimes entre la France et les Côtes de l'Océan Pacifique* (1909), p. 123 *et seq.;* Burney, *op. cit.,* vol. 4, p. 375 *et seq.*

[71] Scelle, *op. cit.,* vol. 2, p. 71.

[72] *Ibid.,* p. 171.

[73] Dahlgren, *op. cit.,* p. 131; Burney, *op. cit.,* vol. 4, p. 302.

[74] The De Lisle map is in Visscher, *Atlas* (1708), plate 103. On De Lisle *cf. Die Reformation der Kartographie um 1700* (1905).

[75] Frézier, *Relation du Voyage de la Mer du Sud* (1716), p. 259.

Other navigators soon followed in Beauchesne's foot-steps in rather rapid succession.[76] Notices of these visits are preserved by Frézier. In 1706 the vessels *Le Maurepas,* and *Le Louis* of the *Compagnie des Indes* visited and named the southern shores of the Falkland group. Frézier states that they found water in a pool near Port St. Louis, a cir-cumstance that may explain why ships thereafter found the islands a convenient port of call; hitherto the reports had uniformly declared that no fresh water was obtainable. The southern coasts were again visited in 1711 by the vessel *Jean-Baptiste* commanded by Jean Doublet de Honfleur. According to Frézier, Doublet followed the coast to a greater extent than his predecessors had done, and he visited the so-called Iles d'Anican, which are depicted in Frézier's map as a cluster of small islands lying southeast of the East Falklands, and which had been named by Fou-quet, another sailor of St. Malo.

The northern coasts of the Falkland group were explored in July, 1708, by Porée of St.-Malo, who named this shore *Côte de l'Assomption.*[77] The uncertainty of the reckonings at sea during this period are shown by the fact that Porée believed himself to be east of the so-called *Iles Nouvelles* of his fellow townsmen. Frézier himself did not touch at the islands on his journey to South America in 1711-1713.[78] His map and the data in his works were collected with much care from the accounts of various voyagers and constituted the most reliable source of information regarding this re-gion for many years to come.

During the War of Spanish Succession there took place another voyage, this time by an Englishman, of which we have an account where the Falklands are mentioned. This was the voyage of Captain Woodes Rogers, who sailed from

[76] *Ibid.,* p. 264. *Cf.* Dahlgren, *op. cit.,* p. 379 *et seq.*

[77] Dahlgren, *op. cit.,* p. 550.

[78] *Ibid.,* p. 530. *Cf.* also Dahlgren's note on the name *Iles Malouines,* p. 382. *Cf.* the note on the *Iles d'Anycan,* p. 311 and chart, p. 312.

Bristol in September, 1708.[79] The expedition sighted the Falkland group on December 23, 1708, but owing to the wind they were unable to land. It is interesting to note that William Dampier accompanied the expedition as a pilot.

The termination of the great war in Europe brought the explorations of the French in the South Seas to an end. Frézier relates how the news of the Peace of Utrecht reached Peru while he was in the harbor of La Concepción and how the president of Chile forthwith issued a proclamation ordering the French vessels in port to depart.[80] This was characteristic of the Spanish policy, both during the war and after. There was, indeed, no reason for vast enthusiasm for the projects of their allies who had brought them little if any benefit, and the Spanish accordingly greeted the end of the war with every indication of relief. The French crown itself appears to have been anxious to assist in wiping out as far as possible any causes of friction that might have arisen during the years of the political association with Spain, and yet some years were to pass before any effectual remedy was resorted to in respect of the contraband trade carried on by the French.

There can be no doubt but that the foothold in South America which the French had gained under cover of the treaty of alliance, the assiento and the general measures of defense, was not to be shaken merely by signing the treaties at Utrecht, although the English government demonstrated throughout the peace negotiations that its purpose was to secure a monopoly of the trade of the Indies, to the total exclusion of former enemies and of present allies as well. Indeed, the commercial aspects of the negotiations so far exceeded in importance the political aspects that one might be led to regard the War of Spanish Succession as having been fought solely over the question of American trade rather than the succession to the crown of Charles II.

[79] Burney, *op. cit.*, p. 459.
[80] Frézier, *op. cit.*, p. 256.

There is no clear evidence of when the English crown
fully matured its plans for the absorption of Spanish commerce in the Americas.[81] The advantages that had accrued
to the kingdom from the possession of Jamaica and the Ber-
mudas were not merely direct; these islands, as we have
seen, formed the *point d'appui* of the huge trade in contraband which had so effectually sapped the Spanish colonial
system of its vitality, and in this way the English had made
an indirect advance upon the Indies that was of greater
importance than the mere acquisition of undeveloped territory. It was doubtless from the lesson learned from the possession of these bases thrust in the very centre of the Spanish domain that the English policies which culminated in
the Peace of Utrecht were fashioned.[82]

At no stage during the war was the hand of the British
more clearly disclosed than in the negotiations with the
Archduke Charles in 1706. This prince, it will be remembered, had attained sufficient military success in Spain to
warrant his allies in dealing with him as if he were *de jure*
monarch of Spain and his succession an accomplished fact.
During the discussion of the plan for the partition of the
Spanish empire prior to the outbreak of the war, William
III had informed the French ambassador that both England
and Holland would require from the power to whom the
Indies might be allotted a favorable treaty of commerce
which would contain proper guaranties for their trade, and
that in the event the partition failed of execution, the English would require certain places as surety for their com-

[81] Already forecast by Lord Sandwich in a paper enclosed by Godolphin to Arlington, Dec. 24 (o.s.), 1667, in *Hispania Illustrata*, p. 93.

[82] Documents in *A Report from the Committee of Secrecy* (1715) (here-
after cited *Walpole Docs.*); Freschot, *Treaty of Utrecht* (1715), 2 vols.;
A General Collection of Treatys (1732), vol. 3; Bolingbroke, *Letters and
Correspondence* (1798), *passim; Harley Papers*, vol. III, in *Portland
MSS.*, Hist. MSS. Comm. (1899). For a general discussion, Weber, *Der
Friede von Utrecht* (1891); Scelle, *op. cit.*, vol. 2, lib. 6; Baudrillart, *op.
cit.*, pt. IV; Maintreu, *Le Traité d'Utrecht* (1909).

merce.[83] This declaration of William III was the keynote of the future diplomacy of England; indeed, not only during this period but for many years to come. That it was in direct opposition to the plans of Louis XIV and the Spanish crown is obvious. Louis himself had been unable to wrest from his grandson any such concessions as the British were dreaming of, and we can well understand, therefore, that the Spanish would offer a long and stubborn opposition.

The British view of their interests in the approaching conflict were embraced in the Treaty of the Grand Alliance signed on September 7, 1701, by the States General, the emperor and the British king.[84] Article VI of this treaty provided that it should be lawful for Great Britain and the States General "by common advice and for the benefit and enlargement of the navigation and commerce of their subjects" to seize the lands and cities of the Spanish in the Indies and "whatsoever they shall take, shall be their own." The eighth article of this convention after establishing the principle of no separate peace went on to say that no peace should be made unless measures were taken that the French should "never get into the possession of the Spanish Indies, neither shall they be permitted to sail thither on account of traffick, directly or indirectly on any pretense whatsoever"—obviously a reference to the assiento. Furthermore, no peace was to be made unless full liberty should be granted to British and Dutch to exercise and enjoy all the same rights and privileges of commerce in the Spanish dominions that they had enjoyed at the time of the death of Charles II of Spain. The British plan of campaign, therefore, contemplated attainment of three distinct objects: first, the acquisition of territory in the Indies; second, the restoration of the *status quo* of the Treaties of Madrid of

[83] Legrelle, *La Diplomatie Française et la Succession d'Espagne* (1888-1894), vol. 2, c. 5, on these negotiations between France and England.

[84] Freschot, *op. cit.,* vol. 1, p. 1 *et seq.*

1667 and 1670; and third, the exclusion of France from any particular benefits in the Indies.

After the abandonment of Barcelona to the allies in 1706, Lord Stanhope was sent by the British government to negotiate with the Archduke Charles a treaty which would realize in concrete form the programme announced in the treaty of the Grand Alliance.[85] Stanhope's instructions dated January 5, 1706,[86] provided for the renewal of the treaty of 1667 and for the establishment of facilities for the English imports into Spain and a uniform customs duty. With regard to the Indies, Stanhope was instructed to secure the renewal of the Treaty of 1670, but far from reestablishing the legal order of a closed sea which the treaties of 1667 and 1670 had set up, Great Britain demanded the right of sending English products on Spanish vessels with the payment of no higher duties than were paid by Spaniards. The treaty was to contain a most favored nation clause.

Unfortunately for the British schemes, the initial success of the allies was not of sufficient duration to permit the immediate realization of the plan outlined in the first instructions to Stanhope. The latter, however, fully aware of Charles' reliance upon continued support, asked and received new instructions which were designed to increase the advantages to England from the conquests in Spain.[87] The two most striking provisions of these new powers, which were dated November 21, 1706, were, first, the direction to authorize by treaty the formation of an Anglo-Spanish company to control the American trade; and, second, the concession by treaty of the assiento, which was hereafter to be a purely English monopoly.[88]

[85] The Methuen treaty had just been concluded with Portugal, a fact that made the effort under discussion of particular economic importance.

[86] Summarized in Scelle, *op. cit.,* vol. 2, p. 461 *et seq.*

[87] *Ibid.,* p. 465.

[88] For text of proposed contract, *ibid.,* vol. 2, appendix no. 7.

The Stanhope Treaty was signed on July 10, 1707,[89] and provided for the reëstablishment of commercial relations between England and Spain. In a separate and secret article, provision was made for the participation of the English in the commerce of the Indies in the manner outlined in the instructions to Stanhope of November 21, 1706, *i.e.*, by means of a joint corporation which would completely assure English enjoyment of this trade to the total exclusion of France. The secret form was adopted as a means of avoiding any complaint by the Dutch that the rights guaranteed them by the Grand Alliance had been violated.

It is scarcely necessary to state that the system which this treaty was intended to establish was never put into effect. The incident has been recited largely because of the light it throws upon the subsequent negotiations of England, France and Spain. It further illustrates the fact that the colonial system of the time was so definitely an international legal order, that only through the agency of solemn treaty could it be altered even in favor of an ally. This is a fact which we are prone to forget in these modern times of more or less unimportant legal barriers upon the economic relations of states. It was a system, comparable in our own experience with the restrictions upon trading with enemy universally adopted in the Great War, resting as it did upon internal legislation and yet receiving, of necessity, an international recognition.

It is beyond our purpose to trace in detail the various attempts at pacification that took place after the conclusion of the treaty of 1707, and prior to the fall from power in England of the Whigs and the formation of the Tory government that finally led to the ending of hostilities.[90] Throughout these diplomatic advances and retreats, the control of Spanish America was a predominant goal. It was held out in 1708 by Louis XIV to the Dutch as a bait to se-

---

[89] Cantillo, *op. cit.*, p. 48.
[90] Roscoe, *Robert Harley* (1902), p. 92 *et seq.*

duce the latter from the alliance. It appeared again in the discussions at Gertruydenberg, but in the end the English were able to cling to the position that they had staked out for themselves in 1707, for the latter conference resulted merely in a reaffirmation of the principle of solidarity of interest between Great Britain and the States General, the indivisibility of Spain and her overseas empire, and the exclusion of France from the benefits of Spanish colonial trade.[91]

The peace project of 1710 that was discussed at Gertruydenberg treated the question of colonial trade in a purely negative fashion; France was to have nothing, and she could not buy any concessions from the Allies which contemplated her participation in the *quid pro quo*. As far as the Allies were concerned, however, there was no definition as to what share each was to get from a possible surrender of privileges in the Indies. Louis XIV, if he was to secure peace, was faced with the absolute surrender of his schemes for French commercial aggrandizement in the South Seas. He was well aware of the fact that he could purchase peace from either ally for this price. With characteristic sagacity he turned to England and prepared to save what he could for France at the expense of Spain.[92]

In April, 1711, instructions were drawn up for the Abbé Gautier, an agent of Marquis Torcy, the French foreign minister, to be presented to the government of Queen Anne.[93] The first point in these instructions dealt with the question of commercial preferment. England was to be given "real security" for the exercise of her commerce in Spain and in the Indies. When this was laid before the English ministers, they demanded a further amplification, and stated their view that "real securities" should include Port

---

[91] Lavisse, *Histoire de France*, vol. 8, pt. 1, p. 116.

[92] Louis was very loath to negotiate with the Dutch.

[93] Summarized in Scelle, *op. cit.*, vol. 2, p. 487. *Cf. Walpole Docs.*, Appendix, p. 1. Gautier had been Lady Jersey's chaplain.

Mahon, Gibraltar and several ports in America.[94] At the same time the French proposals were sufficiently vague to warrant their transmission to the States General, from which presently a favorable reply was elicited.

In the meantime the English ministry sent to France Matthew Prior, more widely known as a poet than as a diplomat. Prior was given a *mémoire* which contained the British demands in precise form; and he was particularly charged to secure from Louis a preliminary assurance that the French were authorized to treat for Philip V. This Louis had already attended to. In May, 1711, he had written to Vendôme at Madrid[95] advising him that the English would demand Gibraltar and Port Mahon and probably a place in America. Simultaneously, his minister, Torcy, stated as his master's opinion that the most that Philip could save would be Spain and the Indies, and the deduction obviously to be drawn was that Philip would have to give way on the point of ports in America. Philip, however, was by no means tractable. He stated that he was willing to cede Port Mahon and Gibraltar, but to cede a port in America seemed to him "a very terrible thing" and he put off making a categorical answer.[96] His grandfather, however, was obdurate and insisted upon Philip's giving in on this point. At the same time Louis wrote to Vendôme that he trusted that this concession would not have to be made, as it would operate as well to the injury of French as of Spanish commerce.

Prior's proposals were dated July 1, 1711.[97] The first part

[94] Weber, *op. cit.*, p. 34.

[95] On Prior *cf.* Bickley, *Life of Matthew Prior* (1914), esp. p. 163 *et seq.*; Legg, *Matthew Prior* (1921), p. 144 *et seq.*; *Prior Papers, Bath MSS.*, vol. 3, Hist. MSS. Comm. (1908).

[96] Scelle, *op. cit.*, vol. 2, p. 490, note 1.

[97] *Walpole Docs.*, appendix 2. Prior's *Journal of Negotiations* is in *Portland Papers*, vol. 5, p. 34-42, Hist. MSS. Comm. Torcy's memorandum is in *English Historical Review* (1914), vol. 29, pp. 525-532.

dealt with the demands for the Allies; the second part with Great Britain's particular requirements. First of all, the British asked "that our trade and commerce should be settled and agreed on such a foot as will be to the satisfaction of the subjects of Great Britain." Gibraltar and Port Mahon were to remain in British hands; the assiento was to pass to them and in matters of commerce the rights accorded France by Spain should equally be granted to Great Britain. In America the *uti possidetis* was to govern. The other demands do not concern us.

It is interesting to note that in the print of this instruction by the Walpole Committee of the House of Commons of 1715 nothing is said of places in America. The clause regarding the assiento reads, "That the *Assiento* should be entirely in the hands of Great Britain and that France nor no other should pretend to meddle in it, but Britain enjoy it after the peace as the French do now." The memorandum handed to Torcy by Prior reads:[98] "The assiento contract shall be made with the English in the same manner as the French now possess it; and such places in Spanish America shall be given to those interested in this trade for the refreshment and sale of their negroes as may be found necessary and convenient." Then a further clause, "And for the better protection of the commerce in Spanish America the English are to be put in possession of such places as may be named in the treaty of peace."

There can be no doubt that the concessions made in the subsequent negotiations led to a severe editing of the original Prior proposals before they were laid before Parliament. The paper published in 1715, and what Prior first submitted to France, differ strikingly in the important point of the *uti possidetis*. This was precisely what Louis XIV hoped to secure and the point on which all the commercial questions pivoted.

[98] Text in Scelle, *op. cit.*, vol. 2, p. 492, note 1.

Prior subsequently elaborated his demands.[99] England, he said, would require more than one place as "real securities"; she needed two places in the North Atlantic and two in the South Sea. This, he explained, did not mean large cities, but merely places of retreat for merchants where goods could be deposited and safeguarded from pirates; and there was, he added, no objection to France having a similar privilege. As for the assiento, this was a demand made necessary by the ruinous costs of the war. To this Torcy replied that the article requiring places in America would retard the conclusion of peace and that they would be the subject of great dispute. In vain he sought to elicit some clue as to what advantages England would offer France in exchange for these concessions. Prior replied it was enough that England tolerated a Bourbon prince on the Spanish throne.[100]

Largely because the demands with respect to the commercial concessions with all their implications were considered unacceptable, Louis XIV determined to send to England one of the best informed and most adroit of his many negotiators. This man was Nicolas Mesnager, a member of the *Conseil de Commerce* and a director of the *Compagnie de l'Assiento*. An answer to the British demands was prepared and passed upon by the Council on July 30, 1711, and Mesnager departed for London.[101]

The seventh paragraph of this reply dealt with the commercial question. Louis cited as an example of his good faith his promise to secure Gibraltar, and then went on to say that he could not believe that a nation as enlightened as the English would insist upon conditions that would completely destroy the commerce not merely of France and Spain, but of all Europe; and hence he believed that this

[99] *Prior's Journal,* p. 35 *et seq.*
[100] Weber, *op. cit.,* p. 38.
[101] Text in Weber, *op. cit.,* p. 41.

part of the project required a further discussion, for which purpose he was sending over an especial negotiator.

Mesnager's instruction[102] contained a more precise delineation of the French position than did the formal reply. He was advised in regard to the claims made by England for advantages in the Indies, that as this was the chief reason for the opening of negotiations, as little as possible was to be conceded. Louis declared his willingness to concede the assiento, together with places for the refreshment of the negroes, and furthermore to guarantee the enjoyment by England of the same rights as the French enjoyed. The true difficulty arose with regard to the "real securities"—what today are known as "sanctions."

The original intention of France in offering the real securities had been the formation of an Anglo-French trading company, in which the English would have the most important privileges. The *plein pouvoir* of Philip V to Louis XIV did not authorize any cession of places. Accordingly Mesnager was instructed to offer certain commercial advantages in Spain, or perhaps the execution of promises made by the Archduke Charles.[103] No places were to be conceded if this could be averted; in the event the English demands could not be met in any other way, Porto Rico or Trinidad might be ceded.[104] The power to make the latter concession was given to Louis a month after Mesnager had been instructed,[105] through the agency of the Marquis de Bonnac, who led Philip V to believe that the concessions involved a greater loss to France than to Spain. At the same time the Spanish minister, Bergeyck,[106] convinced Philip that by

---

[102] At this time Pequet, first *commis* of Torcy, pointed out with much force that even to give England the most desert places, such as Juan Fernandez, would be a virtual delivery into her hands of all the commerce of the South Sea.

[103] Scelle, *op. cit.*, vol. 2, p. 498.

[104] Weber, *op. cit.*, p. 46, gives a long summary.

[105] Scelle, *op. cit.*, vol. 2, p. 508.

[106] On Bergeyck *cf.* Bandrillart, *op. cit.*, vol. 1, p. 349, note 1.

working on the fears of the Dutch, the eventual losses to Spain might be greater than at first anticipated.[107]

When Mesnager arrived in London, the South Sea Company[108] had just been launched and one of its promoters was the prime minister, Robert Harley, Earl of Oxford, whose creature Matthew Prior was. Under the circumstances, therefore, the refusal of Spain and France to effect the cession of places was bound to be looked upon with disfavor. The English insistence on this point was demonstrated at the first meeting in which Prior demanded two places at which English merchants could sell goods brought in Spanish vessels. Mesnager's reply was to submit his plan for trade with the Indies.

The important points about which the first negotiations between Mesnager and the English ministers revolved were, on the part of France, the wresting of some reciprocal engagement from England, and, on the part of England, the restriction of the *pourparlers* to matters strictly of interest to England. The negotiations very rapidly reached an *impasse,* and Mesnager, unwilling to commit his country to proposals more definite than had up to this time been known, succeeded in securing a new *mémoire* from the English ministry which the Abbé Gautier took to France on the ninth of September.[109]

The fifth and seventh articles of the memorandum dealt with the commercial question and the cession of places.[110] Article V read: "The assiento contract shall be made with the English after the same manner that the French now possess it; and such places in Spanish America shall be allotted to those interested in the said commerce for the re-

[107] Philip did not give Louis a very far-reaching authority. He excluded all "strong places" from cession.

[108] Roscoe, *Robert Harley,* p. 147.

[109] Weber, *op. cit.,* p. 51-52.

[110] *Walpole Docs.,* appendix, p. 4. The old forms of capitalizing are not followed in the quotation.

freshment and sale of their negroes as shall be thought necessary and convenient.'' The seventh article, however, stated in part:

And for the better protecting the commerce in the Spanish America, the English shall be put in possession of such places as shall be named in the treaty of peace.

France having offered a real security for the commerce of the subjects of Great Britain in the Spanish America, it was never doubted but France thereby meant some places; and we have been confirmed in this opinion, since France hath proposed Gibraltar as a security for the commerce of Spain and of the Mediterranean. The advantages and privileges offered by the Sieur Mesnager are not regarded as real securities because it will always be in the power of Spain to resume them: Therefore, 'tis believed that Spain is obliged either to cause to be yielded to Great Britain, the places demanded in this article, or to procure it new advantages, such as the love of peace may make it accept as an equivalent. Upon which we shall think ourselves obliged to insist that this minister be furnished with a sufficient power. And further to testifie the sincerity wherewith we treat and the desire that Her Majesty of Great Britain hath to advance the General Peace: She hath thought fit to declare that the difficulty arisen upon this article may be removed in granting to her the following articles:

That the Assiento contract be made with Great Britain for the term of thirty years.

That the whole Island of St. Christopher be secured to Great Britain.

That the advantages and exemptions of Duties promised by the Sieur Mesnager and which he pretended amounted to 15 per cent profit upon all merchandises of the growth and manufacture of Great Britain, be effectually granted to that kingdom.

Great Britain may refresh their negroes at Jamaica and make a distribution of those whom they shall send to Vera Cruz, Porto Bello and other factories in that part of the Indies; But as on the side of the River de Plata, they have no possession of any colony they demand that there be assigned to them in that river some extent of land upon which they may not only refresh their negroes but keep them safe until they be sold to the Spaniards. And as no artifice is intended in making this demand they will submit themselves in this respect to the inspection of the officer that shall for this purpose be named by Spain.

The *mémoire* embraced conditions which appear to have been largely of English origin. In an effort to preclude the possibility of any cessions in the Americas, Mesnager had produced one by one his projected temptations. The offer of a fifteen per cent reduction of duties was put forth and accepted, but this was not a real security. He suggested that Cadiz be put in the hands of the Swiss. This was refused. Finally he offered Port Mahon, but this, it was pointed out, did not guarantee American commerce.[111] At this juncture St. John came forward with the suggestion that the assiento contract be extended for a period of thirty years. To this Mesnager consented, but he declared that this was the utmost concession he could make. St. John then replied that this was not enough and he would further formulate his claims in a *mémoire*. The articles just cited contain these promised amplifications. The demand for St. Kitts was a part of the compensation for the surrender of their earlier demand, and as it was a French possession this sort of revision was particularly unpalatable to France.

The most significant feature of the British demands, however, and one which directly threatened the legal order in the western hemisphere, was the provision for an assignment of territory on the La Plata in connection with the assiento. The Rio de La Plata region was important largely because of its position as a general port of call on the journey to and from the west coast. The least sort of foothold at this place, even in the disguise offered by England, involved not only the possibility of an illicit participation in the trade of both coasts of South America, but it also opened up vast possibilities in the sphere of naval control— a rôle which the Falklands were later destined to play.

[111] Scelle, *op. cit.,* vol. 2, p. 514.

The reply of Louis XIV to these proposals was immediate,[112] as the sacrifices called for were largely to be made by Spain and Louis hoped by speedy action to secure favorable terms for his own state. With reference to the fifth article of the English demands, he replied:[113]

The English shall have after the Peace is concluded, the Treaty of Negroes of Guinea to the West Indies, alias the Assiento contract upon the same conditions that that convention was made by the King of Spain with the French; so that the company which shall be established for this effect in England shall have the prerogative of refreshing, vending, and selling their negroes in all the places and ports of America upon the North Sea in that of Buenos Ayres and generally in all places and ports wherein the importation was permitted to the ships of the company formed in France under the name of the Assiento.

Regarding the seventh article Louis' reply was more diffuse. He declared that Philip V, having need of money at the outset of the war, had been inclined to favor the French, and yet he had given the assiento to the French for no more than ten years. Twenty years seemed to Louis enough of a concession and yet he would concede the demand for thirty years. The cession of St. Kitts was likewise agreed to, as well as the modification of the Spanish tariff duties. With reference to the assignment of land on the La Plata, the king's reply was as follows:

The General peace being made; there shall be assigned to the English Company of Assiento, an extent of land in the river de la Plata upon which they may not only refresh their negroes, but keep them safe until they be sold according to the conditions which shall be stipulated by the convention which is to be passed for the Assiento, and to hinder any abuse of this permission, the King of Spain shall name an officer to intend the affair, to whose inspection the inter-

112 *Ibid.*, vol. 2, p. 516.
113 *Walpole Docs.*, appendix, p. 4.

ested in the said company and generally all those they shall employ in their service shall submit themselves.[114]

The chief point of difficulty in the discussion which ensued over the reply of Louis was in regard to the North American cessions.[115] These questions were reserved for the peace conference. With this obstacle out of the way, the preliminaries were signed on October 8. There were three documents, one dealing with the Duke of Savoy, the second with the general bases of peace, and the third with the demands of England, which we have in part examined.

The conclusion of this negotiation left Louis with the task of persuading his grandson to accept the sacrifices which he had laid upon him. It left England with the task of separately embracing the terms of the third memorandum into a treaty with Spain herself. Up to September 30, Louis had kept Philip V more or less in the dark as to the progress of the *pourparlers* with England. On that date his minister, Bonnac, was able to advise the Spanish king of the content of the latest English demands.[116] How much more his heart was with France than with Spain, Philip disclosed by his expressions of gratitude to his grandfather, Louis.[117] His sole cause of disquietude he found in the provision regarding the La Plata assignment, but Louis with his usual skill pointed out that the Spanish intendancy was an adequate safeguard, and Philip V was secure as long as he prevented the fortification of the place. Further than this the question seems not to have been aired, as Bonnac reported that Philip felt this point so keenly that he had deemed it wiser not to discuss the matter further.[118]

The attitude of England's allies when the details of the preliminaries became more or less generally known was one

[114] *Ibid.,* appendix, p. 6.
[115] Weber, *op. cit.,* p. 56 *et seq.*
[116] Scelle, *op. cit.,* vol. 2, p. 518.
[117] *Ibid.,* p. 516.
[118] Text in *ibid.,* p. 521.

of profound chagrin. With the exception of the States General, the interest of the continental powers had been the defeat of Louis' scheme of a Bourbon dynasty in Spain. This purpose of the Grand Alliance was now disclosed to be a matter of complete indifference to the English ministry. The Allies, however, carried their point so far that they refused categorically to receive the Spanish plenipotentiaries at Utrecht[119] until the matter of the succession, again made a burning question by the death of the Duc de Bourgogne, had been definitely determined. Philip was consequently compelled to submit to the humiliation of having Louis treat for him at Utrecht. As far as the interests of both Louis and England were concerned, nothing could have been more satisfactory. The exclusion of Spain from the conference prevented Bergeyck from carrying out his known scheme of juggling a settlement with the States General that would render nugatory the diplomatic victories of the English; and it enabled the latter to consolidate their gains by concluding with Spain a separate treaty embracing the concessions wrung from France.

The Spanish policy following the signature of the preliminaries appears to have been an attempt to effect a restoration of the *status quo ante bellum*.[120] The powers given to Louis for use at the general conference made no mention of any of the concessions to England. At the same time Bergeyck urged upon Torcy the necessity of using the *status quo* of 1701 as the basis of any future concession to the other Allies. The English, however, were equally insistent on their own point of view.[121] They demanded the right of fixing the limits of the La Plata assignment, and, what was even more galling to Spain, the suppression of the Spanish intendant provided for in the preliminaries. To

---

[119] Bandrillart, *op. cit.*, vol. 1, pt. IV, c. 1.

[120] Scelle, *op. cit.*, vol. 2, p. 526.

[121] *Ibid.*, p. 527. On the British policy of getting a colony in South America *cf.* Defoe to Oxford, July, 1911, *Harley Papers*, vol. 3, p. 66.

this Louis rejoined that his powers did not allow any further concessions and he referred the English to Madrid. In these circumstances the British ministry named as ambassador to Madrid, Lord Lexington,[122] and Philip dispatched to London the Marquis de Monteléon, but more than a year was to pass before the treaty between the two powers was actually signed.

It is not necessary to dwell long upon the details of this negotiation. Lexington was instructed to secure the reaffirmation of the former treaties of commerce and the restoration of all prizes and confiscated property as well as to secure confirmation of the preliminary articles. With regard to the Indies the English at Cadiz demanded the right of full exportation, subject to a two per cent tariff on profits, and the entry of certain English-made goods. Spain, on her part, through her plenipotentiaries, Grimaldo and the Marqués de Bedmar, sought to escape the promised exemption of fifteen per cent tariff duties and to restrict the assignment of La Plata territory.[123] As the conferences proceeded these latter restrictions were explained to mean that England was not to establish herself in any definite manner; houses were to be of wood and no earthworks were to be thrown up. To this Lexington agreed, and after some demur the British government likewise gave way on the question of the fifteen per cent tariff exemption. It is interesting to observe that this was the result of Lexington's advice who counselled his government as follows:

. . . if they grant it [the fifteen per cent exemption] to us they must grant it to all the world, then the French and Dutch will carry their commodities to the West Indies custom free which will glut the market so that they will be of no value when they come. Therefore, I think we had better stick to our clandestine trade which by

[122] On Lexington *cf.* Manners-Sutton, *The Lexington Papers* (1857). For correspondence, *Harley Papers,* vol. III, pp. 231, 237, 239 (Hist. MSS. Comm.).

[123] Scelle, *op. cit.,* vol. 2, p. 529.

the Assiento we have to ourselves exclusively to all the world . . . and make it as difficult to others as we can. . . .[124]

The concession suggested by Lexington was made only on condition that the Spanish would give in on matters connected with the assiento. These negotiations were committed to an English expert sent for the purpose to Madrid.[125] The definitive treaty arrangements between England and Spain embraced the treaty of peace, the assiento treaty and the final treaty of commerce. The former treaty was signed July 13, 1713,[126] the second, March 26, 1713,[127] and the latter, December 9, 1713.[128] An examination of these treaties disclosed the fact that the assignment of territory on the La Plata having been embraced in the assiento agreement and having been made, in terms, to further this project, was to have life only for the duration of the treaty —thirty years. It was, therefore, not a cession, nor a real security, such as had been demanded at the outset of the negotiations, but merely a temporary concession auxiliary to the main purpose of the assiento. For this reason it is correct to state that the La Plata concession did not vary or change the legal system of the colonies which had received general international sanction.

Article IX among other things made provision for the assignment :[129]

It being hereby declared, that her Brittanic Majesty and the Assientists in her name may hold in the said river of Plata some parcels of land, which his Catholick Majesty shall appoint or assign, pursuant to what is stipulated in the preliminaries of the peace from the time of the commencing of this Assiento, sufficient to plant, to cultivate and breed cattle therein, for the subsistence of the per-

---

[124] Text in Scelle, *op. cit.*, vol. 2, p. 531, note 1.

[125] Text in *ibid.*, vol. 2, p. 532.

[126] Jenckinson, *op. cit.* (1785 ed.), vol. 2, p. 66.

[127] *Ibid.*, vol. 1, p. 375.

[128] *Ibid.*, vol. 2, p. 88.

[129] *Ibid.*, vol. 1, p. 379. This is the so-called "Assiento Treaty."

sons belonging to the Assiento and their negroes, and they shall be allowed to build houses there of timber, and not of any other materials and they shall not throw up the earth or make any the least or slightest fortification. And his Catholick Majesty shall also appoint an officer to his satisfaction, one of his own subjects, who shall reside upon the aforementioned lands, under whose command are to be all such things as relate to the said lands; and all other matters as concern the Assiento shall be under that of the Governor and Royal Officers of Buenos Ayres. . . .

In general, the assiento treaty with England was patterned after the preceding arrangement with the French. It was marked, however, by this distinguishing feature, that it was purely a public international agreement and was no longer a mere private concession of a public interest. For this reason its provisions had a significance for the public law of the time which antecedent arrangements had not possessed. The theory of such concessions as the right to have factories, to cultivate land about them,[130] to bring vessels with fruits from the Canaries to the ports of distribution[131] and particularly the rights involved in the carriage of negroes across the isthmus, was that these rights were all proper incidents of the trade. Precautions were taken to prevent smuggling and the celebrated annual vessel of permission,[132] in the profits of which the Spanish king shared as he did in the slave trade, was a device to insure against illegal trade. The whole tenor of the agreement was to the effect that the existing system was not to be disturbed; if this, in fact, took place, the disturbance would be extra legal, and without official governmental support. Thus the legal form would be preserved even if the substance was destroyed.

This view of the international effect of the assiento is

[130] Art. 35.
[131] Art. 36.
[132] "Additional Article."

borne out by the treaty of peace. The eighth article of this document stated:[133]

That there be a free use of navigation and commerce between the subjects of each kingdom, as it was heretobefore in time of peace and before the declaration of this late war, in the reign of Charles II of glorious memory, Catholic King of Spain, according to the treaties of friendship, confederation and commerce which were formerly made between both nations according to ancient customs, letters patent, cedulas and other particular acts; and also according the treaty or treaties of commerce which are now and will forthwith be made at Madrid.

Having thus formally restored the *status quo*, the article proceeded to define in greater detail what this status was—sentences of the most decisive importance in later days.

And whereas, among other conditions of the general peace it is by common consent established as a chief and fundamental rule that the exercise of navigation and commerce to the Spanish West Indies should remain in the same state it was in the time of the aforesaid King Charles II. That therefore this rule may hereafter be observed with inviolable faith and in a manner never to be broken and thereby all causes of distrust and suspicion concerning the matter may be prevented and removed, it is especially agreed and concluded, that no licence nor any permission at all shall at any time be given to the French or to any nation whatever in any name, or under any pretence directly or indirectly to sail to traffick in, or introduce negroes, goods, merchandizes or any things whatsoever into the dominions subject to the crown of Spain in America, except what may be agreed in the treaty or treaties of commerce aforesaid and the rights and privileges granted in a certain convention commonly called El Assiento de Negros whereof mention is made in the twelfth article. . . .

To secure the proper performance of this provision and as an added insurance against French aggression the article continued:

[133] *Ibid.*, vol. 2, at p. 69.

. . . neither the Catholic King nor any of his heirs and successors whatsoever, shall sell, yield, pawn, transfer or by any means under any name alienate from them and the Crown of Spain to the French or to any other nations whatever any lands dominions or territories or any part thereof belonging to Spain in America. On the contrary, that the dominions of Spain in America may be preserved whole and entire, the Queen of Great Britain engages that she will endeavour and give assistance to the Spaniards, that the ancient limits of their dominions in the West Indies be restored and settled as they stood in the time of the abovesaid Catholic King Charles II, if it shall appear that they have in any manner or under any pretence been broken into and lessened in any part since the death of the aforesaid Catholic King Charles II.

Before proceeding to discussion of the legal portent of this document, it will be necessary for us to examine the provisions of the treaty of commerce to the terms of which reference is made.

In the negotiation of this treaty,[134] the English again sought to effect a relaxation of the Spanish colonial system in their favor, while Spain endeavored merely to secure a renewal of the treaty of 1667 and Lord Godolphin's American Treaty of 1670. In this the latter were generally successful. The chief concessions sought by Lord Lexington were an extension of the right of free navigation of Spanish waters—the Caribbean, the Gulf of Mexico, etc., on the ground that it was necessary to English access to Jamaica and the Barbadoes. He also attempted to secure logging rights in Campeche on payment of duty, and the right of securing provisions for English colonists off the Spanish coasts. All of these demands Philip V categorically refused to concede. The treaty of commerce, therefore, merely embraced in terms the 1667 treaty, and the substance of the American Treaty of 1670 with such modifications as the

---

[134] Discussed in Scelle, *op. cit.,* vol. 2, p. 572.

assiento had made necessary. The article dealing with this latter treaty reads in part as follows :[135]

Moreover, the treaty of 1670 made between the crowns of Great Britain and Spain for preventing all differences, restraining depredations and establishing peace between the said crowns in America is again ratified and confirmed without any prejudice however to any contract or other privilege or leave granted by his Catholick Majesty to the queen of Great Britain or her subjects in the late treaty of peace or in the contract of Assiento as likewise without prejudice to any liberty or power, which the subjects of Great Britain enjoyed before, either through right, sufferance or indulgence.

The legal result of the two treaties signed at Utrecht and the assiento signed at Madrid, was to reëstablish the system that had obtained before the War of Spanish Succession, subject only to the exception that the slave trade was to be in British hands, and to the further exception of the annual vessel of permission. It may be argued in the light of Lexington's candid advice to his ministers that the régime introduced by the treaties was a purely formal cloak for a projected destruction of the Spanish colonial legal order. This was, in fact, the case, but the perseverance of the existing legal system had many implications that were of international importance. In the first place, the contraband trade was extra legal and could receive no official support in the event of forcible measures on the part of Spain to destroy it. Secondly, the access to the seas about the Spanish possessions in South and Central America except for purpose of carrying slaves had been refused by Spain and its refusal had been embodied in the treaties. Thirdly, as against all other states except England there was no possible relaxation of the legal system of exclusion, and England herself, in the eighth article of the Treaty of Peace of Utrecht, guaranteed this order, which was also—as far as territorial

[135] Text in Cantillo, *op. cit.*, p. 145; English text in Jenckinson, *op. cit.* (1772 ed.), vol. 1, at p. 230.

concessions were concerned—applicable to herself. It is idle
to argue that the exception destroyed the rule. All the resources of British diplomacy had been employed for the
purpose of maintaining the rule for the benefits of violations which the British were put in a position most easily to
effect. In the negotiations with France after the signing of
the preliminaries and up to the final Treaties of Utrecht the
British ministry maintained the position that the treaties
of 1667 and 1670 were to be revived and the *status quo ante
bellum* restored.[136] Finally, we need only allude to the origin
in the colonial system of such rules of law as the Rule of
Warfare of 1756[137] to understand that the system restored
by the Peace of Utrecht was recognized as legally binding
on the powers for practically a century to come.

Not only Spain but England and France as well were anxious to maintain the colonial system in all its pristine vigor
—the Spanish because they desired to preserve their economic integrity, the British and French because they wished
as far as possible to exclude each other from the benefits of
illicit trade. The English attitude is well illustrated by the
sharp protest lodged by them against the issue by Bergeyck
of six passes to St.-Malo ships for a voyage to the Pacific[138]
while the treaty of commerce was being negotiated. This it
was said violated the spirit of the treaty about to be made,
and the queen offered to pay to Philip the 360,000 crowns
which he received for the contract, and to help him in re-
fitting his navy so that commerce in these regions could be
prohibited. It is needless to add that Philip, although he

[136] Thus the report to St. John of the plenipotentiaries, March 6, 1712
(*Walpole Docs.*, app., p. 25; *Weber, op. cit.*, p. 208), *"The offers of
France to England, the demands for England and the King's answers,"*
Art. VII, X, XI, XII, XIII, all of which show the old point of view.

[137] Moore, *A Digest of International Law*, vol. VII, p. 383.

[138] Lexington to Oxford, March 6, 1813; Bolingbroke to Harley, October, 1713, *Harley Papers*, II, pp. 270 and 241. Scelle, *op. cit.*, vol. 2, p.
533.

declined this latter offer, did not fail to withdraw the permission to the St.-Malo men.

On the other hand, the French were conscious of the necessity of avoiding any cause of complaint from England because of the activities of their sailors. Steps were taken to forbid the commerce of the Pacific to the St.-Malo privateers but without avail.[139] It was not until 1716 that a determined stand was taken by the regent in the issuance of an order forbidding such commerce under pain of death. At the same time a joint squadron was fitted out by France and Spain which sought vigorously to sweep from the seas vessels which were preying upon the Spanish commerce, a measure which fell with equal severity upon the smugglers of all nations.[140]

We have related the prompt and unfeeling action of the president of Chile in ordering Frézier and his countrymen from the Pacific ports. This was characteristic of the policy henceforth pursued by the Spanish government. In June, 1714, a circular *cédula* was issued by the king of Spain to the authorities in America ordering them to use the greatest severity in dealing with smugglers.[141] Pursuant to this order many French ships were confiscated, but on the whole the task was too great and the incessant English protests were met only with a confession of impotence to deal with the situation. At the same time, in relation to the English themselves the Spanish court attempted to restrict any encroachments that the treaties had made possible. The English assiento had, as we have seen, opened up to the contractants the La Plata as well as the city of Buenos Aires.

[139] Dahlgren, *Le Comte Jérome Ponchartrain et les Armateurs de Saint Malo* in *Revue Historique* (1905), vol. 88, p. 225, esp. 235.

[140] Alcedo, *Piraterías in la America Española*, p. 407. Mention should be made of the voyage of Roggeveen, a Dutchman, in 1722. He did no more than give the Falklands a new name—*Belgia Australis. Cf. De Reis van Mr. Jacob Roggeveen ter Ondekking van het Zuidland*, 1721-1722 (Mulert ed., 1911), esp. p. 86.

[141] Scelle, *op. cit.*, vol. 2, p. 538.

This had not been the case in the French contract. The Spanish refused to permit the English to install themselves on the river but restricted them to Buenos Aires, and as the treaty gave the Spanish king the right of designating the place on the Rio de la Plata, the latter simply suspended his action.[142] The company, however, seeing no immediate benefit from such a cession did not press the matter, for the factories set up in Buenos Aires proved to be sufficient for their purposes, and the cession accordingly never took place. Moreover, no mention was made of the matter in the supplementary assiento treaty of May 15, 1716,[143] nor after the war of the Quadruple Alliance in the treaty of June 13, 1721,[144] when the Treaties of Utrecht, including the assiento, were renewed. The British king in the first article of this treaty pledged himself to put in execution the points settled by the eighth article of the Treaty of Peace, "which mention leaving to the Spaniards the free commerce and navigation of the West Indies and the maintaining the ancient limits in America, as they were in the time of King Charles II."

The treaties making up the Peace of Utrecht were the new foundation of the public law of Europe, and we have suggested that they were the foundation of everything relating to international politics in the eighteenth century. What they sought to effect was identical with the aim of the Peace of Westphalia—to set up a legal order, not only with regard to matters that we today regard as peculiarly susceptible of legal regulation, but in regard to things that are now looked upon as purely political. The pitiful cries that had gone up from time to time in the seventeenth century against Louis XIV for the various outrages committed by him upon the public order, were based for the most part upon his violation of the public law established by the Peace

[142] *Ibid.,* vol. 2, p. 558.
[143] *A General Collection of Treatys,* vol. 4, p. 449.
[144] Jenckinson, *op. cit.,* vol. 1, p. 366.

of Westphalia. Not only this series of public acts but the Treaties of Utrecht were designed to effect a solidification of the *status quo* that would have the permanence of and receive the respêct accorded to a code of law. The political arrangements that were effected were matters of general interest to all the European powers. We need only recall the senile and desperate efforts of Emperor Charles VI to secure the adhesion of all the powers to the pragmatic sanction, to understand how definitely the western world was committed to this policy of a legal regulation of political matters. It is true that outside the limits that had been fixed in the way of successions, boundaries and commercial systems, the activity of states in forming alliances could have free sway. But this was regarded as a purely political matter—the problem of the balance of power—and left unaffected the question of the *status quo,* legally instituted, unless, perchance, as in the events which gave rise to the War of the Spanish Succession, the *status quo* itself was threatened.

These notions are strangely unfamiliar to us at the present day, although we may observe a last reminder of them in the general conferences of the nineteenth century regulating colonial questions, the concert of Europe and finally the arrangements growing out of the late war. In all of these cases, however, the notion that an order established by law has been involved seems to be absent. States are expected to abide by these arrangements, not because they are members of a sort of polity that has been created by law, but because they have signed treaties for the performance of which their word is pledged. The mighty force of individualistic theories has exploded the ancient view of legally ordered political and economic systems for Europe and what has been left us is the international law of today—a rather loose-jointed structure of rules for particular transactions between states. Bismarck was the last statesman who seems to have been conscious of the old public law of

Europe, and with his retirement the last possibility of a restitution of the old system disappeared.

It has been difficult to outline with any degree of sharpness the main features of the political and economic systems that lay at the basis of the eighteenth century diplomacy. What has been said, however, has been more or less indispensable in arriving at a just appreciation of the merits of the legal position of the various powers in the Falkland question some sixty years after the Peace of Utrecht was concluded. For in that dispute the very fundamentals of the legal order were involved, and in the eyes of the eighteenth century statesmen no rules of international law were more sacred than those which secured the permanence of the political arrangements on the Continent and the economic system of the New World.

CHAPTER IV

THE CHALLENGE TO THE SPANISH MONOPOLY

IT was the frustration of the English dream of a great over-seas commerce carried on under the rose that led to the adoption of a policy of territorial aggrandizement which in-cluded the first seizure of the Falkland Islands. The com-mercial policy inaugurated by the assiento of 1713 had em-braced the ingenious association of legal with extra-legal trade aided by the control of certain places as *points d'ap-pui* for these operations. By elaborate treaty provisions it was sought to guard against any outside interference in the English monopoly, and against the seizure of the property of the "assientists" in war time.[1] These treaty arrange-ments were predicated upon two assumptions: first, the in-ability of Spain to enforce its revenue and colonial laws; and secondly, the immunity of private property on land in time of war—a principle far in advance of what was then actu-ally practiced. No one could foresee that in respect to both these assumptions the English had been mistaken, and that Spain would undergo an economic renaissance which was ultimately to drive the English to adopt the more aggres-sive policy of "real securities" which had been contem-plated in the peace negotiations of 1712, and then aban-doned. The eighth article of the Treaty of Utrecht was presumably designed to prevent the realization of such a policy. We must, consequently, inquire minutely into the interpretation put upon this article in the various disputes of the eighteenth century to determine its actual validity as a legal bulwark of Spain's monopoly.

The same difficulties which had faced the French assien-tists were to annoy the English. There was a constant re-sistance by Spain of the English attempts to press their

[1] Article 40.

bargain beyond the word of the bond, and this led to incessant friction for the duration of the assiento.

The South Sea Company, to which the slave trade was intrusted, was organized shortly before the conclusion of the Peace of Utrecht. The assiento was assigned to it by the crown in 1713, and shortly after the treaty was signed the company began operations.[2] It is beyond our purpose to follow minutely the course of events in the succeeding years. The policies pursued by the Spanish minister, Alberoni, following the Peace of Utrecht were directed chiefly toward improving the position of Spain in European politics. Questions of colonial trade, however, were also involved. The London merchants were full of their grievances at the hands of the Spanish and their complaints that the treaties were not being fulfilled contributed not a little to precipitate war only three short years after peace in Europe had been established. At a moment when the policy of England hung in the balance the South Sea Company submitted to the king a lengthy memorandum on the state of the difficulties of their trade and prayed for relief.[3] As all the great English politicians were interested in this company, George I, in his address from the throne, which was delivered shortly after the receipt of this petition, depicted the necessity of protecting English trade and asked for support from Parliament. As a matter of fact, hostilities had already taken place in the battle of Cape Pasaro,[4] where the English had defeated the Spanish fleet, and in October the Spanish crown had issued letters of marque and reprisal. The declaration of war in November, 1718, was, therefore, no more

---

[2] On the South Sea Company cf. Roscoe, *Robert Harley, passim;* *Harley Papers* (Hist. MSS. Comm.), vol. 3, *passim;* Briscoe, *The Economic Policy of Horace Walpole* (1907); Batt, *Zur Geschichte der Englischen Südsee Gesellschaft* (1904). On the transfer of the contract cf. *Harley Papers,* vol. 3, p. 385.

[3] Michael, *Englische Geschichte im Achtzehnten Jahrhundert* (1896-1920), vol. II, pt. 1, p. 152.

[4] Mahan, *The Influence of Sea Power on History* (1904), p. 267.

than the legalizing of what had for some time existed in fact.

The most important Spanish war measure of interest to this discussion was the sequestration of the property of the South Sea Company.[5] The company's works in America were seized and trade was completely suspended. The significance of this lay largely in the fact that at one stroke the Spanish crown was able to cripple the English establishments, and no amount of future compensation could wholly repair the damage done to a new and as yet not completely established enterprise.[6]

The main objective of the Spanish in the war had been to secure the restitution of Gibraltar and Port Mahon.[7] As late as 1720, when Alberoni's fall had been effected and negotiations for peace were under way, Philip V insisted on making this object the condition *sine qua non* of peace and as a means of securing a treaty in these terms he withheld the license of the annual ship of the South Sea Company until the British should acquiesce in his demands. Philip's determination, however, gave way before the exigencies of the political situation.[8] The English ministry, wise in the manipulation of popular control of foreign relations, had thrown the question before the Parliament with an effect that had been well calculated. The demand of Spain for Gibraltar was flatly rejected,[9] and thus the guaranty of England's peaceful possession of the Mediterranean trade for which the war had been chiefly fought was saved.

War came to a close with the adhesion of Spain to the Quadruple Alliance treaty in 1720, and relations with Eng-

---

[5] Anderson, *Historical and Chronological Deduction of the Origin of Commerce* (1790), vol. 3, p. 305; McPherson, *Annals of Commerce* (1805), vol. 3, p. 62.

[6] Batt, *op. cit.,* p. 60.

[7] Armstrong, *Elizabeth Farnese* (1892), p. 129.

[8] Michael, *op. cit.,* vol. 2, pt. 1, p. 256 *et seq.*

[9] Text in *ibid.,* p. 272.

land were settled by the Treaty of Madrid of June 13, 1721.[10] The treaty of alliance of the same date, signed by England, France and Spain,[11] was in effect a treaty to guarantee the Peace of Utrecht, together with such arrangements respecting the relations of Spain and the emperor as might be effected at a forthcoming congress to be held at Cambrai. In this agreement the Treaties of Utrecht were mentioned only in general terms. In the Anglo-Spanish Treaty, however, specific provision was made for the restoration to full vigor of all the treaties antecedent to the war; in so far as this had not been done before the English agreed to put in effect the eighth article of the Treaty of Utrecht, which was the covenant of quiet possession executed by England in respect to the Spanish control of the Indies. The Spanish, in addition to an agreement that the assiento was to be restored, undertook to restore in kind or equivalent value all property that they had confiscated in Spain and the Indies in violation of the Treaty of Commerce of Utrecht and the thirty-sixth article of the treaty of 1667. Under this article restitution to the amount of £200,000 was made.

It will be observed that the general effect of the pacification of 1721 was to restore the system set up by the Treaties of Utrecht. In other words, the public law established in 1713 was reaffirmed and restored to *status quo*. This was a great victory for England. But it proved eventually that, although the principles of this public law system were thus reaffirmed, the *mala fides* which underlay this submission to the form was not to pass unchallenged. Not only the provisions of the treaties themselves, but the system that they were designed to cloak were to be subjected to repeated attack.

Following the War of the Spanish Succession, a great attempt had been made by Spanish statesmen, and notably

---

[10] *A General Collection of Treatys,* vol. 4, p. 119.
[11] *Ibid.,* p. 123.

Alberoni and Patiño, to reorganize the economic and fiscal system of the country.[12] This effort embraced not merely the navy and merchant marine, but also the fundamental principles of the colonial system as it was then understood. It was sought by adopting the system under which the English and Dutch commerce had risen to preëminence, to revitalize the Spanish colonial trade and to render the crown independent of those factors which, in the end, threatened to spell the ruin of the empire.

The foremost exponent of these changes was Geronimo Ustariz,[13] who was not merely the leading Spanish economic publicist of the time, but who likewise held the office of secretary and later minister of the *Junta* of Commerce which enabled him to carry his views into operation. That portion of Ustariz' theory which directly involved the enforcement of the treaties is of particular interest to us. This was the plan of increasing the coast guards (*guarda costas*) not only as a means of enforcing the revenue and colonial laws, but also as a means of training the personnel of the navy.[14] Provision for these guards had been made in antecedent legislation,[15] but now measures were taken to increase their number and to make their activity more effective.

At this time the contraband trade carried on by the English was of two kinds. The assiento ships and the annual vessel both used their legitimate business as a cloak for forbidden trade. At the same time the colonists in the British American possessions carried on a lively smuggling business under no color of right whatever. The *guarda costas*, however, made no distinction between the two classes of smugglers, and hence relying upon their commissions and

[12] On this *cf.* Mounier, *Les Faits et la Doctrine Economique sous Phillipe V* (1919); Wirminghaus, *Zwei Spanische Merkantilisten* (1886).

[13] Mounier, *op. cit.,* p. 177.

[14] Ustarriz, *Theory and Practice of Commerce and Maritime Affairs* (Kippax trans., 1771), vol. 2, p. 16 *et seq.*

[15] *Recopilación,* lib. XI, tit. 35.

the principle of non-access to Spanish shores, English vessels were halted on the high seas, searched, and taken prize
—usually under circumstances of cruel and inhuman treatment. The assertion has been made[16] that secret *cédulas*
were issued to governors of Spanish colonies to hamper the
trade of the assientists as far as possible, but this seems
unlikely, as the rule in the books had long been that trade
of aliens was to be prevented and the governors had ample
authority for the exercise of their powers in regard to illegal trade.

The conclusion of the peace in 1721, therefore, brought
no respite to the English traders; the restoration of the
assiento merely resulted in the revival of Spanish efforts to
restrict it to its proper legal bounds. At this time, Robert
Walpole dominated British politics. He realized the value
of a programme of conciliation as regarded Spain, if the
full benefit of the treaties both promised and appropriated
were to inure to England.[17] His ideas of national honor
were by no means quixotic, for he was more concerned with
the general success of his economic policies than in the
occasional losses which his execution of the British programme entailed. The enormous coast line of South America
and the few vessels which guarded it were circumstances
that facilitated illegal trade. Over a period of twelve years
the number of confiscations by the Spaniards were said to
have numbered no more than thirty-one ships.[18] These seizures occasioned considerable popular uproar, but they did
not constitute any real threat to British trade. A real danger, however, existed in the shape of the Ostend Company
of the emperor, and the Spanish attitude toward it.

[16] Williams, *The Foreign Policy of Horace Walpole* (in *English Historical Review,* vol. 15), p. 273; *cf.* also Robertson, *Bolingbroke and Walpole* (1919), p. 152, for an account of Walpole's foreign policy. Morley,
Walpole (1899), p. 200 *et seq.*

[17] Williams, *loc. cit.*

[18] *Ibid.*

In the Treaty of Utrecht[19] it had been stipulated that the inhabitants of the former Spanish Netherlands were to continue in the enjoyment of the privileges of the Indies trade. The implications of this provision were by no means important as long as Philip V and the emperor, in whose hands the Netherlands now were, remained at daggers' ends. In 1725, however, largely through the efforts of the Duke de Ripperda, the Spanish ambassador, treaties of peace, alliance and commerce with the emperor were signed and by the treaty of commerce[20] the trade of the Indies was opened to the Ostend Company, an undertaking organized by the emperor for the purpose of rehabilitating the commerce of his country. This provision was a direct challenge of the English monopoly, and it rendered a war inevitable unless measures could be taken to prevent the fulfilment of the treaty.

The hostile intentions of the Spanish court were obvious from the first. Confident of the military success of the new alliance, open boasts were made by Ripperda that war with England would take place forthwith. The Walpole cabinet on the other hand, fully aware of the Spanish purpose, sought to avoid this catastrophe by detaching the emperor from his new ally and by staging naval demonstrations which were intended to have the effect of a blockade without its legal consequences. A fleet was stationed off the Spanish coast and in the Indies off Porto Bello to intercept the treasure fleet. The Spanish retaliated by seizing the

[19] Barrier Treaty, Article 1 and Article 26, Jenckinson, *op. cit.*, vol. 2, p. 148. *Cf. Representations du Roi d'Espagne contre la Compagnie d'Ostende*, April 26, 1714, in Rousset, *Recueil d'Actes, etc.* (1728), vol. 2, p. 76, and the *Dissertatio de jure quod competit Societati privilegiatæ Fœderati Belgii, ibid.*, p. 43. On the Ostend Company *cf.* Hinsman, *La Belge Commerciale* (1902); Dullinger, *Die Handelskompagnien Osterreichs* in *Zeitschrift für Social und Wirtschaftsgeschichte*, vol. 7, p. 44, esp. at p. 74; Hertz, *England and the Ostend Company*, in *English Historical Review*, vol. 22, p. 255.

[20] Treaty of May 1, 1725, Cantillo, *op. cit.*, p. 218.

Prince Frederick,[21] the South Sea Company's ship at Porto Bello. Subsequently the assiento was suspended, and war was begun in 1727 by opening a siege of Gibraltar.

The defection of the emperor from the alliance and the absence of any military successes soon inclined the Spanish court to peace.[22] The preliminaries[23] with England were signed at Paris for the emperor on May 31, 1727, and the Spanish minister at Vienna accepted them for Philip, though without express authority. The mere signing of the preliminaries, however, by no means involved the restoration of peace, for the Spanish soon made it clear that unless concessions were obtained they would not carry out the terms of the agreement. It was to effect compliance with the preliminaries that Benjamin Keene, former consul general at Madrid, and who also represented the South Sea Company, was sent to Spain. Keene[24] was a man of considerable ability and his dispatches are illuminated with much of the same biting humor which later characterized the correspondence of George Canning.

The English cabinet was well aware of the fact that for them the real issue of the conflict was the commercial situation.[25] This was likewise the view of Patiño, and consequently it became difficult for Walpole to put in effect the usual English formula of continental concessions in exchange for colonial privileges. No difficulty had been had with the question of the Ostend Company, but Spain, reluctant to subject the negotiations to such hazards as a continuation of the blockade of the West Indies and her own coast involved, declined to release the *Prince Frederick* unless the blockade were lifted. After much dispute the Span-

[21] Williams, *op. cit.,* vol. 16, p. 78.

[22] Armstrong, *op. cit.,* p. 216; Coxe, *Memoirs of the Bourbon Kings of Spain* (1815), vol. 3, p. 173.

[23] Rousset, *op. cit.,* vol. 3, p. 399.

[24] *Dictionary of National Biography,* vol. 30, p. 301.

[25] Williams, *op. cit.,* vol. 16, p. 320.

ish finally agreed to execute the preliminaries on condition of the recall of the English squadrons, but they were to hold the *Prince Frederick* as security for damages that might be awarded them for contraband trade for which the congress presently to be held might find the English responsible.[26]

The temper of the English ministry was at once made clear by the repudiation of this agreement. The government declined to discuss at any congress the question of damage done to the Spanish colonies, and refused to treat the *Prince Frederick* as a hostage.[27] It was not until March 6, 1728, therefore, that the so-called Convention of the Pardo was signed.[28] The English had given way to the extent that they consented to discuss at the forthcoming congress questions of contraband and disputed trade problems. They further agreed to withdraw their fleets and on their part the Spanish undertook to raise the siege of Gibraltar and to restore the commerce of the English to *status quo*.

The congress mentioned in the treaty was duly called at Soissons,[29] where the questions previously under discussion were somewhat languidly considered. In the meantime, however, negotiations were carried on both at Madrid and Paris which encountered every conceivable difficulty, due to the reluctance of Spain to arrive at an accommodation with England. This was the result, in part, of the Spanish queen's Italian schemes and in part of Patiño's commercial programme. The negotiations finally terminated in the Treaty of Seville signed November 9, 1729, which was a de-

[26] Correspondence between de la Paz and Stanhope in Rousset, *op. cit.*, vol. 4, p. 45 *et seq.*

[27] Armstrong, *op. cit.*, p. 218 *et seq.;* Williams, *op. cit.*, vol. 16, p. 316; Baudrillart, *op. cit.*, vol. 3, p. 400.

[28] *A General Collection of Treatys,* vol. 4, p. 182.

[29] Documents in Rousset, *op. cit.*, vol. 5, p. 45 *et seq.; cf.* Armstrong, *op. cit.*, p. 222; Williams, *op. cit.*, vol. 16, p. 320; Coxe, *op. cit.*, vol. 3, p. 221.

fensive alliance between England, France and Spain.[30] The treaties of 1725 with the emperor were annulled, and Spain promised to restore the English commerce in the Indies to the situation of 1725. At the same time the Spanish king undertook to make reparation for all the damages suffered by the English in Europe and America. The French and English agreed to make reparation for similar cases; and there was, moreover, a reciprocal engagement to prevent future violences.

Of considerable interest for the development of international arbitration was the sixth article of the treaty, which provided for the appointment of "commissaries" by the English and Spanish "to examine and decide what concerns the ships and effects taken at sea on either side," subsequent to June, 1728. These commissaries, who were to finish their work within three years, were to examine and decide according to the treaties the "respective pretensions" relating to the abuses that were supposed to have been committed in commerce "whether with respect to the limits or otherwise." Report was to be made to the two crowns who were to execute the decisions. In addition to articles relating to European settlements, a separate article provided for the restoration of the treaties antecedent to 1725. The assiento was to be restored and reparation to be made for the confiscated property.

The Treaty of Seville marked an important change in the course of European diplomacy, but it effected no substantial improvement in the relations of Spain and England in the Americas. It was largely due to the forbearance of Walpole and his keen appreciation of the true objectives of English policy that another war was averted. The delay in executing the Italian provisions of the treaty had aroused the ire of Queen Elizabeth of Spain, whose heart was set on the possession of these lands.[31] At the same time the elabo-

[30] *A General Collection of Treatys,* vol. 4, p. 201.
[31] Armstrong, *op. cit.,* p. 240.

rate promises to respect English commerce in America were not fulfilled. The English members of the commission to assess damages[32] arrived in Madrid, but the Spanish resolutely neglected to appoint their own representatives. In the meantime the acts of outrage by both English and Spanish ships continued. Vessels were stopped, boarded and usually confiscated, and where resistance was offered it was done under circumstances of unusual cruelty. It was at this time that the unhappy Captain Jenkins lost his ear, which he was obliged to bottle for eight long years before justice was done him.[33]

The report of the commission on colonial depredations

[32] It is impossible to determine whether the report of the commissioners was ever published. The papers were laid before the House of Commons May 13, 1735. *Cf. Journal of the House of Commons for the year 1735*, p. 490, where a list of papers is printed.

In Ralph, *A Critical History of the Administration of Sr Robert Walpole* (1743), there is a discussion of the British and Spanish claims based upon what appears to be an examination of these papers. He points out that the Seville Declaration of February 8, 1732 (n.s.) provided that when privateers were fitted out to prevent contraband trade "pursuant to the Laws and Ordinances of the Indies which have not been derogated from by the Treaties," they should give security, a provision which he regards as an implied acceptance of the laws of the Indies, particularly the laws which staked out a course for British ships that they had to follow to avoid seizure. The Spanish commissioners, pursuant to this, asserted that by Article 8 of the Treaty of 1667 British commerce was under the same restrictions as was Holland by Article 6 of the Treaty of Münster, and consequently, the British ships were compelled to observe the course set by Spanish law. Ralph also quotes from a note of La Quadra to Keene as follows: "The only Navigation that can be claimed by the *English* being that to their Islands and Plantations while they steer a due Course; their ships are liable to seizure and confiscation, if it should be proved that they have altered their Route without necessity in order to draw near to the Spanish coasts." *Cf.* pp. 451, 461-462.

[33] Temperley, *Causes of the War of Jenkins' Ear* (*Royal Historical Society Publications*, series 3, vol. 3), p. 201. On depredations following the treaty of Seville *cf.* Hist. MSS. Comm., *Egmont Papers*, vol. I, pp. 131, 142, vol. 2, pp. 440, 442, 489.

was finally rendered on February 8, 1732.[34] Reparation was granted by Spain, and an attempt was made to stay the progress of further spoliation in the New World by requiring the Spanish governors to exact bonds from the coast guards not to commit acts of piracy. Six months previously (July 22, 1731)[35] a tripartite convention had been signed by England, Spain and the emperor, designed to settle the differences between the two latter courts, and it accordingly appeared that there had been a sufficient satisfaction of Spanish interests in Europe to assure the execution of the recommendations of the commission. Any hopes, however, that the British government may have had on this score were doomed to disappointment. It was at this juncture that the disputes over the action of colonial governors took a new form and one which was of considerable importance for the development of international law.

We have seen how the public law established by the general international agreements and the special treaties between the interested states had given recognition to the colonial systems then in vogue, and how access to the ports of the several European colonies in the Americas was a right which was enjoyed only by virtue of special permission. Not only were the waters which washed the shores of the Spanish colonies closed seas, but the same rule applied with equal vigor to what we may call the French and English colonial waters. At this time, moreover, there were no generally recognized rules as to what constituted territorial waters. It is true that in 1712 Bynkershoek[36] had expounded the rule that the power of a state over territorial waters was coextensive with the ability to control them by arms from the shore (one marine league), a rule which he later (1737)[37] put in terse form—''imperium ends where ends

---

[34] Williams, *op. cit.*, vol. 16, p. 447.

[35] *A General Collection of Treatys*, vol. 4, p. 231.

[36] Bynkershoek, *De Dominio Maris*, c. 2.

[37] Bykershoek, *Quæstiones Juris Publici* (1751), lib. 1, c. 8.

the force of arms." But this rule was far from enjoying universal acceptance, and states were in the habit of committing acts of violence in support of their alleged sovereignty far from their shores.[38] Indeed, it was in exercise of a claim of this sort over the channel that the English had been in constant collision with the Dutch.

The great extent to which smuggling[39] was indulged in at this time necessarily involved the use of naval forces beyond what are now recognized as the marginal seas, and in the exercise of this revenue power, the English were most active. At the same time, the Spanish, adhering to the old notion that the seas to a distance of one hundred miles were territorial waters, attempted to exercise similar rights in waters contiguous to their possessions. In addition to this claim, there entered into account the prohibition in Spanish law governing the entrance of foreign vessels into the colonial ports, the elaborate provisions for visit and search, and the requirements of registration.[40] All of these laws led to the conclusion that a vessel approaching the coast was presumptively violating the colonial regulations, and hence the validity of any British demands of narrow marginal jurisdiction was greatly limited. The Spanish case was certainly clear in waters south of the equator, where there were no foreign colonies. In the West Indies, however, where other powers had colonies, the case was somewhat different. The treaties had sanctioned the theory of the

[38] Fulton, *The Sovereignty of the Sea* (1911), p. 543 *et seq.*

[39] *Cf.* Harper, *The Smugglers* (1909), *passim,* wherein are retold many stirring incidents of contemporary smuggling.

[40] *Recopilación,* lib. 9, tit. 33 and 35. The writer has been unable to ascertain when the *guarda costas* were instituted. In Atuñez, *Memorias Históricas* (1797), app. 15, is reproduced the *Real Approbación de 28 de Abril de 1732 sobre lo que se capítulo con el comercio acerca de la contribución del quatro por ciento de guarda costas,* which indicates that in this year the forces were heavily augmented. *Cf.* also the cédula of July 20, 1738, in Ortega, *Questiones de Derecho Público* (1747), p. 197. The Spanish view of their rights is well set forth in *ibid.,* c. 23 and 24.

closed sea, but they had not attempted to define the lines
of demarcation. It was in these waters, in particular, therefore, where encounters between *guarda costas* and foreign
merchantmen were the most frequent. To the Spanish, the
right of visit and search was a corollary of the principle of
closed sea, and it was the exercise of this right on the high
seas that led to fresh .difficulties between Spain and England.

It is difficult to visualize the situation in the early eighteenth century. The treaties, it is true, had laid down certain
general rules regarding the possession of territory in the
New World, and as we have seen they had in some instances
expressly and in others by implication sought to prohibit
navigation in waters that washed these lands. But beyond
laying down these principles in a very general way there
was no clear understanding as to how the rules were to be
enforced. We have seen in respect to logwood cutting that
the limits to which Spain might go in punishing these in-
fractions of her boundaries were tacitly assumed to be considerable, and the available state papers of the time show
that the right to visit and search suspected vessels was not
at first questioned. This may have been due partly to the
fact that the English government was well aware of the
illegal nature of log-cutting expeditions as a direct violation of territorial sovereignty and explicit treaty provisions, and partly to the fact that the Caribbean was then
so infested with pirates that visit and search necessarily
was the rule rather than the exception. At the time of which
we are writing, however, the cause of Spanish complaint
was the illegal trade which violated the closed seas, the limits of which were in dispute, and not the lands themselves,
and as the buccaneers had been generally eliminated from
the seas, the reason for a right of search appeared to have
lapsed.

The Spanish view of the matter was, as we have suggested, radically different from the English. The question

at issue was at once a matter of treaty interpretation, and a more or less new problem of international law. It was in a sense the outgrowth of the rule of the papal bulls, for the Spanish, compelled to abandon the claim to a complete jurisdiction in the widest sense, sought to retain such fragments of it as were still possible in the guise of revenue and navigation laws.

Some records of the ferocity with which the Spanish claims were carried out and the equally cruel zeal with which they were resisted by English sailors have been published.[41] They form, however, but a slight part of the unprinted accounts of outrages that were to move the pacific Walpole into a position where war was inevitable. It was partly the effect of the Vienna Treaty, heretofore mentioned, and partly the recollections of the reprisals twice taken by Spain on the property of the South Sea Company that stayed Walpole's hand for some time.[42] Undoubtedly the claims for material damages were on the whole equal, but as the English losses were the result of a far-sighted foreign and colonial policy in which force was a necessary element, it is curious that so much insistence should have been placed upon compensation for isolated acts of violence.[43] It is true that under later conditions such claims would normally have been arbitrated and would not have been treated as a major issue, but the commission which had just completed its labors had shown the futility of this sort of settlement as long as the causes of the evil were not removed. Thus, between 1732 and 1737, some twenty-one British ships were captured, and in 1738 the British am-

[41] Texts in *English Historical Review,* vol. 4, p. 741-749. The Spanish complaints are to be found in Alcedo, *Las Piraterías en la America Española, passim.*

[42] Temperley, *op. cit.,* p. 203.

[43] On the general situation *cf.* Armstrong, *op. cit.,* p. 286; Coxe, *op. cit.,* vol. 3, chapters 41 and 42.

bassador at Madrid presented twenty-eight bundles of claims.[44]

In 1738 the British government advised the Spanish crown that letters of marque were to be issued, and as at this time Parliament was moved to the passage of resolutions that strengthened the stand of the ministry, a very bold demand was made on Spain. Unfortunately for the logic of the English position, however, their case was expressly posited upon the right of free navigation granted by the treaty of 1667. This treaty, the Spanish minister, La Quadra, with some asperity pointed out, had no application to the Indies and was drawn with reference to Europe alone. Nevertheless, *pourparlers* at London regarding the settlement of claims had progressed far enough to permit the effective pacific intervention of Walpole in the negotiations, with the result that on January 3/14, 1739,[45] the Convention of the Pardo was signed, by which all outstanding claims to December 10, 1737, were to be discharged by the payment by Spain of £95,000. Four commissioners were to meet to settle the outstanding questions of principle, among which was the matter of navigation and search.

The agreement to pay this large sum was treated by England as an admission, as a matter of law, of her assumed right of free navigation. The Spanish government, however, was not disposed to agree to this view, and as the sum was never paid there is no reason to suppose the law governing the situation underwent any change.[46]

[44] Temperley, *op. cit.*, p. 209. The situation is well summarized in Keene to Newcastle, December 13, 1737, in Stanhope, *History of England* (5th ed., 1858), vol. 2, p. 266.

[45] *Cf.* La Quadra to Keene, January 21, 1738, Rousset, *op. cit.*, vol. 13, pt. 2, p. 8; Keene to La Quadra, February 10, 1738, *ibid.*, p. 15, for the treaty, *ibid.*, p. 56; Jenckinson, *op. cit.*, vol. 2, p. 339. See also the declaration of La Quadra, Rousset, *op. cit.*, p. 65; Ford, *Admiral Vernon and the Navy* (1907), p. 118, gives the usual British view, which time has apparently not corrected.

[46] Temperley, *op. cit.*, p. 218. The pamphlets pro and con with reference

The Convention of the Pardo made no attempt to settle the account between Spain and the South Sea Company. The former claimed the sum of £68,000 to be outstanding. Benjamin Keene, as the representative of the company, was charged with the settlement of this cause, but unfortunately for the maintenance of peace he was less successful as a private than as a public negotiator. The South Sea Company alleged that as more than the sum stated was due them for confiscations,[47] they would decline to pay the Spanish counter-claims. The Spanish king threatened to suspend the assiento and finally, on May 6, La Quadra announced that this had been done. On May 29 (o.s.) came the formal refusal to pay the £95,000 and as the Pardo Convention had been the chief reliance of the British ministry vindicating the cause of peace, this last barrier was swept away and war was begun.

The War of Jenkins' Ear soon became merged in the general European conflict over the Austrian succession and did not come to an end until the Peace of Aix-la-Chapelle in 1748. The original issues over which the war was fought became dim, as matters of general European concern absorbed the various chancelleries, and yet the English government never lost sight of its own interest. On the part of the Spanish, the war was entered into primarily to vindicate the eighth article of the Treaty of Utrecht and the rights that were theirs under previous treaties of navigation revived after the successive wars of the early eighteenth century. That their claim to a right of search was in some respects justified seems clear. In any event, the defense of free navigation in the Indies made by the English ministry was, as far as the treaties were concerned, effectually rebutted, and Newcastle was eventually driven to a vague re-

to the declaration are in Rousset, *op. cit.*, vol. 13. Hertz, *British Imperialism in the Eighteenth Century* (1908), p. 7 *et seq.*, discusses the pamphlet literature.

[47] *Cf.* the Merchants' memoire in Rousset, *op. cit.*, vol. 13, pt. 2, 47.

sort to the general law of nations in support of his alleged right. Estimating the evidence[48] as far as such is available it would appear that the legal position of Spain was the better. Even the most rabid advocates of the exemption from search took the view that search along the coasts was permissible and resisted only the claim to search on the high seas.[49] As for the latter it would appear that as long as the seas were closed by treaty the Spanish were not wholly wrong in assuming the right to police them.

Like the Peace of Ghent of 1814, the Treaty of Aix-la-Chapelle, by which the wars of the Austrian Succession and of Jenkins' Ear were brought to a close, failed to regulate or even to mention the question of law, the dispute over which contributed so largely to the outbreak of war.[50] At the time of the accession of Ferdinand VI to the throne of Spain in 1746, the new minister of state, the Marqués de Ensenada, prepared for the new monarch a very detailed memorandum on the state of the nation in which he dealt exhaustively with the question of visit and search and how it might best be regulated. This is the most comprehensive available outline of the Spanish position,[51] and it shows in particular how broadly the Spanish interpreted their jurisdiction over the seas. Ensenada's memorandum, however, was drawn with a view to secure peace and although he was not disposed to surrender the right of search he was willing to make certain concessions in the West Indian waters where the probability of dispute was greatest and where the

[48] Temperley, *op. cit.*, p. 219; *cf.* also *Hare Papers* in Hist. MSS. Comm., *14th Report*, App., pt. 9 (1895), p. 243-244.

[49] *Cf.* Lord Carteret's speech in Cobbett, *Parliamentary History of England*, vol. 10, p. 746.

[50] Beer, *Der Friede von Aachen* (*Archiv für österreichische Geschichte*, vol. 47, 1871); Broglie, *La Paix d'Aix-la-Chapelle* (1895); La Fuente, *Historia General d'Espana* (2d ed., 1869), vol. 19, p. 279.

[51] Text in Villa-Rodriguez, *Don Cenón de Somodevilla, Marqués de Ensenada* (1878), p. 31, esp. at p. 37.

English could make out the best case for exemption from search on the high seas.

The pacification between England and Spain was initiated by secret *pourparlers,* in which Ferdinand's Portuguese queen and Benjamin Keene, who was at Lisbon, assisted. Coxe, in his *Memoirs of the Bourbon Kings of Spain,*[52] states that an informal accommodation was reached as a result of these negotiations, and that the right of search, as well as other claims, was admitted by Great Britain. This statement is reproduced by Lafuente,[53] but no documentary evidence is cited in support. On the other hand, it is certainly true that when the congress at Aix-la-Chapelle assembled, the Spanish were determined to cast off the shackles laid on their colonial system at Utrecht—a stand in which the French were obliged to lend them some aid. The English plenipotentiaries, however, declined to give in.[54] They had been instructed that not only should the treaty of 1713 be mentioned, but also the commercial treaty of 1715 and the supplementary assiento treaty of 1716. The tenth article[55] of the preliminaries signed at Aix-la-Chapelle on April 30, 1748, had stated that "the Assiento treaty for the negro trade signed at Madrid, March 26, 1713, and the article of the annual vessel are confirmed by the present preliminary articles for the years of non-enjoyment." Neither France nor Spain desired any amplification or change in these conditions, and in the latter days of September, 1748, the debate over the expansion of the article was especially acrimonious, both the Spanish and French plenipotentiaries threatening to prolong the negotiations by wait-

---

[52] Coxe, *op. cit.,* vol. 4, p. 12, and his *Memoirs of the Pelham Administration,* vol. 1, p. 395.

[53] La Fuente, *op. cit.,* vol. 19, p. 200. But *cf.* Danvila, *Fernando VI y Doña Bárbara de Braganza* (1905), p. 249.

[54] Broglie, *op. cit.,* p. 88. *Cf.* Bentinck's memorandum of April 21, 1748, in Beer, *op. cit.,* p. 94.

[55] Beer, *op. cit.,* p. 79. *Cf.* Bentinck's memorandum of September 22, 1748, at p. 106. Text in Broglie, *op. cit.,* p. 309.

ing for instructions if the English demands were complied with. At this juncture the French offered a new project which enabled the Spanish to overcome their scruples and the treaty was eventually concluded on October 18, 1748,[56] and was signed by Spain on October 20, 1748.

In the third article of the treaty, the Treaties of Westphalia of 1648 and those between England and Spain of 1667 and 1670 were revived, as were the subsequent general pacifications including the Treaties of Utrecht. In view of the fact that by the fifth article, all the conquests made in Europe and the Indies were restored we may assume that as far as the Spanish were concerned, the *status quo ante bellum* was reinstituted in the matter of navigation and the colonial system. The sixteenth article dealt with the restoration of the assiento and read as follows:

The treaty of the Assiento for the trade of negroes signed at Madrid on the 26th of March 1713, and the article of the annual ship making part of the said treaty, are particularly confirmed by the present treaty, for the four years during which the enjoyment thereof has been interrupted, since the commencement of the present war and shall be executed on the same footing and under the same conditions as they have or ought to have been executed before the said war.[57]

The Peace of Aix-la-Chapelle by no means restored the relations of England and Spain to a footing satisfactory to both parties. Keene was again commissioned to Madrid and the negotiations for a new treaty of commerce were commenced. The public law of the Peace of Utrecht had been restored, but, as we have seen, the Spanish were not satisfied with a guaranty of their overseas possessions which involved at every turn insistent and harrowing violations of their sovereignty. The English on their part had secured a renewal of their commercial privileges, but they sensed the

[56] Jenckinson, *op. cit.*, vol. 2, p. 370.
[57] *Ibid.*, p. 384.

necessity of a much more precise definition of their rights, and it was for this reason that they cast about for means to effectuate their ends and under more favorable conditions involving what appeared to be great guarantees for their trade. It was at this juncture, therefore, that their policy to secure a foothold in the South American trade assumed a new aspect and the Falkland Islands for the first time became the subject of diplomatic discussion.

To understand why the Falklands should at this time have been brought on the diplomatic tapis, it is necessary to advert to certain events which took place during the war. The chief purpose of the English naval operations in the opening years of the conflict had been, through concerted action on the east and west coasts of South America, to bottle up the South American trade and to control the Caribbean as well as the Pacific by conquering the Isthmus of Panama. It was to this end that Vernon's attack on Porto Bello was followed by an expedition around the Horn to seize the ports on the Pacific. This expedition was organized in 1740 and was under the command of Admiral Anson. The squadron, composed of six vessels, left St. Helens on September 18, 1740. After a stop at the St. Catherines, off the coast of Brazil, the ships proceeded along the coast to Port San Julian. There one of the vessels was refitted and passage was then made through the Le Maire Straits under circumstances of incredible hardship, which cost the squadron three ships.[58] Similar misfortune continued to harass the expedition so that Anson was compelled to abandon the original scheme of attacking Panama and to decide to content himself with taking prizes. In this the expedition had

[58] Anson, *A Voyage Round the World in the Years 1740, 1, 2, 3, 4* (compiled from his papers by Richard Walter, Edinburgh, 1812), 2 vols., p. 183. On Anson, *cf.* Anson, *Life of Admiral Lord Anson* (1912); Richmond, *The Navy in the War of 1739-48* (1920), vol. 1, p. 97. *Cf.* the criticism on the authorship of *A Voyage* in *Dictionary of National Biography*, vol. 59, p. 261.

some success, as they captured in addition to other prizes the annual ship from Acapulco to Manila bearing a treasure of a million and a half dollars.[59] The other important exploit was the sacking of Paitá.

After the return of the Anson expedition and at the close of the war, there appeared the relation of the voyage edited by the chaplain, Mr. Walter.[60] The account of the difficulties in rounding Cape Horn was followed by a chapter in which suggestions were made for facilitating the passage.[61] These observations were undoubtedly those of Anson and not of his compiler, and in view of the important bearing they had upon British policy deserve some scrutiny.

After setting forth in blunt language the futility of relying upon the friendship of the Portuguese as a means of interrupting Spanish trade from Brazil as a base of operation, Anson proceeded to point out how the fact that Spanish trade adhered tenaciously to a single course over the seas rendered their ships peculiarly subject to attack and capture by a few cruisers stationed along this track. The Spanish, however, were in the habit of laying an embargo on their trade as soon as they were apprised of the presence of an enemy, a circumstance which made concealment very necessary. These two facts led Anson to suggest that some point south of Brazil might be discovered as a base of future operation, and in this connection he proposed either Pepys Island or the Falklands,[62] to which he was moved in the case of the former by Cowley's glowing description of a harbor where five hundred ships could ride at anchor, apparently not suspecting its correctness, although in another connection he reflects bitterly on the frivolous manner with which the buccaneers gave notices of places which did not exist. As for the Falklands, Anson relied upon the Woodes

[59] Anson, *A Voyage,* p. 205.
[60] Coxe, *Memoirs of the Pelham Administration* (1829), vol. 2, p. 115.
[61] Anson, *A Voyage,* p. 105.
[62] *Ibid.,* p. 113.

Rogers description, which, as we know, was none too sanguine, but he made the suggestion that an expedition be sent
to survey the islands and added[63] "if, on examination, one
or both of these places should appear proper for the purpose intended, it is scarcely to be conceived of what prodigious import a convenient station might prove situate so
far to the southward, and so near to Cape Horn." Anson
concluded by recommending that Tierra del Fuego also be
surveyed with the same end in view.

The fact has been mentioned that negotiations were entered into by Keene for the arrangement of the commercial
relations of England and Spain. They came at a time when
Spain was governed by two ministers of considerable
ability—Carvajal and Ensenada—and when the influence
of the French was at a low ebb. Ensenada, as a protégé of
Patiño, was anxious to pursue the policies of his master,[64]
and hence, although the Spanish court was more favorably
disposed to Great Britain than it had been for many decades,
there was no great probability of the English gaining in
all the details of their programme. The recent war, as
we have seen, had demonstrated very clearly that expeditions against Spanish colonies south of the equator and in
the Pacific were impracticable simply for the reason that
there was no near naval base that would permit a long-
sustained campaign to be made. Consequently, in a future
war against Spain there would be no means of profiting by
the weakness of her colonial defense. The success of colonial
campaigns necessitated the complete military conquest of
the colony, as in the case of India and Canada. The mere
acquisition of a single post was not sufficient. A second lesson learned by the war had been the futility of the assiento
as a means of peaceful penetration in South America.
Three times the property of the company had been confiscated, and on the last occasion for a period of ten years the

[63] *Ibid.*
[64] Keene to Bedford, June 30, 1749 (*Library of Congress MSS.*).

company had been unable to profit by its franchise. These facts in connection with the changing views of British colonial policy that led to the reforms of William Pitt[65] were all of the greatest consequence for the negotiations initiated by Keene.

At the time of which we are writing Anson was the chief executive officer of the admiralty.[66] In this office there was projected an expedition for the purpose of carrying out the scheme which was the chief fruit of Anson's expedition.[67] Two frigates were to be sent out for the ostensible purpose of making discoveries in American seas that might tend to the improvement of commerce. This proposal of the admiralty was approved by the king, and the vessels were fitted out in the Thames. The Spanish ambassador at the Court of St. James was Richard Wall, an Irishman in the service of Spain, and one of the romantic figures for which the eighteenth century is famous. To Wall's ears came the news of the expedition, and he undertook at once to make representations to the English courts against the dispatch of the fleet, alleging that it would cause uneasiness and suspicion between the two countries. In view of this protest the Duke of Bedford instructed Keene to lay the project before the Spanish ministry.[68]

According to Bedford, the projected expedition had two purposes; first, the full discovery of the Pepys and Falkland islands, and, secondly, the exploration of the South Seas. As the latter part of the project involved wooding and watering at Juan Fernandez, and possibly coming in sight of the west coast of South America, Bedford stated that it was apprehended in some quarters that the British were preparing to attack the Spanish in these regions on some future occasion. These fears were undoubtedly those ex-

[65] Beer, *British Colonial Policy, 1754-1765* (1907), p. 4.
[66] Sandwich was First Lord.
[67] Bedford to Keene, April 29, 1749 (*Library of Congress MSS.*).
[68] *Ibid.*

pressed by Wall, as the British king undertook to direct the admiralty to proceed only with the first part of the project, and for the ships to return home after the seas about the Falkland and Pepys Island had been sufficiently explored. Bedford went on to say: "As there is no intention of making any settlement in either of those Islands, and as his Majesty's sloops will neither touch upon or even make any part of the Spanish Coast, the king can in no shape apprehend that this Design can give any umbrage at Madrid." Furthermore, as it was the firm intention of the king not only to adhere strictly to the Treaty of Aix-la-Chapelle, but also to do everything to improve the relations of the two courts, Keene was to discuss the matter with the Spanish ministry. Wall having shown that he was not averse to the first part of the project provided the second part was abandoned, Bedford seems to have entertained some hope of securing Spanish acquiescence in the plan.

Upon the receipt of this instruction, Keene interviewed Carvajal upon the matter.[69] The latter stated that he was sorry that so soon after signing a treaty for the reëstablishment of friendship, new matter should be projected which would throw the two courts into the same or worse disputes than those which had occasioned the last war. The English, he said, knew by experience that when the two countries each had possessions in the same neighborhood and commerce and navigation were both prohibited, they had been exposed to disagreeable accidents. The projected expedition Carvajal declared he must regard as a new attempt to keep alive old jealousies and suspicions, a matter which he was anxious to prevent. Moreover, he said, he was no stranger to the rise and intent of the expedition, as it was fully explained in the printed relation of Anson's voyage.

Replying to Carvajal's animadversions, Keene stated that he was sorry and surprised to hear these views, as the

[69] Keene to Bedford, May 21, 1749 (*Library of Congress MSS.*).

expedition was incapable of injuring the navigation, trade or possessions of Spain. In fact, Spain, having the greatest interests in this part of the world, should reap great benefits. He thereupon entered into a complete account of the expedition, emphasizing the good will of the English king in abandoning, on Wall's protest, the part of the project which could give rise to suspicion.

Carvajal seems to have been unimpressed by the disingenuousness of this act of the English crown, for, reports Keene:

whatever I could say did not seem to render the scheme more palatable. When he appeared to give credit to our not having any design to settle in the Islands in question, he fell upon the inutility of pretending to a further discovery of them and affirmed they had been long since first discovered and inhabited by the Spaniards; who called them the *Islands de Leones* from the quantities of these amphibious animals to be met upon their coasts and that there were already in the books in their offices very ample descriptions of the dimensions, properties etc., of those islands; That if we did not intend to make any establishment there, what service could this bare knowledge be of to us? We had no possessions in that part of the world and consequently no passages nor places to refresh in; That he hoped we would consider what air it would have in the world to see us planted directly against the mouth of the straits of Magellan, ready upon all occasions to enter into the South Seas; where the next step would be to endeavor to discover and settle in some other Islands, in order to remedy the inconveniency of being obliged to make so long a voyage as that to China to refit our naval force, upon any disappointment we might meet with in our future attacks upon the Spanish coasts as happened to my Lord Anson.[70]

Keene replied to this with some asperity that it would be difficult to take any step for the improvement of navigation and the procuring of more exact knowledge of geography that could not be subjected to the same twisted interpreta-

[70] These events are also recounted in Coxe, *Memoirs of the Bourbon Kings of Spain*, vol. 4, p. 39 *et seq.*

tion and imaginary objections, and that if such principles had always been in force, Spain would not have had such vast possessions nor have been able to make use of them. He insisted that there was not the slightest ground for suspicion.

Keene next called upon Ensenada, who told him he had heard from Wall, and that he hoped the whole project would be set aside. Ensenada added that he regarded the existing time as improper for such an undertaking, and that the French, who were full of suspicion, would regard this as a joint enterprise to strip them of their possessions. Keene replied in the same sense as he had answered Carvajal. In his communication to Bedford, however, Keene spoke with some contempt of the "whimsical notions of exclusive right in the South Seas," and he pointed out that there was not a single objection advanced against the *right* of the English to put their project into execution.[71] Their chief arguments, said Keene, were that the matter would give rise to "future inconveniences." Ordinary arguments, he added, were not effective at the Spanish court because the government desired to keep its possessions as mysterious as possible—"and the utility and preservation of them depend upon their not being known, nor having any other possession or competitor in their neighborhood."

The anxiety of the British court at this time to effectuate a *rapprochement* with the Spanish is evidenced in the reply of the Duke of Bedford to Keene.[72] After signifying the king's approval of Keene's conduct, Bedford went on to say that his majesty could in no respect agree to the rea-

[71] Brown, *Anglo-Spanish Relations in America* (1923), p. 393, gives a totally incorrect impression of the Spanish point of view in 1749, by relying for her account on Egmont to Grafton, July 20, 1765 (*R. O. State Papers, Spain, Supp.* 253), where the bull *Inter Cætera* and the theory of territorial propinquity are mentioned as the basis of Spain's claim. These points were not raised in 1749.

[72] June 5, 1749 (*Library of Congress MSS.*).

soning of the Spanish ministry as to his right to send out ships for the discovery of unknown and unsettled parts of the world, as this was a right indubitably open to all; yet, as his Britannic Majesty was desirous of showing his Catholic Majesty his great complacency in matters where the rights and advantages of his own subjects were not immediately and intimately concerned, he had consented to lay aside for the present every scheme that might possibly give umbrage to the court of Madrid. Accordingly, he had given orders to the lords of the admiralty to proceed no further in their projects. This concession by the king, Bedford suggested, might be used to good advantage in the negotiations with which Keene was charged—the conclusion of the commercial treaty. Bedford expressed the hope that England would make some advantageous commercial gain by this move as well as assisting in the preservation of the peace.

In view of the subsequent attitude of Great Britain on the subject of the Falklands, it is interesting to note that in this first diplomatic exchange over these islands the question of the right to settle does not appear to have been raised. The British took the view that their expedition was purely a scientific one, although its true intent was never concealed from the Spanish. The latter, on their part, declined to agree to the project largely on grounds of expediency, but also on the ground that the British having no possessions in the region had no business there. As the question of the right to settle was not raised, this aspect of the matter was not discussed. The real question at issue, however, was whether the British had any right to enter the regions. The mere fact that the project was laid before the Spanish crown tends to show that they were well aware of the fact that they had no such right under the treaties, but attempted to secure it in the guise of sending a scientific expedition. This was a purpose not forbidden by the treaties, which contemplated only commercial navigation, and consequently the British request could be denied only on grounds of general expediency, or, as the Spanish did, by traversing the alleged scientific purpose.

The Falklands issue having been temporarily arranged, Keene proceeded with the negotiations of the treaty, to secure the favorable conclusion of which he was liberally supplied with funds.[73] Unexpected difficulties arose in the discussions over the provisions of this agreement.[74] Wall was eventually summoned from London to join in the negotiation and the treaty was finally signed October 26, 1750.[75]

The chief feature of this treaty was the first article, which provided for the retrocession to the Spanish crown of the British rights to the assiento and the annual vessel, a privilege which had four years to run by the terms of the sixteenth article of the Treaty of Aix-la-Chapelle. For this concession the Spanish king agreed to pay the sum of £100,000 and there was a mutual remission of claims on both sides. The advantage which the British gained was a substantial improvement of their commercial privileges in Spain itself that, in view of the then operation of the colonial system, promised to net them more than had the assiento. They were also given the right to take salt on the Island Fortudos. By the ninth article the Treaty of Aix-la-Chapelle was confirmed except in such instances as it conflicted with the new instrument. The attempt to secure confirmation of the especial privileges granted the British by the Treaty of Santander of September 12, 1700,[76] and confirmed by the Treaty of Madrid of December 14, 1715,[77] was unsuccessful.[78]

The anxiety of the British to secure Spanish friendship

---

[73] Keene to Bedford, June 30, 1749 (*Library of Congress MSS.*).

[74] Coxe, *Memoirs of the Bourbon Kings of Spain*, vol. 4, p. 37.

[75] Cantillo, *op. cit.*, p. 409.

[76] *Ibid.*, p. 1.

[77] *Ibid.*, p. 170.

[78] *Ibid.*, p. 412 (note).

was evident in the years following the Peace of Aix-la-Chapelle. There was not a chancellery in Europe which did not share the view of Frederick II of Prussia that this treaty was a mere truce and that war was inevitable within a short space of time. The temporary eclipse of French influence in Spain and the favorable disposition of the Spanish ministry all seemed to point to a possible alliance, and as the British were embarking upon a more statesmanlike colonial policy than had been practiced in the past, some of the causes of friction between the two countries were kept in abeyance. Shortly after the treaty of 1750 was concluded Ensenada, who had been depending on the queen's favor, fell from office, largely, it has been charged, as a result of the machinations of Keene.[79] In any event the Irishman, Wall, was transferred from London to take charge of foreign affairs, and from 1754 until just before his retirement (1763), the Spanish court maintained an attitude of steadfast neutrality in European politics—an attitude largely to be attributed to the favorable inclinations of Wall to England.

The wisdom of Wall's policy was apparent as soon as the Seven Years' War broke out. The diplomatic blandishments of both England and France were practiced upon Spain, but Ferdinand was unwilling to abandon the peace which was so necessary to the Spanish economic rehabilitation, and hence, until his death in 1759, neither belligerent was able to draw Spain into the war.

Ferdinand was succeeded by his half-brother, Charles, king of Naples.[80] This monarch was a man of ability, and under his rule the Spanish dominions experienced a remarkable renaissance. Charles combined a genuine desire

---

[79] Villa-Rodriguez, op. cit., p. 270. Cf. Coxe, Memoirs of the Bourbon Kings of Spain, vol. 4, p. 120.

[80] On Charles III cf. Fernan-Nuñez, Vida de Carlos III (Morel-Fatio ed., 1896), 2 vols.; Danvila y Collado, Reinado de Carlos III (1892), 6 vols.; Rousseau, Regne de Charles III d'Espagne (1907), 2 vols.; Ferrer del Rio, Historia del Reinado de Carlos III (1856), 4 vols.

to promote the interest of his subjects with a sure hand in their government. He was not only imbued with a pronounced sense of justice unusual in a king, but he likewise possessed that quixotic regard for honor characteristic of the Spanish aristocracy. These traits of character were strikingly exhibited in his conduct of foreign relations.

When Charles III left Naples to assume his new crown he carried with him the memory of an old grievance[81] suffered at the hands of England, a circumstance which affected his views on the attitude of Spain toward the war. Moreover, while still king of Naples, Charles had, in April, 1759, so far succumbed to the representations of the Marquis d'Ossun, the French ambassador, that British conquests in the New World threatened to impair his succession, that he had instructed his own minister at London, Albertini, to warn the British ministry that a descent upon Santo Domingo would bring the Spanish garrison on their necks. This communication led to a conference between Wall and Lord Bristol, the British ambassador at Madrid, in which the former reiterated the Spanish intention to stay clear of the war.

It is interesting to observe the astuteness with which the Duc de Choiseul, French minister of foreign affairs, proceeded to build his scheme for drawing Spain into the war upon Charles' personal aversion to the British and his conviction that Spain would in the end suffer from a British victory.[82] Choiseul's plan of action seems to have been, on the one hand, to convince Charles of the identity of Spanish and French interests, and, on the other, to engage the mediation of Spain for the conclusion of a reasonable peace, a project designed to draw Spain into active participation in the diplomatic side of the conflict. The strong probability

---

[81] Rousseau, *op. cit.*, vol. 1, p. 29.

[82] On Choiseul's policy at this early stage *cf.* Soulange-Bodin, *La Diplomatie de Louis XV et le Pacte de Famille* (1894); Bourget, *Le Duc de Choiseul et l'Alliance Espagnol* (1906), *passim*.

that the mediation would be rejected, and that the pro-English policy of Wall would thereby be checked was a factor which entered into the Frenchman's reckoning. Choiseul's programme, however, was not aided by the fact that Charles, averse to changes in the persons who were about him, secured the promotion of Ossun to the Spanish embassy at Madrid, for Ossun was a person of mediocre parts and at this time a very young man; he was incapable of being more than a mere agent for the transmission of dispatches and although he enjoyed the intimate confidence of Charles, Choiseul was not able to profit much by this fact.[83]

After Albertini's conference with Pitt, while Charles was yet only king of Naples, another interview was held, at which the former had suggested the mediation of his sovereign, but Pitt had replied evasively and the matter went no further.[84] When Charles reached Spain, his desire to intervene seems appreciably to have lessened, and the pacific intentions of Wall and Queen Amelia influenced him to maintain the policy of neutrality. At the same time, as an antidote to the Spanish mediations, Pitt proposed a congress in which England, France, Russia and Prussia were to participate, and this move was vigorously supported by Frederick the Great, who had everything to gain from a general pacification and everything to lose by a separate peace between England and France. This, of course, was precisely what Choiseul desired, but his insistence on dictating the very form of Spanish diplomatic intervention led to the complete collapse of his schemes in the spring of 1760.[85]

The diplomatic victory of the anti-French forces at Madrid was only temporary. Queen Amelia died in the fall of the year 1760, and thenceforward Wall's policy found small support at Madrid, while the depredations of the English

---

[83] Soulange-Bodin, *op. cit.,* p. 112.

[84] *Ibid.,* p. 114; Rousseau, *op. cit.,* vol. 1, p. 35.

[85] Soulange-Bodin, *op. cit.,* p. 131.

on Spanish commerce made it increasingly difficult for him to maintain his position. Indeed, the fortunes of war had so definitely favored the English arms that, as is not unusual in such cases, this government became correspondingly careless of neutral complaints. At the same time, other points of dispute between England and Spain, chiefly concerned with the rights of the Spanish to fish in Newfoundland waters and with the illegal logwood cutting in Honduras, were brought forward for adjustment.

Early in the year 1761, Charles III recalled Don Jaime Masones, his ambassador at Paris, and appointed in his stead the Marqués de Grimaldi, who had been serving as ambassador at The Hague. Grimaldi is reported by his contemporaries to have been an accomplished courtier.[86] He had owed his rise to Ensenada, and his continued presence in the service of the king to his own abilities. A Genoese by birth, his sympathies were pronouncedly French, and his ambition at this time was to have a share in arranging the peace. At his first interview with Choiseul (February 11, 1761), Grimaldi very clearly indicated his feelings in the matter of an alliance.[87] Choiseul, already engrossed in a plan of his own for effecting the restoration of peace, maintained a close reserve, although he did not hesitate to play on the fears of the Spaniards with regard to the integrity of their colonial possessions.[88]

From this time forth, the negotiations between France and Spain advanced with some rapidity. Choiseul, in his first interview with Grimaldi, had unsuccessfully attempted to get an assurance that in the event his peace negotiations failed, the king of Spain would declare that he would no longer tolerate British operations in America. This was his

[86] *Ibid.*, p. 146. Harris, *Diaries and Correspondence* (1844), vol. 1, p. 55. But see Bristol to Pitt, March 5, 1859, in Thackeray, *History of William Pitt* (1827), vol. 1, p. 389.

[87] Soulange-Bodin, *op. cit.*, p. 147.

[88] Rousseau, *op. cit.*, vol. 1, p. 56.

formula in the ensuing months. On March 26, 1761, *pourparlers* were initiated at London for the discussion of peace terms. De Bussy was dispatched by Choiseul to London and Hans Stanley was sent to Paris by Pitt.[89] Choiseul had suggested that the *uti possidetis* should be the basis of the peace, a principle stoutly resisted by Frederick the Great, as he was at this moment in an unfavorable military situation. At the same time the Austrian court, likewise suspecting its interests would be sacrificed, opposed any idea of a joint discussion of continental and colonial questions.

The negotiations for the alliance initiated by a French project of March 3, 1761, were resumed in May, 1761.[90] Grimaldi submitted a counter-project of a treaty in which provision for future aid was made, but the Spanish king stipulated that he was not to enter the existing war, as he intended offering peace on terms that could not be rejected. This document clearly revealed the fact that Charles' interest in the conflict than raging was solely with reference to the effect of British victory on his own empire, and he drew the treaty simply for the purpose of guaranteeing and protecting himself against the future consequences which Choiseul had assured him would result from French defeat. The latter, however, would not tolerate such an arrangement, and he refused absolutely to be party to a treaty which did not stipulate immediate aid by Spain. To these representations the Spanish finally succumbed.

In the interim the negotiations for peace had advanced but little. Pitt was aware of the growing intimacy between the two Bourbon courts, and the maintenance of his own position in England, depending as it did upon his indispensability for the prosecution of war, rendered him more inclined to a continuation of the war than toward peace. On July 23, 1761, some three weeks before the treaty be-

[89] Bourget, *Le Duc de Choiseul et l'Angleterre (Revue Historique,* vol. 21, 1899), p. 2.

[90] Text in Rousseau, *op. cit.,* vol. 1, p. 62-63, note.

tween Spain and France was signed, De Bussy handed Pitt a memorandum[91] in which it was proposed that as the treaty should serve as a basis for a solid reconciliation between the two crowns which the interests of a third party should not disturb nor any engagements entered into by the belligerents prior to peace, the king of Spain should be invited to guarantee the peace. The memorandum went on to say that the French king was alarmed by the differences between Spain and England, in that they threatened a new war and that the Spanish king had intrusted him with the settlement of the outstanding difficulties between the two crowns. These differences, it was stated, were over the seizure of Spanish ships, the fisheries and the logwood cutting.

Pitt's annoyance with the French must have been profound. The memorandum was in substance a notification of the alliance still to be signed and at the same time a covert threat of further hostilities in the midst of negotiations for peace. He forthwith advised De Bussy[92] that the king would not tolerate the *immixion* of Spanish issue into the peace *pourparlers,* and returned the memorandum. He also addressed the Earl of Bristol, British ambassador at Madrid, directing him to inform Wall of the offensive nature of the memorandum, and that the British king would not alter his course toward Spain by reason of any covert threats.[93] The negotiations for peace were then broken off and although Pitt insisted upon war with Spain, his colleagues refused to support him in his demand. Accordingly on October 5, 1761, Pitt laid down his office.

Nearly two months previous to Pitt's resignation the alliance of France with Spain, known as the Family Compact, had been concluded (August 15, 1761).[94] This treaty is

[91] Text in *Papers Relative to the Rupture with Spain* (1762), p. 14 *et seq.* (hereafter cited as *Spanish Papers*).

[92] Pitt to de Bussy, July 24, 1761, *Spanish Papers,* p. 18.

[93] Pitt to Bristol, July 28, 1761, *ibid.,* p. 2.

[94] Cantillo, *op. cit.,* p. 468.

so remarkable, not only for its effect upon European diplomacy, but also in its connection with the Falkland Islands crisis which arose some ten years after its conclusion, that its provisions must be set forth in some detail.

The first article declared that by virtue of the intimate ties of relationship and friendship between the two crowns, ''any power which shall become the enemy of one or the other of the two crowns'' would in the future be the enemy of both.[95] The two kings mutually guaranteed ''all the states, lands, islands and places'' in each other's possessions wherever situate without reservation or exception.[96] On the principle that who attacked one crown attacked the other, the treaty went on to fix the aid that one power would grant the other in such an event—twelve ships of the line and six frigates to be supplied three months after requisition;[97] 18,000 infantrymen and 6,000 cavalry if the requisition was made by France, and 10,000 infantrymen and 2,000 cavalry where the requisition was made by Spain,[98] except in case of wars in stipulated regions.[99]

This supply of troops was paid by the sovereign[100] lending them, but they were to be under the command of the king who had requisitioned them.[101] Moreover, and this was the most extraordinary provision of the treaty,[102] the supply was to be made on demand and without any further explanation than that they were needed, and under no pretext was compliance to be eluded; hence the question of offense or defense had no application to this stipulation, for these troops were given pursuant to the obligation arising out

[95] The treaty was later ratified by the King of Naples and the Duke of Parma, who were admitted to its benefits.
[96] Article 2.
[97] Articles 4 and 5.
[98] Article 6.
[99] Articles 7 and 8.
[100] Article 14.
[101] Articles 10 and 13.
[102] Article 12.

of the relationship and friendship of the two crowns.[103] This obligation, when war was actually declared, ripened into an obligation to go to war with all the national resources.

The seventeenth article provided that there would be no separate peace made without the consent of the other power, and all matters of mutual interest were to be communicated by one crown to the other, particularly in regard to questions of pacification. This provision was given vitality and political significance in the following article by which it was agreed that the losses of one power would be compensated by concessions from the gains of the other, so that in peace as well as in war the two monarchies throughout their dominions would form but a single power.[104]

The same intimacy which was to govern the political relationships of the two crowns was also to extend to their subjects, and to this end the treaty contained certain far-reaching economic clauses. These provisions included the declaration that the citizens and subjects of the contractants were no longer to be accounted aliens in each other's dominions, the *droit d'aubaine* was abolished, and the right to dispose of property by will, donation or otherwise, was to subsist. Moreover, the subjects of the two kings were to have the liberty of export and import, and equal treatment in the matter of taxes, navigation and trade.

On the same day that the Family Compact was concluded, another secret treaty was signed by which Spain agreed to enter the war on May 1, 1762,[105] if peace were not concluded before that date. France agreed to assume the Spanish complaints as her own, and to make no treaty until these

[103] Article 14.

[104] Article 20—the provisions, however, were to extend to Parma and Naples.

[105] Text in Blart, *Les Rapports de la France et de l'Espagne aprés le Pacte de Famille* (1915), appendix 2, p. 214.

were settled, and Portugal was to be forced to join the alliance.

It is easy to imagine the surprise that this treaty created in the chancelleries of Europe, and the consternation with which the English greeted it. The reforms carried out by Ensenada and confirmed by Charles III, especially in the navy, had resulted in a widespread overestimation of Spanish military strength, and it was undoubtedly this belief in Spanish prowess that had led Pitt to insist upon an immediate attack on Spain in order to profit by the surprise. The element opposing Pitt, however, resisted this counsel primarily because it was an issue on which the latter had staked his political future. On September 11, 1761, Bristol's dispatch had arrived recounting his interview with Wall regarding the De Bussy memorandum.[106] Bristol reported that Wall had acknowledged the authenticity of the memorandum, and although Bristol had endeavored to demonstrate the great offense that this paper had given to England, and at the same time to give the Spanish a means of retreat, Wall had bluntly refused to accept the British overtures, and had retaliated by rebutting all the claims of the British on the three main points of disputes. The Spanish position was set forth at length in a memorandum[107] which Wall eventually handed to Bristol. Shortly after the receipt of this paper, the cabinet meeting was held which resulted in Pitt's fall.

With the advent of Lord Bute to the leadership of the British government, the policy of that country toward Spain underwent no great change except that a further attempt was made to maintain the peace, an effort that was, of course, foredoomed to failure.[108] The Spanish crown was unwilling to accept the adjudications of British prize courts as final determinations of neutral rights, and the refusal of

[106] Bristol to Pitt, August 31, 1761, *Spanish Papers*, p. 21.
[107] *Ibid.*, p. 47.
[108] Egremont to Bristol, October 28, 1761, *ibid.*, p. 81.

the British to make a formal renunciation of their alleged rights to cut logwood in Honduras was resented as an incursion of Spanish sovereignty over the land itself, although the British declared their willingness to recognize the sovereignty of Spain subject to this servitude.[109] The conference with Spain was finally suspended, the ambassadors were recalled by each court, and war was declared by England on January 2, 1762.[110]

From the very outset of the war between England and Spain misfortune followed the arms of the latter. By August, 1762, a British fleet had reduced Havana to possession; and in the East, Manila was captured and exempted from pillage by a ransom of four million pesetas, one half of which was paid on the spot and half of which was secured by a draft on the Spanish treasury signed by the archbishop of Manila. In Portugal, after an initial success, the Spanish were compelled to withdraw.

It was not so much the military defeats of Spain which hastened the conclusion of a peace, as the series of events beginning with the death of Elizabeth of Russia and culminating in the suspension of hostilities between Prussia and Russia. At the same time, Bute's intention to abandon Prussia became apparent by the failure to renew the subsidies and by his proposal to Russia and Austria that a new alliance be formed to impose peace on the world. It was then obvious that as between Prussia and Austria a military stalemate was inevitable, and negotiations for the restoration of peace on the continent were begun. Choiseul was quick to see the significance of the British withdrawal from war on the continent; it did not require the conquest of Havana to make clear that the war on the sea could now be prosecuted by England with greater vigor. Indeed,

[109] Egremont to Bristol, November 19, 1761, *ibid.*, p. 133; Bristol to Egremont, December 7, 9, 11, 1761, and enclosures from Wall, *ibid.*, p. 241 *et seq.*

[110] Text in *Annual Register*, 1761, p. 285 *et seq.*

shortly after the entry of Spain into the war, Martinique fell, and this blow was followed by the occupation of Sta. Lucia, Grenada and St. Vincent.

On April 16, 1762,[111] Choiseul instructed Ossun to suggest to Spain the advisability of seeking peace, for he had been thoroughly disillusioned about the military value of the Spanish alliance, and hence the most he could hope for was the rescue of the remnants of France's colonial domain.[112] Indeed, Choiseul was at the moment attempting to reopen *pourparlers* with London through the Sardinian minister there. In this effort he was successful largely because King George III and Bute were both strongly inclined against the further continuance of the war. Accordingly the English ministry indicated its willingness to reopen negotiations on the basis of the last two *ultimata* of the previous attempt. Choiseul then dispatched Nivernais[113] to London and Bedford[114] was sent to Paris.

There is a certain ironic element in Choiseul's situation at this moment. The discussions at London and Paris were proceeding in manner as satisfactory as the French could hope, and there was every prospect that peace would be concluded. On the other hand, the Family Compact prevented him not only from making a separate peace but required him to keep the Spanish fully advised of what was going on. Perhaps the overwarm Gallic sympathies of Grimaldi led Choiseul to believe that Charles III would be the silent partner of the new association, and perhaps he counted too much upon his own abilities as an intriguer. In any event, his new ally, although professing he would listen to reasonable and honest conditions, in effect refused

[111] Blart, *op. cit.,* p. 26, gives text.

[112] Rousseau, *op. cit.,* vol. 1, p. 90.

[113] On Nivernais, *cf.* Broglie, *Le Secret du Roi,* vol. 2, p. 106; Soulange-Bodin, *op. cit.,* p. 175.

[114] On Bedford's views at this time, Lecky, *England in the Eighteenth Century* (1899 ed.), vol. 3, p. 207; Bedford, *Correspondence* (Russell ed., 1846), vol. 3.

to consider any peace proposal, for what Charles III regarded as reasonable scarcely appeared to the British victors as such.[115]

The chief objection of Charles III to the conditions of peace which the military *status quo* made inevitable, was the fact that the cession of Canada and the Mississippi Valley would give the English access to the Gulf of Mexico, a body which he regarded as a closed sea. The same exception was taken to the English establishments on the Honduras coast. Accordingly, his outline of reasonable proposals included not only a prohibition of these settlements but a revocation of the rights of commerce hitherto given to England by treaty, in which wise Charles expected to restrict the use of the Gulf of Mexico should the Mississippi Valley be ceded.

Choiseul now had recourse to the formula on which the alliance negotiations with Spain had been posited—that Spain's declaration of war was the vehicle of peace[116]—a rather meaningless phrase, but one by which Choiseul hoped to refire the earlier aspirations of Charles to be the great pacificator. But this design was not to be carried on unless the Spanish were first subjected to a signal defeat, for Charles' interpretation of the formula now was that peace was to be bought with military success. This was doubtless also the view of the English, for although the proposal made to France showed a certain magnanimity, there was no disposition to treat the Spanish with anything but severity.

On August 2, 1762, in the face of the most ardent demands from Choiseul, Charles III eventually indicated his willingness to recede from his earlier conditions in so far that he agreed to give a provisional right of logwood cutting and would keep the treaties of commerce in force for six months pending the conclusion of a new convention.

[115] Blart, *op. cit.,* p. 28.
[116] Choiseul to Ossun, August 17, 1762, in Blart, *op. cit.,* p. 29.

Grimaldi was further given full powers to negotiate with Bedford along these lines. What Charles regarded as concessions, however, were in Choiseul's eyes, as well as in Lord Egremont's, merely obstacles to peace. On September 20, therefore, Choiseul[117] addressed Ossun in brutally frank language, advising him of the immediate necessity of Spain's deciding for peace and threatening the withdrawal of France from the conflict. The British having by this time conceded to France the possession of New Orleans, Choiseul sugar-coated his bitter pill by insisting that the cession of Louisiana would be the *quid pro quo* of Spain's acquiescence.

Shortly after this letter was dispatched, the news of the capture of Havana reached Madrid, and although Charles received this intelligence with the greatest aplomb,[118] the whole basis of negotiation was changed. The issue between England and Spain no longer was the settlement of the ante-bellum disputes, but at once became a question of cession or an equivalent for Havana. Choiseul, foreseeing this contingency, prevailed upon Louis XV to address to Charles III[119] a letter on October 9, 1762, in which New Orleans and Louisiana were offered outright to Spain as a means of securing the retrocession of Havana.

Three days later Lord Egremont delivered to Nivernais the English demands on Spain. These included the cession of Cuba or an equivalent—either Porto Rico, the whole of Florida or a part of Yucatan—and the renunciation of fishing rights in Newfoundland. On October 15 Choiseul counselled the abandonment of Florida, and Charles III, suddenly capitulating, forwarded to Grimaldi full powers to negotiate the peace on the basis of England's demands.

On November 3, 1762, two preliminary treaties were

[117] Text in Blart, *op. cit.,* p. 33.
[118] Rousseau, *op. cit.,* vol. 1, p. 100. On the receipt in England, Soulange-Bodin, *op. cit.,* p. 194.
[119] Text in Blart, *op. cit.,* p. 39.

signed at Fontainebleau, one the preliminaries of peace between the three powers, and the other the preliminary act of cession by which New Orleans and Louisiana were transferred to Spain. This latter treaty was made definitive on February 10, 1763,[120] the same day on which the Treaty of Paris,[121] which ended the Seven Years' War, was concluded.

The Treaty of Paris, following the model of earlier pacifications, expressly renewed and confirmed the "treaties" of Westphalia and the whole series of treaties beginning with the conventions of 1667 and 1670 between England and Spain and ending with the Treaty of Madrid of 1750 that we have had under discussion, excepting, of course, the special assiento treaties. In other words, the whole system of public law previous to the war was confirmed for Europe and America, except as it was modified in the new arrangement.

These modifications were, however, more important in detail than in principle, for the fundamental basis of the existing colonial system was not disturbed. On the part of Spain, in return for the retrocession of Havana,[122] Florida and all of Spain's possessions east of the Mississippi were relinquished to the British.[123] At the same time Charles III was obliged to give up his claim to the Newfoundland fisheries[124] and to accept the decisions of British prize courts as final.[125] The only important concession made by the English was the agreement to demolish all fortifications on the Bay of Honduras[126] and other places on the territory of Spain, wherever these might be. In exchange for this act, the king of Spain agreed that British subjects would not be

[120] In Cantillo, *op. cit.*, p. 496, note, are given the articles of the Fontainebleau preliminaries which differed from the final treaty.

[121] *Ibid.*, p. 485.

[122] *Ibid.*, p. 486.

[123] Article 19.

[124] Article 20.

[125] Article 18.

[126] Article 16.

molested in their business of cutting and shipping logwood, and would be permitted to build and occupy dwellings.[127]

It is not necessary to detail at this place the vast cessions made by France to England. Suffice it to remark that France was stripped of her colonial empire and the balance of power in the western hemisphere was completely upset. We have already remarked that by the Treaty of Paris there was no actual disturbance of the principle of exclusive use of colonial possessions and its corollary, the closed sea. Indeed, the provisions for the evacuation of territories occupied by the British were drawn up to assure the most careful observance of Spanish prohibitory regulations; and the same rule was laid down for the French possessions which were to be restored. The treaty not only required the vessels which were to take off British subjects to arrive in ballast, but the ships were to have passports and there were to be officers of the restored sovereign on board. On the other hand, however, the removal of a third power from the western world really made a further conflict between British and Spanish inevitable, particularly as the cession of Florida and of Louisiana now brought these two powers into a situation of physical juxtaposition more extensive than had ever before existed; and the collisions which had occurred in the West Indies were now threatening in other parts of the Americas.

The Seven Years' War, however, had taught the continental powers a lesson which should have been learned long before; it was that although colonies could be won for England by the battles of her allies on the continent, the rule did not apply with equal force to the other powers. In the previous wars, the employment of British forces on the continent had been negligible[128] and the government had

[127] Article 17.

[128] There is, of course, little available data on this. An exhaustive study made by the writer of troops actually employed in battle and the losses sustained bears out his contention. *Cf.* Moore, *International Law and Some*

been able to engage its military strength overseas while the winning battles in Europe which affected the partition of colonial possessions at the end of the war had been fought by Austrians, Prussians and Hollanders. The French and Spanish, on their side, had been obliged to carry on the wars with divided strength and the toll that the pacifications from Utrecht to Paris had taken showed the futility of this method.

The diplomatic isolation of England at the end of the war created a situation in which both France and Spain found hope for the future. Prussia had been definitely alienated from England by the latter's defection in an hour of need; Catherine II of Russia had indicated her resolve to remain neutral in future disputes; Austria was firmly allied to France. At the same time, the French had been left with few colonies to defend, and hence the division of military operations would be a much easier task than it had been in previous wars. There remained, however, the serious economic situation of France as the chief obstacle to a future conflict, and this Choiseul, with the aid of Spain, undertook to remedy.

That there would be a war with England in the near future seemed to be inevitable. At the time of the Louisiana offering, Choiseul wrote to Ossun that the task of the two nations was to devote themselves to the building of their navies and to resume hostilities in five or six years, this time forestalling their enemies. The Family Compact was admirably designed to promote the maximum of mutual assistance in the process of economic and military rehabilitation. Indeed, the significance of this instrument for the peacetime relations of France and Spain far exceeded its value as a wartime alliance. The formal abolition of the limitations of alienage upon the citizens of the two

Current Illusions (1924), p. 1 *et seq.;* Bodart, *Militär-historisches Kriegslexikon* (1908); and data in von Alten, *Handbuch für Heer und Flotte* (1909), 9 vols., *sub voce.*

countries, and their admission to equal rights in respect to trade, navigation and taxation, promised to remove the most difficult barrier to an economic revival.[129]

We have seen how the Spanish monopoly of the importation or exportation of goods to and from her colonies had resulted in a lively contraband trade in the Americas. Simultaneously, due to the decay of her industry and the exclusive employment of Spanish vessels in the overseas trade and the consequent necessity of relying upon other nations for finished goods and for their carriage to Spain, the same conditions of illegal trade had sprung up in Spain itself. The treaty of 1750 had given to the English the utmost facilities for exercising this sort of traffic. Choiseul now sought to gain for France this monopoly by the introduction of the free trade principle. At the same time Charles III, in a firm effort to bolster up his administrative and financial system, endeavored to force all business through the channels of revenue. Indeed, his programme went even further, for he sought to enjoin all special privileges hitherto exercised by foreign merchants. This programme brought the Spanish government into sharp conflict with the French, and it was only after a serious warning by Choiseul, to the effect that a war would find Spain alone, that a more satisfactory basis of relations was reached.

As a matter of fact, the irritation aroused by the effort to carry into practice the provisions of the Family Compact was supplemented by political friction that had no place in an alliance as intimate as the formal instrument asserted the relations of France and Spain to be. And yet both courts understood that their future salvation depended upon their determination to stand together. Besides, the consuming desire of France for revenge, not uncharacteristic of her policy

---

[129] On Choiseul's economic policy, *cf.* Blart, *op. cit.*, p. 43 *et seq.*, and Muret, *Les Papiers de l'Abbé Béliardi et les Relations Commerciales de la France et de l'Espagne au Milieu du XVIIIe siécle* (1757-1770) (in *Revue d'Histoire Moderne et Contemporaine*, vol. 4, 1902-1903, p. 657).

throughout the ages, commanded adherence to the Spanish alliance at any cost. These considerations were never forgotten by Choiseul, for he preached the gospel of the Family Compact even in the darkest days of his ministry. That the treaty did not fulfil what it had seemed to promise was due not to his lack of loyalty to his ally but to the suspicion and caprice of his sovereign.

CHAPTER V

THE COLONIZATION OF THE FALKLAND ISLANDS

THE Seven Years' War brought to England immeasurable territorial and economic riches, and one might assume that the energies of the nation would have been consumed in the absorption of these new acquisitions. This process of assimilation, on the part of the English, however, has always been a more or less unconscious one, and so we find the foreign policy of that nation devoted to the pursuit of minor advantages assured it by the treaty and to the quest of additional possessions, in part desired to buttress the lands already occupied, and in part intended as *points d'appui* for further expansion. To a certain extent the British government was driven to the pursuit of these objects by the political alignment on the continent, and by the unreserved expressions of dislike from all quarters that promised war in a short space of time, a conflict in which the British would have to stand alone. An attempt to remedy the situation by an effort to restore the good understanding with Spain, lately fostered by Keene and Wall, resulted in a repulse, the intent of which was obvious. In every other direction the paths to an alliance were closed and, except for the general economic exhaustion, the implications of the situation would have been most disquieting. At that, the restless activity of Spain and France to effect a reorganization of their affairs both externally and internally was full of foreboding for the future.[1]

In spite of his avowed desire to renew hostilities with England at an early moment, Choiseul was too shrewd to manœuvre himself into an *impasse* before he was ready

---

[1] Renaut, *Etudes sur le Pacte de Famille et la politique Coloniale Française* (*Revue de l'histoire des Colonies Françaises*, vols. 9-11, 1921-1923), part 2, p. 78.

again to take up arms. He applied himself, consequently, to the execution of the terms of the treaty as rigidly as the financial situation of France would permit,[2] and he sought to exact from Spain a similar fidelity in carrying out the Treaty of Paris in spirit as well as letter. Simultaneously Choiseul undertook to repair the French colonial empire[3] by the formation of new settlements in such localities as had not yet been occupied by other nations. In this latter part of his programme of reform he stood alone.[4] The French court was not in the least interested in colonial enterprises, for even during the war the heroic struggles overseas had failed to stir the group about the king. Individuals of political independence also displayed the same indifference to Choiseul's schemes, and hence, although his hand was free in this direction, he was obliged to perfect and execute his colonial designs without support from any outside source, relying largely for his success upon the intimacy of his contact with Louis XV. This situation, however, was fraught with embarrassment, for despite the fact Choiseul enjoyed a definite liberty of action in colonial matters, if his policies brought him into conflict with other powers he was likely to be left alone in maintaining what he might conceive to be French rights.

Choiseul's schemes for a colonial renaissance show the same lively imagination which characterized his conduct of diplomacy. Out of the wreck of the French overseas empire he dreamed of establishing French suzerainty over a chain of islands in the West Indies and in conjunction with a settlement in Guiana to found an Antillean empire. In the east he turned his attention to Madagascar and to revitalizing the remains of French settlements in India. At one time,

[2] *Ibid.*, p. 59.

[3] On Choiseul's policy the standard work is Daubigny, *Choiseul et la France d'outre Mer* (1892), but Renaut's work deals more fully with the international aspects of the matter.

[4] Renaut, *op. cit.*, p. 78.

too, he entertained hopes of securing a base in the Philippines, but in this direction his aspirations were speedily checked.

All of these designs involved a thorough renovation of the army and navy as well as of the finances of France. They involved, likewise, the most cordial coöperation of Spain and the absence of any dispute between the two crowns over regions that the French might desire to settle. At the same time, the success of Choiseul's ventures demanded the utmost circumspection in the conduct of his relations with England, not only to avoid a fatal collision at some isolated spot in the world, but to prevent the English ministry from embarking upon measures to prevent the realization of his desires. The Seven Years' War had marked the triumph of the British policy of annihilating French overseas strength and French maritime power. It would not require, at this time, a very decided impulse to bring about a renewal of warfare for the crushing of the desire in addition to the reality of imperial expansion. Furthermore, the mere fact that the British, too, were engaged in seizing likely places for colonial establishments was itself a circumstance that seriously hampered Choiseul, particularly as neither party was in a mood for amicable discussion.

An illustration of what has been said may be found in the clash between England and France over the Turks Islands,[5] a group forming a part of the Bahamas. These islands the Count d'Estaigne, governor general of the Leeward Islands, on May 26, 1764, ordered a subordinate to occupy for the purpose of suppressing piratical establishments. The British local authorities forthwith protested the occupation and the French governor replied that he was merely acting as the agent of the Spanish, who were the true sovereigns. The British government, however, reiterated the claims of its local officials, and Choiseul, unwilling at this

[5] *Ibid.*, p. 214.

moment to precipitate a conflict, was obliged to order a withdrawal. The Spanish, it may be added, supported the French by proving an antecedent recognition of Spanish sovereignty by the British; and as the latter were then engaged in cultivating Spanish friendship, the French colony was not immediately replaced by an English settlement.

In 1764 a far more serious dispute was pending between Spain and Great Britain.[6] It has been related how at the capture of Manila by a squadron fitted out by the East India Company, the victors had levied a huge contribution of four million pesetas, half to be paid on the spot and half payable in drafts drawn by the archbishop of Manila on the Spanish treasury. Only a million of the sum was actually paid over to the captors, as the latter had not entirely forgone the pleasure of pillage. The treaty had made no mention of the circumstance, as it was not known at the time the Peace of Paris was executed. The drafts, however, were presented for payment and were protested. The company then turned to the British government, and in February, 1764, Lord Rochford, the British ambassador at Madrid, opened the discussion of the matter with Grimaldi.[7]

The Spanish government maintained the view that the levy of a ransom as an exemption from pillage was a violation of international law and that the archbishop of Manila had had no authority to sign any capitulation or to draw drafts on the Spanish treasury. Having disposed of the legal validity of the convention of Manila, Grimaldi pro-

[6] On the origin of this dispute cf. Ayerbe, *Sitio y Conquista de Manila* (1897); Clowes, *The Royal Navy*, vol. 2, p. 239; Beatson, *Naval and Military Memoirs* (1804), vol. 2, p. 496; Hervey, *The Naval History of Great Britain*, vol. 5, p. 341; Blair and Robertson, *The Philippine Islands*, vol. 49. The expedition was sponsored by the East India Company.

[7] Renaut, *op. cit.*, p. 224. *Cf.* Secretary of War to Conway, July 30, 1765 (*Calendar of Home Office Papers, 1760-1765*), p. 582; Halifax to Draper, July 27, 1754, *ibid.*, no. 430; Halifax to Chairman East India Company, August 14, 1764, *ibid.*, no. 1414; Halifax to Wayland, October 7, 1763, *ibid.*, no. 1026.

ceeded to show that it had not been respected by the British even as a *de facto* arrangement. The British ministry, of course, rejected the Spanish view and the discussion dragged through the year 1764 into the fall of 1765. In September of that year the conversations between Grimaldi and Rochford were resumed,[8] and the ill-concealed choler of both negotiators seemed at the time to presage hostilities. At this juncture Choiseul entered the discussions, as he was loath to be embroiled in a war over an object which seemed to him of relative unimportance. He suggested arbitration, but although the Spanish court indicated its acquiescence in this suggestion, the British were unwilling to consider the submission of their interests to a third power.

Shortly before the Manila ransom had been brought up for discussion, Choiseul's quest of colonies had led him to consider an expedition to the Falklands. This was the first time that the colonization of the Falkland group had been seriously considered and Choiseul's attention had been undoubtedly drawn to them by the proposal of a young officer, Antoine Louis de Bougainville,[9] who had served with distinction under Montcalm at Quebec. Bougainville proposed to the Minister of Commerce that he undertake an expedition at his own expense assisted by his relatives, residents of St.-Malo, M. de Nerville and M. d'Arboulin. The St-Malo sailors and merchants were well acquainted with the Falklands, for they had named them Les Malouines after their

[8] Rousseau, *op. cit.*, vol. 2, p. 56. *Cf.* also Halifax to Deputy Governor of the Bank, December 13, 1763, *Calendar Home Office Papers, 1760-1765,* no. 1116; Halifax to Governor of Bank of England, January 4, 1764, *ibid.,* no. 1179. On the Spanish counterclaim, Marriot to Halifax, Report, October 23, 1764, *ibid.,* 1486.

[9] On Bougainville *cf.* Roy, *Bougainville* (1882); Goepp and Cordier, *Les Grands Hommes de la France (Navigateurs),* 1873; Desplantes, *Marine et Marins* (1912), pp. 10-107; Délambre, *Notice sur la vie et les ouvrages de Bougainville* (in *Inst. Mem. Sci., Math. et Phys.,* 1811, pt. 2); La Roncière, *Un Grand Navigateur Parisien (Rev. Hebdomadaire,* 1920), vol. II, p. 335.

own town, and Bougainville was doubtless privy to the local traditions regarding the islands. In any event, the government having indicated its consent to his plan, Bougainville equipped two ships, upon which he embarked the necessary supplies as well as a number of Acadian families.

Setting sail from St.-Malo on September 15, 1763, Bougainville touched at Montevideo and finally made land on January 31, 1764. Finding no good anchoring ground, the expedition sailed from the West Falkland to the East Falkland, where they entered what is now Berkeley Sound.[10] The place for the new settlement was selected on March 17, and a fort, St. Louis, was erected, together with several huts. Formal possession in the name of Louis XV was taken of all the islands on April 5, 1764, under the name of Les Malouines. Three days later Bougainville sailed for France, and left the small company of Frenchmen to face the cruel rigors of the southern winter.

Bougainville returned to his colony in January, 1765, and forthwith repaired to the Strait of Magellan to secure a supply of timber and young trees. He again left the colony in the following April and upon his arrival in France further colonists and stores were sent out, so that the number of settlers was raised to one hundred and fifty and the colony was in every sense well established.

The planting of the French colony had been observed by Spain with no little disquiet. When the two French ships had touched at Montevideo, the government at Madrid was apprised of the fact, and Grimaldi forthwith addressed the Conde de Fuentes, the Spanish ambassador at Paris, requesting him to ascertain the object of the expedition, drawing the attention of the French government to the fact that this was not the route to India and that the French officials

[10] Bougainville, *A Voyage Round the World* (Forster trans., 1772), vol. 1, p. 40; St. Germain, *Le Routier Inédit d'un Compagnon de Bougainville* (*Géographie,* vol. 35, p. 217), 1921; Pernety, *Histoire d'un Voyage aux Isles Malouines fait en 1763 et 1764* (1770).

in America should be advised that the Family Compact did not authorize this action.[11]

Choiseul's reply to this inquiry was disingenuous enough, for he stated that the ships had gone to the South Seas to discover an island which would facilitate the passage around the Horn, and that the commander was aware that he had no right to enter Spanish colonies or to traffic with them, his visit to Montevideo being occasioned solely by the necessity of repairs.[12]

By September, 1764, however, Grimaldi was in possession of the facts. He had in the interim determined to take steps to interest Charles III in the possibility of an establishment in the Falklands, for he was fully alive to the necessity of protecting Spanish trade by fortifying the islands which commanded the Straits and the Cape Horn passage.[13] Fuentes was instructed to represent to Choiseul that a French settlement at this place was prejudicial to Spain, for it would be the signal for the British to undertake a similar expedition. He was formally to request the abandonment of the station and to inform Choiseul that it was a mystery to Spain why the court had not been advised officially of a fact of which they had heard indirectly from Montevideo and the foreign journals.[14] It was proposed that there should take place a conference between the Duc de Choiseul, Grimaldi and Don Fernando Magallon, secretary of embassy, at which the abandonment of the French settlement and Spain's undertaking the settlement were to be discussed.[15]

The idea of surrendering his new colony was distasteful to Choiseul. The Spanish had placed their claim primarily

[11] Danvila, op. cit., vol. 4, p. 93. This was on June 11, 1764.

[12] Ibid., p. 94. Fuentes to Grimaldi, July 6, 1764.

[13] Ibid., p. 96.

[14] Renaut, op. cit., vol. II, p. 232. The notice first appeared in the Gazette de Hollande of August 13, 1764.

[15] Danvila, op. cit., vol. 4, p. 96.

on grounds of political expediency, but they also claimed as a legal ground the theory of territorial proximity[16]—a principle which we shall presently examine. These grounds were reinforced by an offer to purchase the settlement, a move which indicated that the Spanish were none too sure of the validity of their protest.[17] The French, at first inclined to rebuff all these overtures, eventually gave in. Bougainville, who had returned from his second visit to the Falklands, was dispatched in April, 1766, to Madrid to make his terms with the Spanish court.[18] These included the transfer of the islands to Spain and the payment to Bougainville of a sum by way of reimbursement and compensation.[19] This arrangement was ratified by France some

[16] Bougainville, *op. cit.*, vol. 1, p. 1.

[17] Renaut, *op. cit.*, p. 233.

[18] De Visme to Conway, May 19, 1766 (*R.O. State Papers, Spain*, 174). De Visme writes, "I find it is now agreed between the French and Spanish courts that the former shall renounce all claim to these Islands and that M. de Bougainville shall be reimbursed by Spain the expenses of his settlement, but this last matter is left to be finally adjusted by Count de Fuentes who sets out from Madrid this very day on his return to his embassy at Paris."

[19] The *Acte* for the release of the islands reads: "Moi, Louis de Bougainville, Colonel des Armées de Sa Majesté Très-Chrétienne, ai reçu 618,108 livres, 13 sou et 11 deniers, montant de l'Estimation que j'ai donné des Dépenses faites par la Compagnie de St. Malo, pour équipements et fondation de ses établissemens illégitimes dans les Iles Malouines appartenant à Sa Majesté Catholique, savoir:

"40,000 livres, payées en à compte à Paris par son Excellence le Comte de Fuentes, ambassadeur de Sa Majesté Catholique pour lesquelles j'ai donné quittance.

"200,000 livres qui doivent m'être comptées à la même cour de Paris, suivants des Traités souscrites en ma faveur par le Marquis Zambrano, Trésorier-Général de Sa Majesté Catholique, sur Don Francisco, Ventura Llovera Trésorier Extrordinaire de Sa Majesté.

"Et 65,625 gourdes, 3 quarts, equivalents aux 378,108 livres, 13 sous, 11 deniers dus aux faux de 5 livres par dollar que j'ai à recevoir à Buenos Ayres, en à compte de Lettres de change, qui m'ont été délivrées, tirées par son Excellence le Baylio Fray, Don Julian Arriaga, Secrétaire d'État

months later,[20] and Bougainville returned to Madrid[21] for the final arrangement. The matter of compensation was adjusted by Grimaldi in a liberal manner.[22] Two hundred thousand francs were to be paid at Paris, and the balance at Montevideo.[23]

It was at first intended that Bougainville should embark on a Spanish frigate which was to be sent with another to effect the transfer to Spanish sovereignty.[24] This, however, was not carried out, for the ships were sent ahead to Montevideo to await the arrival of Bougainville. The latter, hav-

du Département Général des Indes et de la Marine de Sa Majesté Catholique.

"En consideration de ces payemens, aussi bien que par soumission aux ordres de Sa Majesté Très-Chrétienne, je m'oblige a remettre en due forme, à la Cour d'Espagne ces Établissements, ainsi que les Familles, Maisons, Travaux, Bois de construction, Vaisseaux en chantier ou Employés à l'Expedition; et enfin, tout ce qui, sur les lieux appartient à la Compagnie de St. Malo, tel que porté sur l'Inventaire, ainsi que ce qui appartient à Sa Majesté Trés-Chrétienne, qui en fait la cession volontaire, renonçant pour toujours à tous droits que la Compagnie ou tout autre intéressé, ait su ou pourrait produire sur la Trésorie de Sa Majesté Catholique, sans qu'ils puissent à l'avenir faire aucune demande d'argent, ou compensation quelconque.

"En foi de quoi, je signe le present Acte et le garantis, comme étant un des principaux intéressés, aussi bien qu'autorisé à recevoir le montant de toute la somme, conformement au Registre minute du Département de l'État.

"A St. Ildefonse, le 4 octobre, 1766.   Louis de Bougainville."

British and Foreign State Papers, vol. 22, p. 1383. Note the admission of the illegal character of the settlement.

[20] De Visme to Shelburne, September 15, 1766 (*R.O. State Papers, Spain,* 175).

[21] Ossun to Choiseul, September 22, 1766 (*Archives des Affaires Etrangéres, Espagne,* 547, hereafter cited *Aff. Etr.*).

[22] Ossun to Choiseul, September 29, 1766 (*Aff. Etr., Espagne,* 547).

[23] Renaut, *op. cit.,* p. 223, states the total indemnity to have been 680,000 livres, 13 sous, and 6 deniers. This is made on the basis of Ossun's dispatch. Rousseau, *op. cit.,* vol. 2, p. 60, says the payment was made in *livres tournois.*

[24] Ossun to Choiseul, September 22, 1766 (*Aff. Etr., Espagne,* 547).

ing repaired to France, proceeded to fit out the expedition with which he encircled the globe, an exploit which has formed his chief claim to fame.

The frigate *La Boudeuse* bearing Bougainville arrived at Montevideo on January 31, 1767, and he thereupon proceeded to Buenos Aires to concert the necessary measures for the cession of the islands.[25] These were completed on February 8, 1767,[26] and the joint French and Spanish fleet set sail for the Falklands on February 28. After a stormy passage the French port was reached on March 25. On April 1, says Bougainville,

I delivered our settlement to the Spaniards, who took possession of it by planting the Spanish colors which were saluted at sun-rising and sunset from the shore and from the ships. I read the King's letter to the French inhabitants of this infant colony, by which his Majesty permits their remaining under the government of his Most Catholic Majesty. Some families profited of this permission, the rest, with the garrison embarked on board the Spanish frigates which sailed for Montevideo, the 27th in the morning.[27]

The new colony was placed under the governorship of Don Felipe Ruiz Puente, and the latter was made dependent upon the captain general of Buenos Aires.[28] The governor of the latter place was at this time Don Francisco P. Bucareli, a man of some independence of character, as we shall soon see.

While these things were transpiring, the British government was likewise manifesting an interest in out-of-the-way localities and its attention was turned to the Falklands. It has been suggested that this interest was stimulated by the failure of the Spanish government to settle the question of

[25] Bougainville, *op. cit.*, vol. 1, p. 13.

[26] Text in Groussac, *op. cit.*, Annex 1.

[27] Bougainville, *op. cit.*, vol. 1, p. 35. *Cf.* also Rapport de Bougainville (*Aff. Etr., Espagne*, 548).

[28] Quesada to Bayard, May 4, 1887, in Quesada, *Recuerdos de me Vida Diplomática* (1904), at p. 224, citing documents in proof.

the Manila ransom and by the desire to have an object of exchange in the event that the Spanish persisted in their refusal to honor the archbishop's drafts. On the other hand, it seems more likely, in view of the interest of Admiral Anson in the Falkland Islands and in view of the unremitting efforts of the British to share in the benefits of the South American trade, that the Falkland colony was intended as a permanent establishment, the chief purpose of which would be the preying upon Spanish trade in peace as well as in war. In any event, an expedition was organized in the spring of the year 1764, and on June 21 of that year Commodore John Byron on H. M. S. *Dolphin* with the *Tamar* frigate set sail from the Downs. Byron was the grandfather of the poet, and a man of great courage. He had earlier in his life performed the feat of crossing Patagonia[29] under circumstances of unbelievable hardship. He was chosen for his task, presumably, because of his familiarity with the regions.[30]

It was not until the ships had reached the Brazilian coast that the true object of the cruise was disclosed. The expedition, presumably destined for the East Indies, had actually been ordered to carry out the design long before projected by Anson. Byron was to call at "His Majesty's Islands call'd Falkland's and Pepys' Islands situate in the Atlantick Ocean near The Streights of Magellan in order to make better surveys thereof, than had yet been made, and to determine a place or places, most proper for a new settlement or settlements thereon."[31]

Byron shaped his course by the chart in Anson's *Voyage*, and after some difficulty he finally made Puerto Deseado. Using this place as a base, the expedition sought to locate

[29] Byron, *The Narrative of the Hon. John Byron, etc.* (1769), *passim*.

[30] Byron, *An Account of a Voyage Round the World* (*Hawkesworth Voyages*, vol. 1, 3d ed., 1785).

[31] Conway to Lords of Admiralty, July 20, 1765 (*R.O. State Papers, Spain, Supp.*, 253).

Pepys Island, using Halley's chart as a guide.[32] After combing the marginal seas for a week, Byron finally concluded that there could be no such island as Cowley had claimed he had seen,[33] and he accordingly set sail for the Islands of Sebald de Weert, which had been seen by enough vessels to make a landfall there more probable than at Cowley's Fata Morgana. Such storms were encountered, however, that Byron was obliged to make for land in order to secure wood and water. He entered the Strait of Magellan and proceeded as far as Port Famine.

On January 4, 1765, Byron left Port Famine to resume his search for the Falklands. Cape Virgins was passed on the eighth and on the eleventh land was sighted. This proved to be the island later known as West Falkland. Byron carried on comprehensive surveys of the coast of this island, naming several harbors and points, and using as his base a spot in Byron Sound that he named Port Egmont in honor of the first lord of the admiralty.[34] He writes: "Of this harbor and all the neighboring Islands, I took possession for his Majesty, King George, the Third, of Great Britain, by the name of Falkland's Islands."[35] It is interesting to note that Byron does not give the date on which he executed this formality.[36]

Byron left Port Egmont and coasted about the northern shores of the islands and past Berkeley Sound, at the end of which the French colony was snugly ensconced. As Byron had left Europe before the public announcement of the French occupation (August 3, 1764), he knew nothing of the settlement and he made no investigation of the sound

[32] Byron, *Account of a Voyage,* p. 28.

[33] *Ibid.,* p. 30.

[34] *Ibid.,* p. 58.

[35] *Loc. cit.*

[36] Brown, *op. cit.,* p. 395, note 146, cites a passage from the 1767 edition of Byron's book to the effect that the flag raising took place January 23d.

itself. Apparently he went no further than Cape Pembroke, for he deemed a point which he observed at 52° 3' to be the southernmost point of the island. He then sailed northward and then set his course for Puerto Deseado. Here he met with the *Florida,* storeship, which he later sent back to England with the news of his discoveries. It is an interesting circumstance that in the following month, Byron sighted the *Aigle,*[37] in which Bougainville was exploring the strait for wood for his colony.[38]

We shall consider elsewhere in detail the legal aspects of Byron's acts, by which he sought to assure British sovereignty over the islands. It is sufficient here to advert to what has already been said regarding these formalities and their total lack of legal portent. In addition to Byron's so-called act of possession, the surgeon of the *Tamar* "surrounded a piece of ground near the watering place with a fence of turf and planted it with many esculent vegetables as a garden, for the benefit of those who might hereafter come to this place." This act of benevolence is mentioned here because it was later used as proof of possession![39]

The *Florida,* storeship, reached England on June 21, 1765, and Byron's report of the islands and the intelligence that no signs of any people "either then subsisting or who had ever set foot thereon" moved the British gov-

[37] Byron, *Account of a Voyage,* p. 75.

[38] Bougainville, *op. cit.,* vol. 1, p. 41.

[39] It is proper to advert here to the account of the Falkland Islands dispute given in Brown, *Anglo-Spanish Relations in America in the Closing Years of the Colonial Era,* p. 387 *et seq.* Dr. Brown not only fails to deal critically with the geographical material, but is also wholly at a loss when discussing the legal aspects of the relations of England and Spain. It is indefensible that Dr. Brown's account of the settlement of the Falklands is so composed as to give the impression that the British expedition was the act necessary to ripen to sovereignty the so-called inchoate title supposed to be conferred by discovery. That the Falklands were *res nullius* and for this reason subject to the jurisdiction of the first occupant is totally overlooked.

ernment to plans for the immediate settlement of the region.[40] On July 20, 1765, Henry Conway, secretary of state for the Southern Department, addressed the lords of admiralty advising them of the king's decision that another expedition should be sent to the Falklands as soon as the weather would permit. This expedition was to consist of a frigate, a sloop and a storeship, the military equipment of the colony to be twenty-five marines. The commanders of the ships were to be instructed "that they do immediately compleat the settlement begun last year at Port Egmont, which they are to accomplish in all events." It is curious that the mere planting of a vegetable garden mentioned earlier in this note was considered by the secretary of state as the beginning of a settlement—and this circumstance discloses how anxious the British government was to utilize whatever facts might support its claim to the islands.[41]

The new colony was to have a ship constantly stationed as a protection, and the other vessels were to be employed in making surveys and to continue the search for Pepys Island, which the king did not as yet despair of finding and reducing to possession.[42]

The notice of the French settlement having been published, the instructions regarding this are of great interest. Conway states:

If any lawless persons should happen to be found seated on any Part of the said Islands, they are to be compelled either to quit the said Island, or to take the oaths, acknowledge & submit themselves

[40] Conway to Lords of Admiralty (*R.O. State Papers, Spain, Supp.*, 253).

[41] *Ibid.* Conway also states: ". . . if any savage people should be found inhabiting any of the said Islands, His Majesty directs that they shall be treated with the greatest Prudence & Humanity, invited by Presents and Kind Usage to trade, & prevailed upon by mild methods to enter into Treaty & to acknowledge His Majesty's Title."

[42] This quest continued until the 19th century. *Cf.* Angelis, *Colección de Obras y Documentos Relativas a la Historia Antigua y Moderna de las Provincias de la Rio de la Plata* (1837), vol. 6, no. 67.

to His Majestys government as subjects of the Crown of Great Britain.

And if, contrary to Expectation, the subjects of any Foreign Power in Amity with Great Britain, should under any real and pretended authority, have taken upon them to make any settlement of any kind or nature whatsoever upon any part or parts either of the said Falkland's or Pepys' Islands, the commanders of His Majestys ships aforesaid are to visit such settlement, and to remonstrate against their proceedings, acquainting them that the said Islands having been first discovered by the subjects of the Crown of England, sent out by the government thereof for that purpose, and of right belonging to His Majesty, and His Majesty having given orders for the settlement thereof, the subjects of no other power can have any title to establish themselves, therein without the Kings permission; acquainting them further, that they are directed to warn them off the said Islands & to transport themselves with their effects within a time limited, not exceeding six months from the day of the notice so to be given.

It is important to note, in view of the later proceedings, that Conway especially cautioned the admiralty that if "contrary to expectation"—which was of course utterly misleading—a settlement was found and no notice was taken of the warning the commanders should avoid "proceeding to measures of hostility or violence, unless compelled thereto by hostility or violence first committed upon them and in their own defence." This did not apply to Port Egmont, which was to be established and maintained at any cost. If a colony were found there, the settlers were to be warned off; and if they did not obey, a landing was to be effected and a joint settlement established without acts of hostility, the question of the future rights and possession of the place to be settled by the British king and the sovereign of the other colonists.

A further discussion of the project is contained in the note of Lord Egmont to the Duke of Grafton, who was then secretary of state for the Northern Department. Lord Egmont transmitted to Grafton the proofs of British title, requesting him to lay the matter before only those persons whose opinion could be taken in a matter "of this very great moment and of the most secret nature." The designs of Britain's policy were clearly and frankly set forth, and as the attitude of the crown regarding the possession of the islands was never substantially altered, we may look on Egmont's note as a remarkable exposition of British imperialism.[43]

After stating that the proof of title was complete, Egmont went on to say:

It [the perusal of enclosures] will also show the great Importance of this station, which is undoubtedly *the key to the whole Pacifick Ocean.* This Island must command the Ports and trade of Chile, Peru, Panama, Acapulco and in one word all the Spanish Territory upon that sea. It will render all our expeditions to those parts most lucrative to ourselves, most fatal to Spain and no longer formidable tedious, or uncertain in a future war. . . . Your Grace will presently perceive the prodigious use hereafter to be made of an establishment in this place by that nation who shall first fix a firm footing there.

Having adverted to the commercial advantages which were likely to accrue to Britain from an establishment on the Falklands, Egmont proceeded to dispose of the claims of Spain and France. Regarding the former, he said:

First, as to Spain, it is impossible that even their pretended title from the Pope's Grant or any Treaty (so far as I can recollect) can give them the least claim to an Island lying 80 or 100 leagues in the Atlantick Ocean eastward of the Continent of South America, to which it cannot be deem'd appurtenant. And the attempt of France to settle there seems to confirm this argument against all that can be urg'd hereafter by either of those powers to that effect.

With respect to France the 1st and 2nd Discoverys of this Island were both by the subjects and under the authority of the crown of G. Britain in the reigns of Q. Elizabeth and Charles the Second,

---

[43] Egmont to Grafton, July 20, 1765 (*R.O. State Papers, Spain, Supp.*, 253).

and the French never saw them till in the reign of Q. Anne. . . . It was many months after Capt. Byron's expedition was planned and 6 or 7 weeks after he had sailed that the first suspicion was entertained in England of any Design on the Part of France to attempt this island. In September, 1764 a paragraph in the foreign Gazettes first mentioned that some frigates were return'd to St. Maloes from visiting and exploring the coast there and in the month of March, last, the famous old voyager Frezier himself avowed to a person employ'd to view the Ports of France . . . that he had been consulted by the French ministers upon this undertaking and that 3 or 4 French Frigates were to be employ'd this summer to make the settlement. This being all that we have yet learn'd of the French intentions and coming to us from no avowed authority, and Capt. Byron so far as February last, having rang'd the coast for 200 miles in length and remain'd long upon it without finding the least trace of any possession taken by the French, we may either suppose the Intelligence above ment'd to have been such as deserv'd our notice or pretend a total ignorance upon the subject as it shall best suit the Conduct which His Majesty may think proper to hold upon this delicate affair.

Egmont, in ignorance of Conway's note of the same day, urged immediate action, for he feared that if the French really intended a settlement and the British took no action, the former would not only have a year's start and it might "then probably be out of our power to expell, at least without direct and avow'd hostilities which may bring on an immediate Rupture both with France and Spain, whereas (for many reasons too tedious to be inserted here) this will be less likely to ensue, if as things are now circumstanc'd we take our measures sooner or at least as soon as France."

The ignorance of the French settlement avowed by Lord Egmont seems extraordinary in view of the elaborate system of espionage which existed at this time, and yet we can only assume that Egmont was stating the case as he knew it. Certainly, the extreme secrecy with which the expedition was planned points to the correctness of Egmont's statement. In any event, the preparations for the expedition were pressed and in September the instructions for Captain John McBride, commander of H. M. S. *Jason,* were drawn up.[44]

In the main, the instructions followed the note of Conway to the admiralty. McBride was ordered to sail to the Falklands with the *Jason,* the sloop *Carcass* and the storeship *Experiment.* A blockhouse was to be erected and guns from the ships were to be mounted there and the fort manned by twenty-five marines. Regarding the attitude toward any alien settlement McBride was instructed as Conway had requested.

The British expedition arrived at the Falklands on January 8, 1766, nearly two years after the French had landed, and fourteen months before the Spanish took possession.[45] The settlement was made at Port Egmont and steps were taken to complete the survey. McBride sailed around the islands, but finding it impossible to make accurate surveys in a large vessel, he determined to finish his task in small boats as soon as the weather would permit. On the basis of this hasty examination of the archipelago, however, McBride reported that he had found no trace of the French settlement.

The rigor of the winter prevented further investigation of the presence of others, although McBride's curiosity was piqued by the discovery of a large burned area which Byron had fired, but which the former believed had been done by the French. He devoted himself to fortifying his post. On September 20, 1766, the survey was again resumed. The party landed on the eastern side of the island and having mounted the highest mountain found there a bottle containing a paper that had been left by some French officers who had previously been on that part of the island. The paper

[44] Secret Instructions to McBride, September 26, 1765 (*ibid.*).

[45] McBride to Stephens, April 6, 1766 (*R.O. State Papers, Spain, Supp.,* 253).

was endorsed on the back by other Frenchmen who had more lately been there. The admiralty had notified McBride on March 17, 1766, of the presence of the French and this notice he had just received.[46] He accordingly determined to visit the eastern part of the group to make certain.

On December 2, 1766,[47] McBride anchored in Pembroke Sound, and an officer having ascended a mountain overlooking Berkeley Sound, the French settlement was at last discovered. McBride at once sailed for Port Louis and on December 4, an officer was dispatched on shore with a note demanding by what authority a settlement had been erected there.[48] The French governor, M. de Nerville, unable to decipher the Englishman's note, sent a deputy, Captain Despierre, to McBride with a letter asking the intentions of the party. This was explained both verbally and by a letter in which all hostile intent was denied. On Despierre's return, steps were taken to defend the colony, and the next morning, McBride persisting in his advance, the governor sent out a second communication stating that he was there by his king's orders and that he cared nothing for who had discovered the islands, and if the English intended hostilities, he would defend himself, for he regarded them as the aggressors.[49]

McBride's progress up the sound had been impaired by contrary winds; these having shifted, he was finally able to land. He affirmed his intention to investigate the establishment and demanded the Frenchman's authority. Bougainville's commission, dated August 1, 1764, was exhibited, after which McBride proceeded to look over the settlement, the French offering no resistance. McBride delivered his

---

[46] Stephens to McBride, March 17, 1766 (*ibid.*).

[47] McBride to Stephens, March 21, 1766 (*ibid.*).

[48] Enclosed with Rapport de M. de Bougainville (*Aff. Etr., Espagne,* 548).

[49] *Ibid.*

warning to leave, and then departed for Port Egmont, whence he sailed in January, 1767, for England.[50]

There can be no question that under the existing state of the public law McBride's proceeding was highly irregular, Port Louis as a French colonial port was closed to foreign vessels, and after the warning not to enter this action of the English officer smacked strongly of aggression. The colony, however, was so soon afterward turned over to the Spanish, that the incident was important only in its bearing on the later events.[51]

The three maritime powers came to grips over the Falklands in a very hesitating and faint-hearted manner. This was due primarily to the circumstance that neither side was completely oriented as to what steps had been taken by the other to promote a colony in the South Atlantic. Moreover, there was a good deal of uncertainty, particularly in England, as to whether or not the Malouines and the Falklands were identical. The surveys of both Frézier, on whom the French chiefly relied, and Byron were incomplete, and there was no way of telling whether or not the English and French colonies were in the same group, particularly as both Byron and McBride in their first reports had stated that there were no settlements in the group. The best-informed were of course the Spanish, who claimed exact knowledge of the region, and who, because of the earlier intimation of the English that they wished to survey the islands, were in no doubt as to the overlapping of the claims of sovereignty.

We have seen how McBride had been informed of the French colony in March, 1766, and how the British government had been advised in May, 1766, of the cession to Spain of the Malouines colony of Bougainville. Up to this time no official notice of the existence of the French colony close be-

[50] McBride to Stephens, March 21, 1766.

[51] The French account corresponds in all important details with McBride's.

side the British establishment at Port Egmont had been received. In the preceding year, Lord Egmont, as we have seen, had denied any specific knowledge of it in rather specious language, and the report of McBride was added confirmation that there were no rival claimants to the islands. A short time after the news of the cession of the Malouines had been received, however, the question of the revictualling of Port Egmont and its probable effect on the relations to France and Spain arose in cabinet and here the full disingenuousness of the admiralty's proceedings was disclosed.

For our account of this meeting, we are unfortunately compelled to rely upon the dispatches of the French Chargé d'Affaires Durand, who, as he states, secured his details from a clerk in the admiralty to whom he paid £75.[52] Durand's account,[53] if it is to be relied upon, proves that the admiralty was fully aware of a French colony on the Falklands and the claims of France to sovereignty over the region and thus could not assert with any degree of justification the innocent establishment of a colony on an adjoining island. It is, consequently, easy to comprehend why England was driven to assert title by discovery—a ground which had never been recognized as valid.

The news of the revictualling expedition had reached France some time before its dispatch. On July 5, 1766, Choiseul, in his instructions to the London embassy, reflected rather bitterly that England expected by this expedition to show who was ruler of the seas, and he informed the embassy that the Spanish rested their case upon the Treaty of Utrecht. On August 15, Durand reported that there had been a meeting of the cabinet at which Egmont had stated with considerable force the motives which had prompted the last ministry to decide upon the establishment of a colony at the Falklands, and he had expatiated upon the

[52] Coquelle, Le Comte de Guerchy (Revue des Etudes Historiques, 1908, vol. 74), p. 461.
[53] Ibid.

advantages of sending the fleet which was then ready to sail. The Duke of Grafton denied the motives which Egmont alleged as the object of the fleet, and he showed how its departure could cause great difficulties. He stated that in the short time that he had been in office he had been informed of the efforts made by the French and Spanish to fortify themselves in settlements adjoining those which England desired to procure, and that the silence maintained by these powers seemed to denote a feeling of assurance that they were superior in case they should decide to oppose England. He added that the expedition might produce a rupture which it was in the interest of the nation to avoid, and that such expeditions were represented as having advantages when in reality experience proved the contrary.

Durand went on to say that the lord chancellor[54] and General Conway were of Grafton's opinion, and in order not entirely to reject Egmont's plan they suggested a delay of a week in which the council could prepare to take a vote. Egmont vigorously opposed this idea and insisted that Lord Chatham had approved the scheme during his last tenure of office. Chatham, however, said nothing and the meeting adjourned. Shortly, thereafter, Egmont handed in his resignation,[55] a step which the junior lords, Saunders and Keppel, followed.

It is interesting that Durand should have received from his informant a suggestion of how the British government would be pleased to treat with Spain and France. This suggestion was that the English should withdraw their establishments in consideration of a promise by the Bourbon courts that they would not occupy the islands.

[54] This was Lord Camden.

[55] There is no collateral proof of Durand's statements. *Cf.* further Winchelsea to Rockingham, August 3, 1766, in Albemarle, *Memoirs of the Marquis of Rockingham* (1852), vol. 2, p. 8; Bateson, *A Narrative of the Changes in the Ministry 1765-1767, Camden Soc. Pub.* (1898), p. 97; Winstanley, *Chatham and the Whig Opposition* (1912), p. 65.

The knowledge of these facts was shared by Prince Masserano, the Spanish ambassador, who proceeded to counsel his court that there should be no waiting or negotiation but that steps should be taken to destroy the colony before the English fleet could reach the Falklands, treating the English as persons without right, for their proceedings were pure aggression in the midst of peace, similar to the acts on the Mosquito coast. In view of the fact that Spain had not yet taken possession, Masserano's violent counsel was somewhat hasty, although it did not fail to produce effect at Madrid. In the interim, however, Durand sought to quiet his colleague and to have his court avoid the rupture.

Before a reply to his dispatch was received, Durand was able to notify his court[56] that after Egmont's resignation, Lord Chatham had broken his silence and had given support to the plan to continue the establishment at Port Egmont, on the ground that the opposition would be slight, that the fleet was equipped, and in any event that the expenses would have to be risked in view of the necessity of having a station at this place for use in time of war. Chatham's views met with no opposition, and so the dispatch of the fleet was determined upon, to take place within a week unless Spain and France should make some antecedent objection.

Shortly after the receipt of Durand's note of the twenty-third, Choiseul elaborated his instructions by directing Durand to advise Masserano that he should adopt a moderate tone toward England,[57] a device by which he hoped to avoid a precipitate step by the Spanish ambassador, while he applied himself to cooling the Spanish court, for at this juncture France was in no condition to engage in any sudden hostilities.[58] At the same time Choiseul informed the

[56] Durand to Choiseul, August 23, 1766 (*Aff. Etr., Angleterre*, 471).

[57] Coquelle, *Le Comte de Guerchy* (*Revue des Etudes Historiques*, 1908, vol. 74), p. 463. On Masserano, *cf.* Fernan-Nuñez, *op. cit.*, vol. 2, p. 311.

[58] The energetic disposition of Shelburne had not failed to impress Choiseul. Writing Guerchy early in August (11th) he described Shel-

British ambassador at Paris that Spain had claimed and obtained from France the Malouines "in consequence of the Treaty of Utrecht, as by it all but Spaniards are excluded from settling in that part of the World."[59] He adverted to what he claimed was an acknowledgment of the treaty by England in the incident of 1749, already related, when the objections of Spain had brought about the abandonment of the projected expedition to the South Seas. Lennox reporting the interview stated that Choiseul had added that the report of the destination of the fleet then fitting seemed to contradict the precedent, but that he would not take alarm until matters were further explained, and that he would give the same advice to the Spanish ministers.

The task of calming Charles III was by no means easy. At this moment Bougainville was in Madrid with the ratification of the agreement of cession, and the actual transfer of possession was yet to take place. Durand's notice of the departure of the English fleet had been forwarded to Madrid, and it produced the most profound uneasiness.[60] Charles III told Ossun that he failed to see just what effect the representations of Masserano would have. To Ossun the Spanish king seemed inclined not to tolerate the English establishment, and he shared Masserano's view that unless steps were taken forthwith to dislodge the English, it would become more and more difficult to do this. Ossun, fully instructed with regard to Choiseul's desire to postpone a war, on his own responsibility ventured to suggest to Charles that such steps would mean war, the greatest mistake that the two crowns could make, for they were not

burne's proposals as indiscreet and disquieting, and although he indicated that he would not easily yield to England's demands regarding the Manila ransom, Guerchy was ordered to explain the pacific intentions of France. Cited in Fitzmaurice, *Life of Shelburne* (1876), vol. 2, p. 8, *cf.* Hist. MSS. Comm., *Third Report,* appendix I, p. 142.

[59] Lennox to Shelburne, September 17, 1766 (*R.O. State Papers, France,* 271).

[60] Ossun to Choiseul, September 22, 1766 (*Aff. Etr., Espagne,* 547).

ready to engage in any contest. The wisest course under the circumstances was for Spain to preserve her rights by representations and protest. In the meantime the two powers were to proceed with their preparations until they were in a position to fight on a basis of equality and after they had concerted their plan of attack. On the same day he notified Choiseul in some detail as to the state of Spain's preparations for a naval war, and his account bore out the wisdom of his advice.

Charles III, however, was not easily moved by his ally. Up to this time Choiseul's task had been not merely the cultivation of a close political and economic relationship with Spain, but also the assumption and maintenance of a sort of political tutelage, by which France would have more or less complete direction of the course of Spanish diplomacy. This purpose had been included in the general design of the Family Compact, and it was fostered by Choiseul after the Peace of Paris largely as a means of holding in check Charles' bellicose inclinations until such a time as a war would result in some profit to France. The abrupt refusal of Charles to accede to the British demands in the Manila ransom case, as Choiseul had counselled him to do, demonstrated how slightly the French had succeeded in their design. That the British had not acted more energetically at once justified the wisdom of Charles' course in the premises, and gave him reason to suppose that a similar stand in the new crisis over the Falklands would meet with equal success.

We have seen that Choiseul instructed Durand on September 15 to advise Masserano to use moderation in his demands on England. This instruction he forwarded without delay to Madrid and it was at once laid before Grimaldi.[61] The latter informed Ossun that he, personally, was quite of Choiseul's opinion and that the course which Louis XV and his council had advised seemed to be the wisest

[61] Ossun to Choiseul, September 29, 1766 (*Aff. Etr., Espagne,* 547).

and most practical, as it gave both courts time to prepare for war if this was inevitable. Ossun's fears that the king would not accept the French plan of action was, however, for the moment dispelled, as Charles III expressed his approval of the instructions to Durand.[62]

Before this information reached France the new intelligence from England served still further to disquiet Choiseul. Masserano had approached Lord Shelburne, who was now secretary of state, and had made inquiries regarding the British designs. Shelburne had disclaimed any knowledge of these matters and added that England would observe the treaties.[63] Subsequently he added,[64] however, that the Treaty of Utrecht, which restored navigation to the *status quo* of the reign of Charles II, *merely regulated the acts of individual subjects and not of the states themselves.* It was absurd, he said, to forbid Great Britain not only the navigation of the Atlantic, but of the South Seas as well. Without admitting the existence of the colony, Shelburne stated that things had gone too far to be abandoned and that without regard to consequences the ministry would adhere to their plans. In the English version of the interview, Shelburne is reported as saying that "if the Spaniards in talking of their possessions included the American and Southern Seas and our navigation there gave occasion to them to suspect a war he had no hesitation to say that he would advise one if they insisted on renewing such a vague and strange pretension long since worn out."[65] The conversation terminated with a request from Shelburne that Masserano prepare a memorandum, to which he would reply by writing. The Spanish ambassador answered that he

---

[62] *Ibid.,* fol. 149. The advice of Choiseul that an additional squadron of ships be sent by Spain to the South Seas was rejected by Grimaldi as he claimed that South America was adequately provided with troops.

[63] Coquelle, *op. cit.,* p. 463.

[64] Durand to Choiseul, September 26, 1766 (*Aff. Etr., Angleterre,* 471).

[65] Cited in Fitzmaurice, *op. cit.,* vol. 2, p. 7.

had been prepared to do this, but he had not thought of using this means of demanding the justice due his king, preferring to use the mode of informal amicable discussion as being less subject to inconvenience.[66] Shelburne had nothing to say to this, but he continued his animadversions against attempts to limit British navigation, and asked what were the limits of Spanish possessions; for, said he, it was for Spain to prove her rights to the Falklands, as England had many navigators who could testify as to her own rights.

Durand's reflections on these conversations are very apposite. Commenting on Shelburne's original complaint that Spain had said nothing about the original British expedition—which, however, was not correct[67]—Durand inquired why, if the Falklands and the Malouines were identical, England had not protested against Bougainville's occupation. At the same time he conceded that all reasoning was futile, as England was obviously ready to go to war rather than give up her colony,[68] and that Chatham was taking the lead in the matter.

On October 2 Choiseul proceeded to reinforce his instructions to Ossun by a direct communication to Grimaldi.[69] Masserano's account of his interviews with Shelburne had been exhibited to Choiseul by the Spanish ambassador at Paris, Conde de Fuentes, and he therefore deemed it necessary that the two courts should come to an understanding regarding the steps to be taken in what he conceived to be an exceedingly delicate situation.

In the first place, he believed that, *salva dignitate,* it was necessary to avoid a rupture for a period of eighteen

[66] It is precisely this desire of all the parties to commit nothing to writing which makes the negotiation difficult to follow.

[67] Masserano had made representations to Richmond, a fact of which Shelburne was not advised.

[68] Shelburne said that Anson had died of chagrin because the Falklands were not seized.

[69] Choiseul to Grimaldi, October 2, 1766 (*Aff. Etr., Espagne,* 547).

months. Secondly, it was of first importance for France to put off a break as long as possible in order to avert the disasters of the last war, when fifteen thousand sailors were taken before the declaration of war. Under the existing system, commerce had to be suspended in order to have sailors for employment in the navy, and consequently the date of the opening of hostilities would have to be fixed.

As far as Pitt's desire for war was concerned Choiseul expressed great doubt whether the great Englishman could force one, unless a pretext were given him, despite his obvious enjoyment in and desire for the rôle of war premier. This pretext Choiseul proposed to avoid. Spain, he wrote, had two causes of complaint against England which were common to France in relation to a war which they might occasion. The first of these was the Manila ransom. The suggestion that this matter be arbitrated seemed to him the wisest course, and any difficulties England might make as to arbitration or the arbiter could easily be met.

The second cause of complaint was the new English colony.[70] It seemed important to determine where the colony was situated before making complaint, and hence he reiterated his previous suggestion that a Spanish fleet of investigation be sent to the South Seas, and if a colony were in "such and such locality," to destroy it at once, because it was easier to discuss a possession already destroyed than one which was to be destroyed. A more dangerous and frivolous proposal could scarcely be imagined.

Choiseul's next remark reflects the annoyance he still felt over the Spanish demands for the cession of the French colony. "If," said Choiseul, "the English establishment is on the Falklands and consequently not in the South Sea, I do not believe that the 8th article of the Treaty of Utrecht is opposed to it, at least unless it can be shown that there were Spaniards on the islands in the time of Charles II.

[70] Other writers have failed to indicate that this document was the lodestone of Spanish policy thereafter.

Read the eighth article with care my dear confrère and if you are neutral and bound to judge the matter impartially I believe you will be at a loss to apply the article to the Falkland Islands unless someone presents titles of ownership at the time of Charles.''

There was, according to Choiseul, another matter to be considered, *i.e.*, to what extent the English colony actually injured Spain and whether the injury was comparable with the injuries which a successful war always entailed. If it could be shown that this injury was more harmful than a war, then the two countries should go to war in eighteen months; their conduct would have to be different if a contrary view was taken.

The plan of action suggested for the present was that Spain should send to the South Seas various vessels which were to depart singly for different places and then to assemble at a distant rendezvous for the purpose of clearing out all settlements made in contravention of the treaties. Before the news of this expedition had reached Europe Spain and France would be ready to fight.

With regard to the immediate policy of France, Choiseul wrote that it had been decided by Louis XV that the Comte de Guerchy, who was returning to London forthwith, should act in concert with Masserano on all the points under discussion between England and Spain. Guerchy was instructed to speak to George III regarding the statements made to Durand, and to advise the king of England that the king of France was bound by treaty and by his particular relations with Charles III to enter into war as soon as the latter might be forced into hostilities. The king of France, moreover, felt that it was in his own interest that he should discuss and enter into all matters which might involve Spain in war. Guerchy was to add that Louis was as much inclined to peace as was Charles, and was doing everything he could to avoid setting the spark to war and that it was for this reason that when Bougainville's settlement had been protested Louis had not taken advantage of his royal cousin's affection to request the continuance of the French establishment. Furthermore, although Louis would not hesitate to make any sacrifice essential to the maintenance of peace, it was necessary that England should also do so, for all the sacrifices could not be made by Spain and France, and that other powers should not acquire in times of peace what they could scarcely acquire in war. France wanted peace, but she would not buy it.

While Guerchy was taking these steps, Choiseul wished to ascertain whether Grimaldi would speak firmly to England and supply the *mémoire* which had been requested—a step which Choiseul advised against—or whether he would temporize, sending an expedition to the South Seas and continuing to negotiate verbally. In any event, Masserano should not present a *mémoire*. In a postscript was added the warning that if Grimaldi prepared for war and sent a fleet to America, the expeditions should be contemplated only for the South Seas and not the Falklands.

This letter is in many respects a complete guide to the policy of the two powers not only in the immediate negotiations, but in the action taken later. Several things interposed to prevent Spain from adopting Choiseul's advice at once, but later developments were merely the execution— with Spanish emendations—of the plan outlined at this moment.

Grimaldi had already committed himself to a delay of a year and a half before Choiseul's letter was written. But this decision was reached evidently in the face of some opposition. On September 15 the powerful Conde de Aranda had drawn up a memorandum on the Spanish rights in which he rebutted the points regarding article VIII of the Treaty of Utrecht raised by the English and later by Choiseul.[71] His memorandum was in many respects similar to that of Prince Masserano, who had written from London on

[71] Danvila, *op. cit.*, vol. 4, p. 108.

August 11 urging the necessity of immediately destroying the English settlement. The hesitation of France to go to war was, however, the determining factor, and the policy of temporizing was decided upon while preparations for war went on.

The instruction finally sent to Masserano was colored more by the pacific advice of Choiseul than the belligerent counsel of de Aranda. Grimaldi stated that Byron's expedition and its results were known to Spain from the public prints, and that the project of an expedition for the settlement of a colony in the regions of the Strait of Magellan explored by him had likewise come to the knowledge of the government. If these things were true, the intent to strike a mortal blow at the Spanish crown and its rights was manifest to the king.[72] By the Treaty of Peace of Utrecht, which was the political foundation of Europe, Spain had recognized the British reigning house and the British had recognized the Spanish, and for this reason as well as others it was proper that both crowns should respect and not contravene the terms of the instrument. Article VIII of the treaty had assured to Spain the exclusive possession of the Americas and the adjacent islands, to the extent that her hands were tied against permitting the alienation of any part of these possessions. It had been England who had exacted these conditions, and England in the past had given proofs of the recognition of the obligation of observing the article. In 1740 England had resisted a project of Russia to make discoveries in the Pacific and had openly declared that Spain was the absolute mistress of the Pacific and England her surety. The instance of 1749 and the fact that Louis XV had agreed to the abandonment of the Bougainville colony to Spain were cited as further evidence of the validity of the Spanish claim. Masserano was instructed to present to the king the most solemn protest in the name of Charles III and to state that the latter would never consent to the pro-

[72] *Ibid.*, p. 115, for text.

jected establishment either in the Malouines or in any other place in the vicinity of the Horn, and that he would prevent them at any cost in spite of his grief at being under so cruel a necessity. The dispatch ended with a compliment to George III's sense of justice and a devout expression for the preservation of peace.

The expectation aroused by Choiseul that France would vigorously second the efforts of Spain to dislodge the British from the Falklands, provided nothing was done to incite hostilities, was not, in fact, realized. Just as the Spanish had gone further in their protest than Choiseul had counselled them, so the French ambassador at London failed to act with the determination that Grimaldi anticipated. On October 21 Grimaldi informed Fuentes that Durand had given Masserano to understand that France would not make war for this dispute, and Choiseul was compelled to renew his assurances that France would stand by the Family Compact.[73]

Undoubtedly what Masserano wrote had been due to a misapprehension, for already, on October 18, Choiseul had instructed Count de Guerchy, in a dispatch which is unfortunately lost in the archives,[74] that he should inform George III that the French would stand by the Spanish. This Guerchy at once communicated to Masserano.[75] The latter had not yet received instructions from his own court, so it was decided to suspend making a formal declaration to Shelburne, but Guerchy was to visit the latter and advise him of the interest France took in Spanish affairs and to draw him out on his reaction to French interference.

At the first conference between Shelburne and Guerchy both parties were eager in their protestations of friendship. Guerchy stated that he had no important business to discuss, being in a somewhat different situation than Spain,

[73] Blart, *op. cit.,* p. 89.

[74] Coquelle, *op. cit.,* p. 465.

[75] Guerchy to Choiseul, October 24, 1766 (*Aff. Etr., Angleterre,* 471).

in whose affairs his king, by reason of treaty and blood-relation, was much interested. Shelburne had nothing to say to this—a fact which pleased both Guerchy and Masserano, as the secretary of state had previously told Durand that he did not wish France to interfere in Anglo-Spanish disputes.

On the same day Masserano also called upon Shelburne. The Spanish ambassador raised the question of the English establishment on the Falklands and remarked very bluntly that it was taking a possession from Spain and that although he had not yet received instruction on the subject, his court would certainly be astonished at such an undertaking. Shelburne replied evasively that the colony was a small object compared with the great possessions of Spain in the Indies, and that the English settlement should be a matter of indifference to Spain. He then adverted to the Manila ransom, in an obvious effort to change the course of the conversation, and remarked that *this* was an affair of real importance which he hoped Masserano would impress upon his court. To this the latter replied that his master had done all that could be reasonably expected of him when he had offered to submit the matter to an arbitrator and had even gone so far as to suggest a prince who was not suspected by Great Britain.

The suggestion that the Manila ransom be arbitrated had been advanced in the preceding July and the prince suggested as arbitrator had been the king of Prussia.[76] The British government through the Duke of Richmond had at once rejected the proposal as compromising to the dignity of the British crown. Incidentally, the refusal to agree to the proposal brought disastrous consequences to the northern European policy of England, for Frederick looked on the refusal as a slight to himself, and resolutely declined to entertain proposals for an alliance.[77] It is true that the

[76] Maltzan to Frederick II, July 1, 1766 (*Politische Correspondenz Friedrichs des Grossen,* vol. 25, p. 159).

[77] Fredrick II to Maltzan, August 10, 1766, *ibid.,* p. 189; and August

English based their refusal as much upon the determination not to permit Spain to subject the question to further delay as upon a deep-seated aversion to arbitration. This attitude, however, not only rendered the settlement of the question more difficult, but weakened the diplomatic position of England on the continent still further.

A more ingenious solution, however, had occurred to the English government. At a meeting of the cabinet on October 16, 1766,[78] it was decided that the Manila question could be linked with profit to the Falkland Island issue, and it was this resolution that Shelburne now proposed to Masserano. Choiseul in his note of October 18 had made a similar suggestion as a means of protracting the negotiations, and it was a circumstance of importance that the same idea should have been advanced independently by England. Shelburne suggested that although he was not willing to submit the Manila ransom to arbitration, he was willing to join the two causes. He then asked Masserano whether he believed that his court would consent to submit them both to arbitration. Masserano answered cautiously that he had not used these words in reference to the establishment on the Falklands, as he was without instructions from his court. Moreover, the two causes were of a different nature and had to be treated separately.

It is curious that Masserano should have been so evasive, as Guerchy had previously told him of Choiseul's suggestion of uniting the two causes, as a convenient solution which would save the point of honor involved in both cases. Masserano, however, had told the French ambassador that in spite of his desire to settle both affairs he thought Choiseul's proposal really involved the purchase of England's

23, 1766, *ibid.*, p. 197; Mitchell to Conway, September 13, 1766, *ibid.*, p. 217; Maltzan to Frederick II, October 3, 1766; Frederick II to Maltzan, October 15, 1766, *ibid.*, p. 265; Mitchell to Conway, December 1, 1766, *ibid.*, p. 316.

[78] Von Ruville, *William Pitt* (1905), vol. 3, p. 230.

forbearance, and the compounding of an infraction of article VIII of the Treaty of Utrecht. The consequence of this would be that the English would sometime later put another colony on the islands. Guerchy pointed out to Masserano that Choiseul really contemplated in his proposal that England recognize Spanish right under article VIII, but the Spaniard said he believed the English would never consent to such a proposal. In this opinion Guerchy was inclined to agree, in view of the fact that Shelburne had suggested the submission of both cases to a third power, a device not contemplated by Choiseul, and he consequently proposed to sound out Lord Chatham before pursuing the matter further.

It may be because, as one writer states, the Earl of Hertford[79] had first brought this suggestion to England from Choiseul that the British ministry expected to accomplish the solution of these two troublesome questions in the manner suggested. In any event, Shelburne, in his next conference with Guerchy, on November 2, again refused to arbitrate the Manila case alone[80] and when Guerchy finally had his interview with Chatham, the latter showed no disposition to offer different terms from those advanced by Shelburne. In fact, at a second conference, on November 22,[81] Pitt suggested that the evacuation of Port Egmont would take place only after the Manila ransom had been paid and Spain had conceded the English freedom of navigation in the South Seas.

This latest addition to England's bill of particulars did not tend to facilitate negotiations. Early in November Choiseul, confident that a break had been averted, had told Rochford, the English ambassador, that the credit for avoiding a crisis was his, that he had dissuaded the Spanish from adopting violent language, and that he could settle

[79] Renaut, *op. cit.,* p. 235.
[80] Coquelle, *op. cit.,* p. 466.
[81] *Ibid.*

the question in a half-hour if it were left to him. This remark, of course, seemed to indicate a speedy settlement
along the lines suggested by Shelburne, particularly as
Masserano had disclosed the passionate attachment of
Spain for the Falklands, and had implied a willingness to
make substantial sacrifices for the evacuation of Port Egmont. At almost the same moment, however, that Chatham
had laid bare the underlying purpose of the British demands—free navigation of the South Seas—Guerchy had
undertaken to explain to Shelburne how Choiseul really believed a joining of the Manila and Falkland questions would
settle the pending disputes. This was, in brief, an abandonment of the Falklands in exchange for the payment of the
Manila ransom subject to France's arbitration of the
amount.[82] Shelburne, on the other hand, insisted that there
could be no arbitration of the Manila ransom, but that its
full payment would be accepted as a set-off for the immediate abandonment of the Falklands.[83]

Both sides had now advanced their claims to a position
where further negotiation seemed useless, and this might
indeed have been the case had Lord Rochford at Paris not
misunderstood his instructions. He interpreted Shelburne's
refusal to arbitrate simply to apply to the question of principle and not to the amount,[84] a course which even Spain did
not wish to pursue.[85] This mistake was fortunate only inasmuch as it gave Choiseul further time to persuade Spain to
adopt a course of moderation, and he so far succeeded in
his programme of delay that on January 20, 1767, Grimaldi
definitely instructed Masserano[86] to avoid any appearance

[82] Shelburne to Rochford, November 29, 1766, and December 12, 1766,
in Fitzmaurice, *op. cit.*, vol. 2, p. 13.

[83] Shelburne to Rochford, November 29, 1766, Hist. MSS. Comm.,
Third Report, appendix I, p. 135.

[84] Shelburne to Rochford, January 2, 1767, *ibid.*

[85] Shelburne to Rochford, January 23, 1767 (*R.O. State Papers,
France,* 272).

[86] Cited in Rousseau, *op. cit.,* vol. 2, p. 66.

of brusqueness and to keep the British ministry engaged with all sorts of expedients while the two courts prepared for war. Obviously there was no serious intention on the part of Spain to acquiesce in an exchange of Port Egmont for the Manila ransom. The negotiations on the proposal, however, had continued both at London and Paris. Choiseul sought to manœuvre the British back to their original suggestion of an arbitration of both causes and at the same time toward a reduction of the ransom. Shelburne, however, was not inclined to permit the English interests to be subjected to judicial decision where their legal rights were so open to question. He instructed Lord Rochford, who was now British ambassador at Paris, that no idea of arbitration was contained in Choiseul's first offer, nor could he believe that it was meant, as George III had repeatedly declared his objections to this process to the Spanish when they had suggested Frederick II as arbiter in the Manila ransom case, for he regarded this mode of settlement "as unbecoming His Dignity as well as the justice of His Demands." As for a reduction in the amount of the ransom, Shelburne refused to consider it.

The British appear to have assumed that France had some direct interest in the evacuation of the Falklands, and for this reason placed a good deal of confidence in Choiseul's project for the settlement of the pending questions with Spain. The identity of the Falklands and Malouines was known in England, as was the fact that Bougainville had ceded his colony. Nevertheless, when the Duc de Praslin, in the absence of Choiseul, informed Rochford[87] that Bougainville had gone to turn over the Malouines to the Spaniards, the latter was overcome with astonishment that the French should restore the islands to the Spaniards while negotiating the Manila ransom on the basis of the British desisting in their pretensions to the Falklands. It is

[87] Rochford to Shelburne, February 12, 1767 (*R.O. State Papers, France*, 272).

impossible to say whether Choiseul had, during this period, made any pretense that the French still possessed an interest in the Falklands that would be of service in making the Spanish more inclined to accept his proposed settlement. During the first months of the year 1767, however, Choiseul was faced with the situation where he would have to abandon his rôle of mediator and assume the duty of an ally.[88] As soon as this resolution was taken, therefore, the failure of his earlier scheme was certain, for it had involved lending a temporary diplomatic support to the English in order to bring the Spanish around to an agreement. The announcement to Rochford of the transfer of possession may consequently be regarded as marking the change in Choiseul's position. Unquestionably this news was bound to effect a change in the diplomatic situation, because hitherto the discussions had been proceeding on the theory that the British occupation of Port Egmont was a violation of the principle of the closed sea and *status quo* established by the American Treaty of 1670 and the Treaty of Utrecht. Once the Spanish were in possession under an agreement of cession by which they succeeded to the rights of an occupant anterior to the British, the legal aspects of the question were completely changed, and the Spanish position was immeasurably strengthened. At the same time, the presence of a Spanish settlement increased the possibility of actual collision.

The idea of exchanging the Manila ransom for the Falklands never found favor with the Spaniards, because in both cases it was conceived that a point of honor was involved. We have seen that the scheme had not met the approval of Prince Masserano, and as his opinion was in high favor at the Spanish court, it is not surprising that his continued opposition to Choiseul's peace plan, as well as his avowed espousal of a war for the Falklands, affected the course of Spanish diplomacy. Masserano was as firmly of

[88] Renaut, *op. cit.,* vol. 10, p. 236.

the opinion that England was in no mood for war as was Choiseul that Chatham could not continue a ministerial existence without a conflict; but the fact that Chatham was totally disabled by a stroke rendered Masserano's view more plausible.[89] The latter was convinced that the Manila ransom ought not to be paid, and as these ideas coincided with Charles' the prospect of immediate war drew nearer.

The Spanish court had been advised in September, 1766, that war could not be declared for a period of eighteen months, and although both Grimaldi and Charles had agreed in this conclusion, they apparently determined to hasten hostilities. In November, 1766, Grimaldi had addressed to Choiseul a voluminous report[90] on the state of the Spanish army and navy and outlined a comprehensive scheme of operations which should be undertaken in 1768. Such an enterprise was the matter furthest from Choiseul's mind; but the Spanish were to learn this indirectly.

After the receipt of Grimaldi's instructions of January 20, 1767, Masserano was advised by the Comte de Guerchy that France could not be prepared before the end of the year 1769. The consternation caused by this report when it reached Madrid is easily imagined. Ossun hastened to report it to his superior, adding the comment that Spain would not take any steps to oust the British from their establishments in the South Seas without the previous approval of France.[91] In regard to an alleged British colony on the Bay of St. Bernard on the Gulf of Mexico, Grimaldi was under the impression that France had approved the use of force in ejecting the English colonists without a preliminary complaint at London.

Upon the receipt of this disquieting information from Spain Choiseul immediately instructed Ossun[92] that far

[89] Ossun to Choiseul, March 5, 1767 (*Aff. Etr., Espagne,* 548).
[90] Blart, *op. cit.,* p. 91.
[91] Ossun to Choiseul, March 5, 1767.
[92] Choiseul to Ossun, March 24, 1767 (*Aff. Etr., Espagne,* 548).

from agreeing with the opinion of Masserano that the English did not expect the payment of the ransom, he believed that the whole question depended on Chatham's own interest, and that the East India Company was doing what it could to have the matter treated as one of the important state questions. Regarding the year in which they would go to war, Choiseul stated that when the French had announced they would open hostilities in the course of the year 1768, the idea had been that they would be in a position to operate in the beginning of the year 1769. In any event, the French would be ready for war when Spain would be obliged to fight, but it could not be denied that the two courts would be more ready to fight in 1770 than in 1769 and more ready in 1769 than in 1768. This intelligence Ossun was to convey to Grimaldi.

Before the arrival of this note in Madrid, the Spanish government had taken the first steps in its programme of ecclesiastic reform.[93] On April 2, 1767, a royal proclamation was published banishing the Jesuits from Spain. As this measure was directed not merely against the Society of Jesus, but was intended as a move in a plan to reduce the spiritual and temporal power of the Roman church, it is easy to understand that the Spanish crown for over two years was completely absorbed in these internal questions and that colonial and foreign problems were relegated to a second place.

The refusal of France to be drawn into an immediate war had convinced both Grimaldi and his king of the futility of precipitating a conflict at this moment. Moreover, the Manila question was practically removed from the field of diplomatic discussion in the early part of 1767, just as Masserano had predicted. The latter had again informed the British government that Spain had no intention of paying the ransom, and although this refusal was by no means a

[93] Blart, *op. cit.*, p. 95 *et seq.;* Rousseau, *op. cit.*, vol. 1, p. 117; Danvila, *op. cit.*, vol. 3.

new development in the situation, the British government apparently dispaired of securing a payment. Partly for this reason and partly for the reason that the Spanish had proceeded no further in their protests against the Falkland Islands settlement, which England could regard as a real compensation for waiver of further claims, Sir James Grey, the new British ambassador at Madrid, was instructed on June 26, 1767, on the Manila ransom, as a matter of minor consequence.[94] Grey arrived in Madrid in October, 1767. At this time the burning question between the two courts had to do with an illegal entry of British warships into Havana harbor, and hence the minor matters with which Grey was charged were not pressed.[95] The Havana incident in its turn passed into the limbo, but the colony at Port Egmont remained a blot on the scutcheon of Spain which was not forgotten, and which was soon to be removed.

It is proper at this point, before proceeding to the relation of the crisis which arose over the Falklands in 1770, to examine the legal claims of each side to the islands in the light of international law as it had been practiced up to this time.

The questions of discovery and occupation in international law prior to the year 1625 have been discussed in some detail, and we have seen, moreover, how the fact of possession, about which the doctrine of occupation pivots, became the foundation of all the international discussions and arrangements relating to colonies throughout the seventeenth and eighteenth centuries. The theory that possession was the only true index of title was applied also in the principle of *uti possidetis,* and found the most far-reaching expression in the American Treaty of 1670, which was in

[94] Text in Renaut, *op. cit.,* p. 237.

[95] Brown, *op. cit.,* p. 377, gives a résumé of the incident. Dr. Brown does not apparently understand the international legal status of the colonial system, for she inclines to the view that a right of entry could be established by prescription in the face even of treaty provisions.

substance reëxecuted in the Treaty of Utrecht. It is no-where to be found that the so-called doctrine of discovery, in the sense of merely finding without taking possession, was advanced by any state and successfully maintained prior to this time. As far as international practice was con-cerned, therefore, Great Britain as well as Spain would be obliged to rely upon occupation to support a claim to sover-eignty over the Falklands; and Spain had, in addition to these general grounds, the American Treaty of 1670 and the Treaty of Utrecht to support her rights.

Up to the time of the Seven Years' War the text writers had accepted the doctrines promulgated by Grotius,[96] and as these rules were those which states actually applied, there was no discordant element in the law, as sometimes happened after the science of international law fell into the hands of the natural law doctrinaires of the seventeenth century. In 1758, however, appeared the first edition of Vat-tel's *Droit des Gens*,[97] in which for the first time legal va-lidity was attributed to an act of discovery as a means of acquiring sovereignty over territory. In the *Institutions du Droit de la Nature et den Gens* of Christian Wolff[98] had oc-curred an obscure passage which furnished Vattel with his text. This passage is as follows:[99]

. . . if some one encloses a territory within bounds, or destines the land to some use by an act not merely transitory, or he who declares upon the land so enclosed, in the presence of other men, that he in-tends the land should belong to him, takes possession.[100]

[96] Pufendorf, *The Law of Nature and Nations* (Kennet trans., 1749), bk. 3, c. 6.

[97] Vattel, *Le Droit des Gens* (Lond., 1758), bk. I, c. 18, paragraph 208.

[98] Wolff, *Institutions du Droit de la Nature et des Gens* (Luzac ed., 1772).

[99] *Ibid.*, paragraph 213.

[100] Luzac commenting on this says, "We do not find this sort of occupa-tion in Roman law. It is upon this that are founded the rights which sov-ereigns assume by virtue of discoveries."

Vattel, whose work is really a vulgarization of Wolff's, rendered this passage as follows :[101]

All mankind have an equal right to things which have not yet fallen into the possession of any one, and those things belong to the person who first takes possession of them. When, therefore, a nation finds a country uninhabited, and without an owner, it may lawfully take possession of it, and after it has successfully made known its will in this respect it cannot be deprived of it by another nation. Thus, navigators going on voyages of discoveries furnished with a commission from their sovereign and meeting with islands or other lands in a desert state have taken possession of them in the name of the nation; and this title has been usually respected, provided it was soon after followed by a real possession.

The effect of these statements upon later writers was indeed far-reaching,[102] although Vattel elsewhere limited his language by stating that the law of nations did not acknowledge the property and sovereignty of nations over unin-

[101] Vattel, *op. cit.*, bk. I, c. 18, paragraph 207.

[102] Twiss, *Law of Nations* (1861), vol. 1, p. 162; *The Oregon Territory* (1846); Hyde, *International Law* (1922), vol. 1, p. 167; Hall, *International Law* (5th ed.), p. 101, who speaks of discovery giving an "inchoate title." This, of course, is senseless. If Hall means a legal claim which occupation perfects into a right he at least would be clear, but equally wrong.

A recent and sweeping assertion of the view that discovery confers a right of sovereignty has been made by the United States in the Palmas Island arbitration. As the claim is supported by incomplete research as to the nature of Spain's assertions of right to her former possessions, the conclusions of the American agent scarcely deserve serious consideration. It is characteristic of the whole argument that Chief Justice Marshall's opinion in Johnson v. McIntosh (8 Wheat 543) is cited in the belief it has some value as an authority on discovery. Marshall's decision in a domestic issue is scarcely authoritative in an international case, particularly as historical facts were completely ignored by the Chief Justice. "The Island of Palmas Arbitration," *Memorandum of the United States* (1925), esp. p. 51 *et seq.* Cf. also *The Counter-Memorandum of the United States*, and *The Counter Memorandum of the Netherlands* (1926), the latter a very weak production.

habited territory except actual possession were taken; and he added that where navigators had found in desert regions monuments erected by others to show possession had been taken these signs were as little regarded as the regulations of the pope in dividing the world.

It is interesting that in spite of the qualifications which Vattel put upon his theory, the notion that mere discovery could give title found so much favor among certain nations. An examination of the note of Lord Egmont referred to in the preceding pages, at once raises the presumption that it was written with reference to the passage from Vattel. Not only does Egmont stress the fact that the British navigators had been regularly commissioned by their sovereign, but he also seeks to show that their discovery was first in point of time. Moreover, the attempt to explain Captain Byron's expedition as an undertaking to perfect the supposed inchoate title given by discovery demonstrates that the admiralty was trying to lend its plans the color of right as explained by Vattel.

Nothing could be further from a correct exposition of the law than Egmont's note. Even assuming he was correct in believing that discovery could give a good title, it was by no means certain that the islands had been discovered by Englishmen, and, in any event, as nearly two centuries had passed since Davis and Hawkins had been in these regions, it would require a stretch of the imagination to regard either Byron's or McBride's expedition as the prompt taking possession which Vattel declared was necessary.

In the nineteenth century, when disputes arose over the right of states to lands discovered in the previous centuries, the rule applied was that conflicts of right were determined by the law of nations understood at the time of discovery.[103] This rule has every dictate of reason to commend its soundness, and if we apply it to the situation under discussion, there can be no doubt but that the English claim was totally

[103] Moore, *A Digest of International Law,* vol. 1, p. 259.

devoid of any legal foundation. Not only was discovery repudiated by the maritime states throughout the sixteenth and seventeenth centuries as a ground of acquiring sovereignty, but the text writers were also uniform in rejecting it as the basis of a claim of right. Moreover, if we assume that the law to be applied was that which obtained in the eighteenth century our answer is no different. The passage from Wolff cited above obviously had reference to *inventio* (discovery) in the Roman law sense of the word, and not as it was subsequently understood in international law. Wolff expressly required an anterior act of delimitation to give his declaration of intention any legal significance. What he had in mind was evidently an act by which a claimant to a considerable stretch of territory, having established himself at one point, could affirm in some valid way his sovereignty over a region too extensive to be immediately occupied effectively. This was really what the treaties of the seventeenth and eighteenth centuries sought to do when they fixed a *status quo* and defined the regions within which the colonial activity of states could be carried on. Wolff was by no means referring to a situation such as existed on the Falklands, where, until Byron set foot on the shore a year after Bougainville, no act of formal possession had been executed by any of the British navigators; and even Byron failed to delimit his territory, assuming the rule of Wolff would apply in such a case.

It has already been intimated that Vattel's rule of discovery was not a correct statement of the law at the time it was announced; that is, if we regard the law to be what was actually practiced and not what some publicist might announce it to be regardless of the acts of states. Indeed, at the time, Vattel stood alone, and except for the deference accorded to his views by the British and by later writers whose knowledge of law was not always beyond reproach, his doctrine would have passed into the discard.

Some fifteen years before the Falkland dispute arose

British and French commissioners met to discuss the title to Santa Lucia, pursuant to the Treaty of Aix-la-Chapelle.[104] The current British view of the law is clearly set forth in the memorandum submitted by the British commissioners. There had been a British settlement on Santa Lucia which was given up in 1640 under stress of circumstances and with no antecedent intent to abandon the place. The following month a French settlement was placed on the island. The British claimed prior occupation and involuntary relinquishment *sine animo direlinquendi*. The case really turned upon the question of abandonment, but what is said regarding the acquisition of sovereignty clearly shows that the British lawyers had no idea that discovery played any part in this process.[105] Indeed, as they rested their case upon the views of Grotius and Pufendorf,[106] it is difficult to see how the argument would be different.

This being the law applied in practice, it is strange that the doctrines of Vattel, announced only seven years later, could be treated with respect as an authoritative statement of the law. Certainly no lawyer would be inclined to defer to Vattel's view, although it might serve to furnish political claims with a disguise of pseudo-right.[107]

In view of what has been established regarding discovery, there is little doubt but that the validity of the British claim to the Falklands as against the Spanish would have to rest upon anterior occupation, and this leads us to an examination of the eighth article of the Treaty of Utrecht in its bearings upon the present case.

The intent of the eighth article was, as we have seen, to

[104] *The Memorials of the English and French Commissioners concerning Sta. Lucia* (London, 1755).

[105] Esp. at p. 63.

[106] Citing l. 4, c. 6, § 7: *Igitur regulare est ut occupatio verum mobilium fiat manibus, rerum soli pedibus. . . . Vidisse autem tantum aut scire quid sit nondum at possessionem sufficere iudicatur.*

[107] Both the English and French Commissioners speak of the discovery of Sta. Lucia, but not as the foundation of right.

leave navigation in exactly the same state that it had been in the time of Charles II of Spain and to establish a territorial *status quo,* the motive for which was the exclusion of France from any commercial or territorial benefits in the Americas. Consider the following clause:[108] ". . . it is by common consent established as chief and fundamental rule that the exercise of navigation and commerce to the Spanish West Indies should remain in the same state as it was in the time of the aforesaid King Charles II." Permission was to be withheld to France or any nation whatever to sail to any of the dominions of Spain in America. Moreover, "neither the Catholick King nor any of his heirs, and successors whatsoever *shall sell, yield, pawn, transfer or by any means under any name alienate* from them and the Crown of Spain to the French *or to any nation whatever* any lands, dominions or territories or any part thereof belonging to Spain in America." The British, moreover, agreed to guarantee the observance of the *status quo* of Charles II.

We have already considered at great length the meaning of these clauses and the manner of their observance throughout the period of their vigor. It is clear that the Spanish regarded any approach to their dominions in the South Atlantic and Pacific as an infraction of the terms of the treaty, and that their protests were in general effective. Shelburne's idea that the treaty had application only to individuals was, of course, specious, for the very terms of the instrument indicate that concessions to foreign states and not merely individual subjects were intended to be prohibited. Moreover, as the Spanish themselves correctly held, the 1749 incident was rightly to be interpreted as an admission of the restriction of navigation in the South Atlantic —and this despite the reservations of language made by the British government. Under such an interpretation of the treaty, therefore, the conclusion is inescapable that an expedition to the Falklands was in direct violation of the

[108] Art. 8.

terms of the Treaty of Utrecht and of the express guaranty pledged by England in 1713.

There remains to be considered the question of whether the actual settlement of the region was in derogation of the Treaty of Utrecht. By no perversion of fact is it possible to regard the Falklands as a part of the Spanish dominions as they existed during the reign of Charles II. The mere circumstance that they were known to Spain, as alleged, would not be sufficient to constitute them a part of the domains of the king. Whether or not this could be effected under a theory of geographic propinquity is difficult to say. Such a rule was observed in regard to outlying and unsettled regions of *terra firma,* as, for instance, in the case of the Scotch settlement at Darien. Its applicability to a group of islands lying as far from the coast as the Falklands seems too broad an extension of the rule, unless we revert to the dictum of Bartolus regarding islands, a statement which was the chief and only expression of law on the subject. In this relation, however, it is proper to remark that, considered in connection with the existing prohibition on the navigation of the southern waters, there is some justification for regarding the Falklands as included in the *status quo* agreement embraced in the Treaty of Utrecht; for if access to the place was denied, *a fortiori* a colony was not to be considered.

The precise meaning of the Treaty of Utrecht also enters into consideration in determining as between England and Spain the priority of occupation. The fact is incontrovertible that France settled the islands nearly two years before the English colony reached Port Egmont, and as between these two states there can be no question but that the French as the first occupiers had established a right to the islands, and that the British settlement was in derogation of French sovereignty. The Spanish, however, looked upon the French as intruders, and hence in taking possession of the French colony in 1767 they might well have regarded their own acquisition of sovereignty as original and not derivative through any act of cession, for the French evacuation was no more than a recognition of the anterior sovereignty of Spain. If the Spanish occupation of 1767 was the original act by which Spain acquired sovereignty, then the British occupation of 1766 was a prior act and the Falklands as *res nullius* were theirs by prior occupation. This, however, was not the case, for Spain did not claim the occupation of 1767 as the basis of her title. Furthermore, the British, not recognizing the Treaty of Utrecht as applicable, were bound to regard the French occupation as prior and the Spanish deriving their title through France, for whatever passed between these two was as to the British *res inter alios acta,* and they could regard the transaction as simply an act of cession. The Spanish, however, not wishing to compromise their position under the Treaty of Utrecht, chose to posit their case squarely on the eighth article of this instrument, but there can be no question that from the legal point of view the better claim was of a derivative sovereignty from the French, simply for the reason that the law of occupation was better defined and was free from the political shadows that rendered the legal meaning of the treaty obscure.

Briefly stated, the position of the two states was as follows: Great Britain claimed a right by discovery and by occupation, insisting that the Treaty of Utrecht did not exclude her from settling in the South Atlantic; Spain claimed a right by occupation and the sole privilege of making settlements in this region under the Treaty of Utrecht. Leaving aside the contentious point of the application of the Treaty of Utrecht, the British right rested merely on discovery, a wholly unsupportable ground, for the Spanish, having succeeded to any title of the French, were in law to be treated as prior occupants. On the other hand, if we admit the treaty applied, the whole British position is demolished.

From what has been said there can be no doubt but that at the beginning of the year 1770 the British were on the Falklands without the least color of right and that their act in making settlement was one of pure aggression, involving not merely a denial of the validity of a previous settlement by another power, but likewise the repudiation of a solemn treaty engagement which had subsisted for over a half-century. This was the view of the Spaniards and it was from a deep-seated conviction that an injury had been inflicted upon them that they proceeded to assert their own better right.

CHAPTER VI

THE DIPLOMATIC CRISIS

FREDERICK THE GREAT on one occasion characterized Choiseul as a man of *esprit,* but frivolous.[1] The counsel conveyed by Choiseul to Grimaldi in October, 1766,[2] that Spain should send an expedition to the South Seas to clear them of intruders certainly justifies this caustic judgment, even if we assume, as was certainly not the case, that Choiseul had an immediate desire for war. We have seen how the Spanish had allowed themselves to be lulled into a state of quiescence by promises of French coöperation in a war to be commenced after the lapse of eighteen months, and that the suppression of the Jesuit order had engaged the attention of the Spanish court for a considerable period of time.

There can be no doubt that after the receipt of Choiseul's note of March 5, 1767, in which the latter sought to postpone war indefinitely and to avoid the obligations of the Family Compact, the Spanish court realized that if anything were to be done about the Falklands it would have to be on its own motion, and Choiseul's aid sought only after he was faced with a *fait accompli.* Consequently, long before the Jesuit imbroglio was settled, steps were taken to act upon the earlier suggestion of Choiseul, and on February 25, 1768,[3] an order was sent to Bucareli, the captain general of Buenos Aires, by the Bailli Arriaga in the following terms:

His Majesty orders me to charge you that no English establishments are to be permitted, and you are to expel by force any already set up if they do not obey the warnings, in conformity with the

---

[1] This is somewhat milder than Frederick's usual characterization of the French Foreign Minister. He usually referred to him as a trickster.

[2] Choiseul to Grimaldi, October 2, 1766 (*Aff. Etr., Espagne,* 547).

[3] Text in Danvila, *op. cit.,* vol. 4, pp. 112-113.

law. You need no other orders nor instructions, and in observing these measures you will consider nothing except your own troops and those of the occupants in order that you do not expose yourself in case of inferiority to failure. In such a case or in anticipation of other bad consequences which your excellency can deduce from the state of the province you will resort to protests and accusations declaring that no action will be taken until the king has been informed and his orders received.[4]

The man to whom these instructions were addressed was perfectly capable of supplying the deficiencies of detail. Bucareli was both able and energetic, and although he did not hasten to carry into effect his new instructions, when he finally acted his course was calculated to put the best face on a transaction that was deliberately hostile.

Whether or not Bucareli's delay was due to instructions from Madrid is unimportant. Danvila[5] states he had not been able to act, because of the weather and because the data of the exact location of the British settlement given him by the home government were equivocal.[6] In any event,

[4] *Cf.* also the earlier instruction, Arriaga to Bucareli, December 29, 1766, on the taking of an island by the British, Argentine-Chilean Arbitration, *Esposición de Chile,* vol. 1, p. 83, and apéndice I, no. 12, and the orders to the Chilean government, *ibid.,* p. 85. On Bucareli *cf.* Fernan-Nuñez, *op. cit.,* vol. 2, p. 311.

[5] Danvila, *op. cit.,* vol. 4, p. 97.

[6] It was well known that the coasts of the Falklands were dangerous and the weather treacherous. This may explain the curious fact that the Spanish had not completed their survey of the islands. Moreover, when we consider McBride's difficulty in finding the French settlement, it is easy to understand that the Spanish had trouble in finding Port Egmont. On December 29, 1766, Arriaga advised Bucareli that there was a British colony in these waters, and he ordered the latter to find it and to warn the colonists that they were there in violation of the law (Angelis, *Memoria Histórica sobre los Derechos de Soberanía y Dominio de la Confederación Argentina* [1852], Document 13). February 7, 1767, Arriaga again wrote stating that M. Guyot of the *Aigle* had asserted that if the British were on the Malvinas they could not be found. Accordingly it was suggested that search be made elsewhere (*ibid.,* Doc. 14). Arriaga wrote again on

an expedition was finally prepared consisting of the frigates *Santa Catalina* and *Santa Rosa,* and the xebec *Andaluz.* This fleet sailed in December, 1769, having on board two Englishmen who claimed they knew the situation of Port Egmont.[7] This precaution, however, proved to be unnecessary, for when Bucareli's expedition reached the Puerto de la Soledad, it was greeted with the news of the final discovery of the English settlement.

It appears that in the month of November, 1769, the governor of the Spanish colony, Ruiz Puente, had dispatched a schooner to make a survey of the islands. On the twenty-eighth of that month the pilot, Angel Santos, fell in with Captain Hunt of the English settlement, who was likewise making a cruise.[8] Hunt, pursuant to his instructions, warned the schooner off. A few days later the schooner reappeared at the place where Hunt was anchored, bearing an officer with letters and presents from Ruiz Puente. The latter expressed to Hunt his surprise that the Englishmen should have been so wanting in respect to the Spanish king as to have compelled the pilot to put about, and he requested an answer to his letter.[9] A second letter from Ruiz Puente bearing the same date stated as follows:[10]

August 21, 1767 (Doc. 15), but Bucareli had already replied on the sixteenth explaining why he had not yet acted, and on January 24, 1768, he wrote Arriaga that an expedition had been sent (Doc. 17). On May 2, 1768, Bucareli stated an expedition had been sent to Tierra del Fuego (Doc. 20), and on December 30, 1768 (Doc. 23), he gave notice of another reconnaissance.

[7] There were evidently two or three English sailors, one of whom was one Peter Farrow or Sparrow. There is a considerable correspondence over him in the Spanish archives, for he did not dare return to England, where his wife was destitute.

[8] Hunt to Stephens, June 3, 1770, in *Papers Relative to the Late Negotiation with Spain and the taking of Falkland's Island from the English* (1777) (hereafter cited *Falkland Papers*), p. 10. *Cf.* also Coleman to Grenville, March 4, 1770, *Grenville Papers* (1853), vol. 4, p. 505.

[9] Ruiz Puente to Hunt, November 30, 1769, *Falkland Papers,* p. 10.

[10] Ruiz Puente to Hunt, November 30, 1769, *ibid.,* p. 13.

Supposing, as I really do suppose, your being on these coasts to be purely accidental and that on the first formal warning given you by the said officer to depart, you will totally lay aside all thoughts of any further stay or sailing in these parts; there is no need of enlarging on the matter as you very well know the contrary to be an absolute violation of good treaties and a breach of faith.

The exquisite courtesy of language with which Ruiz Puente garnished his communication made no impression upon Captain Hunt. The latter, writing in the time-honored manner of the bluff sea captain, stated in reply:[11]

In return I am to acquaint you, that the said Islands belong to his Britannic Majesty, my master, by right of discovery as well as settlement, and that the subject of no other power whatever can have any right to be settled in the said Islands without leave from his Britannic Majesty, taking the oaths of allegiance and submitting themselves to his government, as subjects to the crown of Great Britain. I do, therefore, in his Majesty's name and by his orders warn you to leave the said island in order that you may be the better enabled to remove your effects you may remain six months from the date thereof, at the expiration of which you are expected to depart accordingly.

Captain Hunt did not merely express his determination in writing. The Spanish Lieutenant Don Mario Plata who brought the Spanish protest was told that he would be fired on if he prosecuted his commission to survey the islands and he was particularly forbidden to enter the harbor of Port Egmont. Against this treatment Don Mario protested in writing, and in turn he warned Hunt that the latter's entry into La Soledad would be taken as an insult.[12]

These proceedings were reported to the governor and he again addressed Captain Hunt,[13] demanding that he and his

[11] Hunt to Ruiz Puente, December 10, 1769, *ibid.*, p. 15.

[12] *Ibid.*, p. 16. *Cf.* Don Mario's second protest, December 18, 1769, *ibid.*, p. 20.

[13] Ruiz Puente to Hunt, December 12, 1769, *ibid.*, p. 17.

command quit the islands, as he had produced no license to navigate or to make settlements, and that a further stay was in violation of treaty. Captain Hunt's rejoinder was merely a reiteration of his previous ultimatum.[14]

When Bucareli's squadron was advised of what had transpired, Don Fernando de Rubalcava, in command of the *Santa Catalina,* set sail together with the *Andaluz* for Port Egmont, where he arrived on February 20, 1770. He at once addressed to Hunt a letter[15] in which he expressed his surprise at finding a British settlement, asserting that such a proceeding was in violation of treaties which allowed no intrusion into the king of Spain's dominions. Accordingly, he protested against the usurpation of the coasts and announced that he would take no action until he had his king's orders. Hunt replied,[16] stating that the islands belonged to his Britannic Majesty by right of discovery, and warning the Spanish to evacuate. On this occasion he failed to set a time limit.

Rubalcava stayed at Port Egmont eight days and then departed. Meantime, the *Santa Rosa*[17] had been dispatched to Buenos Aires with news of the first encounter with the English, and the *Andaluz* soon followed with the notice of Rubalcava's encounter. Hunt sailed for England in March, 1770, and arrived at Plymouth early in June, 1770.

Bucareli at once took steps under his *plein pouvoir* to organize an expedition sufficiently strong to reduce the British settlement if opposition were offered, and to meet the resistance of any possible reinforcements. The expedition consisted of four frigates and a xebec. Don Juan Ignacio de Madariaga was put in command. On board were some 1,400 troops, one fifth of which were seasoned veterans. After invocations proper to such an extraordinary under-

---

[14] Hunt to Ruiz Puente, December 16, 1769, *ibid.,* p. 19.
[15] Rubalcava to Hunt, February 20, 1770, *ibid.,* p. 21.
[16] Hunt to Rubalcava, February 20, 1770, *ibid.,* p. 20.
[17] Danvila, *op. cit.,* vol. 4, p. 97.

taking the squadron set sail from Montevideo on May 17, 1770.

On June 4, 1770, Madariaga on the *Industria* anchored in the bay of Port Egmont. He addressed a note to Captain William Maltby[18] and "intimated" that the English quit the islands, otherwise he would be obliged to resort to hostilities. At the same time a letter was addressed to Captain George Farmer[19] to the same effect, and the next day (June 9) a third note was dispatched addressed to the two English officers jointly.[20] In this communication Madariaga stated that under the existing law no colonies could be made in these regions without the consent of the Spanish king, and he demanded withdrawal, which, if peacefully carried out, he would facilitate as far as possible. A failure to comply with his demand would, he stated, compel him to resort to hostilities, a step which Hunt's conduct fully justified him in undertaking without notice. He terminated his letter with a warning that operations would begin unless the British capitulated within fifteen minutes after the receipt of his demand.

By this time Madariaga had been joined by the other ships of the expedition. Farmer, who was in command, had already taken steps to defend the island[21] and he ordered the frigate *Favourite,* which was the sole protection of the island, to move in nearer the shore. The Spanish then threatened to fire on her. The Englishmen, however, ignored the threat and Madariaga fired two shots over the vessel. While preparations for defense were carried on, Farmer addressed a letter to the Spanish commander, requesting that he leave.[22] Meantime, the latter's ultimatum arrived, and

[18] Madariaga to Maltby, June 8, 1770, *Falkland Papers*, p. 24.

[19] Madariaga to Farmer, June 8, 1770, *ibid.,* p. 29.

[20] Madariaga to Maltby and Farmer, June 9, 1770, *ibid.,* p. 31. The Spanish commander evidently wanted to be sure he was slighting no one.

[21] Farmer to Madariaga, June 8, 1770, *ibid.,* p. 30.

[22] Maltby to Stephens, September 22, 1770, *ibid.,* p. 23; Farmer to Madariaga, June 9, 1770, *ibid.,* p. 34.

to this Farmer made a short and spirited reply, rejecting the terms of surrender. Madariaga at once landed his troops, fired at the blockhouse, and although the English returned the fire, they were shortly compelled to hoist a flag of truce and to agree to surrender.

The terms of the capitulation[23] provided for the surrender of the blockhouse and the rest of the settlement. The troops were allowed to fly their colors until embarkation, and to transport on their ship everything that could be carried off. The *Favourite* was to stay in port for twenty days after Madariaga had dispatched a frigate with news of the surrender, and to insure this delay the rudder of the ship was to be removed.

The happenings at Port Egmont have been related in some detail because, as often happens in international conflicts, the pettiest incidents are the source of most acrimonious disputes. Both crowns found in the conduct of the commanders of their opponents' forces acts which wounded the national honor, and hence the merits of the dispute were complicated by the absolute refusal on the one hand or the other to give way.

It has been related that Hunt arrived in England two days before the first Spanish demand was delivered to Captain Farmer. The rumor was at once about in London[24] that the Spanish had compelled the English to evacuate. This the government took pains to deny, although it was clear to the ministry, in the face of what had occurred in February, that matters were proceeding to a new crisis. The most discreet silence was observed, and even Prince Masserano was advised merely that there had occurred something on the part of the Spanish commander. The French Chargé d'Affaires Francés, a man of no mean ability,[25] had, however, so far succeeded in ferreting out

---

[23] The full capitulation is in *Falkland Papers*, p. 36.

[24] Francés to Choiseul, June 15, 1770 (*Aff. Etr., Angleterre*, 492).

[25] On Francés cf. Anson, *Memoirs of Augustus Henry, Third Duke of*

the facts that he was able to report to Choiseul an accurate summary of what had occurred, although, of course, Captain Hunt's original ultimatum to the Spanish was not known.

At this moment Lord North was at the head of the British ministry and Lord Weymouth, a person of mediocre talent, was secretary of state for the Southern Department. Chatham had long before resigned, and the vicissitudes of his successors in office had spread abroad the conviction which was not at all unfounded, that the present government was weak and incapable of pursuing a vigorous policy.[26] There can be no doubt that the spectre of Chatham heading the British government in the prosecution of a war had had a quieting effect upon Choiseul four years before, when the Falkland dispute had first come to life. In fact, as we have seen, he had not failed to impress upon Grimaldi the dangers of precipitating a war with England as long as Pitt was in command. At the present moment, however, the persistence of trouble in the American colonies and the vacillations of the ministry seemed to promise weaker opposition.

Francés, on the other hand, was by no means deceived by the fact that failure to deal adequately with internal problems necessarily implied a weakness in foreign policy, much less in war. He did not hesitate to express to Choiseul the belief that, although the ministry were not disposed to war over the Falkland settlement, from pride and weakness they would not dare abandon the colony, particularly as Chatham headed the opposition which would seize upon any

---

Grafton (1898), p. 256; Walpole, *Journals of the Reign of George III* (1894), vol. 4, p. 137: "This (Francés) was a very shrewd artful man who had privately sometime before his public appearance lived here unknown for three years, in which time he made himself master of our language and affairs. He was the confidential creature of Choiseul." *Cf.* on the reception of the news in England, Whately to Grenville, June 10, 1770, *Grenville Papers*, vol. 4, p. 518.

[26] Winstanley, *Lord Chatham and the Whig Opposition*, p. 320 *et seq.*

such act as a means of discomfiting the government. Furthermore, Chatham had denounced the acts of Spain (as they were then known) as a declaration of war and he had openly charged the ministry with having taken no steps for three years to avoid the incident.[27]

As far as public opinion was concerned, Francés reported it to be disinterested and generally leaning to the view that England had no right to the islands,[28] but that the establishment, having been made, could not honorably be abandoned. Francés, however, was of the opinion that if the British should undertake a war it would be a particularly risky undertaking for the present ministry.

The receipt of Francés' dispatch found Choiseul in what the Spanish would have described as a receptive mood. He had recently been advised of an insult to the French flag at Chandernagor in India,[29] and the intelligence conveyed to him from London, involving as it did the interests of his ally, must have struck him as offering a rare opportunity to effect a humbling of England that would satisfy both crowns. Whether or not Choiseul at this moment actually considered going to war it is difficult to say. In any event, he instructed Francés on July 7, 1770, to present a demand for reparation for the Chandernagor incident, and on the same day he addressed both the Marquis d'Ossun[30] and Grimaldi regarding the situation. Having stated that a demand for satisfaction had been served on the English, he desired to learn what Grimaldi thought of the matter and what information he would furnish regarding the Falkland incident of February.

At this moment Choiseul's political fortunes were in a

[27] Walpole, op. cit., vol. 4, p. 77. Cf. Thackeray, op. cit., vol. 2, p. 197.
[28] This was Walpole's view. Walpole, op. cit., p. 113.
[29] Flammermont, Le Chancellier Maupeou et les Parlements (1885), p. 156.
[30] Choiseul to Grimaldi, July 7, 1770 (Aff. Etr., Mémoirs et Documents, 575).

parlous state. He had failed to reckon with the success of Madame Du Barry as an emollient for the king's melancholia, and in cultivating the favorite's displeasure he had seriously endangered his standing with the king.[31] At the same time, he had become involved in a bitter controversy with the Chancellor Maupeou over the powers of the *parlements,* a fact which had ranged powerful opposition against him. It was natural, therefore, that like other politicians he should look to a sucessful war as his salvation. A few months before, Ossun had advised him that the Spanish navy was in a fine state of preparation for war,[32] and when we consider his previous assurance of 1766 that war could be made in eighteen months there seems reason to suppose that he was momentarily determined to go to some lengths to support his ally against England.

Doubtless Choiseul was counting upon the usual truculence of the Spanish court when he sought to revive its interest in a conflict with England. In the preceding month a pragmatic sanction had been issued prohibiting the importation into Spain of English muslins,[33] and as this measure was calculated to arouse the protests of England Choiseul was justified in believing that Charles III was ready to follow his lead. Contrary to his expectations, however, the Spanish failed to respond to his suggestion with enthusiasm. The Jesuit question was still a subject of lively negotiation with the Holy See,[34] and the country as a whole was not yet in an adequate state of preparation for war. Ossun, advising[35] Choiseul of this latter fact, wrote that Grimaldi

[31] Flammermont, *op. cit.,* p. 152 *et seq.;* Goncourt, *Madame du Barry* (1914), p. 87 *et seq.*

[32] Rousseau, *op. cit.,* vol. 2, p. 69. But see Ossun's dispatch of July 23, 1770 (*Aff. Etr., Espagne,* 560).

[33] Danvila, *op. cit.,* vol. 4, p. 122.

[34] Ossun to Choiseul, July 23, 1770 (*Aff. Etr., Espagne,* 560).

[35] Ossun to Choiseul, July 23, 1770, second dispatch (*Aff. Etr., Espagne,* 560).

declined to give an opinion as to the merits of the Chandernagor incident until he had consulted his king; and that both Grimaldi and the king were strongly attached to the policy of peace.

What Grimaldi had to say regarding the Falkland incident of February is of great interest, because it absolves the Spanish court of direct complicity in Bucareli's intemperate proceeding in destroying the English settlement. The action of the Spanish ships, said Grimaldi, had been in accordance with what had been resolved previously, and communicated to the French court. When they had been advised in vague terms that the English had founded a colony in the general vicinity of Port Egmont, the Spanish had decided that if this was true a reconnaissance should be made and if the colony was on the Pacific side of Cape Horn it should be ejected at once, but if the colony was on the Falklands, the Spanish would merely reconnoitre and protest. The reason for this course, he said, was the fact that settlements on the Pacific side of Cape Horn were clearly forbidden by treaty, and that Spanish rights were probably not so clearly established in reference to the South Atlantic.

On August 6, 1770,[36] Grimaldi finally gave the answer of Charles III, that as far as the Chandernagor affair was concerned, he was inclined to peace, at least for several years to come, particularly in view of the state of French finances. Speaking of a proposed treaty between France and the Porte, he indicated that although Spain was ready to go to war obedient to her engagements under the Family Compact, she could not be drawn into conflicts beyond the purview of this instrument. The treaty which Choiseul proposed to make with Turkey unquestionably would mean immediate war with England. The implications of this excursus were obvious—Spain was willing to fight only if her own interests were involved.

Choiseul received this letter in no equable frame of mind.

[36] Ossun to Choiseul, August 6, 1770 (*Aff. Etr., Espagne,* 560).

Replying to Ossun,[37] he remarked with some asperity that Spain was dying of fear whenever an incident occurred that might lead to war. Grimaldi's tactless reference to the state of France's finances, which was a particularly acrid source of dispute between Choiseul and his political opponents, was countered with the boast that France was prepared for war as far as her physical resources were concerned and that money had never been lacking in the kingdom when it was needed. These rather impolitic remarks Choiseul would probably not have made had he known that at the very moment he wrote Spain was already apprised of Bucareli's expedition, and that it was he who would henceforward have to·resist the pressure for hostilities.[38]

On August 11 Madariaga arrived at Cadiz fresh from his triumph at Port Egmont. The Conde de Aranda, to whom this officer reported, at once notified Grimaldi of the event.[39] The Spanish court was fully conscious of the probable results of this new complication. It was, however, determined not to permit the news to leak out,[40] but to endeavor first to assure the support of France before advising its ally of the details of the situation. In view of the fact that England would not receive the news for at least another three weeks, owing to the detention of the *Favourite*, this plan seemed feasible. About this time a letter of Bucareli's dated April 3 had arrived, recounting the events that had taken place in February and the fact that an expedition was planned. Accordingly Grimaldi related these facts to Ossun, who at once notified his court (August 17).[41] He told Choiseul that

[37] Choiseul to Ossun, August 20, 1770 (*Aff. Etr., Espagne,* 560).

[38] For the judgment of the Austrian ambassador at Paris *cf.* Mercy to Maria Theresa, September 19, 1770, in Arneth and Geoffrey, *Marie Antoinette,* vol. I, p. 57.

[39] Danvila, *op. cit.,* vol. 4, p. 122.

[40] *Ibid.*

[41] Ossun to Choiseul, August 17, 1770, text in Flammermont, *op. cit.,* p. 159. There seems no reason to question the correctness of Danvila's statement that Madariaga was in Spain as early as August 11, 1770.

it was clear that England would regard the projected expedition as a hostile act and that she would either take vengeance or demand satisfaction. Spain, he wrote, could scarcely enter into negotiations without prejudice to her rights to the Falklands; on the other hand, if Bucareli's action were upheld, war would be inevitable.

Three days later Grimaldi addressed the Conde de Fuentes, his ambassador at Paris,[42] telling him that the affair of the English colony in the Falklands had become serious and perhaps would precipitate war. The course decided upon by the king, he said, was to avoid the catastrophe of Spain and France being hurried into a war for which neither kingdom was ready. This it was hoped to accomplish by having Masserano inform the British court of Madariaga's expedition. By doing this the Spanish court believed that the English would act with less violence than if they were advised by another and more direct means. It was clear that Grimaldi had little desire to make war over so insignificant an object as the Falklands.

The change of circumstances which produced so sudden a reversal in the dispositions of Charles III and his advisers was at this moment particularly welcome to Choiseul, as it drew from his shoulders the burden of public responsibility for war. At the same time, the shift in Spanish policy fitted in with his own secret designs, and promised to assure him the continuance in office which at this moment was seriously threatened. It is not possible to know to what extent Louis XV was advised of the state of things in Choiseul's department of the foreign office, nor the details which

Nevertheless it is curious that Arriaga should have written to Bucareli on August 24, 1770, in answer to Bucareli's letter of April, ordering him to hold up the expedition (Angelis, *op. cit.*, Doc. 27). This letter was probably written for exhibition to Harris, and to put Spain right on the record.

[42] Apparently Grimaldi only intimated to Ossun that an expedition was *going* to be sent to the Falklands. Text in Blart, *op. cit.*, p. 167.

were supplied him regarding the existing crisis.[43] In any event, on August 20 Choiseul informed Ossun that he had spoken to the king and that he could assure Ossun that his Catholic Majesty "could count on all occasions and in every way upon the king his cousin."[44]

In the meantime Grimaldi had taken steps to carry out the business of quieting the British. This court had preserved throughout the summer a discreet silence on the subject of the Falklands, despite the fact that Hunt's report must have convinced the more astute members of the ministry that trouble was not far off. On the very day that Madariaga arrived in Spain there had appeared in a London paper[45] a malicious libel on the king of Spain of so injurious a character that the Spanish ambassador had undertaken to protest at the Foreign Office against the insult. The agitation over this incident in London was sufficiently great, but fortunately at the moment Masserano was instructed on the Falklands the facts were not yet known in Madrid. Otherwise Grimaldi's recommendations to Masserano that he should do everything to avoid war[46] would probably have had a different tenor—at least, if we may judge by the temper of the Spanish court after the libel was known.

The news that something had happened in the Falklands soon spread abroad. Indeed, notice reached James Harris, the youthful chargé d'affaires in Madrid, whose talents, it may be remarked, have been somewhat overestimated. He at once reported to his government the fact that an expedition had set out from Buenos Aires and that its object was the ejection of the British colony at Port Egmont.[47] This notice reached the British foreign office about the same time

[43] Choiseul to Ossun, August 20, 1770 (*Aff. Etr., Espagne,* 560).
[44] *Ibid.*
[45] Walpole, *op. cit.,* vol. 4, p. 112.
[46] Blart, *op. cit.,* p. 167.
[47] Harris to Weymouth, August 23, 1770, *Falkland Papers,* p. 1.

that Masserano appeared to communicate the facts to Lord Weymouth.

Obedient to his instructions, Masserano[48] informed the British secretary of state that he had reason to believe the Spanish governor of Buenos Aires had taken it upon himself to use force to dispossess the English at Port Egmont. He added that in making the communication he did it to prevent consequences that might arise should the news reach the government by other hands, and he hoped that Bucareli's acts executed without royal authority would not lead the English to take measures dangerous to the good understanding between the two crowns. To this Weymouth replied rather bluntly that if Masserano's fears were realized he could not see how a fatal step in consequence could be avoided. He went on to say that the instructions to the British officers in charge of Port Egmont were merely to warn alien settlers to depart, and if they refused to heed the warning, to make a joint settlement, leaving the question of right to be settled by the respective sovereigns. Weymouth then asked Masserano whether he was authorized to disavow Bucareli's acts, to which the Spanish ambassador replied that he was not advised on this point and would have to ask for instructions.

Upon this conversation being reported to the king, Weymouth informed Masserano that George III demanded a disavowal of Bucareli and that the colony be restored to *status quo ante*. Meantime Harris was instructed to call on Grimaldi to read his dispatch and ask "whether his Catholic Majesty, by disavowing a measure which his ambassador here acknowledges not to have been authorized by his particular instructions and by restoring things to the precise state in which they stood before M. Bucareli undertook this rash expedition will put it into his Majesty's power to suspend those preparations which under the present circumstances, his honour will not permit him to postpone."

[48] Weymouth to Harris, September 12, 1770, *Falkland Papers,* no. 2.

The preparations for war in England hinted at by Weymouth had likewise been proceeding in Spain. As early as August 27 Ossun reported[49] that the king and his ministers were seriously engaged in measures to carry on war with England if the Buenos Aires expedition should make such a course inevitable; not only was the army being mobilized for war but steps for the defense of the Indies were under way. The public, advised of what Bucareli had proposed to do, were enthusiastically supporting the conduct of the governor. On September 3[50] the French ambassador, in a long dispatch, detailed the preparations, all of which showed a surprising amount of energy and capacity, and which gave the lie to Choiseul's impatient characterization of the Spanish. At the same time, Ossun observed a quickening of interest in the Chandernagor affair; nevertheless, he believed the Spanish still dreaded any incident which might lead to war, and Grimaldi apparently entertained sanguine hopes that a conflict could be averted, although the activity in measures of offense and defense was in no wise restrained.

Up to this moment the French apparently were not fully advised of what had happened at Port Egmont. Indeed, it was not until September 10[51] that Grimaldi informed Conde de Fuentes of Madariaga's *coup de main* in all its details. In the same dispatch he further indicated the fact that Charles III was satisfied with the assurance which Choiseul had conveyed to Ossun, and he entered fully into the designs for war which were being carried out in accordance with the plans of 1766.

Grimaldi's course was in general that which he believed would be most acceptable to Choiseul. He was probably not entirely aware of the state in which his colleague's political fortunes then were, and yet he had every reason to believe Choiseul would not desert him in the crisis, but would give

[49] Ossun to Choiseul, August 27, 1770 (*Aff. Etr., Espagne,* 560).

[50] Ossun to Choiseul, September 3, 1770 (*Aff. Etr., Espagne,* 560).

[51] Flammermont, *op. cit.,* p. 161.

him active support. In any event, his failure to make .complete disclosures of the situation to Choiseul was no more a breach of confidence than Choiseul's hesitancy in unmasking the fact that war was more a personal than a court project. The Spaniard's predilection seems really to have been for peace. But in the ministry was the dynamic Conde de Aranda, whose enthusiasm for a conflict with England knew no bounds. Unquestionably de Aranda's forceful personality had a great deal to do with firing his colleagues and the king to a steadfast adherence to an aggressive policy. It will be recalled that in the earlier discussions of the Falkland question, de Aranda had declared himself for vigorous action. At the present juncture it was he again who sought to assume the direction of Spanish policy and to turn the recent defeat into victory.[52]

In contrast with the situation in Spain, the posture of affairs in France was not such as to encourage Choiseul. The rapid germination of the seed sown early in July, promising as it may have been to the design itself, in reality was calculated to force the issue between Choiseul and his enemies.[53] The prosecution of war necessitated the voting of funds and the levying of new taxes. This could be done only by the *parlements,* which would act only in the event that sacrifices of certain men were made who were creatures of Madame du Barry. It is not surprising, therefore, that we find Choiseul, except for the assurances of support conveyed in his letter to Ossun, temporarily abandoning the direction of affairs to Spain—a course which later proved disastrous. In an instruction to Ossun dated September 17 Choiseul left the decision to Charles III:[54]

I think that peace or war depend on the disposition of Spain; you will neglect nothing to advise me what side Spain takes. Moreover,

[52] Danvila, *op. cit.,* vol. 4, p. 131.
[53] Flammermont, *loc. cit.*
[54] Choiseul to Ossun, September 17, 1770 (*Aff. Etr., Mém. et Doc.,* 575).

you will let them know that whatever view they take, that of peace being preferable, it is necessary that they come to a prompt decision in order that they do not have to fight the position of Parliament which meets in November.[55]

It is curious that in taking this resolution Choiseul was, nevertheless, thoroughly impatient with the way Grimaldi had managed things. Pouring out his heart to Francés,[56] he confided that had the Bourbon courts awaited the British complaints they would at once have been advised of what the British wanted and would have been masters of the negotiation. As it was, in approaching the British in a semi-apologetic manner they had let the control of the situation pass to London.[57] This view was confirmed when the instructions to Harris, already outlined, fell into Choiseul's hands.[58] The tenor of this document being fully in accord with Choiseul's own forecast of the British attitude, he could not forbear to place a guiding hand on Spanish policy, despite his resolution to leave the real direction of negotia-

[55] The statement that peace was preferable has been seized upon as evidence of Choiseul's deep duplicity.

[56] Choiseul to Francés, September 9, 1770 (*Aff. Etr., Angleterre*, 403).

[57] It is interesting to observe in this connection that Choiseul with his usual discernment was able to forecast the probable course of George III's ministers. If the British would not negotiate on the basis suggested by Spain, war would be inevitable and nothing could prevent it. If on the other hand they negotiated, this would be either in bad faith to gain time for war preparations, or in good faith. In the latter case, they would ask three things,—restoration to Port Egmont, recognition of the British sovereignty over the islands, and withdrawal of the Spanish establishment, and third, the punishment of Bucareli. If the British sincerely desired peace they would not press the question of exclusive sovereignty. The recognition of British right would in any event be the point on which Spain would balk. This, of course, was undoubtedly what England would demand, and Spain would have to cover her refusal by adroit delay until ready to make war. If Spain decided to surrender Port Egmont this would have to be done before Parliament met.

[58] Weymouth to Harris, September 17, 1770, *Falkland Papers*, p. 9.

tions to Grimaldi. Writing to Ossun on September 26,[59] he urged the necessity that Spain adopt a firm and consistent course. The instructions to Masserano, he complained, showed an immoderate desire for peace and an extraordinary fear of war, whereas it appeared that in reality Spain desired war. A decision, said Choiseul, must be reached, but in any event, after the steps taken by Masserano, there was no doubt but that the two English demands would have to be conceded.

The reason given by Choiseul for this counsel, bound to be unpalatable to Spain, was the state of unpreparedness of France. It was necessary, said he, that the sailors in Newfoundland return, that the French fleet be victualled and that the colonies should all be provisioned. These things could not be accomplished before December. Within three months, however, the English would be active and France would lose all her sailors, as she had done in the last war. The English ministry was the weakest in history, and yet if a clear and satisfying answer were not given to their demands they would be forced to declare war. Choiseul's proposal was, therefore, agreement, and in the event Spain wanted war this could be precipitated during the discussions over the right and sovereignty to the Falklands. In such a case France would be fully prepared in every way, and at the service of Spain.

This proposal was not written until two days after Harris had actually presented his government's demands on Spain.[60] The whole tone adopted by Harris in his interview with Grimaldi was exceedingly conciliatory. He commenced by stating that the dignity of the crown had been attacked and that only the sincere desire of the king for peace could avoid disturbing the peace. The only way this could be effected would be by disavowal of Bucareli and restoration of

[59] Choiseul to Ossun, September 26, 1770 (*Aff. Etr., Mém. et Doc.*, 575).
[60] Harris to Weymouth, September 28, 1770, *Falkland Papers*, p. 9.

the colony, acts which were possible in view of the fact that the whole thing had occurred without the knowledge of or at least appearance of authority from the king of Spain.[61]

Grimaldi was disconcertingly vague in his reply. He stated that as soon as the court had been apprised of the Bucareli expedition a vessel had been dispatched to prevent its consummation, but it was then too late. The English, he said, had reason to foresee the event, as the settlement had been the subject of discussion, and the Spanish had not concealed their disapprobation of it. Bucareli, he thought, could not be blamed, as he had acted in accordance with the established law of America. Despite these facts, however, the king was desirous of peace and of avoiding a war in which he had everything to lose. All Charles wished was to act consistently with the honor of his crown and the welfare of his people. In so far as much of these two points were compatible with the demands of England, Harris might be assured that they would be agreed to.

Three days later Grimaldi advised Harris that the British memorial had been laid before the king and that the latter had decided to do everything in his power to terminate the affair amicably. Accordingly he had admitted the British demand and assented to every point consistent with his honor. The affair, however, had to be settled in London and not at Madrid. Consequently orders had been given to Prince Masserano to lay the Spanish ideas before Weymouth. These differed only in terms and not in substance from what England had demanded. Harris, of course, wanted to know what the Spanish "ideas" were, but Grimaldi, adopting a paternal tone toward the young chargé, declined, saying this was needless, that they were various and England could choose what she liked best.

Grimaldi's vagueness at least had the advantage of con-

---

[61] The British evidently adopted this tack in the hope that Spain, observing the loophole, would grasp the opportunity to negotiate on this basis for peace.

vincing Harris that Spain was most desirous of peace.[62] Unlike Ossun, he found the key to this attitude in the inability to support a war, as well as the attitude of the people, whom he pictured as in subjection to the military. The infantry, he reported, was in bad shape and ill disciplined; the cavalry, though on better footing, was not as good as formerly. The navy was in a fair condition but underarmed. Worst of all were the finances, which resisted all efforts at betterment. "These, my Lord," wrote Harris, "may be looked on as much more secure pledges of peace than any we may infer either from their protestations or good disposition of those who guide here toward us." The great danger, in his mind, lay in the direction of America, where extraordinary measures had been taken to keep out British ships.

The instructions given to Masserano were in due course communicated to Weymouth.[63] It was in substance proposed that a convention be drawn in which any particular orders to Bucareli be disavowed, but at the same time it was to be acknowledged that the governor of Buenos Aires had acted in accordance with his general instructions and on his oath as governor, an inferential acceptance of the Spanish colonial laws and the Treaty of Utrecht. The convention was further to provide for the restitution of the colony without prejudice to the rights of Spain to the islands. Finally, England was to disavow the menace of Captain Hunt which had given occasion to the acts of Bucareli.[64] It was further pro-

[62] Harris to Weymouth, September 28, 1770 (private) (*R.O. State Papers, Spain,* 185).

[63] Weymouth to Harris, October 17, 1770, *Falkland Papers,* p. 17.

[64] Text: "Le Prince de Masserano . . . en vertu des ordres à lui donnés par le Roi son maître pour faire voir combien S. M. C. désire de conserver la paix et la douce harmonie avec la couronne britannique et qu'Elle ne voudrait point que le paix fut rompue à l'occasion de l'évènement du 10 juin dernier, jour auquel les Anglais ont été expulsés de l'île appelée par eux Falkland et par les Espagnols Grande Malouine, et en vertu aussi du pouvoir spécial dont il se trouve muni pour donner une preuve manifeste

posed by Spain that the two powers should evacuate the islands jointly at a time which the British government might

et de la manière la plus authentique des susdites intentions royales de S. M. C.;

"Déclare que S. M. C., considerant l'amour dont elle est animée pour la paix et le maintien de la bonne harmonie (note: Si on ne peut s'en dispenser, ajouter 'et le mécontentement que S. M. B. a marqué.') avec S. M. B., a vu avec deplaisir que Don Francisco Bucareli, lieutenant général de ses armées et gouverneur de Buenos Ayres eut ordonné l'armement destiné à exécuter et qui a exécuté la susdite expulsion, ce général s'y étant déterminé d'une part dans la vue de remplir ses obligations (note: On omet l'expression 'de satisfaire aux loix et au serment sous lequel il a reçu le gouvernement' pour ne point offenser le ministère anglais.), et de l'autre (note: Dans le cas d'une nécessité absolue, substituer 'des fortes raisons qu'il a eues de craindre que les Espagnols ne fussent chassés de la Soledad par les Anglais de la Grande Malouine si on ne les gagnait de vitesse.') y ayant été poussé par la menace que le Sr Hunt, capitaine anglais commandant de l'île appelée Falkland ou Grande Malouine avait faite à Don Philippe Ruis Puente, gouverneur de l'île de Soledad (qui est une autre île des Malouines) qu'il irait dans six mois le chasser de la dite île avec les autres Espagnols; et le Prince de Masserano fait la presente déclaration d'après l'assurance à lui donnée ministériellement que le roi de la Grande Bretagne a appris avec un égal déplaisir cette menace du susdit Hunt, commandant de Falkland (note: Ou 'les motifs qui ont donné lieu à Bucareli de faire effectuer cette expédition.'), en tant qu'il en résulterait l'interruption de la bonne harmonie que S. M. desire de maintenir entre les deux nations espagnole et britannique.

"Le Prince de Masserano déclare aussi que S. M. C. consent que les Anglais retournent (note: Le mot retourner doit faire entendre que les Anglais aient à y aller d'eux-mêmes, ce que est important.) s'établir dans l'île de la Grande Malouine ou Falkland comme ils y étaient avant le 10 juin de cette année jour auquel ils ont été expulsés par violence, afin que de cette manière il soit notoire (note: Par cette explication, l'outrage dont ils se plaignent se trouve réparé; vouloir d'autres satisfactions c'est prétendre nous humilier sans aucun avantage pour eux. Ce passage peut être omis ou remplacé par 'avant l'expulsion et avant que les motifs qui l'ont précédée eussent eu lieu.') qu'ils sont remis dans l'état ou ils étaient avant la menace faite par le capitaine Hunt et avant l'éxpedition par laquelle Don Francisco Bucareli a obligé ce capitaine de sortir de cette île avec les autres Anglais.

"S. M. C. promettant, comme S. M. B. promet aussi, l'un par la pre-

fix. The demand of England that Spain convey the settlers to the islands was flatly rejected for the reason that the question of sovereignty would otherwise be compromised.[65]

These terms were at once conveyed to Choiseul, and at the same time both Ossun[66] and Grimaldi[67] assured the former that although Spain wanted peace she was not afraid of war. Simultaneously, in view of the state of preparations in both France and Spain, Masserano was told to delay the

sente déclaration et l'autre dans celle par laquelle Elle admettra cette même déclaration et que fera aussitôt par son ordre et avec son pouvoir spécial le lord Comte de Weymouth, que dans le terme de . . . (note: On peut laisser ce terme à la volonté des Anglais.), les deux souverains feront abandonner l'un l'île de la Soledad par les Espagnols et l'autre l'île de la Grande Malouine par les Anglais et que toutes les Malouines resteront désertes afin qu'il ne puisse plus s'élever de discussions sur les établissements qu'on pourrait y faire, d'autant que le peu d'importance de ces îles n'est en aucune manière comparable aux avantages bien plus précieux d'une bonne harmonie entre les deux nations (note: Ce dernier article sera celui qui arrêtera de nouveau les Anglais; il est le plus épineux quoiqu'à dire vrai ils aient bien l'air de l'être tous. Ils pourront bien dire qu'il atténue la satisfaction portée par notre déclaration. En ce cas, le Roi autorise Masserano à répondre que la déclaration finira par les mots 'les autres Anglais' . . . mais il ajoutera qu'il faut que dans la contre-déclaration anglaise on promette l'abandon réciproque dans le délai qu'ils jugeront à propos quoiqu'on demande qu'il soit positif et fixé. S'ils ne voulaient pas non plus faire cette promesse dans la contre-déclaration, on leur proposera de la faire par une convention particulière et d'une date postérieure. Masserano peut convenir d'antidater ou de posdater selon ce qu'il estimera nécessaire, mais il prendra garde malgré cela de ne point lâcher d'une main la déclaration, à moins qu'en même temps il ne tienne la contre-déclaration, ou seule—s'ils se déterminaient à y comprendre tout—ou avec la convention s'ils préféraient qu'il y eut l'une et l'autre.)." Renaut, op. cit., vol. 11, pp. 48-49.

[65] Ossun to Choiseul, October 3, 1770 (Aff. Etr., Espagne, 561). It is interesting that Harris was not advised of these latter proposals. They were conceived in the belief that England must at all costs be excluded from the South Atlantic and Pacific. Grimaldi to Choiseul, October 3, 1770 (Aff. Etr., Espagne, 561).

[66] Ossun to Choiseul, October 3, 1770 (Aff. Etr., Espagne, 561).

[67] Grimaldi to Choiseul, October 3, 1770 (Aff. Etr., Espagne, 561).

negotiations as far as possible and to raise the hopes of the British for an accommodation, in order to avoid an immediate declaration of war. In this wise it was hoped to give Choiseul time to have his house in order. The reports from London all indicated that the ministry would not dare declare war before Parliament met, and that the attitude of the opposition, headed by Chatham, would be determinative. Grimaldi, in his writing to Choiseul, plaintively rejected the idea that the decision of war or peace lay in Spain's hands, and insisted that the real arbiters were the British ministry, who in turn were governed by their fear of the opposition.[68]

While these exchanges of view were being made on the continent, the *Favourite* had arrived at the Mother Bank on September 22, and the full details of the events of the preceding June were communicated to the Foreign Office.[69] Preparations for war were at once undertaken on an even larger scale than heretofore. The ministry, which had clearly been disposed to an accommodation at the outset of the trouble and might even have gone so far as to acquiesce in the arrangement suggested by Spain, which was yet to be dispatched, now found itself in the situation where only extreme measures would silence popular clamor. The fear of the opposition, so vividly depicted by the French and Spanish foreign ministers, was no mere chimera. Lord Chatham was a popular figure and, having made his name in the successful conduct of a war, was likely to emerge as a bitter champion for English rights—a rôle which would secure him not merely public support but the leadership of the gov-

[68] Ossun gives in some detail the extent of Spanish preparations, all of which give the lie to Harris' reports. The plan of campaign was to avoid a continental war and carry on the fight overseas. The fact that so many ships and munitions were sent to America may account for Harris' being misled in his estimates. For Choiseul's plan to invade England *cf.* Morison, *The Duc de Choiseul and the Invasion of England,* 1768-1770, in *Transactions of the Royal Historical Society,* 3d series, vol. 4 (1910), p. 83.

[69] Maltby to Stephens, September 22, 1770, *Falkland Papers,* p. 23.

ernment. This was a contingency which neither the king nor Lord North desired to have happen, and hence the position of the ministry in respect to war was no less delicate than was that of Choiseul. The situation was not unlike that existing in 1914, where all sides were unwilling to precipitate a conflict, and yet where none could conveniently move.

The mood of the British ministry having thus blackened, and report of the fact having reached Choiseul, one can readily imagine his consternation at learning that the English actually were inclined to engage in war. His letter advising acceptance of the British terms had crossed the dispatch containing the instructions to Masserano. When the latter were displayed to him before their delivery, as was the custom between the two courts, he at once saw that what Charles III was willing to concede fell far short of the demand, and that the British ministry would be less disposed to accede to them than Grimaldi had surmised. His advice had arrived too late at Madrid, but he yet hoped to avert untoward consequences. Accordingly he instructed Francés at London to do all in his power to persuade Masserano to follow the French plan of procedure in preference to that contained in the instructions from Grimaldi *"qui n'ont pas le sens commun."* Convinced that the matter would go before Parliament, Choiseul added that when this happened it was necessary that there be a party for peace, a thing which would be impossible if the nations were not reasonable. If England wished peace she could find a mediator in France, because "we can do what we wish with Spain in such an event," and he pointed out that mediation of this sort would cover him with honor.[70]

This curious dispatch is almost unprecedented, not only in that it violated the sacred canons of diplomatic usage, but in the fact that it was virtually a diplomatic abandonment of Spain. Some weeks later Frederick the Great, writing to his ambassador at Paris, described the situation

[70] Choiseul to Francés, October 7, 1770 (*Aff. Etr., Angleterre,* 493).

trenchantly in a sentence—that Choiseul was like one who had hit a timid man and was overwhelmed with surprise that the victim had hit back.[71] This characterization was sufficiently apt, but at the same time it does not fully explain Choiseul's change of front. Involved in the gravest sort of inner political difficulties, it was not unnatural that he should seek some means of saving himself, and as mediation offered a way out, he no doubt felt justified in his resort to it.

Choiseul's advice arrived too late, for Masserano on the receipt of his instructions proceeded to acquaint Weymouth with their purport.[72] The latter laid the Spanish proposals before the king, who regarded them as inadequate and expressed himself as dissatisfied with the solution proposed.

George III and his ministry were fully aware of the dangers of delay, not only from the military but the parliamentary point of view. In these circumstances Weymouth was directed to inform Masserano that the king had laid down the minimum which he would accept, and there was nothing left for Spain to do but to discuss the means of carrying into execution the disavowal and restitution. Masserano was told that without entering into the "insurmountable *matter*" of the proposed convention the *"manner"* alone was totally inadmissible, and that the king would never consent to a convention which was supposed to give him satisfaction for insults and yet which compelled him to enter into engagements to procure it. The reparation, it was declared, would lose all its value as soon as it became conditional and was obtained by stipulations on the part of the king.

When this was imparted to Masserano, he remarked that he had no power to proceed further in the matter and that

[71] Frederick II to de Rohd, October 28, 1770, *Politische Correspondenz Friederichs des Grossen,* vol. 30, p. 224.

[72] Weymouth to Harris, October 17, 1770, *Falkland Papers,* p. 17.

he would have to ask for new instructions. Weymouth, impatient at the delay, instructed Harris to demand the Spanish king's answer immediately after laying the matter before Grimaldi.[73]

Before these orders were dispatched to Harris, Choiseul's note of September 20 had reached the Spanish court. Conferring with Grimaldi regarding the minor sources of complaint,[74] Harris observed the former to be in an ill humor, because, as he supposed, of the news received from Paris that extensive naval preparations were under way in England. From the conversation which ensued,[75] however, it appears that Grimaldi was really chafing under Choiseul's rebuke for having informed England too soon of the Port Egmont affair, particularly, as the English preparations confirmed the Frenchman's attitude. Grimaldi, speaking with some passion, remarked to Harris that the naval armaments the English were making were an ill return for the early intelligence conveyed to them by Spain of the expedition to the Falklands. Obviously, said he, the English must be considering some treacherous stroke by the warmth with which orders for preparation were given and the speed with which they were being carried out. Harris replied that the king, his master, could not of course sit idly by when an act of direct hostility had been committed against him, of which, though he had not yet been advised, he had no positive assurance of the consequences it would produce. Harris then went on to assure Grimaldi that his fears that the English were contemplating a hostile stroke was a supposition injurious to the crown, particularly because they had demonstrated their consideration for the Spanish crown. The preparations would cease if Masserano's reply to their demands was satisfactory. Grimaldi then cried, "I hope in

[73] *Ibid.*

[74] Harris to Weymouth, October 4, 1770 (*R.O. State Papers, Spain,* 185).

[75] *Ibid.* Cf. also Harris to Weymouth, October 11, 1770, *ibid.*

God, and I call Heaven to witness that I desire nothing so much as peace and dread nothing so much as war.''

Unquestionably Choiseul's pessimistic reports of the conditions of things in France had disquieted Grimaldi as much as his colleague's rebuke had angered him. That he ever meant to convey an abject fear of war which both Harris and Choiseul thought they discerned in his conduct seems unlikely. The anxiety for peace that Choiseul found so distasteful, Grimaldi seems to have been unable to suppress as time went on. Naturally, in view of Harris' earlier report of the condition of army and navy, the British ministry was confirmed in their decision to insist on the original terms. Even the later report,[76] sent in by Harris, of the rapid advance of preparations could not alter this impression, particularly as Harris remarked that in his daily conversations with the Spanish foreign minister the latter kept reiterating his desire for peace.[77] Of course this incongruity between the irreconcilable instructions to Masserano and the wavering talk of Grimaldi must have been puzzling to the British, and, between the two, the verbal protestations of the foreign minister no doubt appeared the more credible in view of the state of Spanish armament. Grimaldi, however, was no fool and he was not yet sure that French support would be adequate. As he told Ossun at this time, he feared that he might be sacrificed if his notes were not sufficiently strong.[78]

The apprehensions which Choiseul had aroused in the minds of the Spanish ministry by his earlier communication, and which was reflected in the conversations with Harris did not abate as the month of October proceeded. Apart from the original assurance that Louis XV would not desert his ally, there was little in the situation to raise hopes of active support. Indeed, on October 15 Grimaldi ad-

---

[76] Harris to Weymouth, October 11, 1770, *ibid.*
[77] Harris to Weymouth, October 18, 1770, *ibid.*
[78] Ossun to Choiseul, October 3, 1770 (*Aff. Etr., Espagne, 560*).

dressed Fuentes, demanding an explanation for the apathy and lack of interest in France.[79]

These explanations were soon en route, for Choiseul, after directing Francés to dissuade Masserano from following the Spanish instructions, addressed Grimaldi and Ossun[80] to the same effect, hoping to put the Madrid court in a favorable mood for what he had undertaken. He implored Ossun to do his utmost to persuade Grimaldi to follow French counsel either in a reply to Harris or by authorizing Masserano to make the requested declaration. Three days later (October 24), after he had probably been informed in detail of Grimaldi's note to Fuentes, Choiseul again addressed the Spanish minister. In the covering note to Ossun,[81] he entered at some length into his reasons for an acceptance of the British demands. He asked that Grimaldi reply to Harris in writing, clearly and briefly, upon the two propositions of disavowal and restitution, announcing a declaration which would be sent to Masserano on the subject. "Nothing," said Choiseul, "could be less dangerous than such a declaration, because if war supervenes the whole declaration falls and it would serve to give us the necessary time. If the declaration averts war it will have produced a great good and would not injure Spanish interests as the basis of right to the Malouines still remains to be discussed."

Before this latter note had had time to reach its destination, Harris was in receipt of Weymouth's instructions of the seventeenth and on October 29 he called on Grimaldi.[82] After listening to the substance of Weymouth's dispatch the latter remarked that he would like to see an accommodation and that he was concerned that after the concession which the Spanish had made the English were still unsatis-

[79] Rousseau, op. cit., vol. 2, p. 72.
[80] Choiseul to Ossun, October 21, 1770 (Aff. Etr., Mém. et Doc., 575).
[81] Choiseul to Ossun, October 24, 1770 (Aff. Etr., Mém. et Doc., 575).
[82] Harris to Weymouth, November 7, 1770, Falkland Papers, p. 19.

fied. He then said that the king was anxious to make all concession compatible with his honor, and that he wished to
know what the English wanted, for the Spanish had done
so much there was nothing more to be done. Harris replied
that Weymouth's letter was explicit, and that if Grimaldi
considered the difference between the matter of their proposals and the manner of their intended execution, he could
be at no loss to comprehend what was meant, since their
original demands had not changed. These demands were the
only ones which they could make, consistent with honor,
and there was no reason, therefore, for surprise that they
were persisted in.

Grimaldi then remarked that the Spanish had admitted
that they were in the wrong and had offered to make ample
reparation. He could not understand why England would
not give way on the point in which Spain felt insulted. This
statement of Grimaldi is interesting because he put his fin-
ger upon the element in the situation of most importance to
Charles III. This monarch had always entertained the
greatest solicitude for his honor. The present crisis was
looked upon by him as one involving the honor of the crown,
and it was probably for this reason more than any other
that Charles turned a deaf ear on those persons who were
seeking a peaceful solution. It was, therefore, not a mere
diplomatic subterfuge that the threats of Captain Hunt were
allowed to play so large a rôle in the negotiations. It was in
consequence of this mutual sense of injury on both sides
that negotiations were more concerned with a settlement of
the immediate facts than with the ultimate problem of right
on which the matter really depended. At the same time, the
Spanish were fully conscious that an unconditional acceptance of the British terms was likely to prejudice a discussion of the underlying question, if it did not in fact contain
implications of a recognition of British right to the Falklands.

The British, for their part, were aware of both the imme-

diate advantage of an unconditional settlement as well as
its bearing upon any subsequent discussion of the sovereignty. Accordingly, when Grimaldi raised the question of
a disavowal of Hunt, Harris, obedient to his instructions,
replied that the party injured could under no circumstances
agree to a conditional reparation, since in so doing it would
make a sort of conditional disavowal of the injury.

On November 7 Grimaldi sent for Harris and told him
that a messenger had been dispatched to Masserano with
the king's reply. This was in substance[83] that the king, being anxious for an accommodation and to preserve peace,
was disposed to give every reasonable satisfaction to the insult which the king of England believed he had suffered, and
that this satisfaction should be given in such manner as the
English king required. The king, on the other hand, felt that
as he had gone so far to save the honor of the king of England, the latter would be disposed to contribute to the saving of his honor as far as this did not interfere with the satisfaction he would receive. In the second place, Charles
required that the affair should be ultimately terminated
without leaving any traces which might disturb the harmony
of the two courts. In the third place, there would have to be
"reciprocal and authentical" assurance that the whole matter was thoroughly accommodated.

Having read this dispatch, Grimaldi remarked that he
hoped it would produce the desired effect and that by the
affair being thoroughly understood it would be effectually
concluded.

The vagueness of the instructions to Masserano was an
attempt to give the prince the greatest leeway in arranging
the matter without departing from the conditions which
Charles III regarded as essential to the preservation of his
honor. The negotiations at London had not ended merely
with the communication of the first project of a declara-

[83] *Ibid.*

tion.[84] Throughout the month Masserano and Weymouth were actively engaged in an attempt to arrive at a satisfactory formula. The sense of the original declaration had been so far reduced that Masserano was willing to give way on the disavowal of Hunt if the English would agree to the evacuation of the islands.[85] The Spanish ambassador leaned to the view of Choiseul that the reparation question and the question of sovereignty were separate and that negotiations should be carried on on this basis.

During the course of the negotiations the declaration originally proposed had been followed by projects of two others. Early in November Masserano proposed the following:[86]

The Prince de Masserano declares that his Catholic Majesty, considering the love of peace which animates him, as well as the maintenance of good harmony with his Britannic Majesty has viewed with displeasure the expedition which could interrupt these relations, and being persuaded that his sentiments are reciprocated by his Britannic Majesty disavows these enterprises, having ascertained the unwillingness of his Britannic Majesty to authorize anything which might disturb the good understanding between the two nations.

At the same time the Prince de Masserano declares that his Catholic Majesty agrees that the English return to settle in the Island *la Grande Malouine* called by them Falkland, as they were prior to June 10 of this year, the day they were ousted by violence in order that, in this way it be known that they are restored to the state in which they were before this event.

It is not difficult to understand that, although this declaration was framed in a manner to conceal a tacit disavowal of the Hunt menace, it did not satisfy the English. On the other hand, Grimaldi was by no means agreeable to sepa-

[84] Renaut, *op. cit.*, in *Revue de l'Histoire des Colonies Françaises*, vol. 11, p. 52.
[85] *Ibid.*
[86] Text in *ibid.*, p. 52.

rating the questions of reparation and sovereignty. In his reply to Weymouth's second demand he had informed Masserano of his fears that the English would never consent to abandon the island without some other compensation than the mere abandonment of the Spanish settlement. They realized that this was a thorn in the side of Spain and if it were drawn out they intended to make Spain pay dearly. For this reason Grimaldi deemed it inexpedient that the question of right should remain unsettled.

Before the negotiators at London were advised of the conversations between Grimaldi and Harris at Madrid, the prorogation of Parliament had taken place. George III, in his address from the throne,[87] adverted to the Falkland Island crisis by stating that at the last session of Parliament he had expressed his fixed purpose to preserve the general tranquillity, that he had hoped to have been able to continue this policy. Since then considerations of honor had laid him under the necessity of preparing for a different situation.

The king went on to explain the situation:

By the act of the Governor of Buenos Aires, in seizing by force one of my possessions, the honour of my crown and the security of my people's rights were become deeply affected. Under these circumstances, I did not fail to make an immediate demand from the court of Spain for such satisfaction as I had right to expect for the injury I had received. I directed also the necessary preparations to be made, without loss of time, for enabling me to do myself justice, in case my requisition to the court of Spain should fail of procuring it for me; and these preparations you may be assured, I shall not think it expedient to discontinue until I shall have received proper reparation for the injury as well as satisfactory proof that other powers are equally sincere with myself in the resolution to preserve the tranquillity of Europe.

The debate[88] which ensued in the Commons on the address of the king fully justified the prediction of Choiseul

[87] Cobbett, *Parliamentary History*, vol. 16, p. 1030.
[88] *Ibid.*, vol. 16, p. 1032.

that Parliament would be instrumental in forcing the issue of war and peace. Shortly before Parliament had been prorogued, Choiseul, unable to resist the pressure which Grimaldi was putting upon him to hasten the armaments, had laid before the council the necessity of taking steps to avert a surprise such as had occurred in 1756.[89] Accordingly he demanded the sum of eight millions for the navy. This demand, contrary to his expectations, was not resisted by his enemies, Terray and Maupeou, both of whom stated that war was inevitable. Choiseul, doubtless suspecting a plot to compel him to disclose his true policy, had declined to take the same point of view and, with the purpose of reassuring the king who was avowedly against a war, had declared that he had the greatest hopes for peace, that England was pacifically disposed and Spain would make the required concessions. Nevertheless, it was essential that they should arm as a measure of safety. The session terminated when Louis XV exacted a promise from Choiseul that he would do his utmost for peace.

Choiseul was thus definitely pledged to the preservation of peace irrespective of what his personal inclinations may have been. The fact that it was virtually impossible for his cousin, the Duke de Praslin, minister of the marine, to secure any subsidies from Terray served still further to hamper Choiseul in the development of his original designs.[90]

In these circumstances, it is easy to comprehend the mingled feelings of anxiety and hope with which Choiseul awaited the news of George III's address. A few days be-

[89] Flammermont, *op. cit.*, p. 165.

[90] It is difficult to take a position on this much discussed question of whether or not Choiseul actually persisted in a design to precipitate a European war. The dispatches examined unquestionably prove that from time to time, especially in the summer of 1770, he nourished such a scheme, and yet during the intermediate period of the crisis he undoubtedly endeavored to undo what he set in motion. Consistency has never been the outstanding virtue of the politician.

fore the event Choiseul had discussed the situation with
Harcourt, the British ambassador, at some length and had
assured the latter again and again of his desire for peace—
assurances which the British ambassador was the readier
to credit as he believed Choiseul's tenure depended upon
keeping out of war.[91] At this same meeting Choiseul again
repeated his tentatives of good offices and added that if the
English would advise him of any particular obstacle in the
way of a settlement he would use all his influence to sur-
mount it. It is interesting to note that Choiseul in the most
explicit terms denied that what he was doing constituted
mediation. He then adverted to the king's speech and
asked whether it was warlike in tone. Harcourt assured him
that it was not such a speech. The following day, however,
the text reached Paris, and Choiseul, who was entertaining
Harcourt at dinner, with visible agitation pronounced the
speech to be a declaration of war. Harcourt, of course, denied this and at some length explained its content. Choiseul
then remarked that what Harcourt said corresponded entirely with the opinion of Francés, and he again expressed
his hope of a settlement.[92]

Choiseul would no doubt have felt less sanguine of peace
had he foreseen the full power of the attack made upon the
government by the opposition a few days after his conversation with Harcourt. On November 22, in the House of
Lords, the Duke of Richmond moved that an humble address be presented to the crown asking for the copies of
papers relating to any hostilities of Spain against the
king's dominions between September 12, 1769, and September 12, 1770, that the House be acquainted with any claims
of Spain to the Falklands, and finally that information re-

[91] Harcourt to Weymouth, November 20, 1770 (*R.O. State Papers,
France*, 281).

[92] The address reached Spain too late to affect the negotiations. *Cf.*
Grimaldi to Masserano, December 3, 1770 (*Archivo General de Simancas,
Estado*, leg. 6976, fo. 1, hereafter cited, *Arch. Gen. Sim., Est.*).

garding the state of the Spanish navy and the movement of her ships be supplied.[93]

The debate on the motion proceeded with great acerbity. The attitude of the ministry was substantially that the negotiations were under way and that any step to disclose the course of things by publication of the papers would merely tend to make further diplomatic discussion impossible. The opposition, led by the redoubtable Chatham, who delivered a speech well decorated with invective, charged the ministry with criminal delay in preparations for war, and with a total lack of patriotism in the negotiations. The motion was finally lost, and in the House of Commons, where a similar resolution was introduced, the same thing occurred.

The chief fear of the North ministry at this moment was that Chatham and his associates by continuing and protracting their attack would force them out of office on the war issue. Every further day of negotiations with Masserano consequently served to increase their embarrassment, as it gave credibility to the charge that they were acting without the assurance and courage that the situation demanded. At the same time, there was nothing to be gained in an out-and-out attitude of hostility toward Spain, particularly because such a change of position really implied a surrender to the opposition. In view of the previous record of Chatham and the universal admiration for his abilities as a war premier, such a victory would surely spell ruin to the North ministry and would assure Chatham's succession. In reality, therefore, the prorogation of Parliament had the effect at once of compelling the ministry to fix their course in the matter of preserving peace, and simultaneously of giving the opposition an unexampled opportunity to harry them out of existence.

With this latter object in view Chatham, on November 28, renewed his attack by a motion that Captain Hunt should be ordered to attend the House in the following

[93] Cobbett, *op. cit.*, vol. 16, p. 1081.

week.[94] Upon this motion being lost, Chatham moved an address to the king praying that the House be acquainted at what time the first demand was made for reparation from Spain. This was defeated. The next day in the House of Commons Mr. Dowdeswell moved the previous motion in the Falkland matter, but after some discussion the motion was defeated.[95]

All of this was not lost upon the representatives of the two Bourbon crowns. On November 28 Francés had a long interview with Lord North, who was at once first lord of the treasury and prime minister.[96] The refusal of Weymouth, the official primarily charged with the negotiation, to entertain further proposals, had led the Comte de Guines,[97] the new French ambassador, who had lately arrived, to send Francés to North, hoping by this roundabout method to influence the ministry to make a settlement. It may here be remarked, parenthetically, that at this period of history there was not the same bureaucratic punctilio in the matter of diplomatic intercourse as later obtained.

Francés was charged with a message from de Guines to Lord North in which the French ambassador expressed his surprise that Lord Weymouth had rejected all of Masserano's proposals, and particularly his latter offer, which was very reasonable, as these proposals gave England what she demanded in the form desired. The only conclusion to be drawn was that England desired war for an unworthy object. He went on to say that neither Spain nor France desired war, and that Masserano had even exceeded his

[94] Chatham, *Correspondence of William Pitt, Earl of Chatham* (Taylor and Pringle eds., 1839), vol. 4, p. 30, note 1. The speech was not reported.

[95] *Cf.* the enclosure in Masserano to Grimaldi, December 3, 1770 (*Arch. Gen. Sim., Est.*, leg. 6980, fo. 3).

[96] On North, *cf.* Lucas, *Lord North* (1913). At p. 331 *et seq.* is an account of the Falkland incident which is about as misleading as it could possibly be.

[97] On Guines *cf. Nouvelle Biographie Général* (Hoeffer ed., 1859), vol. 22, p. 752.

instructions in the premises. De Guines added, through Francés, that although he had no particular instructions from his king he was so anxious to avoid war that he was making the direct appeal to North to preserve peace on the basis that Spain would give the satisfaction demanded if England would fix a time for an evacuation stipulated for in a counter-declaration or convention simply to assure such evacuation.

North's reply to this appeal did not promise any weakening in the British position, for he stated that the ministry desired complete satisfaction without any convention, and that he understood Masserano's powers were greater than he had admitted. This Francés denied. He then asked whether or not England would abandon the *Gran Malvina* (West Falkland) after they had taken possession. He was led to ask this because North had said several times before that he could not comprehend why the Spanish court had no confidence in them.

The answer of North was important because the subsequent discussions pivoted about his suggestion. He said that he could not speak officially (ministerialment) on this matter, but *if Francés would promise that this conversation would not be made public he would say in confidence that they did not desire to keep the island, that it was worth nothing to them and if Spain would give the satisfaction demanded they would certainly evacuate.* Francés remarked that he did not know whether his court would adhere to what Masserano had previously proposed—an exchange of declarations—and he suggested that what might be done would be an interview of King George and Masserano, at which the former would direct his ministers to settle the question of right to the *Gran Malvina,* and assure Masserano that there would be no difficulty in composing the issue. Francés' suggestion, of course, went beyond the simple expedient of North—that the allies rely upon British faith. It is not surprising, therefore, that North equivocated, and finally promised an answer after he had laid the matter before the king.

This interview with Lord North marked a definite turn in the negotiations. After the categoric refusal of Weymouth to listen to anything except an unconditional acceptance of the British demands, the conciliatory language of North and his unofficial promise to abandon the islands indicated that the activities of the opposition had so far been successful as to produce a certain variety of view in the ministry if not actual differences of a more serious nature. North's attitude and his statements were the first sign of hope that the British would in any way recede from their original stand.

Francés was quick to appreciate the situation. Without informing Masserano, he dispatched a courier to Choiseul telling him to hold Masserano's courier with the latest notice of Weymouth's rejection of the Spanish proposals until he was advised of North's reply. In the meantime, on the twenty-ninth,[98] Masserano had discussed the situation with Lord Rochford, who was now secretary of state for the Northern Department, and very anti-Bourbon in his views. Rochford had declared roundly that there was no doubt of England's rights to the Falklands, but if Spain would give the satisfaction desired the English would then treat on the legal question. Masserano remarked very coolly that Rochford's views were not shared by everyone, and that if they once gave satisfaction without stipulating for reciprocal evacuation, the position of Spain would be hopelessly compromised. Rochford had then said that war was inevitable, and that Chatham's activities in the House of Lords were driving them in this direction.

Immediately after Masserano had left, Francés entered Rochford's office. The Englishman, strangely enough, adopted a totally different tone in this conversation. After bemoaning the fact that war seemed inevitable, he re-

[98] Masserano to Grimaldi, December 3, 1770.

marked that it was incredible that the Spanish would not rely upon the good faith of the English ministry, for *if Spain would only give satisfaction without condition England would abandon the Falklands to them, as she did not desire to make war for the islands.* Francés, hoping to feel out the alignment for peace and war in the cabinet, replied that he knew both the ministry and the king wanted war. This Rochford denied, but he added that North was the only one who had hopes of peace. This remark led Francés to inform him that he had conferred with North, a step which Rochford enthusiastically approved. It is important to note that the North negotiation was thus undertaken with the consent of the Foreign Office.

The proposal made by Francés of a formal confirmation by the king of the secret promise was duly considered at a plenary session of the cabinet, and it was rejected on the grounds that satisfaction must be complete without even the appearance of a secret convention. On their part, the ministry were prepared to send merely a sloop of war to the islands, and for the future Spain would have to rely upon the good faith of the English.[99]

When North communicated this decision to Francés, the latter accused the English of having decided for war. Everything, he said, pointed to it—the forty thousand seamen and the twenty thousand additional soldiers which they were about to vote. All this North denied most vehemently, and he insisted Spain was driving toward war, as evidenced by the fact that Masserano had advised all Spanish ships in the Thames to leave in ballast.

On December 1 Francés again conferred with Lord North, this time using as his text the third project of Masserano mentioned above, which the Frenchman had redrawn in terms somewhat more suave. North, after deciding to take a copy of the project, remarked that he could not go back on what he had said in the House of Commons to the effect

[99] Masserano to Grimaldi, December 3, 1770.

that they were not treating of the question of right but merely of satisfaction. Accordingly, he could not consent to the inclusion of any declaration on their part in the paper which Masserano was to sign. He therefore suggested a counter-declaration, and that after everything was settled they would treat of the right and the abandonment. This suggestion, he added, was not to be taken as a guarantee, for it was unofficial, his office not being that of secretary of state.

Francés replied that he had gone to North because he knew his disposition toward peace and that in reliance upon his answer he had suggested holding the Spanish courier. In response to North's query as to what proofs he had that Spain did not want war and would accept North's proposal, Francés said that he was sure the French king could secure Spanish acquiescence, and that a reply would be in by January 2. On his part, North promised to lay the matter before the cabinet and to have a definite answer by the third of December.

North was politically very timid and the boldness of his conduct on the present occasion filled him with nervous fears, for on the third he opened his conversation with Francés by repeating what he had previously said, that the conversation was not official, and then added some twenty times that it was not Francés' mediation which was moving him to continue treating, but England's love of peace. All Spain needed to do was to rely upon the ministry and their successors, because the Falklands did not suit England nor was the nation interested in keeping them because of expense. He declined, however, to treat of the question of right even verbally, until satisfaction had been given.

After this preliminary, North stated that he had consulted all his colleagues, none of whom would listen to the project which Francés had delivered the day before, because none of the ministers were sufficiently acquainted with the French language. He therefore asked Francés to explain the contents to him. The clever concealment of the British disavowal of Hunt at once caught his eye, but Francés insisted that the Spanish king would never yield on the point, as he believed his honor to be involved. North then remarked that he saw no reason to stickle over a word, and after some discussion the text was slightly revised.

Turning next to the question of possession, North asked that, to avoid any misunderstandings, the orders which were to be sent to the Spanish governor be communicated to the British. It was thereupon agreed that Masserano would make a declaration and that they would give a counter-declaration in the same form. Francés, having gotten this far with North, then renewed his suggestion that George III give Masserano an interview, in which he would prom- ise the Spanish ambassador that the question of right would be dealt with. North, however, said this was impossible, but that Spain would have to rely on their good faith and that they would show that they did not want war. As a sign of their indifference toward the Falklands he went on to cite a proposal of Admiral Hawke of a year before that the is- lands be abandoned. This, he said, had been opposed on the ground that it would arouse too much public antagonism, whereupon it had been decided that evacuation should take place the following year. After some discussion as to the guarantees for this settlement, the conference came to an end.

When the conversation was reported to Masserano, he was, of course, exceedingly dubious as to the good faith of North and his colleagues. The state of preparation for war in England was such, however, that an immediate declara- tion of war was impossible. For this reason, therefore, Masserano urged his court to continue its own armament.[100] In the meantime he did not fail to make an exhaustive re- connaissance of the position of the several ministers with a

[100] Masserano to Grimaldi, December 4, 1770 (*Arch. Gen. Sim., Est.,* leg. 6976, fo. 2).

view to determine whether or not there was complete accord between North and his secretaries of state, particularly as the former had kept insisting that he controlled only his own vote in the cabinet.

In pursuance of his purpose of sounding Weymouth, Masserano, on December 6, interviewed the secretary at length,[101] but was unable to deduce much either from his tone or from his language. He was led to conjecture, however, that negotiations were to be held in abeyance until the return of the courier from Spain to learn whether Charles III would adhere to the latest project and would rely on the good faith of the ministry to evacuate the Falklands after satisfaction was given, and that what North had said had been with approval of the two secretaries.[102] From the various interviews Masserano concluded that peace would not be disturbed if Charles III would give in on the two points, and would rely upon the good faith of the ministry on the point of abandonment.

It is interesting that at this particular moment the fear of war does not seem to have been very great. In fact, the successive victories in Parliament had greatly strengthened the hand of the government. On the other hand, just as Masserano suspected, there was not complete harmony in the ministry, and although North was unquestionably inclined to peace, the tone adopted by the Foreign Office itself was not encouraging. In these circumstances it was undoubtedly a very shrewd move on the part of Francés to approach Lord North and to get what was substantially a commitment of policy.

If we can rely upon Walpole's account of affairs, Wey-

<hr />

[101] Masserano to Grimaldi, December 9, 1770 (*Arch. Gen. Sim., Est.,* leg. 6980, fo. 6).

[102] Francés had an interview with Weymouth on this same day and drew the same conclusions. The Comte de Guines also advised Weymouth that his court was surprised England had not accepted Spain's proposal and that France would stand by Spain; *q. v.* Masserano's dispatch, cited above.

mouth had from the start played for war, believing George III to be thoroughly committed to such a policy, and that he would thus assure himself of a commanding position in a future war cabinet.[103] In the meantime North and the Bute faction, which Walpole describes as the "Scottish junto," apprehensive that Chatham would return to power, had deflected the king from his original martial course, for the king's dislike of Chatham seems to have outweighed his hatred of Spain. A prudent politician would, of course, have made a *volte-face* at this point, but Weymouth chose instead to adhere to his previous determination. At the time Francés approached North the cabinet situation was probably reaching a crisis, for Weymouth resigned within the next month. It was this situation, therefore, which really lent political significance to the North-Francés *pourparlers*.

Weymouth's rigid adherence to his original demands had of course committed Lord North further than he otherwise might have gone. At the same time, the opening of Parliament and the declarations there made by the government had likewise served to ossify the position *vis-à-vis* Spain. North, however, was keen enough to see that if he was to carry out his pacific policy he would have to produce a *douceur* of some variety for the wounded honor of Charles III. He was precluded by the previous course of negotiations from making any direct concessions in the Port Egmont matter itself. He could not consent to a paragraph in the proposed declaration to the effect that the question of right would be later negotiated, so he intimated that if the Port Egmont incident were treated solely as an affair in which an injury to the *honor* rather than to the *possessions* of George III were involved, *i.e.*, a matter requiring reparation only for the insult, carrying no implications on the matter of right, England was prepared to make a subsequent concession in the matter of right. In other words, North wanted the affair to be treated as a direct injury to

[103] Walpole, *op. cit.*, vol. 4, p. 157 *et seq.*

the dignity of the crown and not as an indirect injury through the violation of territory to which the crown laid claim.

Masserano, it will be recalled, had from the very outset proposed the mutual evacuation of the Falklands as a means of disposing of the question of right. What North was now proposing *was the evacuation by England alone, not indeed secured by any declaration, but by a mere verbal engagement,* as a consideration for the Spanish agreement to make reparation. A proposal of this sort went a great deal further than either Grimaldi or Masserano had dared to hope. Both of these men from the first had been concerned with how the rights of Spain might properly be safeguarded. The insistence upon the impropriety of Hunt's action had been the chief means by which they had sought to effect this. If the proposed evacuation, however, should actually take place, it rendered the threat of Captain Hunt which Charles III could so illy stomach purely academic, for there was no longer any necessity of safeguarding Spanish rights by an English disavowal of Hunt if the English were going to abandon their settlement. The question of the right to the islands would by such a promise and its fulfilment no longer be involved. In these circumstances it was obvious that the road to peace was open—the only question of importance being whether or not the Spanish king would be disposed to rely on the good faith of England.

The discussions of North and Francés had, therefore, really cleared the way to a settlement, for a totally new basis for negotiation had been laid. But in neither Paris nor Madrid were the courts fully advised of the internal situation in England, and from their point of view the situation was indeed desperate. Desperate, too, was the situation of Choiseul, and it was this fact which was to provoke the next move in the drama, and which was to affect so profoundly the ultimate settlement of the dispute.

CHAPTER VII

THE SECRET PROMISE

IF Lord North's dilemma in December, 1770, grew out of the political embarrassments of democracy, Choiseul's predicament at this time was due chiefly to the hazards inherent in serving an absolute monarchy. Quite apart from the fact of whether or not he was playing for war or peace, it is clear that Choiseul had from the outset been confident that it lay in his hands to shape the course of French politics. Certainly this had been his conviction in 1766, when the war with England had first been broached, and it undoubtedly was the case even as late as October, 1770, when he first saw fit to counsel Grimaldi to use caution. The month of November, however, had brought many disillusionments. We have seen how Terray and Maupeou had sought to trap Choiseul into a disclosure of his warlike aims, and how the latter, avoiding any commitments, had succeeded in postponing a breach with Louis XV, whose pacific sentiments were well known. His cleverness, however, had not brought the subsidies so necessary to the pursuit of his policy of waiting but arming.

At the Spanish court Choiseul's situation was understood, but by no means appreciated. In fact, the probable defection of France from the alliance was so thoroughly bruited about, that Harris[1] jubilantly reported to his government that if there was war Spain would stand alone. This was also the substance of a conversation between Choiseul and the Conde de Fuentes in the latter part of November.[2] On the twenty-ninth of that month, at a meeting of the council, Choiseul, who still had hopes that the king would not aban-

---

[1] Harris to Weymouth, November 26, 1770 (*R.O. State Papers, Spain*, 185).

[2] Flammermont, *op. cit.*, p. 169.

don his cousin, undertook to speak of the preparations for war. The king, however, interrupted him and postponed the session to another time.

The second of December having been chosen for another council meeting, Choiseul determined to prepare the king for a favorable reception of his plans by having Fuentes make representations to Louis asking for a statement of the extent of French armaments for transmission to his court to abate his government's misgivings. Louis expressed himself in friendly terms and added that his cousin's interests were his own. On the following day, however, when Choiseul sought to bring up the question of the pace of preparation in France, the king again abruptly adjourned the meeting.

In this posture of affairs it is not surprising that the arrival of news of Masserano's latest interview with Weymouth, and the consequent hopelessness of averting war should have determined Choiseul upon a step decidedly irregular from the diplomatic point of view, but which he hoped would save the situation. On December 3 he drew up a project which he dispatched to Masserano and which the latter was to present in lieu of instructions from his sovereign.[3]

The declaration[4] opened with the statement that the king of Spain, "forgetting and taking no notice" of the motive which had occasioned the events of June 10, was desirous

---

[3] *Projet de déclaration*. Choiseul to Masserano, December 3, 1770 (*Aff. Etr., Angleterre*, 494).

[4] The text is as follows: Le P^{ce} de Masseran ambassadeur, etc., "en vertu des ordres à lui donnés pour faire connaître combien sa Ma^{te} Catholique, dissimulant et oubliant le motif qui a occasionné l'événement du 10 juin, désire de conserver la paix et la bonne harmonie avec la Couronne Britannique, et en vertu aussi d'un pouvoir spécial dont il se trouve muni, pour donner une preuve manifeste et de la maniére la plus autentique, des intentions amicales et pacifiques de S. M. Cat^l, déclare, que S. M. Cat^l considérant l'amour dont elle est animé pour la paix et son amitié particulière pour S. M. B^{que}, désavoüe l'entreprise qui occasionna le 10 juin

of maintaining peace. Accordingly, he disavowed the enterprise of June 10, which had occasioned the expulsion of the
English who were on the Falklands. The declaration went
on to say that the king consented to the return of the English to the Falklands, as they had been on the day when the
violence disavowed had occurred. The king further agreed
that he would have the captured effects returned to the
English. In conclusion, it was stated that the declaration
was an authentic proof of the king's chagrin over an event
which might have disturbed the good understanding between the two crowns, but it (the declaration) could not
prejudice the anterior rights of the king to the Falklands—
rights founded upon ancient and prior discovery, upon possession and upon treaties, rights which the restoration of
the English consented to could not impair.

The project was worded in a manner intended to cover
Charles III's insistence upon a disavowal of Captain Hunt.
The words "forgetting and taking no notice of the motive"
were drawn to satisfy this point. The reservation of right
was beyond anything theretofore agreed upon by the English, but Choiseul doubtless expected concession on this

dernier l'expulsion des Anglais qui se trouvoient dans les Iles Malouines
ou Falkland au port dit Egmont.

"Le Prince de Masseran déclare aussi que S. M. Cat. consent que les
Anglais retournent s'établir dans l'Ile de la Grande Malouine par eux
appellée Falkland, comme ils y étoient avant le 10 juin de cette année jour
auquel la violence désavoüée a été exécutée. Et S. M. Cat¹ se charge de
leur faire remettre, à leur retour, par un officier préposé de sa part, les
effets qu'ils ont laissé au Port dit Egmont le 10 juin selon l'Inventaire qui
en fut fait alors.

"La dᵉ déclaration du Pᶜᵉ de Masseran est une preuve autentique du
chagrin du Roy son Maître, sur un fait qui aurait pu troubler la bonne
intelligence entre les deux couronnes, mais ne peut pas préjudicier aux
droits anterieurs de S. M. Cat¹ sur les Isles appellées Malouines et par les
Anglais Falkland; droits fondés sur l'ancienneté et la primauté de la dé-
couverte, sur la possession, et sur les traités; auxquels droits S. M. Cat¹
déclare que le rétablissement des Anglais consenti de sa part au Port dit
Egmont, ne pourra donner atteinte."

point in view of the regal manner in which the Hunt episode was glossed over.

Due to stress of weather this project, together with the dispatches accompanying it, was delayed at Calais for a week. In the interim another council meeting had taken place[5] at which Terray had demonstrated that the treasury was empty and that France's credit was exhausted. This report was counter to an earlier one showing a favorable balance, and yet the king exhibited not the least interest in the situation. Choiseul, believing discretion to be the better part of valor, maintained an astute silence. On the other hand, his cousin, the Duc de Praslin, at the next session of the council (December 9) proceeded to attack the comptroller general with such violence that the king at once adjourned the meeting.[6]

Choiseul's position at this moment was that of a juggler who has sent into the air more objects than he can conveniently control. He had practically lost the royal confidence and he was unable to assure a complete fulfilment of the military terms of the Family Compact, although he had so far relied upon that same treaty as to ask the Spanish ambassador at London to ignore his monarch's instructions and to follow those of an ally. He had yet to make his peace with Grimaldi for taking this unprecedented step, and when the news of the North-Francés negotiations arrived he notified his colleague of what he had done.[7]

Choiseul began his communication by intimating that the Spanish negotiations with England were at an end, and that nothing but war remained, as Charles III undoubtedly would not go back on what he had already said. This being

---

[5] Cf. Flammermont, op. cit., p. 170. Cf. also Memoires de l'Abbé Terrai (1776), p. 52.

[6] Fuentes, reminding the king at this moment of his promise to furnish him with an inventory of French preparations, was rewarded for his importunity by having Louis turn his back to him.

[7] Choiseul to Grimaldi, December 10, 1770 (Aff. Etr., Espagne, 561).

the state of affairs and Choiseul having received intimations from Francés that negotiations might be continued, he had sent to London a project which was drawn in the sense in which he had always understood the affair and which did justice to both courts. He then proceeded to explain how his project met what he conceived to be the difficulties of the case: 1, The reciprocal disavowal of Hunt and Bucareli; 2, The fault of Bucareli; 3, The reciprocal evacuation of the island, which Spain required at the same time that she gave satisfaction.

The justification for his act Choiseul declared to be, first, that the negotiation be sustained in a simple, amiable form and satisfying to everyone; second, to demonstrate that if the project was not used as a basis of negotiation the English and not Spain wanted war; and third, that Charles could disavow his ambassador without any embarrassment to him in case the negotiation did not please the king, and without prejudice to his case could make a new project. Masserano, he added, was to take up the matter "*sub spe rati.*" Choiseul informed his colleague that he was sending the dispatches relative to the Francés-North negotiation, stating that he feared Francés and North were falling into a trap and that he did not believe the two courts could go further than he had proposed in his project. In conclusion, he remarked that Grimaldi might be angry at what he had done, but that he should remember, while the Falklands and all the accessories of the affair belonged to Spain, the war belonged to France as well as to Spain.[8]

The new project arrived in London on the thirteenth.[9] Francés at once applied himself to the task of persuading Masserano to accept the French instructions, but the latter insisted that Choiseul's proposals were too radically differ-

[8] On the same day Choiseul advised Ossun of what he had done. Choiseul to Ossun, December 10, 1770 (*Aff. Etr., Mém. et Doc.*, 575).

[9] Masserano to Grimaldi, December 11, 1770 (*Arch. Gen. Sim., Est.*, leg. 6980, fo. 8).

ent from those of his own government. Moreover, he was convinced that the British government would not accept them, and in view of these circumstances he could not incur the censure of his government. Francés resorted to every argument to convince Masserano, but in vain, and even the arrival on the fourteenth of a copy of Choiseul's letter to Grimaldi did not shake the Spaniard's resolution. In these circumstances Francés decided, at Masserano's suggestion, to lay the matter before the British government on his own initiative, so that, in the event of an acceptance, Choiseul could notify Grimaldi and a courier with the Spanish reply could return before January 15, the day on which Parliament again assembled after the Christmas holidays.[10]

[10] The Duke of Grafton tells a story in this relation which does not in every respect match up with the dispatches. He says: "The restless disposition of the Duc de Choiseul, prompted him to consider the moment favorable for forwarding his favorite purpose of reducing the power of Great Britain. With this view, through the channel of Grimaldi, he did everything to foment the commencing quarrel with England; and, as I believe, trusting that he should be able to shew to his Royal Master that if called on by Spain for troops or ships, under the Pacte de Famille, these might be duly furnished, as an auxiliary, and not as a principal in the contest. Choiseul's design, however, was so veiled over, as to be kept away from the knowledge of the French King; and the rivals of Choiseul's power did not fail to improve the advantages they had obtained. The French King with much anger charged his Minister to take care, that there should be no rupture between Spain and England; well knowing that Spain would acquiesce when France was firmly decided. At this moment a courier arrives with such dispatches, to Prince Masserano, the Spanish Ambassador to our Court, as would at once have plunged the two countries into an inevitable war. The messenger brought also other letters communicating to their ambassador at Paris the directions sent to Masserano. Immediately on Choiseul's reading the letters, he saw but one way left by which he could obey his master, and hope to preserve his power, he dispatched a courier to Monsieur Francés, left Chargé des Affaires at London; where the two couriers arrived the same morning. Francés flew directly to the Spanish Ambassador, whom he found on the point of setting out for an audience of the Secretary of State, on the subject of the dispatches he had just received. The Duc de Choiseul's letter was given to

According to Francés,[11] the internal situation in England was such as to render the diplomatic situation more and more critical. North was too timid and not a sufficiently dominating person in the cabinet to overcome Weymouth, whom Francés regarded as maliciously inclined, and to effect the acceptance of any step suggested by France, whose actions were viewed with the greatest distrust. Masserano was convinced that the ministry would not dare to present a conditional settlement to Parliament even though Francés looked on the reservation of right as a mere matter of form and believed that North's proposals of December 3 represented their best offer. His own view of the latter was that British promises in the matter of evacuation were open to grave doubt.

As the favorable outcome of the negotiations seemed to depend upon the difference of view of the members of the cabinet, Francés proposed to lay the Choiseul project before Lord North and Weymouth jointly, hoping not only to ascertain whether the two were in agreement, but if possible to play them off against each other. Accordingly he requested an interview, stating that he had a proposed settlement from Choiseul satisfying to both crowns.[12] North

Masserano to read; wherein he ventured to intreat him not to enter on the orders he had received from his own Court; as he might be assured, that he would receive instructions of a different nature, as soon as time would allow them to come from Madrid. Masserano, having read his own dispatches over again, as also those addressed to Francés, with some difficulty was brought to comply with the latter; for he was undoubtedly not ignorant that the weight of French councils would preponderate at his Court; thereupon he submitted. I was well acquainted with Mon^r Francés while he was with Mon^r de Chatelêt in England. After the American war he passed over into this country to visit all those from whom he had received civilities; I saw him a great deal, and we had many interesting conversations; and from him, in one of these, I had the anecdote above related." Grafton, *Autobiography and Political Correspondence* (Anson ed., 1898), pp. 255-256.

[11] Francés to Choiseul, December 14, 1770 (*Aff. Etr., Espagne,* 561).

[12] One is constantly struck with the shrewd political sense of Francés.

replied that he was always glad to hear new proposals, but he could receive them only *ad referendum*. Weymouth, he feared, in view of the system which he had adopted as the only one compatible with the honor of the crown, would probably not be willing to listen to propositions different from those made by him, or which did not emanate directly from Spain.[13] Francés, however, insisted that the proposal was not only acceptable but that Choiseul would undertake to secure Spanish consent.[14]

The difficulty of getting Weymouth to be present at a conference was as great as North had anticipated. The former finally agreed, however, to appear at a meeting on the sixteenth, although he stated he would not assist in any conference.[15] The meeting was accordingly held at North's house and Francés opened proceedings by exhibiting three papers, one containing the disavowal and restitution of the colony, the second, the reservation of Spanish rights, and the third, an admission by the British ministry approving the satisfaction and the reservation.

North at once stated that this was an entirely new and

Of course his friendship with men like Grafton and Walpole, who were repositories of all the court gossip, was a great aid to his natural sagacity.

[13] In a separate dispatch to Choiseul of December 14, 1770 (*Aff. Etr., Espagne*, 561), Francés discussed in detail the acceptability of the project of December 3. He stated that even if Masserano would agree to it, he doubted whether the effect would be as great as Choiseul hoped, for he was convinced that the project would be regarded by the British as totally inadmissible. The British Ministry were totally devoid of imagination and neither desired nor were able to depart from their demands. His earlier proposals to North were made with this in view and because he wished to be able to negotiate during the parliamentary holiday. Otherwise he feared that Parliament would not be adjourned. He was convinced further that the desire for peace which animated North would aid in the prolongation of negotiations.

[14] The Comte de Guines, so Masserano reported, had orders not to present his credentials if Masserano was advised to withdraw.

[15] Masserano to Grimaldi, December 19, 1770 (*Arch. Gen. Sim., Est.*, leg. 6980, fo. 10).

different project from that decided upon and sent to France on the third, and asked whether the French court had not made any proposals relative to the latter, adding that all they did was to make new and more difficult proposals which led him seriously to doubt their desire for peace. Francés replied by saying that France was really using its good offices to effect a settlement and was not trying to interfere and play the arbiter. The proposals of December 3 were made unofficially and he had no knowledge whether the Spanish court would agree to them; that, moreover, Choiseul was also ignorant of their attitude, and hence had sent proposals more admissible and more agreeable to all. Thereupon North read the three papers, remarking that the words "forgetting and taking no notice of" were superfluous. He added that they would never admit the Spanish claim to prior discovery, possession and treaty rights. As for the paper which the British were to sign, he stated that they would never sign it because it was conceding Spain a right which they had always denied.

Francés, answering these objections, declared that they need not be concerned with rights maintained by Spain, provided they were restored to the island, and he added that North could not expect the Spanish to give them a paper by which it would appear that the British were being put in possession of something which Spain pretended was her own, because England would use it as if it gave her a legitimate right. North then said that he did not want to increase his rights nor those of Spain, but he could not admit a proposal so different from the antecedent ones. The present circumstances, he said, were such that no conditional satisfaction was acceptable, but if settlement were made along the lines of his earlier suggestion England would ask for no indemnity of any sort. The conference closed with a promise by North to lay Choiseul's proposals before the cabinet.

There is no means of knowing exactly what transpired

between North and Weymouth after this meeting. In any event, the difference of view between the two had become so ineradicable that Weymouth resigned,[16] but without going over to the Bedford party, which was grimly pressing for war,[17] and Rochford was given the seals of the Southern Department. The change was viewed by the two Bourbon ambassadors with great complacency, partly because Weymouth was the most ardent war man in the cabinet,[18] and partly because Rochford, having resided as ambassador both at Madrid and Paris, was regarded as more sympathetic to the two courts, a feeling which the new secretary very soon dissipated. At the same time, the move presaged the ascendancy of North in the cabinet, and consequently the prospects of a pacific settlement were brighter.

The resignation of Weymouth involved a temporary suspension of negotiations, and in the interim the foreign ministers visited about with great assiduity, endeavoring to ascertain what the new orientation was to be.[19] Masserano, discoursing at length with Lord Hillsborough, who was at the time secretary of state for the Colonies and president of the Board of Trade, a not particularly discreet person, was told that Weymouth was strongly for war and that the other ministers had opposed him. The new proposals had been laid before the ministry, but not one of them was dis-

[16] Masserano to Grimaldi, December 18, 1770 (*Arch. Gen. Sim., Est.,* leg. 6978, fo. 1). *Cf.* also Walpole, *Memoirs of the Reign of George III,* vol. 4, p. 157.

[17] Both the Duke and Duchess of Bedford, as well as Lord Hillsborough, in conversations with Masserano denied that the Bedford party was out for war, but in London generally a contrary impression seems to have prevailed. Masserano to Grimaldi, December 19, 1770.

[18] In Weymouth's last dispatch to Harris (November 28, 1770, *Falkland Papers,* p. 28), he advised the latter that the negotiations were at an end and that he should notify the British vessels in Spanish ports of the fact.

[19] On the Weymouth resignation *cf.* Chatham, *Correspondence* (Taylor and Pringle eds., 1840), vol. 4, p. 60 *et seq.*

posed to accept them. After a considerable discussion, Hillsborough adverted to the North proposals of the third and intimated that these would be acceptable. Masserano retorted that the essence of these was that they should rely upon the faith of the ministry and the resignation of Weymouth showed that ministries were of short duration. Furthermore, the proposals were unofficial and, without any writing to rely on, such promises were easy to forget. Within six months they might be in a war because the promise was forgotten. Hillsborough, however, denied very emphatically that they wanted the Falklands, but he insisted that unless Spain would act for peace, war would be inevitable.[20]

It was obvious from this interview that the ministry was generally behind the North proposals, and for this reason Masserano advised his court[21] to adhere to these rather than to the Choiseul project, for, said he, although the proposals of North were merely verbal and unofficial, they at least dealt with the evacuation of the *Gran Malvina* (West Falkland), whereas in Choiseul's project nothing was said of evacuation, and protests and reservations would be of little avail once the English were in possession.

On December 20 Francés again interviewed North, with not very different results.[22] The prime minister expressed himself satisfied with the first paper and was willing to forego his previous objections to the terms "forgetting and taking no notice," on the ground that, while they might seem

[20] The war preparations were meanwhile going on at a lively rate, as were the impressments for the supply of the navy. *Cf.* Masserano to Grimaldi, December 11, 1770 (*Arch. Gen. Sim., Est.*, leg. 6980, fo. 8); December 21, 1770 (*ibid.*, leg. 6978, fo. 2); December 22, 1770 (*ibid.*, leg. 6980, fo. 11); December 28, 1770 (*ibid.*, leg. 6978, fo. 6); December 31, 1770 (*ibid.*, leg. 6978, fo. 5).

[21] Masserano to Grimaldi, December 19, 1770 (*Arch. Gen. Sim., Est.*, leg. 6980, fo. 10).

[22] Francés to Choiseul, December 22, 1770, no. 66 (*Aff. Etr., Angleterre*, 494).

to weaken the disavowal, they should not prevent a conciliation, as the phrase was intended to avoid any idea of reciprocity, which was inadmissible in view of the insult. North
also seemed to be agreeable on the article dealing with the
reëstablishment of the English colony, but he asked that
words be added to the effect that the action taken was to the
end that it be notorious by this action that things were restored to the same condition that they had been at the time
of the expulsion.

The real difficulty arose over the papers England was to
execute. North declared very positively that if the maintenance of peace depended upon a written acceptance of
the declaration of reservation of right by Spain, war was
inevitable. Francés insisted that it was impossible for
Spain to give a writing by which she consented to a colony,
when such an instrument could be used against her as a
title, unless England could in her response give Spain some
guaranty in the matter. He then asked if England received
the reservation whether she would make a reply and what
this would be. North requested more time for an answer.

Two days later North again sent for Francés and at once
raised difficulties over the disavowal. The two words which
he had previously been inclined to admit he now said he
could not formally engage to approve. Francés said they
were essential, and he could scarcely believe England would
make war for two words when they would obtain restitution
of the colony. North answered that he himself wanted the
words suppressed, and he could make no engagement on the
score of acceptance by the government unless they were
dropped, as two members of the council were absent at the
moment.

Passing next to the discussion of the reservation of right,
Francés asked North whether the English had ever contested the rights of Spain to the islands. He insisted that
there was no state paper which proved either a claim or a
contest on the part of England. A furtive establishment,

said he, not recognized by Spain could not serve to divest
that power of her rights and it was consequently equitable
that if the British were restored this act should not be
turned against Spain. Lord North admitted the justice of
this principle, but he added that it was also not equitable
that by a mere act of violence Spain should acquire title
and an advantage which she had not previously enjoyed.
Acquiescence in the reservation of right would have the
effect of a recognition by England of this right which, although she had never contested, she nevertheless had never
recognized. Moreover, England must not lose anything in
receiving satisfaction which might appear as if purchased,
and Spain in giving satisfaction should gain nothing. England, he declared, would never accept the reservation of
right, but she would accept and reply *mutatis mutandis* to
a declaration by which the king of Spain declared that he
consented to make satisfaction for the acts of June 10
alone and without affecting his anterior rights to the Falklands. In this manner the *status quo ante* would be restored
and neither side would gain or lose.

It may here be remarked that this proposal was of signal
importance for subsequent negotiations. North does not
seem to have been inclined to attribute great importance to
the Port Egmont colony. The fact that he was so ready to
promise evacuation in the event Spain would give satisfaction, although this was beyond anything Charles III had
asked, is evidence of his feelings on the matter. At the same
time, as he explained to Francés,[23] the reservation could

[23] Francés to Choiseul, December 22, 1770 (*Aff. Etr., Angleterre,* 494,
2d letter). In this dispatch Francés stated that he regarded North's ultimatum as doing everything to avert a war. He stated that the king, the
ministry, and the people were for once agreed, but only in the maintenance of the position taken and not for the purposes of any softening of
the demands on Spain. Regarding Weymouth's resignation he stated that
it had been brought about by friction with North and by the fact that the
former had demanded a rejection of all negotiations with France, the recall of Harris, and additional demands on Spain for the expenses incurred.

not be agreed to because occurring simultaneously with the agreement to give satisfaction it could only be looked upon as an abandonment of British rights,—the price paid for the reparation. And what bothered North the most in this situation was that any restrictions on the reparation would arouse such opposition in the nation that he would be compelled to resign.

Francés fully appreciated the difficulties to which parliamentary interference subjected a negotiation as delicate as the one then in progress. On the other hand, he had no idea of permitting Lord North's domestic policies to operate so as to force Spain into an untenable position. He was fully conscious of the fact that the sort of reservation proposed by North was not a sufficient safeguard for Spain. He accordingly told North that his *mutatis mutandis* declaration would never be acceptable to Spain, that they would not allow England to keep the Falklands, and, furthermore, that any suggestion of indemnity for the armaments occasioned by the incident—a proposition recently raised in Parliament—was also not to be considered. North replied that if Spain gave prompt satisfaction indemnity would not be

His departure had consequently produced greater harmony. Francés asked that the most explicit instructions should be given to Masserano in case Choiseul was able to bring Spain around, in order that the negotiation could be terminated with all possible speed as the British were fearful they were being played with. He also requested that if Choiseul approved North's ultimatum, he be informed positively and that North be encouraged. He added, "no one has confidence in Lord Harcourt, and Mr. Walpole [respectively ambassador and secretary of embassy at Paris] is suspected. Moreover, they are neither one in correspondence with the Prime Minister, who would never compromise himself by putting any of his intentions in writing. The two secretaries of State are equally circumspect, writing nothing either officially or confidentially, in their delicate position where they believe they will be attacked in Parliament and they desire to be in a position to deny positively that they did not turn to France to obtain satisfaction."

What he says about Harcourt is borne out in Weymouth to Harcourt, November 28, 1771 (*R.O. State Papers, France*, 281).

thought of. He then said, regarding the question of right, that although he could not enter into any formal engagement even verbally in this regard, Spain could and must be assured that if England would not make war on account of an affront, she would not do so for the Falkland Islands.[24]

North's temper during the interview was reported by Francés to have been not too genial. He insisted that they could not be put off longer than the return of the courier. Francés asked him very coldly whether they wanted war or peace, because if they desired the latter they had to give Francés time to lay the English point of view before Spain, as up to this time the English had been very short and had conducted negotiations in an equivocal and obscure manner. If England precipitated action before the end of January she would stand before Europe accused of having wanted war from the first. North at once said that England did not want war and that she would take no action until Spain had positively refused satisfaction.[25]

While Choiseul's lieutenant was making these desperate efforts to effect a settlement, Masserano's accounts of his

[24] The projects sent to Choiseul were enclosed with Francés' no. 66 of December 14, 1770, and were substantially the same as Choiseul's original in form.

[25] Francés was more than ever convinced of North's pacific disposition when on the night of Thursday, the twentieth, in response to a summons from the Prime Minister, Francés found both North and Sandwich, with whom North was dining, very talkative and very frank, his Lordship being "drunk as a cabby" (*ivre comme un fiacre*). Francés retailing the ensuing scene to Choiseul stated with great positiveness that not only did the Ministry not want war but they would make no difficulties on the score of the question of right. Francés came to this conclusion because he was positive North knew he could not continue to hold office if there was war. In the midst of his drunkenness Francés said that North adhered to the same fundamental principles and the same course of ideas as he pursued when sober, "because these gentlemen by force of habit, mechanically preserve their logic and reasoning powers when intoxicated." At the conference on the twenty-second North was very morose and captious because he feared Francés might try to take advantage of the circumstances of the

interviews with Weymouth in November had reached Madrid.[26] Grimaldi, by this time thoroughly disgruntled by the news from France, was equally disturbed by the intelligence that Weymouth declined to abate his demands in any particular. The refusal to give in on the point of Captain Hunt's menace was bitterly received, but Grimaldi succeeded in dissuading Charles from pressing the matter further, and Masserano was instructed, on December 6, that the king abandoned this demand and consented to the reëstablishment of the English at Port Egmont in the state prior to June 10. Charles was further willing to disavow the governor of Buenos Aires, but Masserano was expressly advised that the king insisted upon an instrument providing for the reciprocal evacuation of the Falklands at such time as the English might choose. These instructions were to be submitted to Louis XV, and if he agreed to them, Masserano was to proceed, but if he did not, the instructions of November 5 were to govern his conduct.

These instructions are cited not so much because they played a rôle in the negotiations, for even when they were drawn up events in London had so far progressed that they were no longer apposite, but because they indicate that Spain was not so resolved upon a war as has sometimes been charged,[27] although, of course, the attitude of France was responsible for these amended views.

Ossun, writing to Choiseul on December 10,[28] gives a very

previous meeting. Francés to Choiseul, December 14, 1770 (*Aff. Etr., Angleterre*, 494, 2d letter.) Quoted also in Flammermont, *op. cit.*, p. 184, n.

It is a curious circumstance how various historians with their unfortunate penchant for the trivial have quoted liberally from this dispatch and have overlooked the more important official communication of the same day.

[26] Grimaldi to Masserano, December 6, 1770 (*Arch. Gen. Sim., Est.,* leg. 6980, fo. 4).

[27] This has been too frequently assumed. *Cf.* Brown, *op. cit.*, p. 431; Hertz, *British Imperialism in the Eighteenth Century*, p. 110 *et seq.*

[28] Ossun to Choiseul, December 10, 1770 (*Aff. Etr., Espagne,* 561).

gloomy picture of the Spanish court torn between a too lively sense of injury at the hauteur of the British, and disillusionment over the French attitude. Fuentes had given very circumstantial accounts of the state of French finances as well as of court politics, so that when the news of England's latest refusal to alter her terms was received, a caucus was held of the whole ministry, all the facts from both England and France being laid before them.[29] As late as December 17[30] Grimaldi was still in the dark as to what the king would do. As the attitude of England seemed to Grimaldi absolutely uncompromising, for the North proposals of December 3 had not yet arrived, Masserano was given discretion to demand his passports[31] should difficulties be put in the way of further negotiation, and he was to proceed to Paris, where he was to await his king's orders.[32]

Before these instructions had arrived in Paris on their way to London the fortunes of Choiseul had taken an apparent turn for the better. On December 13 he was confidentially apprised of the fact that his enemies proposed to lay before the king certain charges that he was involved in the resistance of the *parlements* to the king. Choiseul at once resolved to take the bull by the horns. Meeting Louis XV that same evening, he stated that he knew he had been charged with two breaches of faith, the first being an at-

[29] *Ibid.* Danvila, *op. cit.*, vol. 4, p. 137 *et seq.*, gives the substance of a long and elaborate opinion of d'Aranda. *Cf.* Ferrer del Rio, *Historia del Reinado de Carlos III*, vol. 3, p. 80 *et seq.*

[30] Grimaldi to Masserano, December 17, 1770 (*Arch. Gen. Sim., Est.*, leg. 6980, fo. 9).

[31] *Ibid.*

[32] On the same date Harris reported that a messenger had been sent to Masserano with instructions probably to explain the king's views. He added that he was convinced that Grimaldi would do everything in his power to effect a settlement. Harris seems to have had a wretched spy service, an inexcusable breach of duty in the days when such methods had reached a high degree of perfection. Harris to Weymouth, December 17, 1770 (*R.O. State Papers, Spain*, 185).

tempt to force France into war, the second an alleged inci-
tation of the *parlements*. With regard to the first Choiseul
reviewed the whole Falkland case in such a manner as to
absolve himself, and on the latter charge he demanded a
trial. The king forthwith expressed to Choiseul his confidence and good will. Choiseul was, of course, enchanted, for
he was completely taken in by Louis XV's assurances. Apparently he was actually convinced that the king was frank
in what he said, and that the control over the situation was
in his hands.[33]

The restoration to royal favor did not, unfortunately for
Choiseul, render him master of the situation. The eighteenth of December brought Francés' dispatches of the fourteenth relating his interviews with North with reference to
the Choiseul project. The Duc was already in possession of
Grimaldi's instructions to Masserano of the sixth, in which
the latter was ordered to cleave in every event to the mutual
evacuation as the only means of leaving the question of
right unprejudiced by the restoration of the colony. It was
only too patent that, unless some satisfactory means of saving Spanish rights could be found, war was inevitable.
Choiseul accordingly recurred to the North proposals of
December 3, which he had at first looked upon with grave
suspicion.

The day after their receipt, Francés' dispatches were
forwarded to Grimaldi with a personal letter from Choiseul
in which the policy to be pursued was fully described.[34] It
was clear, wrote Choiseul, that his proposal regarding the
question of right was not acceptable and that his project of
the third was therefore of no use. On this point he had conferred with Fuentes and they had agreed that the only way
of maintaining peace was to make the declaration alone and
to trust the English in the matter of the discussion of right,
making simply a verbal declaration of this score. Choiseul

[33] Flammermont, *op. cit.*, p. 172.
[34] Choiseul to Grimaldi, December 19, 1770 (*Aff. Etr., Espagne,* 561).

added that he still thought that a reservation in writing was entirely equitable, and so he did not advise Grimaldi to depart from this point. Indeed, this requirement was so evidently fair that he believed, in spite of the news from London, the English would accept it, the chief difficulty being to get some sort of a response from them. To keep the peace it would be necessary to authorize Masserano to make the reservation in a declaration trusting the English for their response, and at the same time declaring verbally that if their conduct was not such as Spain was entitled to rely upon after their promise, his Catholic Majesty would not disarm until their action fitted their words.

After the dour warning from Ossun that the Spanish were thoroughly disgusted with the inaction of France, Choiseul hesitated to press his colleague too far. He told Grimaldi that he was not advising him but merely suggesting that his was the only way to assure peace. If he should come to a contrary decision it would be necessary to declare war by the end of January, in which event he wished to be advised when the general embargo on vessels would be put in effect, as he desired to do the same. In conclusion he again remarked that the decision lay with Spain whether a war for such a petty object was justifiable. No one, he wrote, should sacrifice the honor of the crown, but he did not believe that here the honor of the crown was compromised. A mere question of interest was involved in the question of right and the problem really was whether this interest was worth the hazard of a war.

At the time this dispatch was composed Choiseul was, in the nature of things, much more fully and recently advised of the turn taken by the negotiations at London than was the Spanish court. He knew, of course, that the discussions had long since passed beyond any consideration of the question of mutual evacuation, and that Spain's claim of rights to the Falklands could only be saved by an acceptance of North's verbal promise to abandon the islands or by an express reservation of right. What he contrived, therefore, in his note of the nineteenth was to effect an amalgamation of the two schemes, flattering himself doubtless that his project of the third had found sufficient favor in the eyes of King Charles to render his new formula more acceptable.

If Choiseul, however, cherished any illusions regarding his influence at the Spanish court he was gravely mistaken. His letter of the tenth informing Grimaldi of the steps taken did not reach Madrid until the eighteenth and was not laid before the king until the twentieth.[35] It arrived, however, at a moment when the intrigues of the war party were at their height, so that although Ossun reported Grimaldi personally inclined to the plan, he feared the king would succumb to the representations of the Conde de Aranda that to admit the two demands of England would fatally compromise his honor. In view of this situation, Grimaldi, who feared he might be ousted, declined to assume any responsibility and referred the whole question to the other ministers.

The king's view of the matter was embraced in an instruction to Masserano of December 24, 1770.[36] By this time the accounts of the first meetings of North and Francés had likewise reached Madrid, the results of which Grimaldi remarked drily were substantially nil. As for the Choiseul project, the king expressed the hope that Masserano had not presented it, for he was fully instructed of the extent to which Spain was willing to go, although he hinted that depending on what the outcome of Francés' efforts were the king might change his attitude.

On the same day Grimaldi replied to Choiseul's letter of the tenth,[37] giving a very detailed and circumstantial account of the situation in Madrid. In the first place, he stated

[35] Ossun to Choiseul, December 20, 1770 (*Aff. Etr., Espagne,* 561).

[36] Grimaldi to Masserano, December 24, 1770 (*Arch. Gen. Sim., Est.,* leg. 6980, fol. 12).

[37] Grimaldi to Choiseul, December 24, 1770 (*Aff. Etr., Espagne,* 561).

the king was animated by a high sense of honor which the
arrogant and "legislative" manner of the English ministry
had excessively piqued. In the second place, as it had
seemed proper that the whole council be consulted, an unanimity of feeling had developed against sacrificing the
honor of the king. In the third place, all of Grimaldi's efforts to move the king were stultified by constant rumors
that he was immolating the royal honor, a fact which compelled him to act with circumspection. The Spanish view of
the case was that it would be humiliating to disavow Bucareli, dishonorable and a mark of weakness to restore Port
Egmont, except a simultaneous agreement or convention be
made providing for the evacuation, whereby it would be
made known that Spain had gained her object of not allow-
ing the English to settle in this part of the world.

In view of these facts Grimaldi pleaded that he was not
master of the situation, and he doubted whether there was
any man who could move the king when he believed his
honor was at stake. This feeling was so acute that even
Francés' action in approaching the English ministry after
repeated refusals to treat was looked on as inappropriate.
The one ray of light which Grimaldi could cast on the situation consisted in the fact that the king had dispatched a letter to Louis XV by the same courier in which he stated with
respect to the project of Choiseul that he would await news
as to how it was received before reaching a decision.[38]

Ossun, writing on the same day,[39] supplied further facts
which indicated that Grimaldi's task of dissuading the king
from war was not wholly hopeless. It appears that de
Aranda had imprudently written to Grimaldi a very sa-
tiric criticism of the king's conduct in the present negotia-

[38] The king of Spain writing to Louis XV on December 22, 1770, explained the attitude of his court and attributed the failure of the English
to settle to his own lack of vigor. He further urged Louis to hasten his
preparations. Text in Blart, *op. cit.*, pp. 181-182.

[39] Ossun to Choiseul, December 24, 1770 (*Aff. Etr., Espagne,* 561).

tion. This letter had been exhibited to Charles, who was so much incensed that he had ordered that de Aranda should not be consulted with regard to matters outside his office. Grimaldi, whose position had been seriously threatened by de Aranda, was profiting by this incident to win adherence to his policy. Grimaldi himself confided to Ossun that the king would undoubtedly feel his honor sufficiently salved if the disavowal of Hunt could be wrung from the English; he would then not only disavow Bucareli but agree to the restoration of Port Egmont with a reciprocal reservation of right. This would also justify the king in the eyes of the people, who were so far excited by the events as to make them a real factor to be considered.[40] Indeed, the popular feeling had run so high that the king, in the event France did not fulfil her obligations under the alliance, was prepared to go to war rather than acquiesce in the British demands.

When these letters reached France, Choiseul was no longer minister. The cabal which had been working so long for his dismissal finally was able to utilize the Anglo-Spanish crisis as the means of his downfall. According to the Baron de Besenval,[41] Louis XV was a particular stickler for having all transactions with foreign states officially conducted. Choiseul, primarily at the instance of an official in his department, the Abbé de Ville, was accused by the cabal of carrying on a secret correspondence with Spain of which the king was not informed.[42] The abbé, being questioned by the king of the state of negotiations with Spain, informed his master that he could not answer, because Choiseul drew up his own dispatches and did not communicate them to

---

[40] To understand how solicitous the court was of popular feelings one need only recall the riots in Madrid three years before.

[41] Besenval, *Mémoires* (1821), vol. 1, p. 255 *et seq.*

[42] This the king regarded as his privilege. Louis' private spy system was the bane of his ministers' existence. *Cf.* the account in Broglie, *Le Sécret du Roi* (1879).

anyone. The king thereupon asked Choiseul to draft a letter to Charles III to the effect that the king absolutely desired peace and that no consideration would induce him to take part in a war if it was declared. Choiseul demurred on the ground that he had given assurances of his support of the Family Compact. The king thereupon succumbed to the incessant demands of his mistress and to the threats of Maupeou that he would resign if Choiseul were kept any longer. The dilemma between his obligations of honor and loyalty to his ally, on the one hand, and his fear of the *parlements* and his mistress, on the other, was solved by abandoning the former.

The Abbé de Ville was ordered to prepare a letter to Charles III, and Louis himself is said to have penned the order of exile to Choiseul. On December 23 a final interview was had between the king and his minister, which Walpole reports[43] as having been very stormy. That same day Choiseul wrote his last dispatch to Ossun,[44] enclosing the latest letters from Francés. Once more he insisted that the decision on war and peace lay with the king of Spain. England, he said, clearly did not want war, but that country could not without great risk depart from her simple demands. If Charles III really desired peace he would have to accept the declaration of disavowal and restitution and if he desired to add anything war was certain. Whether the object was worth fighting for Spain alone could decide. France for her part would be disgruntled at having to fight for such a petty object. Choiseul then added that if he were advising the king he would tell him to give satisfaction in a declaration and make a verbal declaration on the basis of right, waiting some time then to negotiate on the legal question. "This," said Choiseul, "is my opinion; the King authorizes you, Monsieur, to tell this to his Catholic Majesty."

[43] Walpole to Mann, December 29, 1770, in Walpole, *Letters* (Cunningham ed., 1854), vol. 5, p. 273.

[44] Choiseul to Ossun, December 23, 1770 (*Aff. Etr., Espagne*, 561).

It was after his final interview with Choiseul that Louis decided to send his own letter to Charles III,[45] which Ossun was ordered to present.[46] Several drafts were made and in the final form it read as follows:

Your Majesty is not ignorant how the spirit of independence and fanaticism has spread in my realm. I have been governed by patience and kindness up to the present, but now pressed to extremity, and my Parlements forgetting themselves to the extent of wishing to combat my royal authority which I hold only from God, I am resolved to make myself obeyed by all possible means. War in these circumstances would be a fearful evil for me and my people. But my extreme tenderness for your Majesty, the intimate union which subsists between us, cemented by our Family Compact, always leads me to forget all else but that. My ministers are but my agencies, hence when I believe myself obliged to change them, nothing can bring a change in our affairs for as long as I live we shall be united. If your Majesty can make some sacrifice to preserve peace without injury to your honor, you will render a great service to humanity and to myself in the circumstances in which I now find myself. . . .

The following morning the Duc de la Vrillière, who had been designated to succeed Choiseul, dispatched the king's letter which exiled the former minister to Chanteloup.[47]

Choiseul's dismissal was a nine-days sensation in the European chancelleries. Frederick the Great, who entertained a particular dislike for the discredited statesman, hailed with delight the disappearance from European poli-

[45] Louis XV to Charles III, December 21, 1770 (*Aff. Etr., Espagne,* 561).

[46] There appear to have been three drafts made, the one actually sent, another in *Aff. Etr., Espagne,* 561, which is given by Daubigny, *Choiseul et la France d'Outre Mer,* p. 264, and a third in Boutaric, *La Correspondance Sécrète Inédit de Louis XV* (1866), vol. 1, p. 413. The one cited above was the letter dispatched and is to be found in Flammermont, *op. cit.,* p. 190, and Blart, *op. cit.,* p. 188.

[47] Maugras, *Le Duc et la Duchesse de Choiseul* (1904), p. 447 *et seq.* *Cf.* also on the incident, Jobez, *La France sous Louis XV,* vol. 6, p. 486 *et seq.*

tics of a minister "so full of intrigue, so restless and so ridiculous."[48] Choiseul's reputation abroad, however, was not so black as the Prussian king painted it, and yet the general sentiment appears to have been one of relief, coupled with the belief that his removal imported a radical change in French politics. At this moment, of course, the apprehension that war was imminent was very general and the consensus of opinion in the European courts was to the effect that ultimately the decision lay with France, because Spain was believed incapable of undertaking hostilities single-handed. The dismisal of Choiseul, of course, was on the face of things a rejection of the war programme. This was, indeed, the immediate reaction on the European diplomacy, although, as between England and Spain, the event was finally to be of less weight in the negotiations than was generally thought.

The immediate effect of Louis XV's action in Spain was profound. Masserano's dispatch, relating his refusal to have anything to do with Choiseul's project, had arrived prior to the notices from France, and the king had scarcely had time to enjoy his relief[49] over Masserano's refusal to depart from his instructions, when Ossun presented Louis' letter and the news that Choiseul had been dismissed by the king. Charles remarked very bluntly, "So much the worse for him," but the event moved him far more than any previous pleas for peace, for only four days before Ossun had delivered Choiseul's note of the nineteenth,[50] and had reported the fact that there seemed not the remotest possibility of deflecting Charles from his resolve to make no further concessions.

During all of this period no answer had yet been pre-

[48] Frederick II to Sandoz Rollin, January 8, 1771, *Politische Correspondenz Friedrichs des Grossen*, vol. 30, p. 379.

[49] Grimaldi to Masserano, December 31, 1770 (*Arch. Gen. Sim., Est.,* leg. 6980, fo. 14).

[50] Ossun to Choiseul, December 27, 1770 (*Aff. Etr., Espagne*, 561).

pared for Masserano in regard to North's proposals, and in regard to the discussions over Choiseul's project. At this moment, however, faced with the probable scrapping of the Family Compact, Grimaldi and his colleagues realized that further delay was impossible. The situation was again laid before the members of the council, who were asked to give their written opinions, and finally on January 2, Spain's new proposals were dispatched to Masserano.[51]

These instructions[52] opened with a statement that, animated by his ardent desire for peace and of freeing mankind from the horrors of war, and moved particularly by the instances of the king his cousin, who had asked for all possible sacrifices in view of the situation of his kingdom, and particularly as Choiseul, who was the chief exponent of the Family Compact, was gone, the king had determined upon a new expedient. This plan contemplated that the French ministers should present to the English another project of declaration which Masserano was to execute and which it appeared there was no reason for the English to refuse to sign. This declaration[53] stated that on June 10

[51] Grimaldi to Masserano, January 2, 1771 (*Arch. Gen. Sim., Est.*, leg. 6980, fo. 15).

[52] Grimaldi took no chances. He sent about a memorandum of the instructions and received a written note of approval from the other members of the Consejo de Estado. (For these papers *cf. Arch. Gen. Sim., Est.*, leg. 6980, fo. 15.)

[53] Anexo al oficio de Grimaldi de 2 de enero, 1771 (*Archivo Histórico, Madrid*). The text from the Spanish source is as follows:

"Le 10 juin de l'année de 1770 quelques frégattes espagnoles instruites de ce que les anglais établis dans la Grande Malouine à un endroit appellé par eux Port Egmont avoient menacé de chasser les espagnols établis dans une autre de ces Isles, les sudites frégattes obligérent avec la force les anglais a évacuer le sudit Port.

"S. M. Britannique s'étant plaint de la violence qu'avait été commise, offensante à l'honneur de sa couronne dans une affaire qui aurait du préalablement être arrangée à l'amiable avant que d'en venir aux voies de fait:

"Le Prince de Masseran a reçu ordre de déclarer: Que S. M. Catholique considerant l'amour dont elle est animée pour la paix et pour le maintien

some Spanish frigates, having been advised that the English established at Port Egmont had threatened to drive off the Spaniards established in another island, had with force obliged the British to quit the Port. His Britannic Majesty having complained of the violence as offensive to the honor of his crown in a matter which should have been previously arranged before resorting to violence, the Prince de Masserano was ordered to declare that his Catholic Majesty in view of his love for peace and for the maintenance of good relations with Great Britain, and considering that so petty an object should not disturb the peace, had viewed with displeasure the expedition, and, assured of the reciprocity of his Britannic Majesty's sentiments in not wishing to authorize anything which might disturb the good understanding between the two courts, disapproved of the enterprise. In consequence Masserano declared that his Catholic Majesty consented that things at Port Egmont be restored to the condition they were in prior to June 10, 1770, for which purpose a Spanish officer would be charged with returning

de la bonne harmonie avec S. M. Britannique et réfléchissant qu'un aussi petit objet pourroit l'interrompre, a vu avec déplaisir cette expedition capable de la troubler, et assurée comme Elle a ètè de la réciprocité de ses sentiments de S. M. Britannique pour ne pas autoriser tout ce qui pourroit interrompre la bonne intelligence entre les deux cours désaprouve la soudite entreprise violente et en conséquence le Prince de Masseran déclare:

"Que S. M. Catholique consent qu'on remette les choses dans la Grande Malouine au Port dit Egmont dans l'état ou elles étoient avant le 10 juin, 1770 auquel effet, un officier espagnol sera chargé de remettre aux anglais les effets qu'ils y ont laissé.

"L'unique objet de la présente déclaration est de donner une preuve authentique des sentiments de S. M. C. sur un fait qui aurait pu troubler la bonne intelligence entre les deux Couronnes; et cette déclaration ne pourra pas prejudicier aux droits anterieurs de S. M. Cath[l] sur les Isles appellées Malouines et par les anglais Falkland, mais seulement rétablir les choses pour le droit et pour le fait telles qu'elles étoient avant l'expulsion des anglais de l'établissement dont il s'agit."

the British effects. Here followed the most important paragraph, which read as follows:

The sole object of the present declaration is to give an authentic proof of the sentiments of his Catholic Majesty on a matter which might disturb the good intelligence between the two crowns, and this declaration shall not prejudice the anterior rights of his Catholic Majesty to the Islands called Malvinas and by the English Falkland, but is solely to restore things as a matter of law and of fact, to the state they were before the expulsion of the English from the establishment in question.

It will be observed that this declaration was made in substantial accord with what Choiseul had counselled in his letter of December 19. The further instructions of Grimaldi indicate even more explicitly how completely the Spanish were ruled by the last words of the departed minister. Masserano was to drop the earlier paragraph that the Falklands be evacuated, as the English were of the opinion that the satisfaction would be weakened if it were made conditional, *"but as they assure us they will evacuate the Falklands later, and that we should rely on their promise, the King has determined to concede that which is to save his honor and leave for later the negotiation on the evacuation of the island, accepting their offer although it be merely verbal.* Your Excellency should secure this in the best way possible either by an explanation of the British king as Francés previously suggested, or at least by his ministers at the time when your Excellency executes the declaration, if this takes place."

Grimaldi went on to say that this project seemed at once honorable and drawn in a manner acceptable to the British ministry in view of their constitution and what had been reported to him. The opening narrative was necessary because it made clear the origin of the complaint for which reparation was made. The reservation was also cast in an inoffensive manner. Masserano was, however, given power to change the phrasing if necessary, and, as to the confirmatory act of the British, Grimaldi proposed that the secretary of state should hand Masserano a paper stating that the declaration had been received, and that thereby the difference had been terminated. Spain would regard this as sufficient and the less words used the better.[54] Finally, the French ambassador or Francés was to present this proposal and ascertain whether it was acceptable. Masserano was not to treat directly with the British ministry until he knew whether the project was acceptable.

On the same day that this instruction was dispatched to France, Charles addressed a letter to his cousin Louis in reply to his unwelcome note of December 21.[55] He stated that he had always been distressed to see the disobedience of the French *parlements* and the way they took of flouting royal authority. Consequently he could only commend his cousin's resolution to preserve his sovereign power and to make himself obeyed, and Charles offered his assistance in case it should be necessary. Acting on this principle he declared that he would do everything possible to avert a war, and his ambassador would inform Louis of the new orders sent to settle the difficulty.

But [said he] I fear this very situation of France, which has determined us to such great sacrifices and of which England is not ignorant, do not lead her absolutely to desire war; it is for this reason that it would have been well if the just resolution of your Majesty with regard to the Parlements could have been deferred until this very critical moment was passed. For the same reason I am very

[54] The confirmatory act or counter declaration could be made in a separate paper, but the king wished, if possible, that it be joined as a part of the declaration. It is curious how the Spanish adhered to Choiseul's suggestions even after they knew he was disgraced and that his policies were probably discredited at the French court. It is not unlikely that in this way Charles III hoped to hold Louis to the course previously followed, as the most favorable for his own interest.

[55] Charles III to Louis XV, January 2, 1771 (*Aff. Etr., Espagne,* 561).

vexed that the Duc de Choiseul at this very moment should have displeased your Majesty, for our enemies will assume, although without foundation, that as he was the instrument of the Family Compact his removal might lead to coolness between the two crowns, a matter for which they have long hoped.

It is evident from the cold and censorious tone of this communication that Charles was deeply injured and incensed by the base desertion of his ally. When we consider how deeply Charles' honor had been injured by the threats of the obscure Captain Hunt, the wound caused by his own cousin's unchivalrous conduct must have been unforgetable. According to the accounts of Ossun, of Harris and of Grimaldi, Spain was in a certain sense prepared to make war alone. At the same time, the whole plan of campaign which had been concerted four years before had contemplated the coöperation of France. Consequently the defection of the latter at this moment, which was the most critical of the whole negotiation, really compelled Spain to make diplomatic concessions in order to gain time for a rearrangement of the military and naval plans. The French alliance, which involved also the Austrian court, was in view of England's isolation really a guarantee against a continental war. The only prospect of an ally for England was Russia and as long as this power was engaged with the Porte there was no chance that Catherine II would accept any further commitments. Furthermore, Kaunitz, the Austrian minister, had undertaken to sound Frederick II[56] on a plan to guarantee the neutrality of central Europe. This move, of which Spain could not have been unaware, was undoubtedly undertaken at the instance of France, for Austria, though allied with the latter, was not allied with Spain. In these circumstances, the damage wrought by the strum-

[56] Memorandum of a conference between Frederick II and van Swieten, December 30, 1770, *Politische Correspondenz Friedrichs des Grossen*, vol. 30, p. 345.

pet intrigues of Versailles was momentarily irremediable. Spain had no alternative but to submit. At the same time, it is a mistake to assume that Spain's acts portended a complete surrender to the British. The fact that the diplomatic control of the situation now passed from Paris to Madrid was the only benefit Spain derived from the situation, and she was thereafter to go her own road.

The sensation caused in Madrid by Choiseul's fall was paralleled only by the excitement in England.[57] The event formed the great topic of gossip, and the consensus of opinion was that nothing could have been more fortunate for England in the existing circumstances. The sovereigns themselves were unable to conceal their joy and made no secret of the fact that they believed a complete change in the system of the French court was impending, that she would abandon her ally if Spain now refused to give satisfaction, and that the latter would be alone involved in war.[58]

Masserano, communicating to his government his estimate of the situation, stated that he believed the British ministry would profit by the occasion and, adhering to their earlier demands, attempt to disrupt not only the Family Compact but the Franco-Austrian alliance as well, both of which instruments were the creations of Choiseul. The ministry had up to the present been inclined toward peace, and they would doubtless wait until they were apprised of the attitude of the new ministry in France. Masserano's advice to Grimaldi—and it was of decisive importance for the future—was to come to an understanding with England. Peace was not at the present moment to be disturbed, but Spain should remain armed and await the fulfilment of the promises by the British ministry to the effect that Spain should trust them in the matter of the evacuation of the *Gran*

[57] Masserano to Grimaldi, December 31, 1770 (*Arch. Gen. Sim., Est.,* leg. 6980, fo. 13).

[58] *Cf.* also Walpole to Conway, December 29, 1770, Walpole, *Letters,* vol. 5, p. 273.

Malvina, for, said he, it was cheaper to stay armed than to go to war.[59]

The English ministry was not slow to take advantage of the changed situation. On January 3, 1771, Masserano had his first conference with Rochford, who had succeeded Weymouth.[60] Rochford opened the conversation with some formal remarks regarding his desire for peace and desultory reflections with regard to the detention of the couriers at Dover on account of the weather—an event which threatened to retard Spain's reply beyond the reconvening of Parliament. Masserano remarked they would probably have no difficulty coming to an arrangement if they would deal frankly with him, for Weymouth's ambiguousness and lack of good faith had been a constant impediment. Rochford, thereupon, swore upon his honor that they would have peace if Spain gave satisfaction, for no one wanted war, and he added hastily that he was speaking unofficially, as he considered negotiations with Spain at an end since Masserano had had no new instructions. To this the latter rejoined that since the North-Francés conferences he had hopes of peace.

At this juncture Rochford, who no doubt had been wanting courage for his task, blurted out that he had given orders to Harris to withdraw from Madrid,[61] but that this step was not to be regarded as manifesting desire for war, as the king and all his ministers desired peace.[62] The Span-

[59] Before Choiseul gained the complete ascendancy in Spanish politics which he enjoyed prior to the Falkland crisis, Masserano was a most influential councillor of the Spanish Foreign Office. The influence appears to have fallen into abeyance at the height of Choiseul's power, but it was subsequently of great importance in questions involving English relations.

[60] Masserano to Grimaldi, January 5, 1771 (*Arch. Gen. Sim., Est.,* leg. 6980, fo. 16).

[61] This step had been determined upon at the meeting of the Council on December 19, 1770. *Cf. Home Office Papers,* 1770-1772, no. 383.

[62] Rochford to Harris, December 21, 1770 (*Falkland Papers,* p. 28).

ish ambassador could scarcely believe his ears, as Rochford babbled on, saying that Harris was needed at home because he was a member of Parliament,[63] and his recall should not affect the good understanding between the courts. Unmoved by these extraordinary words, Masserano replied bitterly that his master would be very much surprised at this resolution of the British and that he was personally grieved that such an inconsiderate step had been taken at the moment when he had been working so hard for peace and urging his court to rely on the good faith of the ministry.

There is no need of going into all the details of this interview. With some difficulty Masserano managed to extract the fact that Harris' orders had been sent on the twenty-first of December, although Rochford impressed upon Masserano that these instructions had directed withdrawal only after a week's delay. This the secretary of state insisted was not evidence of any desire for war, for, said he, they would never have told Harris to take leave had they contemplated such an eventuality. Masserano, however, was not to be satisfied by any such excuses and with some rancor he accused the British of bad faith and of playing with him and Francés while feverishly preparing for war. He insisted that the expedient of having Harris wait was use-

The note reads: "All negotiations having been for some time at an end between Lord Weymouth or myself and the Spanish ambassador to whom his Catholic Majesty thought fit to commit his answer to the King's demand, which answer was totally inadmissible, and it being inconsistent with his Majesty's honor to make further proposals to the court of Spain, I am now to signify to you the King's pleasure that your longer stay at Madrid appearing entirely unnecessary you prepare to return home with all convenient speed after taking leave in the usual manner."

[63] This was not the case—at least no mention of it is to be found in any biographical notice of Harris. It is probable that Masserano misunderstood Rochford. Harris' father was a M.P., and the desire to secure *his* vote—at best a fatuous excuse—might have been what Rochford had in mind.

less, for he would have left before the news of North's ultimatum could reach Madrid.[64]

Masserano's recriminations were delivered with telling effect, for, as the conference drew to a close, Rochford expressed his extreme regret that the step had been taken and his desire to repair the damage. Masserano at once suggested they should either tell Harris to stay or should name the consul general in his place, or nominate a new ambassador. Rochford replied that the best thing would be to tell Harris to remain, but that he would have to get cabinet approval of this step.

Immediately after Masserano's departure Francés entered Rochford's office, and although the Choiseul project with North's counter-proposals were discussed, Rochford, either because he was afraid or had had sufficient abuse for the day, did not communicate the news about Harris' recall. It was not until after the conference that Masserano himself informed both the Comte de Guines and Francés what had happened. All three were agreed that the English had acted in bad faith, and that they had been inspired by ignorance. They were particularly bitter against North, in whom they had reposed the greatest confidence, for having made his final proposals when he knew the courier to Harris was on his way. It was accordingly decided that Francés should call upon North and represent to him the gravity of the situation and its probable resolution in war.

It is difficult to say exactly what had prompted the extraordinary step of recalling Harris. The explanation given by Walpole does not seem wholly adequate. He says:

The fact was, Lord North had been seized with a panic on Lord Weymouth's resignation who, he concluded, would recant of having advised war; he had figured to himself Lord Chatham armed with national vengeance and the opposition bellowing against his

[64] There can be no doubt that Harris' recall was the idea of Weymouth. Francés was advised of it and Hillsborough had likewise mentioned it to Masserano, adding that this idea was being opposed by all the ministers.

pacific inclinations. Instead of striking the peace before any obstructions could be given to it, he had obtained from the cabinet council four days after Lord Weymouth's retreat the absurd direction to Harris to leave Madrid—a rash act dictated by fear from which nothing but Choiseul's fall could have extricated him.[65]

What Walpole wrote was undoubtedly true, and the perturbation exhibited when Masserano pointed out what would probably happen indicates that the step could have been only superficially considered. At the same time, it is possible that the ministry, knowing the poor state of preparation in England, had deemed such a step advisable as a means of gaining the advantage of being the first to break off relations, and of getting English ships out of Spanish ports before they could be embargoed.

There can be no doubt that but for the fall of Choiseul the ministry would scarcely have imparted to Masserano the order to Harris. At this moment, as no dispatches had as yet arrived from France, North and his colleagues were full of high hopes that the change in French politics had appreciably strengthened their position. The Comte de Guines, desiring that there should be no doubt on this score, because of the effect it might have on the Harris incident, took pains to inform the British ministry that there was no change in the diplomacy of his court—but he did this on the basis of old orders, and this the British undoubtedly knew.

On the night of January 4[66] Rochford personally called at the Spanish embassy to inform Masserano of the result of the council meeting. He explained that the king and all his ministers regretted the interpretation which Masserano had put on the incident, and that Harris had been recalled because his presence in Spain after the suspension of direct negotiations on November 28 was regarded as useless. He added that they were doing everything they could to prevent

[65] Walpole, *Memoirs of the Reign of George III,* vol. 4, p. 172.

[66] There seems to have been no order to Harris to remain a week unless there was a secret instruction overlooked by the writer.

war and he promised Masserano that there would be no difficulty over the question of right to the Falklands, as these islands were of no value to them.[67]

Masserano replied very coolly to all these protestations that he was willing to accept what was said about Harris' recall, but he doubted whether he could persuade the king, his master, who would see in this act only a sinister design either to make war or to announce to Europe that a break was near. He thereupon declared that even if the order should come to reopen negotiations he would be compelled to suspend action until he could get orders from Spain subsequent to Harris' actual withdrawal, and such orders could not arrive until the end of the month.

This announcement must have fallen heavily upon Rochford, in view of the fact that the whole ministry had been counting upon a reply before the assembly of Parliament after the holidays. Too proud or too stubborn to accept Masserano's suggestion that the way to avoid an *impasse* was to appoint an ambassador at once, Rochford stated that the best they could do would be to appoint one after they knew the reply would be favorable, and if this did not arrive by the twenty-second he and his colleagues would resign if the king did not declare war.

The conference with Francés and North was held in much the same terms. To Francés' charge that the ministry had proved its word was not to be trusted, North replied with assurances that they all wanted peace and would consequently ask no indemnity nor raise any difficulties on the question of right if Spain would only give the satisfaction asked.

On the ensuing days further conferences,[68] all equally fruitless, were held. Lord Sandwich,[69] who had taken over

[67] Masserano to Grimaldi, January 5, 1771 (*supra*).

[68] Masserano to Grimaldi, January 12, 1771 (*Arch. Gen. Sim., Est.,* leg. 6980, fo. 19).

[69] Walpole, *op. cit.,* vol. 4, p. 171, says, "No man in the Administration

the Northern Department,[70] and was one of the ablest men in the administration, likewise lent his voice to that of the other ministers, for Masserano's threat not to negotiate until he was advised of the king's decision in the Harris matter had aroused the deepest apprehension.[71] The idea was now advanced by the British ministry that the step had been necessary as a sort of sop to Parliament, and Rochford protested very volubly that their heads would have been forfeited had they not recalled their charge. To this Masserano retorted impatiently that Rochford was always holding his head up to him as a scarecrow, and yet there was no instance in English history of ministers being decapitated for such a cause; furthermore, a ministry with North's parliamentary strength could make war or peace at its pleasure.[72] Rochford, however, answered that war was inevitable unless the answer of Spain was in their hands when Parliament reconvened, hoping no doubt by this threat to shake the Spaniard's resolution not to negotiate, not knowing, of course, that Masserano secretly intended to negotiate if the reply from Madrid were favorable, as he was too seasoned a diplomat to permit a point of etiquette to stand in his way.

While these things were transpiring in London, Louis XV

was so much master of business, so quick or so shrewd, and no man had so many public enemies who had so few private; for though void of principles, he was void of rancour, and bore with good-humour the freedom with which his friends attacked him and the satire of his opponents."

[70] Sandwich had been made first lord of the admiralty, but as he had not yet accepted the seals he continued to conduct the Northern Department. Masserano to Grimaldi, January 11, 1771 (*Arch. Gen. Sim., Est.,* leg. 6978, fo. 11).

[71] Masserano had received Grimaldi's instructions of December 17, in which he was authorized to ask for his passports in case the ministry refused to treat with him. This was a particularly dangerous juncture, but Masserano was a man of good sense and not disposed to repair the affront of Harris' recall by an equally foolish step. Masserano to Grimaldi, January 12, 1771 (*Arch. Gen. Sim., Est.,* leg. 6978, fo. 12).

[72] Masserano claimed that letters of marque had been issued, a fact which Sandwich vigorously denied.

and his new advisers awaited the arrival of the courier from Spain in a very ecstasy of impatience.[73] The courier reached Paris on the tenth, but Fuentes, much to Louis' annoyance, did not appear until the next day to hand over the letter of Charles III and to impart the instructions dispatched to Masserano. Louis' delight at Charles' compliance with his request quite overpowered his natural reaction to his cousin's censorious remarks on French politics, particularly as two letters from London had previously been received detailing the reaction of the British government to the fall of Choiseul and reciting the disquieting intelligence of Harris' recall.

It is impossible to know whether Louis was already apprised on January 10 of the decision of the Spanish court, although ignorant of the details. If he was not, his instructions to de Guines of that day served in some measure to repair his honor, of which he had lately been so little solicitous. These instructions read in part as follows:[74]

The recall of Harris from Madrid is a circumstance which seems to announce the real disposition of the English for an early war, and in this event the remarks which the British Ministers make regarding their pacific intentions could not be less in conformity with their true sentiments. However this may be, I await at any moment the final determination of the King of which you will be advised without delay.

The intimate relations of blood and friendship which subsist between myself and the King my cousin and the treaties which unite the interests of our crowns should leave you in no doubt as to the perfect uniformity of principles and views which guide our policy. Therefore, if any of the events which you have anticipated should take place in regard to the Prince de Masserano, it is my will that you and M. Francés should conform exactly to the course of conduct which he may follow, either to remain in England or to withdraw simultaneously with him.

[73] Flammermont, *op. cit.,* p. 193.
[74] Louis XV to Comte de Guines, January 10, 1771 (*Arch. Gen. Sim., Est.,* leg. 6980, fo. 18).

The joy with which the royal command was received in London by the three Bourbon diplomats was equalled only by the consternation it caused among their adversaries.[75] The Comte de Guines forthwith repaired to Lord Rochford's residence and informed him of the contents of Louis XV's instruction, adding some reflection of his own on the manner in which the British had conducted the affair. Rochford was visibly embarrassed and exclaimed that he had never imagined France's policies had changed by reason of Choiseul's dismissal, nor had he ever dreamed that Harris' recall would be interpreted in the manner it had been by France. He was very voluble in his explanations of Harris' recall and the British desire for peace, until de Guines reminded him of his remark to Masserano some days earlier that unless an answer was received within a certain time there would be war. The secretary of state thereupon insisted he had explained himself very badly and that a delay of a few days would make no difference.

At the same time that this conference was going on, Francés broke the news to North. The latter was much affected and exclaimed that if Spain would only give satisfaction they would prove within twenty-four hours that they did not want war; all that Masserano had to do was to trust to them. And he cited as evidence of British pacific intent the fact that they had kept their fleet in port while Spain had made great concentrations of troops.

The Bourbon representatives were well satisfied with the result of their announcement. Francés, who had always clung to the belief that North did not want war, expressed his conviction that in view of Louis' declaration the chances for peace were greater than before, particularly as the ministry were thoroughly convinced that the order to Harris had been a great mistake.[76] The situation was therefore a

[75] Masserano to Grimaldi, January 16, 1771 (*Arch. Gen. Sim., Est.,* leg. 6980, fo. 24).

[76] At this very moment the papers printed a notice that a Spanish

most favorable one for the negotiation on Grimaldi's instructions of January 7.

On January 16,[77] two days after the receipt of Louis XV's letter, the Spanish dispatches reached London, but before they had been officially communicated, the British government, from advices received from Lord Harcourt at Paris, was already advised that they were favorable and a sharp rise in stocks took place, an event particularly gratifying to the several officials. Masserano, however, pursuant to his policy not to appear at court functions until the Harris incident had been settled, was absent from the levee of the king, much to the surprise of everyone who had expected him, as he says, "to hurl himself in their arms to settle the cause."

It had been concerted with Francés that Masserano would himself not present Grimaldi's project until he was advised in what manner it was proposed to remedy the false step of recalling Harris at such a critical time, as well as the instructions to order all English ships to leave Spanish ports. Francés was further to state that Masserano did not regard his new instructions to be applicable to the present situation, having issued at a moment when the Spanish court was ignorant of the British belligerent intent, and hence if he received instructions to withdraw he would leave with the project in his pocket. The only reparation which would be at all considered would be the appointment of an ambassador to Spain or a similar measure.

courier had arrived with bad news. Masserano suspected the government of having inserted the notice with the purpose of exciting the people. More probably it was to affect the stock market, which actually fell. Walpole, *op. cit.*, vol. 4, p. 161, mentions Francés' complaints on the subject. "He imputed much of the delays in negotiations to Wood's [Undersecretary of State] stock-jobbing (in which no doubt no man was more capable of detecting another than Francés, who was deep in the mystery himself). . . ."

[77] Masserano to Grimaldi, January 23, 1771, no. 2038 (*Archivo Histórico, Madrid*).

Francés at once proceeded to North's house, where the latter was impatiently awaiting the Spanish answer. Francés advised the prime minister of Masserano's decision in the terms agreed upon, and added that, although he was empowered to use his good offices, he could of course do nothing without the Spanish ambassador's consent, and this could only be secured by making the reparation demanded. North, somewhat nonplussed, again attempted to excuse their precipitate action and said no conclusions should be drawn from it, as Harris was of no use to them in Madrid after direct negotiations with Masserano had come to an end. He stated that he wanted to repair the injury, but could do so only with the consent of the king and the other ministers. All of his efforts to elicit from Francés some inkling of what the project contained were unsuccessful.

North obtained George III's reply that same day, and that night he advised Francés that an ambassador would be named as soon as the Falkland affair was concluded, that it could not be done sooner on account of the Parliament, and if Masserano wished to treat he might do it in reliance on this promise. Masserano, however, was not satisfied with this, and he sent Francés back to North with the demand that Harris be ordered to return and that these instructions be delivered to him in order that he could be satisfied that the British had withdrawn the threat implied in their action. This suggestion seemed reasonable to North, and he promised to consult with Rochford.

North and Francés arrived at Rochford's office at the very moment that warm words were passing between the latter and the Comte de Guines, who, annoyed at the Englishman's flippancy, was about to leave.[78] Francés explained his proposals, and knowing North and Rochford

[78] Rochford seems to have had an irritating habit of making frivolous remarks. On this occasion de Guines remarked hotly that he was not the Minister of Venice and wished to be treated as the representative of the great power whose ambassador he was.

were not fully in accord, added that they had been made confidentially to North as premier. Rochford at once said the ambassador could not be appointed, but that he would order Harris to return. Then he asked for an unofficial view of the Spanish project, but Francés said he could not satisfy him until the orders were actually sent. Here North interrupted, saying that Masserano could be sure they would be, but that they could only be communicated to him when they were sure Grimaldi's project was admissible. As soon as this was communicated the orders would be antedated to the day on which the negotiations were resumed. Francés then communicated the project.

After listening to the whole document North stated that he did not like the preamble for the reason that he had always rejected the idea of disavowing Captain Hunt, but that if it was necessary to have something about the incident the preamble should begin with the arrival of the Spanish at Port Egmont on their survey. After some parley, however, it was decided to begin the declaration with the statement "His Britannic Majesty having complained." The discussion then turned to other phrases in the document and the conference ended.

On the twenty-first Rochford sent for Francés and informed him that they wished to conclude the matter the following day, the declaration having met with their approval, including the reservation of right.[79] Francés on that same night brought to Masserano the completed declaration which he was to sign and the counter-declaration of acceptance by the British king. The Spanish ambassador after some demur decided to execute the document, despite the fact that with some details he was by no means satisfied. His

[79] Masserano, very cleverly, was able to suppress the recital of his full powers, averting thereby the necessity of ratification, a circumstance which the reference to the powers would have made obligatory, and which he wished to avoid, for he feared the consequent delay would give the British an excuse for delaying their disarmament.

chief concern had been that England should make no mention in the "Acceptance" of their alleged rights to the islands, and he was successful in securing this, for he believed it portended acquiescence in Spanish right when the question of evacuation or abandonment arose. On this point Francés advised him that the ministry declined to speak at present, for they would give no official or confidential statement in view of their desire to say in Parliament that they had received unconditional satisfaction. After a few days, however, they would discuss the matter fully and Masserano would see the favorable manner in which they would deal.

The declaration having been decided upon, it was yet necessary to arrange the matter of Harris' recall before Masserano would sign the final act. These instructions were drawn up and dated January 18, 1771,[80] and were handed to Masserano before he signed.

On January 22 Masserano called at Rochford's office. After some discussion, in the course of which the Spaniard succeeded in obtaining some important changes in verbiage which Francés had not been able to extract, the two negotiators signed their respective documents. The declaration read:[81]

His Britannick Majesty having complained of the violence which was committed on the 10th of June, 1770, at the island commonly called the Great Malouine, and by the English Falkland's Island, in obliging, by force, the commander and subjects of his Britannick Majesty to evacuate the port by them called Egmont; a step offensive to the honour of his crown;—the Prince de Maserano, Ambassador Extraordinary of his Catholick Majesty, has received orders to declare, and declares, that his Catholick Majesty, considering the desire with which he is animated for peace, and for the maintenance of good harmony with his Britannick Majesty, and reflecting that this event might interrupt it, has seen with displeasure this

[80] Rochford to Harris, January 18, 1771 (*Falkland Papers*, p. 31).

[81] Jenckinson, *op. cit.*, vol. 3, p. 234; Cantillo, *op. cit.*, p. 519.

expedition tending to disturb it; and in the persuasion in which he is of the reciprocity of sentiments of his Britannick Majesty, and of its being far from his intention to authorise anything that might disturb the good understanding between the two Courts, his Catholick Majesty does disavow the said violent enterprise,—and, in consequence, the Prince de Maserano declares, that his Catholick Majesty engages to give immediate orders, that things shall be restored in the Great Malouine at the port called Egmont, precisely to the state in which they were before the 10th of June, 1770: For which purpose, his Catholick Majesty will give orders to one of his Officers, to deliver up to the Officer authorised by his Britannick Majesty the port and fort called Egmont, with all the artillery, stores, and effects of his Britannick Majesty and his subjects which were at that place the day above named, agreeable to the inventory which has been made of them.

The Prince de Maserano declares, at the same time, in the name of the King, his master, that the engagement of his said Catholick Majesty, to restore to his Britannick Majesty the possession of the port and fort called Egmont, cannot nor ought in any wise to affect the question of the prior right of sovereignty of the Malouine islands, otherwise called Falkland's Islands. In witness whereof, I the under-written Ambassador Extraordinary have signed the present declaration with my usual signature, and caused it to be sealed with our arms.

The British acceptance read:

His Catholick Majesty having authorized the Prince of Maserano, his Ambassador Extraordinary, to offer, in his Majesty's name, to the King of Great Britain, a satisfaction for the injury done to his Britannick Majesty by dispossessing him of the port and fort of Port Egmont; and the said Ambassador having this day signed a declaration, which he has just delivered to me, expressing therein, that his Catholick Majesty, being desirous to restore the good harmony and friendship which before subsisted between the two Crowns, does disavow the expedition against Port Egmont, in which force has been used against his Britannick Majesty's possessions, commander, and subjects; and does also engage, that all things shall be immediately restored to the precise situation in which they stood before the 10th of June, 1770; and that his Catholick Majesty shall give orders, in consequence, to one of his Officers to deliver up to the Officer authorised by his Britannick Majesty, the port and fort of Port Egmont, as also all his Britannick Majesty's artillery, stores, and effects, as well as those of his subjects, according to the inventory which has been made of them. And the said Ambassador having moreover engaged, in his Catholick Majesty's name, that what is contained in the said declaration shall be carried into effect by his said Catholick Majesty, and that duplicates of his Catholick Majesty's orders to his Officers shall be delivered into the hands of one of his Britannick Majesty's Principal Secretaries of State within six weeks; his said Britannick Majesty, in order to shew the same friendly disposition on his part, has authorised me to declare, that he will look upon the said declaration of the Prince de Maserano, together with the full performance of the said engagement on the part of his Catholick Majesty, as a satisfaction for the injury done to the Crown of Great Britain. In witness whereof, I the under-written, one of his Britannick Majesty's Principal Secretaries of State, have signed these presents with my usual signature, and caused them to be sealed with our arms.

Upon exchanging the two documents Masserano stated that he had orders from his king to bring to Rochford's attention the great sacrifice his Majesty was making in permitting the British to return to territory which belonged to him, and that he had done so to preserve good harmony with Great Britain, relying upon the promises of the ministry in the matter of the evacuation of the island and the port. Rochford replied that he and his colleagues truly desired peace and that for the moment he could make no categoric reply, but that the Spanish would see that they would act after a week or ten days, within which he hoped the party of opposition which would attack the declaration would be overcome. He added that they would never make war for the Falkland Island (*sic*), in the preservation of which the nation had no interest, and experience would make the Spanish see that this was true.

To this assurance Masserano retorted that he knew that

everyone was aware of the little use these islands were to the British, but nevertheless it would bring on war if when treating of evacuation they demanded any compensation. Rochford then stated that the Spanish would observe the effects of their promises, and he added that the courier to Harris would be sent at once and that an ambassador would be named within the week.

In the evening of the following day Masscrano attended the king's levee.[82] George III greeted the ambassador most effusively, hailing him as the author of their well-being, and he added that Masserano would learn the usefulness of trusting to his good faith and the advantages of establishing it between two such great courts as theirs. Masserano replied that it was in reliance on this good faith that the king, his master, had directed him to do what he had just done and that his Catholic Majesty would be very pleased to learn by his intermediary that his Britannic Majesty had said that they could rely upon his good faith in the treaty.[83]

To the bystanders these words no doubt were mere hollow amenities appropriate to the occasion.[84] They were, however, more than this—they were the royal ratification of the promises of North and his colleagues that the island was to be abandoned, in reliance upon which the satisfaction had been given and which remained the great question yet to be settled.

It is proper at this place to add some comment upon the declaration and counter-declaration from the legal point of view, for the negotiations leading up to its conclusion have

[82] Masserano to Grimaldi, January 25, 1771 (*Arch. Gen. Sim., Est.*, leg. 6980, fo. 23).

[83] The same day Rochford advised Masserano of the appointment of Lord Grantham as ambassador.

[84] The rumor that there was a secret agreement seems to have been in circulation at once. *Cf.* Barré to Chatham, January 22, 1771, *Chatham Correspondence*, vol. 4, p. 72.

been minutely detailed chiefly for the purpose of demonstrating exactly what legal result was accomplished by the exchange of these two documents. In the first place, the Spanish declaration was a mere act of satisfaction. The disavowal of Bucareli and the restitution of the colony were the two acts constituting the reparation, and the latter, in view of the reservation of right, was a mere restitution of possession. It was an act by which the physical *status quo* previously obtaining was restored. The question of right, however, was not affected by the act of the Spanish king, for the reason that as the negotiations progressed the English demand had been sharpened down to satisfaction to the injury to the crown which the attack of Bucareli had involved, a claim which, as we have seen, was based not on any violation of territorial sovereignty but upon the fact that a royal force had been attacked. The distinction may be more forcibly brought out if we cite in illustration the Tampico incident of 1914 when American sailors were fired on by the Huerta troops and an act of satisfaction was demanded for the affront. In this, as in the present case, the essence of the offense was the injury to the sovereign as represented by the troops.

In this connection, the failure of the British to make in turn a reservation of right is, as Masserano wished it to be, a circumstance of singular importance. On the one hand, it necessarily added force to the view that what Spain was offering was a mere act of reparation for injury to the British crown, and, on the other hand, in the face of Spain's express reservation there was a tacit waiver of any particular claim of right. We are led to this conclusion not only by the fact that Masserano and Francés sought to avoid a British reservation because it would weaken the Spanish claim, but also by the antecedent assurance of the British that the islands would be evacuated in due course. The British ministry insisted that the assurances were given "neither officially nor confidentially," and yet it cannot be denied that they *were* given and that they were the motivating inducement for the Spanish action. To deny them legal effect would be to deny the validity of all contracts made under similar conditions.

In these circumstances it was undoubtedly true that the declaration, restoring, as it did, the *status quo ante* as far as the physical situation of the British was concerned, did not leave the question of right in the same situation as it was before the expedition of Bucareli. The promise of North to abandon was not merely an act which left the question of right untouched so that at some future time the British could return and set up a claim. It was, in the light of all the surrounding circumstances, a waiver of all question of right and was so understood by Masserano at this moment. The fact that the British did not see fit to ask for a mutual and reciprocal evacuation was taken as sufficient proof that they were willing by withdrawal to admit the Spanish claim to a better right. The admission, however, would acquire legal validity only by an actual abandonment in fact whereby the union of intent and act necessary to an abandonment in law would occur. For this reason the fulfilment of the British promise was to be in the months to come a question of as great importance as the questions settled by Masserano's declaration.[85]

[85] The effects of British propaganda at this time are interestingly illustrated in the account of the Falkland affair in the anonymous work, *Beschreibung der Spanischen Macht in Amerika* (1771), appendix, pp. 3, 15. The account is obviously based upon British sources and is so phrased as to accord all the equities in the controversy to England.

CHAPTER VIII

THE DIPLOMATIC SETTLEMENT

THE expression of joy which attended the signing of the declaration of January 22, 1771, emanated chiefly from members of the British government. Their relief was shared by the French, and in the various European courts there was likewise a feeling of satisfaction when the news got about that the peace would not be broken. The general feeling of elation, however, by no means stifled the expressions of contempt which North and his colleagues were believed to have earned for the sort of reparation accepted by them. The jibe of Frederick that the declaration was a shameful monument of British pusillanimity was typical of this feeling, for men could not easily forget the glory that was Britain's at the end of the Seven Years' War, and the international code of honor at this moment dictated that any settlement of a national injury other than a military one was a humiliation. Doubtless had the full extent of the British surrender been known the prestige of the government both at home and abroad would have suffered to an even greater extent. Lord North was fully aware of the fact that the action of his government was understood to have been taken more in the interest of the preservation of power than of peace. The issue had in reality not been so much of his own making as of the opposition's, and one can therefore comprehend why the Falkland affair, especially in its latter stages, was treated more as a question of domestic than of international politics. Indeed, in the weeks ensuing upon the submission of the declaration to Parliament, the matter passed temporarily out of diplomacy into the battlefield of party politics, and it was not until the menace of continued preparation for war became so acute that the subject was again made the subject of negotiation.

On the very day that the declaration was signed, notice was given both in the Lords and the Commons that the documents would be presented on January 25.[1] The wildest rumors as to its content and manner of conclusion[2] were circulated, but the exact tenor of the document appears to have been kept secret until the moment of presentation. The opposition, however, did not delay in marshalling its forces in anticipation of the government's action,[3] and a resolution for the production of the papers relating to the dispute was prepared.[4]

True to its word, the ministry submitted the declaration on the day stated. The original document having been signed in French, the translated version laid before Parliament was couched in the most extraordinary English, a circumstance which, of course, laid it open to the attacks of the purists of style, as well as of politics. In the House of Lords, after the document had been laid on the table, a profound silence ensued.[5] The Duke of Manchester then arose and observed that on its face the declaration appeared very inadequate and insufficient, but that he would withhold final judgment until he was in possession of further information. He then moved that there be laid before the house copies of all "claims and propositions of Spain relative to the Falklands since first settled by the English together with all replies, together with the correspondence and papers relative to any hostilities actually undertaken or indicating a hostile intent of Spain, and all papers relative to the question of reparations." This motion was forthwith amended by Rochford to restrain it to the "business of Falkland's Island." Thereupon Lord Sandwich added a second amend-

---

[1] Chatham, *Correspondence*, vol. 4, p. 77.

[2] *Ibid.*, p. 78. *Cf.* Schlosser, *History of the Eighteenth Century* (1845), vol. 5, p. 823.

[3] Chatham, *op. cit.*, p. 78.

[4] *Ibid.*, p. 80.

[5] Hansard, *Parliamentary History of England*, vol. 16, p. 1338.

ment which still further limited the question. After some debate Chatham entered the lists. Without awaiting detailed information he declared that the declaration was ignominious on its face; it was not satisfaction, nor reparation; the right was not secured and even restitution was incomplete, for Port Egmont alone was restored.

The last point raised by Chatham was, of course, one of the most obvious defects in the declaration, the existence of which the government had discovered too late to avoid. On the night of the twenty-fourth Rochford had dispatched his secretary to the Spanish embassy with the "Acceptance" and with the request that Masserano add to the declaration at the point where was mentioned the restoration of Port Egmont the words, "and its dependencies," which the English had added to their "Acceptance." The reason given for this request was the probable censure of the opposition for a failure to add the words.[6] Masserano of course declined to agree to this, and when Rochford's secretary sought to press him he declared very shortly that he had sent the document to his court and he could add nothing. It is interesting that in the copy finally sent him the additional words were left out. The circumstance is mentioned here largely because of the light it throws on the legal situation.

Following Chatham other lords of the opposition continued to press the government with such determination that Rochford finally abandoned the amendment and the original motion was agreed to. The Duke of Richmond, who had been Shelburne's ambassador at Paris in the early days of the Falkland dispute and knew the interest of France in the matter, then moved the production of papers that had passed between the government and the French ministers on the seizure of Port Egmont, if any such negotiation had taken place. Rochford promptly said he objected because there were no such papers. Richmond then retorted that if

[6] Masserano to Grimaldi, January 25, 1771 (*Arch. Gen. Sim., Est.,* leg. 6980, fo. 29).

any negotiation with France had been carried on it was the public's privilege to know about it and to punish it, for such an act would be giving efficacy to the Family Compact. He added that with reference to the declaration he had one observation to make distinct from all the information the papers might produce; it was that he wondered how any minister dared accept a declaration in which the sovereignty was brought into question, for when he was in the administration the Spanish ambassador had attempted to make it a matter of discussion and that he believed all ministers up to this day had never suffered it to be so much as made a matter of doubt. A vote was then taken and the motion was lost.

In the Commons Lord North appeared as the protagonist of the treaty, but he deferred making any statements until the matter was the order of business before the house. Dowdeswell, who was leading the opposition, raised much the same points as were brought out in the House of Lords, and presented the motion in the terms agreed upon by the leaders of the opposition. North moved an amendment to restrict the production of papers to those bearing on the injury to the crown, leaving out the question of the rights of the people, for these had been in dispute no further than as the honor of the crown included them.[7] The general tone of the ensuing debate, in which Colonel Barré and Burke subjected both North and his declaration to vicious attacks, was much fiercer than in the upper chamber. Barré reminded North that before the holiday the government had declared that Spain would have to pay a part of the expense for the war preparations, and although North denied this, Burke at once backed up Barré's charge, insisting— very characteristically—that the satisfaction from the Spaniards was adequate to the injury, as they had taken a barren desolate rock and had restored as barren and deso-

---

[7] Hansard, *op. cit.*, vol. 16, p. 1342. It was stated by the opposition that the words of the motion were taken from the king's speech.

late a rock, but that the people deserved satisfaction for the treasure expended, in the form of recompense for the outlays. In spite of these demands North's amendment was agreed to.

These debates were but opening flourishes preliminary to the meeting on February 5, when the matter was to be the order of the day. One fact of importance, however, was brought out in the Commons by North, when he declared that the rights of the people had not been in dispute. This was a virtual denial that a question of right was involved, and an attempt to have the declaration treated simply as reparation for an affront to the crown. The opposition was, of course, intent upon compelling the government to disclose what disposition had been made of the question of right and failing this to impeach the declaration for leaving in suspense the fundamental issue. North's statement was furthermore of interest for the reason that it furnished additional evidence that from the international law point of view the declaration was a mere act of satisfaction for an affront to the crown, and that apart therefrom had not the least international significance in the matter of title to the islands.

The declaration having been made public property, the discussions pro and con on the action of the government served to fan the flame of general interest and to define the specific grounds of attack. So great, indeed, was the popular concern in the matter, that on January 30, Junius, that spectre of British politics,[8] who had been accustomed to vent his spleen on far different subjects, addressed a lengthy letter to the *Public Advertiser* in which the government, and particularly the king, was excoriated with great gusto. Junius' letter followed the line of attack already projected in Parliament—he pointed out the fact that mere possession was restored, and that, Spain having expressly reserved her rights, the implication was obvious that a sur-

[8] Junius, *Letters* (Woodfall ed., 1772), vol. 2, p. 132.

render of the British claim of right was imminent. Junius further assaulted the distinction drawn by North between the honor of the crown and rights of the people,[9] insisting that the two were inseparable and that the failure to secure the latter entailed the abandonment of the former.[10]

The determination of the opposition to blast the declaration by a concerted blow at the question of right culminated in the preparation by the Earl of Chatham of two questions which he proposed should be submitted to the law lords. The first of these was: ''Whether in consideration of law the imperial crown can hold any territories or possessions thereunto belonging otherwise than in sovereignty?'' The second question read: ''Whether the declaration or instrument for restitution of the port or fort called Egmont to be made by the Catholic King to his Majesty, under a reservation of a disputed right of sovereignty expressed in the very declaration or instrument stipulating such restitution, can be accepted or carried into execution, without derogating from the maxim of law before referred to touching the inherent and essential dignity of the crown of Great Britain?''[11]

The day before the motion was introduced Chatham submitted the matter to Lord Camden, sometime lord chief justice of the Court of Common Pleas and lord chancellor. Camden, after a hasty consideration of the matter, advised his colleague that he had his doubts as to the illegality of the king's acceptance, for he could not satisfy himself that the reservation of right in the declaration of the Spanish king in any way touched the right of the king of Great Britain.

[9] Cf. the letter of Philo-Junius, ibid., vol. 2, p. 146.

[10] The incident of these letters and the supposed connection of Sir Philip Francis with them is discussed at some length in Parker, Memoirs of Sir Philip Francis (1867), vol. 1, p. 248. Francis lost £500 gambling in the market. He and Calcraft anticipated war and the return to power of their patron, Lord Chatham.

[11] Hansard, op. cit., vol. 16, p. 1355.

The right of sovereignty [wrote Camden] becomes absolute *jure coronæ* from the moment the restitution takes place. Nor does it seem to me the King's title is abridged or limited; inasmuch as the reservation neither denies the right on one side nor asserts it on the other. The question remains as it stood before the hostility; the King of Spain declaring only that he ought not to be precluded from his former claim by this act of possessory restitution.[12]

The learned lord, unacquainted with the complete facts of the case and regarding the question primarily as a matter of English constitutional law, reached a conclusion which has been the conventional judgment on the legal effect of the declaration. The question of international law, however, in no wise depended upon the view of the common law regarding British sovereignty. As we have seen, the declaration, in the light of the secret promise which induced its signature, was no more than a restoration of such possession as the crown previously had. To speak of sovereignty attaching when this restitution took place was not in accordance with the facts, for the form of the instrument was expressly conceived to exclude any implications of sovereignty.

Lord Camden's views, however, appear to have been those of the house. When the matter was raised on February 5, all strangers were excluded and no record of the debate is preserved other than a note by Walpole that Lord Mansfield remarked it was needless to refer the matter to the law lords, as the queries answered themselves. The final vote resulted in a defeat of the motion.[13]

The debates on the papers themselves[14] took place in the Commons on February 13 and in the Lords the next day. Dowdeswell again led the opposition in the lower house,

---

[12] Chatham, *op. cit.*, vol. 4, p. 90.

[13] Hansard, *op. cit.*, vol. 16, p. 1355.

[14] *Ibid.*, p. 1358. *Cf.* also the full account in *Arch. Gen. Sim., Est.*, leg. 6980, fo. 55.

moving an amendment in thirteen counts to the original motion for the presentation of an address of thanks to the crown.[15] This amendment was aimed chiefly at the failure to safeguard British sovereignty and was very inadequately supported, except for a long but incisive speech by Governor Pownall. The discussions in the House of Lords were equally long drawn out, but in the end the government was sustained in both chambers.[16]

There is no doubt that the opposition which developed in the Parliament was much more violent than the ministry had anticipated. When the declaration was signed, the Spanish ambassador had been assured that a definite arrangement would be made regarding the evacuation within a few days, as soon as the attacks of the opposition abated. The storm raised by Chatham and his friends, however, precluded any such speedy action. And at the same time Masserano was disinclined to enter into any *pourparlers* until he was apprised of his government's reaction to Harris' recall. It was inevitable, therefore, that diplomatic negotiations should languish and that both sides remained armed.

The Harris incident, and particularly what transpired at Madrid after the orders of December 21 were received, probably because of a certain dramatic quality, has always been treated by historians as the high spot of the negotiation. The really important aspect of the matter—the effect upon the London conversations—has already been dealt with. The effect upon the Spanish court we may mention with greater brevity.

The instruction of December 21 arrived in Madrid two days after Grimaldi had dispatched to Masserano the no-

[15] Richmond to Chatham, February 20, 1771, Chatham, *op. cit.,* vol. 4, p. 89.

[16] For the protest of the minority *cf.* Hansard, *op. cit.,* vol. 16, p. 1380. It is also to be found in a French translation in *Arch. Gen. Sim., Est.,* leg. 6980, fo. 55 bis.

tice of Spain's concessions.[17] Harris at once advised the British consuls of his orders[18] and having waited eight days for the messengers to reach their destinations he proceeded to acquaint Grimaldi with the facts. The latter, he reported, was much affected and expressed great concern at the disagreeable turn things were likely to take. Grimaldi then asked Harris whether he would leave anyone in charge, and being informed that he would not, exclaimed that the king would certainly recall Masserano. Harris then requested an interview with the king as well as a post license, adding that he intended to stay in Madrid a few days to arrange his personal affairs.[19] The interview was duly accorded and Harris' official relation was terminated.

Charles III immediately determined to recall Masserano.[20] The latter was given a personal letter of Charles to George III[21] in which nothing was said of the reasons for the ambassador's departure, but Masserano was instructed to inform the British ministry that the step was taken solely for his king's honor and in imitation of their own action. The Spanish king, however, showed his superior good sense by qualifying his order to take leave with specific instructions regarding the Falkland negotiations. If the French minister had presented the project of January 2 and the British had agreed to it, Masserano was to have his audience with the king and take leave. If, however, the British offered to appoint an ambassador forthwith, he was empowered to delay his actual departure on the pretext of arranging his affairs pending the actual execution of such an offer. The same conduct was to be followed in the event that the British did not agree to the project but made an

[17] Harris to Rochford, January 13, 1771 (*R.O. State Papers, Spain*, 186).

[18] *Ibid.*

[19] *Ibid.*

[20] Grimaldi to Masserano, January 13, 1771 (*Arch. Gen. Sim., Est.*, leg. 6980, fo. 20).

[21] Enclosure in *ibid.*

offer to name an envoy, and Masserano was to be careful to do nothing to aggravate the situation. If, however, the British ministry had precipitated a breach of negotiations Masserano was to leave without an audience.[22]

Harris' zeal for the service fortunately was qualified by "a passion which made his separation from the court exceedingly hard."[23] Loitering in the vicinity for the purpose of dining nightly and in secret with his belovèd, the delay in his departure was so protracted that the courier charged with Rochford's order of January 18 found him at the village Algora, no further than twenty leagues from Madrid.[24] Harris at once made a *volte-face* and posted back to the capital and the arms of his inamorata.[25] His first business, so he relates, was to interview Grimaldi. The latter, already in possession of Masserano's account of the signing of the declaration, was very affable, but he declined point-blank to present Harris to the king in the absence of new credentials, and he ended with a long lecture on the etiquette—or lack of it—of the British that they treated the Spanish court so shabbily in the matter of diplomatic representation.[26] In

[22] In the event negotiations had reached a critical stage, Masserano was to sign the declaration and then take leave. *Ibid.,* confirmed also, Grimaldi to Masserano, January 21, 1771 (*Arch. Gen. Sim., Est.,* leg. 6980, fo. 26, and fo. 27). The Spanish were moreover thoroughly irritated that the English had kept an envoy of inferior rank at Madrid for so long a period.

[23] Fernan-Nuñez, *Compendio,* vol. 2, cap. 2. Cited in Ferrer del Rio, *Historia del Reinado de Carlos III,* vol. 3, p. 86 n. Fernan-Nuñez declares he was a friend of both parties and attended these little dinner parties.

[24] Harris to Rochford, February 9, 1771 (*R.O. State Papers, Spain,* 186).

[25] The spectacle of North negotiating with a heavy cargo of spirits aboard, and Harris philandering in Madrid in the midst of a situation of utmost gravity is at once amusing and deplorable, but it had the very flavor of the eighteenth century.

[26] Harris to Rochford, February 9, 1771. There is a copy of this note in Malmesbury, *Diaries and Correspondence,* vol. 1, p. 73, in abbreviated form, with no notice that it was cut by the editor.

vain did Harris seek to induce him to alter his determination. Grimaldi was adamant, and England was as before without official representation at the Spanish court.[27]

Although there is no question that Grimaldi's attitude in the premises was in all respects correct, his proceeding under the circumstances of a hardly won pacification certainly seemed but slightly conciliatory. On February 8 he addressed Masserano approving the declaration and enclosing duplicates of the orders to Ruiz Puente which were necessary under the settlement.[28] Although Harris' return was expected momentarily, acting upon the determination to go no further than the circumstances had forced them, Grimaldi instructed Masserano to conduct himself as previously ordered unless the French king, through the Conde de Fuentes, should in the interest of peace advise the suspension of these instructions.[29]

Masserano had in the interim been in that most difficult

[27] Grimaldi to Masserano, February 11, 1771 (*Arch. Gen. Sim., Est.,* leg. 6980, fo. 53).

[28] Grimaldi to Masserano, February 8, 1771 (*Archivo Histórico, Madrid, Estado*). The orders were enclosed. They state: "The King and His Britannic Majesty having agreed in a convention signed in London on last January 22nd by the Prince de Masserano and Count Rochford, on the prompt restitution of the Gran Malvina, called by the English Falkland, to the precise situation in which it was prior to their evacuation on June 10th of last year, I advise your Excellency of the order of the King that as soon as the person commissioned by the court of London presents himself with this order, your Excellency will arrange to effect the delivery of the Puerto de la Cruzada or Egmont and its fort and appurtenances as well as all the artillery munitions and effects which were found there of his Britannic Majesty and his subjects, according to the inventory which was signed at the time of their departure on July 11th of the same year by Mr. George Farmer and Mr. William Maltby and of which I herewith enclose copies for your Excellency signed by my hand; and having carried out these things with proper formalities, your Excellency will carry into effect the immediate retirement of the officials and other subjects of the King who are now living there. . . . February 7, 1771."

[29] Grimaldi to Masserano, February 8, 1771 (*Arch. Gen. Sim., Est.,* leg. 6980, fo. 50).

of positions—an ambassador who acts against instructions. The orders to withdraw had arrived three days after the declaration was signed,[30] and Masserano, disinclined to disturb the favorable atmosphere which he had with difficulty succeeded in creating, deemed it wiser to await a reply to his dispatch advising Grimaldi of the signature of the declaration. Moreover, he believed the predating of the order to Harris remanding him to Madrid to be an ample satisfaction, particularly as Lord Grantham had immediately been named ambassador. Besides these points of policy a more urgent reason held him in London; he suffered from the universal malady—the gout. In these circumstances the Prince simply suspended all business and awaited the reply of his sovereign.[31]

In the meantime Masserano watched with keen interest the progress of debate both within and without the Parliament. He reported to Spain the general satisfaction among all except the persons engaged in foreign trade, and the serious handicap to commerce occasioned by the continuation of armament. The attacks on the government for the failure to secure the question of right were of greatest interest to the Spaniard in view of the fact that the British had declined to discuss this question. At this moment the ministry realized too late the embarrassment into which its policy had thrown it. Rochford, preparing the papers for Parliament, searched feverishly for some memoranda on the earlier negotiations and finally sent to Masserano for information.[32] The full consequences of Chatham's and Shelburne's refusal to deal with the matter in writing was then

[30] Masserano to Grimaldi, January 25, 1771 (*Arch. Gen. Sim., Est.,* leg. 6980, fo. 28).

[31] Apparently the war preparations showed no signs of ceasing. *Cf. The Public Advertiser,* January 31, 1771; Masserano to Grimaldi, January 29, 1771 (*Arch. Gen. Sim., Est.,* leg. 6980, fo. 32); February 1, 1771 (*ibid.,* leg. 6980, fo. 35); February 5, 1771 (*ibid.,* leg. 6980, fo. 41).

[32] Masserano to Grimaldi, February 1, 1771 (*Arch. Gen. Sim., Est.,* leg. 6980, fo. 35).

apparent, for no memoranda from the hand of the Spanish ambassador existed, and Rochford, whom Masserano suspected of wishing to prejudice the negotiations of right by a publication of the earlier protest of Spain, was able to lay before Parliament only the few notes which had passed between the foreign office and Harris since September.[33]

Reassuring as was the final vote in Parliament,[34] the continuation of the British armaments was excessively disquieting. Masserano was accordingly full of foreboding in respect of the future discussions on the question of sovereignty, for he suspected that the state of military preparations presaged some sort of diplomatic offensive which had not been previously contemplated. It seemed under the circumstances highly improbable that the British contemplated an abandonment of right as well as of possession when North had given the promise to evacuate. The Spanish ambassador, therefore, counselled his court to suggest a reciprocal evacuation as the likeliest plan to succeed, in place of a discussion over the right, for he entertained the gravest doubts whether the British would give in. Disarmament would be a necessary consequence of a decision along the lines suggested.[35]

Pending the arrival of the duplicate orders to the governor of the Malvinas, the British were certainly justified in maintaining the *status quo* in respect to armament. Anticipating their future action, moreover, Lord Halifax, who now had the Northern Department, questioned Francés about the Bougainville incident and whether any payment

[33] These were the *Falkland Papers* to which reference has been made previously in the notes.

[34] The debate in the Commons on February 4, 1771, is recorded by Masserano in the enclosure to his dispatch of February 5, 1771 (*Arch. Gen. Sim., Est.*, leg. 6980, fo. 41). North took great pains to explain that all the papers were submitted, from the beginning of the dispute to its settlement. The debate raged over the question of French mediation.

[35] Masserano to Grimaldi, February 8, 1771 (*Arch. Gen. Sim., Est.*, leg. 6980, fo. 46).

had been made. Francés told him that the colony had been surrendered as soon as Spain had made her requisition. The payment to Bougainville had been an act of grace by Charles III because the navigator's family had been bankrupted by the enterprise. Francés added that the Spanish had not permitted the French to stay and he doubted if they would ever consent to the presence of the English. Halifax responded that the whole Falkland colony was a chimera of Anson's which Egmont had carried into execution.[36]

The importance of Francés' last reflection lay primarily in the fact that de Guines had received new instruction from his court[37] after the order to leave had reached Paris, confirming the previous mandate of Louis XV that he should pattern his conduct on that of Masserano, once these orders had been communicated to Lord Rochford. The ministry knew that the two courts were continuing to make common cause, and in the case of the Falklands France had a particular reason that England should not settle in a locality from which she herself had been excluded.

Despite this veiled insinuation that France had an interest equal to that of Spain in excluding England from the South Seas, North in his defense of the declaration before the Commons on February 13 was so bold as to declare[38] that he held with those who believed that England should have a base for operations in the South Seas and he hoped the English nation would always maintain the right which it had to visit and navigate these seas, for it was of greatest consequence to England for the purpose of discovery in the South as well as for her commerce and navigation. Little wonder that cold chills should have aggravated Masserano's gout when he heard so forthright a repudiation of

[36] *Ibid.*

[37] Masserano to Grimaldi, January 29, 1771 (*Arch. Gen. Sim., Est.,* leg. 6980, fo. 31); and February 8, 1771, (*ibid.,* leg. 6980, fo. 47).

[38] Masserano to Grimaldi, February 19, 1771 (No. 2054, *Archivo Histórico, Madrid, Estado*).

Spain's claims under the Treaty of Utrecht, a statement scarcely compatible with Lord North's verbal assurances. Indeed, the whole tenor of the debates impressed the ambassador with the advisability of reciprocal evacuation as the only means of avoiding the opposition of Parliament behind which the ministry could hide as an excuse for failure to make good its promises.

Grimaldi's instructions of February 8 arrived in London on the twentieth.[39] The following day Masserano called on Rochford and informed him of the orders to Ruiz Puente, governor of the Malvinas, and to the governor of Montevideo and the commandante of Buenos Aires to return the British property. The king, he said, had not ordered anyone to proceed to the *Gran Malvina,* from which Rochford could surmise how little their own possession of the island concerned them, but that occupation by other powers was a matter of great consequence. He then conveyed the expressions of Charles III's satisfaction that peace was established through the agency of George III, in whose good faith the Spanish king had relied, and who, he hoped, "would now effect what was lacking, which was not the least essential thing to end the affair amicably."[40]

Rochford replied that the point of honor having been saved—the chief consideration—he regarded the rest as accomplished. To which Masserano remarked that it was necessary to see these things effected. Rochford then declared himself ready to listen to any proposals, but Masserano, much astonished, assured him he had no orders to make any proposals, for he did not regard it as necessary. Not satisfied with this, Rochford asked the ambassador point-blank whether he had no instructions to make proposals. Masserano answered that the king, his master, wished to rely on

[39] Masserano to Grimaldi, February 22, 1771 (*Arch. Gen. Sim., Est.,* leg. 6978, fo. 28).

[40] Masserano to Grimaldi, February 23, 1771 (*Arch. Gen. Sim., Est.,* leg. 6980, fo. 61).

the good faith of the British king and the statements made by the latter to Masserano after the declaration was signed, and that his king wished to see how the promises of the ministry in regard to the evacuation of the *Gran Malvina* and the suspension of armaments would eventuate.

Rochford hastened to reassure Masserano, stating that they were about to order the levies of seamen to be suspended, and that he was glad to hear Masserano explain himself as he did. The ministry could not admit that they had made any promises, having always refused to speak of the future. For the moment they were going to send two small frigates to take possession and a storeship with victuals for the few people they were sending, which was less than Spain had there, "because they desired the establishment gradually to diminish."

These last words pleased Masserano the most, for they alone contained the implication that the British were going to evacuate. He read Rochford the duplicate orders to Ruiz Puente, and impressed upon the secretary the good faith of his court. The conversation then turned to Harris and his position at Madrid, and Masserano having explained Grimaldi's attitude suggested that Harris be made minister plenipotentiary, a step which was at once carried out.

After his conference with Rochford, Masserano proceeded to the palace, where he repeated the message of Charles III already communicated to the secretary of state, and reminded George III of the conversation of January 23. The king repeated his assurances of acting in good faith, and his desire to avert war.

There followed a long conference with Rochford on the question of disarmament, at which the latter stated they could not disarm at present in view of the opposition of Parliament as long as Spain and France were armed. Masserano replied that they would probably never disarm if they expected the Bourbon courts to take the initiative. Rochford then suggested that a precise day be set, a proposal to which Masserano was willing to agree provided some ratio were worked out by which Spain would have a force corresponding with the new peace footing decided on by the British.

While these conversations were going on at the Foreign Office, Francés had gone to interview North confidentially on the subject of the evacuation of the *Gran Malvina,* and the mutual disarmament. Having ascertained that North was aware of the instructions from Spain, Francés opened the discussion with remarks about Spain's relying on the good faith of the British ministry and that the former never would consent to an establishment on the Falklands either of the English or anyone else and hence it was necessary to regulate the questions of law and of disarming.

North replied that actual reductions of armament were taking place, and that orders to suspend the levies of seamen had been issued, all of which were signs of peace. Francés was not impressed with these facts, and pointed out that the existing state of the navy was far beyond what was necessary to keep the peace. North, however, insisted that the British needed a greater number of ships than the other great powers. To this statement Francés retorted that Spain and France would certainly follow the British example in the status of their fleet. These discussions proceeded without result. In the matter of the right to the Malvinas, however, Francés having asked how the ministry proposed to carry out its word and preserve peace, North inquired what he meant by the question of right. The sovereignty of the islands, said Francés. North thereupon remarked that the offer of reciprocal evacuation had been inadmissible when the attack on Port Egmont had previously been discussed and besides he did not wish the Spanish to do them out of their right of free navigation in the South Seas, where they had a legitimate right to go.

North undoubtedly was thinking of the remarks he had made in Parliament, and how he would be able to back up his words with deeds. Francés soon relieved his anxiety by pointing out that the questions of the evacuation of the *Gran Malvina* and the freedom of navigation were two distinct questions, the latter being fully regulated by the Treaty of Utrecht, which it was necessary to observe. North at once objected that all the Treaty of Utrecht did was to prohibit to all non-Spanish states entrance to Spanish ports in America, and that it did not prohibit navigation in these seas. Francés' reply was the stock argument of the Spanish that a nation having no ports in these seas had no business there, and he added a subtle thrust to the effect that North was talking more like a parliamentarian than a minister who wished to end a task which he had undertaken, and that he well knew the two questions should not be joined. Lord North then admitted that Francés was right, and that he would see that the Spanish were not held up in being fully content with having relied upon the British king, for his ministry desired peace and they would do everything to avoid a disturbance. It lay, however, entirely with Lord Rochford to settle the evacuation of the *Gran Malvina*, but he (North) was always ready to intervene personally to smooth out any difficulty that might hinder a settlement along the lines agreed upon.

Any encouragement which the Spanish ambassador may have drawn from these conversations was presently dissipated. The orders to Ruiz Puente, it is true, were approved in Parliament,[41] and a resolution Governor Pownall introduced on March 5[42] to require Spain to explain her colonial policy was voted down. On the other hand, the naval preparations were maintained at such a rate[43] that it was entirely

[41] Masserano to Grimaldi, March 1, 1771 (*Arch. Gen. Sim., Est.,* leg. 6978, fo. 32).

[42] Hansard, *op. cit.,* vol. 16, p. 1385.

[43] Masserano to Grimaldi, March 8, 1771 (*Arch. Gen. Sim., Est.,* leg. 6980, fo. 65).

impossible to quiet public apprehension that war was intended, despite the declaration of January 22.

On February 28 Masserano[44] had been advised of the intention of the ministry to discuss a plan of Lord Sandwich for the new peace footing of the navy, a step which was of great consequence to both France and Spain, as there appeared to be no other alternative than to maintain an equally augmented force. Moreover, the fact that fleets had been sent by the British both to the East and West Indies was regarded as evidence either of hostile intent or of forcing a condition of armed peace. The Spanish were naturally opposed to the latter policy, for they were able to mobilize more quickly than the British in case of threatened war, and the maintenance of a great British navy was regarded as a constant challenge to their pretensions in the matter of navigation and control of waters adjacent to their coasts. These views in a somewhat altered form were laid before Rochford. The latter hastened to assure Masserano that the expeditions mentioned were merely for the relief of those already stationed in East and West Indian waters. The British, however, he added, could not carry on with as small a fleet as they had had before the Port Egmont incident, and he saw no reason why Spain should not follow their example.

A suggestion of this sort in the existing circumstances of a most delicate transaction still unsettled was received with great disfavor. Masserano, however, put his objection upon the fact that the British warships had made a practice of protecting contraband trade, and that an increase in the fleet would be met with measures by Spain to exclude all ships from her European ports except for supplies. Masserano then suggested some sort of project based on mutual good faith by which the danger of war be definitely averted, for, said he, he and his king would believe themselves de-

[44] Masserano to Grimaldi, March 9, 1771 (*Arch. Gen. Sim., Est.*, leg. 6980, fo. 64).

ceived until they saw the fine promises of the ministry actually carried into effect.

Rochford's response to this proposal was that the king and all his council were anxious to settle the matter, but that Spain should not hurry them, knowing their constitution. The government was sending only a single frigate, a sloop and a storeship to the *Gran Malvina,* and the frigate was to return with the notice of having taken possession, upon receipt of which notice the affair would be regarded as terminated. Masserano interjected here that it would be ended when the island was abandoned.[45] To this Rochford replied that the French had suggested a reciprocal evacuation, the question of law not to be touched, and that the arrangement be made by means of conversations without any writing. Rochford had, however, declined to discuss this with de Guines, as the matter concerned only the Spanish. Masserano at once asked if the proposal was an official one. Rochford temporized and said he would have to ask his colleagues, but that whatever was the method chosen they should arrange for disarmament. In other words, they were not willing to treat the two matters as phases of the whole subject under discussion. Having received satisfaction from Spain, the North ministry was inclined to regard the remaining issues as isolated questions of policy. This was, however, a position Masserano was unwilling to admit. The British had armed to compel reparation; the Spanish were remaining armed to ensure the performance of the British promises. Up to this moment the divergence of policy had not become fully defined, but in the ensuing days the difference of view became increasingly clear.

On March 1 Rochford summoned Francés and told him that he was anxious to settle the pending questions, but that he could not deal directly with Masserano as he feared that

[45] Masserano here gave Rochford a second duplicate of the orders to Ruiz Puente to give the commander of the sloop in case the latter arrived before the frigate, hoping in this way to avoid difficulties for Ruiz Puente.

the latter would charge him with bad faith and that difficulties might consequently arise. What he desired was a conference of all three ministers to discuss the peace footing, and to decide on a day when disarmament might take place. He did not know whether Masserano was authorized to make any sort of proposals in regard to the matter. In any event, he wished a general disarmament.

Francés replied very shortly that he did not know what Masserano's instructions were, but that although it was necessary to talk of disarmament he knew the Spanish ambassador was primarily interested in the evacuation of the *Gran Malvina* after the British had taken possession. Rochford then advised him that he had laid before the cabinet all that had transpired at the conferences of February 28 and that the ministers were of the opinion that Spain was in a great hurry to have the island abandoned when the British had not even taken possession. Moreover, the orders of the king to the governor of the Malvinas had been examined by the cabinet and all were of the opinion that Spain, by making the British go to Soledad for the order to receive possession of Port Egmont, showed great astuteness, for by this act they were seeking an inferential recognition of their right. Consequently, added Rochford, he would warn Spain that if the British ships were compelled to go to Soledad it would be necessary that the ministry adhere to the instructions given earlier to Captain Byron and others, *i.e.*, to intimate to the Spanish governor that he must leave the islands, as they belonged to the British king. This notice he would give in order that the ministry should not be charged with bad faith in the premises. To avoid any such contingency he suggested either that the British squadron be permitted to go to Buenos Aires, armed with a letter directing the governor to send an officer and ten men to Port Egmont to effect the reëntry, the captured English property being sent from Montevideo and Soledad, or that the British squadron be held until it was known that the Spanish king had ordered the governor to send a man to Port Egmont to effect the restitution.

This statement fell like a thunderbolt. It portended a complete change in British policy. Before the declaration had been signed the promises of evacuation had contained all possible implications that the claim as well as the possession would be surrendered. Now the language used seemed to imply an attempt to salve the claim. It was at least an effort to wring from Spain the greatest possible amount of concession. Francés was quick to appraise the situation. He declared flatly that if the British made any such intimation to Ruiz Puente a breach would result, and he warned Rochford that although both Bourbon courts wished to disarm, neither would do so until the question of law was settled.

Rochford then stated that he did not want any written negotiations, but that if the Spanish would let the British take possession, the frigate would be sent back with the notice of this event and that a sloop would thereupon be dispatched for the two remaining ships to abandon the establishment and to return to England; on their part the Spanish should abandon their establishment. He likewise asked Francés to notify Masserano of this, in case he had any other proposal to suggest when the conference on the matter was finally held.

Masserano was sufficiently surprised at the new development, particularly as the orders to Ruiz Puente had at first been declared to be satisfactory. He was inclined to favor the second suggestion for the entry into Port Egmont, but either way seemed to involve the greatest delays. He was even more astonished when he heard that Rochford had given up the idea of a joint conference and summoned the ambassadors singly—the Comte de Guines first. The key to the situation was quickly found in the fact that a public announcement of the conference was made and the stocks of the East India Company dropped six or eight points, and others three or four. Rochford, who was reported to be in bad financial straits, was suspected of trying to affect the market.

The scheduled conferences took place on March 5, and at both interviews the discussions took substantially the same course. Rochford opened his interview with Masserano by saying that the terrific expenses of armament should be stopped and a day fixed for disarming. He pointed out that England had already suspended the conditioning of some ships and had discontinued the levy of seamen. The naval forces, now at 38,000 or 40,000 men, were to be reduced to 25,000, including marines. This latter figure was the number authorized by Parliament, and, although the peace footing of the navy was not decided, England would probably keep the ships now in commission. The period suggested for disarming was from April 1 to 10. This Rochford said he intended to write to the envoys at Paris and Madrid to be laid before the governments there.

Masserano replied that he would inform his court, but that personally he did not regard the British plan as a peace footing, for Spain would have to bring her forces up to the same standard. To this Rochford answered that Spain could do as she liked, and he then took up the orders to Ruiz Puente. He explained himself in practically the same terms as he had previously done in his conference with Francés.[46] The objections made by Masserano were the same as those made by the French minister. He declared that the entry of a British squadron into Buenos Aires was inadmissible, and as for any threats to Ruiz Puente, this was a sure way to declare war. Rochford protested that if they had wanted to declare war they would have done so long ago. And when Masserano insisted they need make no declaration to Ruiz Puente, for the national disapproval of

[46] Rochford stated that they were sending 385 men to Port Egmont. This was 95 more than had been there in June, 1770.

the whole enterprise was too marked, Rochford replied that no ministry would dare admit it.

The Spanish ambassador did not fail to heap recriminations upon Rochford for telling him first the orders were satisfactory and later raising difficulties. He added that in ultimate analysis the only question was execution of the promise of evacuation which had induced the act of satisfaction and that all the difficulties simply put off the first settlement. Rochford retorted that he could not treat of evacuation until they had taken possession and that his intention was that the frigate should return, leaving the sloop and storeship with a very few men as a sign to all Europe that they desired to abandon the island.

Masserano assured him that the Spanish would not be content with this, that they must have an actual abandonment. The king his master had insisted from the first that the question of right and satisfaction be treated jointly, and that they had given up this point in reliance on the British promises. The fulfilment of these Spain was still waiting to observe, and it seemed to him that as all their plantations on the island had by this time died off, it was wisest and most expeditious that the British order back all the ships sent to take possession. This suggestion Rochford said could not be admitted, but a year hence in April, when a supply ship was sent out, if they then wanted to abandon the island an order could be dispatched.

This postponement of the evacuation into the dim future shocked Masserano to the depths of his soul. He inquired sharply whether the secretary of state doubted the necessity of evacuation after the expectations which they had repeatedly aroused that it would be effected. Repeating the assurances given him in the matter as an inducement to make reparation, he reflected bitterly that after all their promises it was clear that the British were not sincere and that Spain should not have trusted them. Then, catching himself, he concluded more quietly that although he did not doubt the evacuation would take place, he was not sure that it would be effected before the end of 1772 or 1773 and that then a new ministry might be in power which would not approve the previous decision, and consequently the question of law should be treated at once.

Rochford, of course, seized on this latter point and declared that he was ready to treat whenever Masserano liked, if the latter would prepare a memorandum on the Spanish rights. This he would lay before Parliament and support, and if the question of abandonment was adversely decided he would resign. Here, Masserano remarked, it was not his (Rochford's) office the Spanish wanted, but the island, because it belonged to them. Rochford replied to this that it was not the discoverers who had the best right, but those who first occupied, and this rule gave to France the best claim. The Spanish ambassador then explained the Bougainville incident, stating that upon the representations of Spain the French king had ordered Bougainville to abandon his establishment. This led Rochford to remark that an abandonment by England in the manner proposed would not involve a loss of right, and the English could return whenever they pleased. On the other hand, if the question of right were decided adversely to them their pretensions would cease. Masserano, knowing the British aversion to arbitration, replied that lacking a competent judge, his expedient was the best. The answer of the incorrigibly frivolous Rochford was that if Spain did not want them on the island she could always eject them. Masserano assured him, however, that this was what they wanted to avoid; he had no intention of hurrying them but he must have an agreement when the evacuation would take place.

Rochford said that he could not give him this assurance either confidentially or officially, but that Spain must not push them because Chatham and the opposition would then be right in charging the ministry with having dealt secretly on the question of abandonment. And even if the ministry did what Masserano asked the question of right would remain unsettled. Furthermore, it was clear that any written communications were inadvisable for both sides, and without losing his head he could give no verbal assurance what they would do. For the present it was necessary not to press the matter.

Endeavoring to wring some sort of commitment from Rochford, Masserano inquired when the hopes with which the Spanish had been deceived would be realized, but Rochford declined to answer. "If that is so," said Masserano, "then even these are lost forever."

Rochford protested that he either had not explained himself or Masserano did not understand him. Masserano answered that he understood him, but he did not comprehend him, and that Rochford wished to be neither understood nor comprehended. As for himself he intended advising his court fully of what had transpired, that his king would see in what bad faith the British had dealt and that they really desired war. The orders for recall he had hesitated to present because he wished to preserve peace, and he regretted deeply that he had not obeyed his king's orders forthwith upon their receipt.

Rochford replied that he knew of the orders and he would have been seriously embarrassed if they had arrived sooner. However, he had trusted to Masserano's candor and love of peace that the Spanish court would be advised of the dilemma of the ministry in respect to Parliament. No one in the ministry wanted war, but they would not let Rochford set a date for evacuation.

Once more Masserano asked when they could expect evacuation, and once more Rochford declined to satisfy him. And after repeating how the king had relied on their good faith Masserano withdrew.

As soon as the Spanish ambassador had ascertained that de Guines' interview had been equally unsatisfactory the two envoys decided that Francés should call on North to

impress upon him the gravity of the situation. The conference being arranged for March 6, Francés took up the
armament question and the explanations given by North
were identical to those already heard. Francés pointed out
to him the dangers involved in the British course, particularly because of the effect upon the minds of the public, and
he launched, thereupon, into a vivid analysis of the situation. He told North that the disarmament was indeed a
question accessory to the main problem of the evacuation,
but that in reality the two could not be separated, and he
knew that when Charles III learned of the refusal to set a
date for the evacuation Spain would remain armed. The result would be that only a truce and not a peace had been
reached. The reaction of the Spanish court to the evident
lack of good faith, no one could foretell, and as Spain had
acted with absolute sincerity the resentment of Masserano
over the objections to the Ruiz Puente orders and the abandonment had led him to decide to ask the king for leave to
present a memorial on the disputed questions and then depart.

North was greatly agitated. He protested that he himself
had seen no sinister intent in the orders to Ruiz Puente, but
that the other ministers had thought differently. There
seemed no reason why the English could not go directly to
Port Egmont and be installed by an officer sent for the purpose. Moreover, he saw no objection to disarmament taking
place at the time mentioned. Francés, however, reminded
him that the Spanish did object to the latter proposal as
long as the question of right was unsettled. It was inadvisable, he said, to exchange memorials and consequently he
suggested that the English force after a brief stay at the
island return to England and the Spanish should thereupon
withdraw their colony.

Lord North declined to commit himself, but he promised
to support the proposal when Rochford presented it to the
ministry and he urged Francés to see the secretary of state

about the matter. The ships destined for Port Egmont, he added, would have to leave at once on account of the attacks of the opposition, but they would be held at Madeira until a Spanish official could be sent to effect the transfer of Port Egmont.

Obedient to North's suggestion Francés called on Rochford, to whom he outlined the situation in the same manner as he had to North. He minced no words in charging the British with insincerity and inconsistency. First, said he, the ministry said it did not want to treat formally of the question of law and now it wanted a memorandum. Spain and France had no alternative but to believe that they were discreting some secret design. Rochford then admitting that he did not want to deal thoroughly with the question of law, Francés asked him whether they desired to retain the island.

"No," said Rochford.

"If that is so," retorted Francés, "why don't you come to an understanding with the Spanish ambassador as he asks, on the time when the Spanish and English should abandon the islands?"

Rochford replied that he could not set a date on account of the opposition and the charges of a secret agreement on the matter. Francés thereupon submitted the proposal he had just made to North, and the latter's reply. The secretary of state agreed to lay the matter before the cabinet on the following day, and if the proposal was approved, the ships would sail for Madeira, arriving at Port Egmont in October. In the beginning of June he would agree on a memorandum with Masserano which would state that in the interests of peace and harmony both powers proposed abandoning their establishments, and the question of law would remain unsettled. Orders to the commanders would then be exchanged and a sloop sent out in April, 1772, with the orders for the abandonment.

On March 8[47] Francés returned to hear the decision of the ministry. He was told that the decision had been unanimous, that it would be contrary to the dignity of the British crown to treat of abandonment before actual possession of Port Egmont had taken place, it would otherwise be impossible to persuade the opposition as well as the rest of Europe that a secret understanding had not been made, particularly if such a decision was made before they disarmed. Francés replied tartly that he did not know whether in view of Rochford's answer they should care to disarm, for the British were in no hurry to do so. Masserano had intimated that the easiest way was to deal with the question after Parliament had dissolved, asking only a guaranty at what time the evacuation would take place, and Rochford had declined to give either an official or confidential assurance. Francés' own belief was that Spain would not disarm; France would not act unless Spain did, and Masserano would undoubtedly ask for leave to withdraw. This course would make war inevitable.

Greatly concerned, Rochford expressed his regret, but he exhibited orders to Harris in which it was stated that Masserano having asked that the time for the evacuation of the *Gran Malvina* be settled, Rochford had replied that he could not treat in this matter until they had received notice of having taken possession. The dispatch further dealt with the time for disarming. These instructions, said Rochford, Harris was to give to Grimaldi, and he added that in view of the explanations which the ministry had made in Parliament regarding the Falklands, Masserano could be assured that they did not wish to retain them, that under the circumstances it was impossible to say more, but that he would not be averse to having Masserano present a *mémoire* in June proposing mutual abandonment. To this Francés retorted grimly that nothing would save the heads of the am-

[47] Masserano to Grimaldi, March 9, 1771 (*Arch. Gen. Sim., Est.*, leg. 6980, fo. 64).

bassadors if the British did not proceed with the good faith with which they had been met.

The interview terminated with some remarks regarding the restoration of Port Egmont, and Rochford steadfastly insisted that the formal restitution would have to take place there.

Masserano was, of course, greatly exercised over the turn taken by things. He was convinced that the ministry was acting in bad faith, and that the evacuation would be indefinitely postponed. Even the anxiety to disarm at once did not move them to any concession, and the Spanish ambassador feared that if Spain did not disarm new subsidies would be voted. The French, he thought, did not seem to worry the English any longer and hence they felt free to take a bold stand with respect to Spain. Masserano accordingly suggested disarmament to avoid any possible future bullying, or a demand for an equivalent, and to rely on the superior ease with which Spain could mobilize in case the necessity should arise.

It will be observed that the Spanish ambassador had throughout maintained with great astuteness the position that the issue was not *whether* evacuation would take place, but *when* it would be effected. The assurances given him before the declaration was signed had led him to believe that the abandonment promised was to be an abandonment in law as well as in fact. It had now transpired that the British pretended that evacuation would effect only the possession and not the sovereignty. Rochford had tried to offer him the alternative of discussing the latter point, but Masserano was much too shrewd to yield the concession already gained in respect of the abandonment of possession. For this reason, even when the discussion had been most heated, he had never allowed the promise itself to evacuate to be called in question.

The change in the British attitude we may attribute primarily to the unexpected vigor of the opposition, and in the second place to the fact that Harris had reported[48] the rumor of a secret agreement being freely circulated at the Spanish court. Even if they had been willing to brave the opposition, every instinct of caution forbade them to enter upon acts which would still further depreciate their diplomatic credit abroad. Moreover, the changes in the French ministry had given them every reason to suspect that Spain was diplomatically isolated and that she would necessarily agree to disarmament.[49]

As we have seen, agreement on disarmament was by no means certain in view of the attitude taken by the British on the question of evacuation. Furthermore, both Charles III and Grimaldi were of the view that Spain had done everything possible to assure peace, and that after the recall of Harris it was only proper that future advances should come from England. It was in this spirit of injured vanity that Grimaldi instructed Masserano[50] on February 18 to make no proposals in the matter of disarmament, as the king regarded such a step as contrary to the dignity of his crown. An instruction of this sort, of course, limited the power of Masserano to deal with what the British regarded as the main question at issue, and as the question of evacuation was the only part of the whole matter in which he had a free scope of action it was natural that he should insist that evacuation was a *sine qua non* to disarmament.

In this posture of affairs, Rochford's proposals for disarmament dispatched directly to Madrid were of considerable importance, for clearly the question could not be settled at London, and the only hope of an arrangement lay in

[48] Harris to Rochford, February 14, 1771 (*R.O. State Papers, Spain,* 186, no. 80).

[49] On Spanish disarmament *cf.* Harris to Rochford, February 14, 1771, (*R.O. State Papers, Spain,* 186), no. 79; February 21, 1771 (*ibid.,* no. 82); February 25, 1771 (*ibid.,* no. 83).

[50] Grimaldi to Masserano, February 18, 1771 (*Arch. Gen. Sim., Est.,* leg. 6890, fo. 58); and acknowledgment, Masserano to Grimaldi, March 9, 1771 (*ibid.,* leg. 6978, fo. 34).

the shifting of negotiations to Madrid.[51] In these instructions[52] Rochford mentioned the necessity of discretion in the matter of disarmament, and stated that the king desired to disarm if the courts of Spain and France would go *pari passu* with him, and to this end "have the most authentick Engagement from Each of Them that They will disarm at the same instant with his Majesty." The dates April 1 to 10 were named for the period of disarmament and Rochford suggested that Harris arrange for a communication of orders. With reference to the increase in the British establishment, Rochford stated simply that France and Spain had set the example and that it was imprudent to reduce their navy to the state it had previously been in.[53]

These instructions had been on their way but a few days when Thomas Walpole, secretary of embassy at Paris, arrived in London, bearing intelligence of the change of heart of France, news which was most reassuring to North and his colleagues. The alteration in the tone adopted toward Spain was immediately noticed. On March 12 Masserano, having met with Lord Hillsborough, complained very bitterly of the course negotiations were taking, and the continual evidence of bad faith which he was encountering.[54] Lord Hillsborough endeavored to reassure him, repeating all the arguments previously aired by North to Francés. He protested that although no official assurances regarding abandonment could be given, both he and North could say confidentially that they would abandon the *Gran Malvina* when Spain abandoned La Soledad (East Falkland). Masserano answered glumly that he had had enough of confidential

[51] Harris had been made Minister Plenipotentiary. *Cf.* Rochford to Harris, February 22, 1771 (*R.O. State Papers, Spain,* 186). He presented his credentials March 9. *Cf.* Harris to Rochford, March 11, 1771 (*ibid.*).

[52] Rochford to Harris, March 8, 1771, *ibid.*

[53] The writer could not find the second instruction mentioned by Masserano.

[54] Masserano to Grimaldi, March 16, 1771 (*Arch. Gen. Sim., Est.,* leg. 6980, fo. 69).

dealings and that what he now insisted upon was official assurance when the evacuation would be effected. Hillsborough then said that he would be exceedingly sorry if war
should now result, because it would be over a misunderstanding. This Masserano denied, for, said he, the tension
proceeded simply from the British refusal to satisfy Spain
and their manner of disarming proved their desire to remain prepared for war. He, himself, had said everything he
could say, and unless some new instructions arrived there
was no use to talk further, even if they discovered new expedients, unless they would deal officially.

Masserano's impatience with the ministry was enhanced
by the fact that his conferences were always accompanied
by a fall in the stock market.[55] And as it was generally
rumored that Rochford was anxious to recoup his fortunes,
the conclusion that the Foreign Office was juggling the negotiations for its own personal profit seemed unavoidable.

A conference was scheduled to take place on March 14
and rumors got about that the French and Spanish ambassadors were going to present a forty-eight-hour ultimatum.
When Masserano entered the Foreign Office, Rochford sent
word to Francés, who was waiting, so that all present could
hear, that he desired to treat privately with the French minister of matters which he could not deal with officially. This
imprudent announcement seemed to Masserano conclusive
proof that Rochford was trying to drive down the stocks.

When Masserano finally interviewed Rochford he commenced by pointing out the injury to the public funds that
the constant rumors were wreaking. Rochford, obviously
embarrassed, regretted that it was impossible to guard
against spies, and that there was actually no remedy. He
then remarked that he understood from de Guines that all
were to remain armed, but that England was willing to disarm when the Spanish did. Masserano replied that England

[55] Walpole to Mann, March 22, 1771, Walpole, *Letters,* vol. 5, p. 286.

had armed first, but that in any event all his court was interested in was the date of evacuation, and he would have to await instructions. Rochford persisted in his refusal to commit himself, adding that he could do nothing without the consent of all the ministry, which had been refused, and he indulged in some maudlin reflections on losing his life if he acted otherwise. This was more than the Spaniard could stomach. He reproached the secretary of state for making such remarks, for his position was simply that he requested a ratification of their promises. The withholding of this ratification could, under the circumstances, mean nothing else than the desire of the ministry to protract affairs until they were fully prepared for war.

The interview now proceeded to become more heated. Rochford declared that the suggested procedure for entering Port Egmont was not intended to delay things, but was merely a precaution because they were afraid otherwise of what would happen. Masserano, greatly incensed, exclaimed this was answering their courtesies with cannon-shot, that it was a declaration of war. Rochford retorted even if they were not ready Spain was also not prepared. There ensued denials and counter-denials. The conferees stopped for breath, and then Rochford proceeded to discuss his orders to the commander of the English squadron which were designed to assure them against any mishaps, particularly a failure of Spain to deliver over Port Egmont. He wound up by stating that Masserano could be assured that the whole nation knew the little use the island was to them, and the fact that only a few men were being sent was proof of their intention to abandon. Masserano, however, remarked that their course was probably induced by reasons of economy and Spain would never tolerate any English in that region.

Once again the conversation flared up when Rochford declared it was an impertinence of Spain to assert such pretensions until after the English had abandoned the island.

"No more impertinent than the English pretensions to something that belongs to Spain," retorted Masserano.

"Be assured," came back Rochford, "that even if we go to war over it, it will be a big war and by no treaty of peace will we cede the island."

Assuming that the secretary was trying to cow him with empty boasts, Masserano replied coolly that if England wanted to pick a quarrel this was easy to do, but everyone knew that England needed peace more than any other European state. Then, fearing the conversation was getting too hot, he asked if Rochford would like a *mémoire* asking for evacuation; but Rochford indicated this would be unwise. The interview came to an end after several other unrelated matters had been discussed.

Francés entered as Masserano left, and the second conference ended as had the first, except that both the French envoys assured Rochford that France's conduct would be governed by Spain's; an assurance which Rochford gave them to understand he did not believe.

The situation was as black as it had been in December. The Spanish ambassador was convinced that England was positive Louis XV wanted immediate disarmament, and was accordingly working for a split between the two Bourbon courts. Furthermore, he regarded the new peace footing of the British simply as a ruse to enable them to indulge in aggressive acts *ad libitum*. The protestations of Hillsborough and Sandwich that the ministers all wished to abandon the Falkland establishment but could not give a formal engagement was looked on by both de Guines and Masserano as a futile device to quiet Spain. For this reason Masserano declined to advise his court to disarm, particularly as the British preparations seemed as feverish as they had been two months earlier.

Despite the tension between the two courts, life in London went on gaily enough. The stock market, reacting under the stimuli applied by the government, responded favorably to the wishes of the inner circle. John Wilkes was embroiled with the Parliament, and Masserano went about refusing to take any further notice of the Falkland business. Only once did he break his silence, and this was to discuss the matter with Halifax on the occasion of his first conference with the new secretary of state for the Northern Department.[56] This discussion, it may be said, was along the same lines as had been followed by both sides since January, and the cause of peace was not furthered in the least degree.

About this time de Guines received instructions from France which fully explained the firmer tone so recently adopted in London.[57] The general tenor of these instructions was that the English ministry should be treated with gloved hands, because Louis XV was convinced of their good faith, and because it would be fatal to put weapons in the hands of the opposition when the present ministry was favorably disposed to France and to the maintenance of peace. As regarded disarmament, Louis declared he would do nothing until he was advised of the attitude of Charles, but it was intimated that the latter would think as he did.

When Masserano learned of these orders, he realized that the English had gained a strategic victory, and that there was nothing to prevent their staying armed and forcing Spain either to accept their terms or to fight without France, a policy which would mean the end of the Family Compact.

The Spanish court, however, had already come to a decision on the matter of evacuation and disarmament. On March 16 Grimaldi addressed a long instruction to Masse-

[56] Masserano to Grimaldi, March 22, 1771 (*Arch. Gen. Sim., Est.,* leg. 6978, fo. 45).

[57] Masserano to Grimaldi, March 23, 1771 (*Arch. Gen. Sim., Est.,* leg. 6978, fo. 47).

rano[58] in which he stated that agreement on disarmament must comprehend the East and West India squadrons recently dispatched, for these included nearly all the ships outfitted during the Falkland negotiation. Under the circumstances only reciprocal good faith would avail to reach an understanding. Masserano was neither to deal directly or indirectly on disarmament, but was to transmit all proposals, and act as if the matter was one of indifference. At the same time he was to use the greatest vigilance in detecting and reporting on the preparations and armaments then going on.

Regarding the evacuation of the *Gran Malvina,* "which the British Ministry and the King had offered" and which they would not recognize formally nor could agree upon, Grimaldi believed it was useless to make a formal agreement if they would not for personal or domestic reasons execute it. The Spanish, wrote he, should know the British and their system by this time. As for the reciprocal abandonment, the suggestion had been advanced earlier at a time when it seemed expedient in view of the demand for satisfaction. The circumstances now were different. Satisfaction had been given, and it was now merely a question of one act for another. He added that he did not mean to imply they should not be on good terms with each other. Masserano was, however, to inform the British that if they wished to assure peace with Spain, it was necessary to remove this thorn. Spain could never regard it with indifference and she would judge British intentions by their acts.

These instructions, as a matter of fact, told Masserano nothing, and enjoined upon him a policy of watchful waiting. They arrived in London March 30.[59] When they were drawn up Grimaldi had not yet heard of the conferences of

[58] Grimaldi to Masserano, March 16, 1771 (*Arch. Gen. Sim., Est.,* leg. 6978, fo. 38).

[59] Masserano to Grimaldi, April 2, 1771 (*Arch. Gen. Sim., Est.,* leg. 6978, fo. 54).

March 5 and 6, and hence Masserano did not feel free to enter into further discussion. He notified his government[60] on April 6 that the ministry was exceedingly impatient at the delay in a reply from Spain, and Rochford had frankly told both Francés and de Guines that he believed Spain would not disarm. Regarding the evacuation, Masserano advised Grimaldi that he had not made a proposal for reciprocal abandonment—this had been made by the British and by the French, but he had never approved it.[61]

The British ministry no doubt suspected that the courier who had arrived on March 30 brought some definite reply. The rumors that Spain wanted war were rife and the stocks reacted accordingly. In an interview with Halifax on April 5 Masserano was pressed by the secretary of state to disclose what he had heard from Madrid, but the Spaniard maintained an astute silence. Halifax later confided to Francés that he suspected Masserano of having a reply, which the Frenchman denied. Halifax then exclaimed that he hoped it would be favorable, for it would be a shame to fight over such miserable territory as Port Egmont, that they intended abandoning the place, but they could not fix a time without risking their offices.

The continued preparations and the suspense felt by the government had no little effect on the public mind. The Wilkes affair had, it is true, diverted general attention from the diplomatic situation, but the opposition was anxiously waiting for a false step by North to pounce upon him and his colleagues. On April 10[62] the prime minister had under-

[60] Masserano to Grimaldi, April 6, 1771 (*Arch. Gen. Sim., Est.,* leg. 6978, fo. 59).

[61] Apparently no effort was made to halt war preparations during these months. Every dispatch of Masserano furnishes details. The effect upon the public funds was most marked, and everyone was kept in a state of ferment over the situation.

[62] Masserano to Grimaldi, April 12, 1771 (*Arch. Gen. Sim., Est.,* leg. 6978, fo. 67, *enclosure*).

taken to explain in the Commons the expenditure of the subsidies voted for the navy and to prepare the way for a new appropriation for further increases. He informed the house that both parties were disarming gradually, but he believed a stronger navy was the best guarantee of peace—words with a peculiarly familiar ring—and hence sought to justify his conduct. This was the signal for a fierce attack upon the government, and Colonel Barré proceeded to charge the ministry with the infamous design of ceding Port Egmont to Spain. This, of course, was the very ammunition which the ministry needed in their discussion with Spain, and Rochford did not hesitate to bemoan the activities of Chatham in his conversations with Francés.[63]

As it turned out, the new offensive in Parliament was superfluous. Masserano's reports of the early March conferences had reached Madrid and the king, acting in the spirit of the earlier instructions to Masserano, determined to abide the event of evacuation. Grimaldi advised Masserano to this effect on March 25.[64]

The first point taken up in this instruction was the orders to Ruiz Puente. Grimaldi insisted that the British had not understood the good faith of Spain in the matter, and that the king had never entertained the least design to take advantage of England by having the ships go to Soledad. The reason for adopting this course had merely been because there was no living soul on the *Gran Malvina*. Ruiz Puente, however, had been immediately advised to send someone to that island to effect the restitution. Regarding the other points, Masserano was to follow his previous instructions. The Spanish had no intention of keeping larger armaments than the British, for they had the sincere wish of avoiding a break.

[63] Masserano to Grimaldi, April 12, 1771 (*Arch. Gen. Sim., Est.,* leg. 6978, fo. 68).

[64] Grimaldi to Masserano, March 25, 1771 (*Arch. Gen. Sim., Est.,* leg. 6980, fo. 73).

The instruction regarding evacuation was the most interesting of all, because it at once discloses the wisdom of the Spanish policy and the chivalrous love of honor of Charles. Grimaldi wrote:

With reference to the evacuation of the *Gran Malvina* we shall see whether they wish there [in England] to give credit by their own acts that their most sacred promises can be relied on.

When the instruction arrived in London on April 12, Masserano was obviously deeply disappointed. He wrote[65] that he would carry out the orders, but he warned Grimaldi that the British had insisted they had made no official promise. He added that he believed England had no intention of disarming and consequently, as he knew how anxious they were to have Spain disarm, he would say nothing until he had an answer how Harris' instructions of March 8 had been received. Accordingly, he merely explained to Rochford[66] the intent of the orders to Ruiz Puente. Rochford declared he himself had had no suspicions, that it had merely been the opposition. Masserano, however, replied coldly that he had been the one to mention it, and without reason, for his court had always shown the greatest good faith.

In the absence of instructions regarding disarmament, no further steps were taken in London. Harris, owing to the Easter holidays, had delayed in presenting Rochford's plan, and it was not until April 1[67] that Grimaldi notified Masserano that the Spanish had decided to disarm on April 20 to 31 and that they would keep a number of ships in commission in proportion to those maintained by England.

Obedient to this instruction, Masserano called on Roch-

---

[65] Masserano to Grimaldi, April 12, 1771 (*Arch. Gen. Sim., Est.,* leg. 6978, fo. 66).

[66] Masserano to Grimaldi, April 16, 1771 (*Arch. Gen. Sim., Est.,* leg. 6978, fo. 70).

[67] Grimaldi to Masserano, April 1, 1771 (*Arch. Gen. Sim., Est.,* leg. 6978, fo. 53).

ford on April 20.[68] He communicated the Spanish decision to his lordship, and added significantly that by this act they could see the sincerity and good faith of the Spanish crown. Their deeds and words corresponded, said he, and he trusted that he could expect an exact reciprocity on the part of England. Rochford then read Harris' dispatch and discussed at length the details of disarmament and the means of exchanging orders.

At the end of this conference Masserano stated that it was desirable to avoid the least suspicion of lack of confidence between the two courts, that the matter of the *Gran Malvina* be settled in order that that "heap of rocks and sand" should never cause trouble. It was not his intent to hurry them, for the king had ordered him to be on watch that the British perform the promises which they had made in the time of their negotiation on abandonment. Rochford replied that Spain did well not to hurry them, for while he was of the opinion the island should be abandoned later, present circumstances did not permit them to take this step. He added, reported Masserano, "that his sovereign had told him all I had said when the duplicates of the orders to restore Port Egmont had arrived, and he [Rochford] having taken the liberty of representing to the King what he could have said to me regarding the extent to which I could place reliance, even for the future, upon the good faith with which this negotiation had been carried on, his Majesty had said he was right; that he regretted he had not done so and that he would speak to me about it upon the first occasion which would present itself."

Masserano replied that he was sure the king, his master, would have more confidence in a promise from his Britannic Majesty's mouth, than in any writing.

There ensued further discussions on the method of dis-

[68] Masserano to Grimaldi, April 20, 1771 (*Arch. Gen. Sim., Est.,* leg. 6978, fo. 72).

armament[69] as well as on the exact number of men and ships which were to constitute the peace footing. At a conference on April 22 Masserano used expressions which led Rochford to think he had further instructions to deal with the matter of evacuation. Masserano replied that he had no orders to speak otherwise than he had already done, as his court wished to avoid all possibility of dissension in the future. Rochford expressed his pleasure that they were not to be hurried, for, said he, the ministry wished to avoid the appearance of having made any promise, *a fact which they always intended to deny.* He added that the reciprocal abandonment of the Falklands was a matter different from the question of right, which had never been settled, and even if they abandoned they could always return and occupy them reciprocally in case of dispute, to which Masserano said nothing.[70]

The negotiation on disarmament soon passed into its final phases and the orders were approved by George III. At the king's levee on April 24[71] Masserano took occasion to mention to his Majesty that Charles III had been greatly pleased at the successful settlement of affairs, and that his policy had been proof of his friendship for the British crown. He added that he hoped in time that George III would free them from doubt by seeing to it that they should not have to bear the thorn in their foot, a thing which would pain them until it was withdrawn. George III replied that Charles could be assured that his affection was reciprocated, and, not to be outdone in flowery compliment, the king compared the late unpleasantness to a lovers' quarrel, which was started for the pleasure of making up. He added that Spain must not put in doubt his good faith.

[69] *Ibid.;* Masserano to Grimaldi, April 24, 1771 (*Arch. Gen. Sim., Est.,* leg. 6978, fo. 75).

[70] *Ibid.*

[71] Masserano to Grimaldi, April 26, 1771 (*Arch. Gen. Sim., Est.,* leg. 6978, fo. 80).

The final word on the Spanish policy regarding the promised evacuation was addressed to Masserano by Grimaldi on April 9.[72] The Spanish minister, having stated the necessity of knowing definitely the extent of the British peace establishment, instructed Masserano to do his best to ascertain the intentions of the ministry. He cautioned the ambassador against exhibiting too great an interest in the matter, for, said he, representations, persuasion and even facts are useless in dealing with the English and "the more one talks the more one loses or at least the less one gains."

He went on to say:

The same applies with regard to the evacuation of the *Gran Malvina*. They know the verbal promises given during the negotiation and these were not dependent upon a reciprocal evacuation of our *Soledad*. Why should we go to them with this proposal immediately? If it suits them they will perform. If it does not suit them, in view of the situation of the Ministry with reference to Parliament or to the public they would run a risk in admitting it, they will not perform and we shall only get a refusal—more or less clear. Why shall we expose ourselves to this? It would be most inopportune to give them cause. Your Excellency has observed that having shown a desire of presenting this demand they have already indicated that they would receive it but as if doing us a favor. They would make a reply which would require an answer one way or another and in the end we would arrive at an extremity, or we would find ourselves deceived. The conduct to be observed is not to press them and only when it can be done accidentally to repeat in conversation that we shall see how you will carry out your promise, how you will convince us of your good faith. The opportune time to do this might be the moment when the duplicates of the orders of restitution are delivered but not for the purpose of urging them that they effect evacuation at once, and really they have said correctly that Spain has been proceeding in the matter with discretion.

If the King had thought in any other way he would have advised your Excellency at the time when the approval of the declaration

---

[72] Grimaldi to Masserano, April 9, 1771 (*Arch. Gen. Sim., Est.*, leg. 6978, fo. 64).

was dispatched sending other duplicates. Nothing was said to you because his Majesty at once decided to be on the watch and to regulate his conduct by what that court did with the others after its promises, not relying greatly upon these and knowing that it was better in this relation to choose a favorable occasion, and not to enter in a negotiation on the law so that in the event of a repulse the [British] could do what suited them.

Spain having thus committed herself to a policy of patient waiting, the second crisis over the Falklands came to an end. Many a day was to elapse before the British ministry was ready to execute its promise. What the Spanish desired above all to avert was the use of the Port Egmont colony as a means of more extensive operations in the South Atlantic and Pacific. They were sufficiently guarded against this by the assurance that the British would post only a small force on the West Falkland, and the maintenance of their own establishment on the East Falkland was a guarantee against any misuse of Port Egmont in connection with violations of the Treaty of Utrecht. Hence it was that they could view the postponement of the promise to evacuate with equanimity. There was no need to imperil their position under the treaties with any discussions of the meaning of these instruments, for it was clear that an evacuation *de facto* would mean the abandonment of the British pretensions to a right of free navigation and settlement.

The actual restitution of Port Egmont to England took place on September 15, 1771.[73] The British squadron, Captain Stott commanding, had reached Port Egmont on the night of September 13. They found there Lieutenant Francisco de Orduna with a number of men. Stott delivered the orders of the Catholic king and after arranging for the restoration of the stores and of possession, the British force

[73] Stott to Stephens, December 9, 1771 (*R.O. State Papers, Spain,* 188). *Cf.* Rochford to Lords of Admiralty, March 15, 1771, *British and Foreign State Papers,* vol. 22, p. 1389.

landed and was formally entered in possession. The British flag was hoisted, a salute fired, and the Spanish then departed. Stott reported that the transaction was effected with the greatest appearance of good faith and without the least claim or reserve being made by the Spanish officer on behalf of his court.[74]

The North ministry were in no hurry to carry out their promise to evacuate. The Foreign Office put to the Admiralty the question of the reduction of the force to a minimum, in accordance with the assurance given to Masserano to that effect. The Admiralty replied that it could suggest no plan for further reduction which would enable them to keep the establishment up at any less expense—the ground upon which the Foreign Office put its request. The Admiralty, however, made the remark that effective possession could not be kept up constantly at any expense, and hence suggested the reduction of the force. A smaller number of men it was said would maintain a *mark* of possession, and the existing garrison was not a security for the defense of the place.[75] The garrison of Port Egmont was accordingly reduced when the relief was sent out in the winter of 1773.[76] It was not until a year later, however, that England finally executed the promises by which the declaration had been induced.

On February 11, 1774,[77] Lord Rochford addressed Lord Grantham, the British ambassador at Madrid, as follows:

I think it proper to acquaint your Lordship that Lord North in a speech some days ago in the House of Commons, on the subject of

[74] *Ibid.;* Lords of Admiralty to Rochford, December 11, 1771, (*R.O. State Papers, Spain,* 188); Rochford to Grantham, December 13, 1771 (*Add. MSS.,* 24157).

[75] Lords of Admiralty to Rochford, February 26, 1772 (*R.O. State Papers, Spain,* 189).

[76] Rochford to Grantham, March 6, 1772, *British and Foreign State Papers,* vol. 22, p. 1393.

[77] Rochford to Grantham, February 11, 1774 (*Add. MSS.,* no. 24160). Also in *Br. and For. St. Pap., loc. cit.*

naval establishment this year, mentioned the intention of reducing our Sea Forces in the East Indies, as a material object of Diminution to the number of Seamen, and at the same time hinted, as a matter of small consequence, that in Order to avoid the Expense of keeping Seamen or Marines at Falkland's Islands, they would be brought away afterwards, leaving there the proper Marks or Signs of Possession and of its belonging to the Crown of Great Britain. As this measure was publickly declared in Parliament it will be naturally reported to the Court of Spain, and though there is no necessity of your Lordship's communicating this notice to the Spanish Minister officially, since it is only a private Regulation with Regard to our own Convenience, yet I am inclined to think from what passed formerly on this Subject that they will rather be pleased at this Event, your Lordship may, if they mention it to you, freely avow it without entering into any other Reasoning thereupon. It must strike your Lordship that this is likely to discourage them from suspecting designs which must now plainly never be entertained in our minds. I hope they will not suspect, or suffer themselves to be made to believe that this was done at the Request, or to gratify the most distant wish of the French Court, for the real Truth is neither more nor less than that Lord North intends [is desirous] to lessen a small part of an economical Naval Regulation.

The same caution which had characterized the British conduct three years earlier was evident in this instruction. North had found that his Parliament was tractable, and he had accordingly carried out his promise. There was of course no word in the dispatch to indicate that evacuation was the execution of an antecedent obligation. The Foreign Office still clung to its policy of having nothing in the record which would disclose what had really been done. But as we know the actual course of negotiations and what was promised by the British, we are justified in dismissing as a mere diplomatic phrase the reference to a policy of economy. Nor was Spain interested in the formal reasons given by the British for their conduct. The only concern of his Catholic Majesty had been the fulfilment of the promise and this had at length taken place. The governor of the Malvinas was instructed[78] that "offers having been made by the English to abandon the island" he was to see that this was actually done and to report any future attempts to colonize. The fact that Spain continued her own colony was regarded as a sufficient safeguard of the right.

The abandonment took place on May 20, 1774.[79] Formal leave was taken and an inscription engraved on a piece of lead was affixed to the blockhouse. This inscription stated:

Be it known to all nations that the Falkland Islands, with this fort, the storehouses, wharfs, harbors, bays, and creeks thereunto belonging are the sole right and property of His Most Sacred Majesty George the Third, King of Great Britain, France and Ireland, Defender of the Faith, etc. In witness whereof this plate is set up, and his Britannic Majesty's colors left flying as a mark of possession by S. W. Clayton, commanding officer at Falkland Islands, A. D. 1774.[80]

[78] Arriaga to Ruiz Puente, April 9, 1774, *ibid.*, p. 1379; Arriaga to Vertiz, April 9, 1774, *ibid.*, p. 1378.

[79] Penrose, *An Account of the Last Expedition to Port Egmont* (1775), p. 76 *et seq.*

[80] One of the curious consequences of the Falkland incident was the scandal which arose over the alleged stock gambling activities of the Comte de Guines. He was accused by his secretary, one Tort, of having speculated, using the latter as his agent. Tort later brought suit against de Guines, who eventually was exonerated. *Cf.* Walpole, *op. cit.*, vol. 4, p. 107; Masserano to Grimaldi, April 24, 1771, no. 2101 (*Archivo Histórico, Madrid, Estado*); *Correspondence de Monsieur le Duc d'Aiguillon au sujet de l'Affaire de M. le Comte de Guines* (Paris, 1775); *Memorial of the Count de Guines . . . against Messieurs Tort and Roger . . .* (London, 1776).

CHAPTER IX

THE STRUGGLE FOR SOVEREIGNTY IN THE NINETEENTH CENTURY

THE legal consequences of the British abandonment of Port Egmont, and its effect upon the claims of Spain to the whole group of islands,[1] are by no means superficially apparent. Nor was the legal situation in 1774, and in 1811 when the Spanish colony was withdrawn, precisely identical. It is, therefore, necessary to consider in some detail the implications of evacuation at the moment it took place.

In 1771 the position of the two parties was substantially as follows: the British government, by promising speedy abandonment, had secured from Spain an act of satisfaction by which possession of Port Egmont was restored, with a reservation of right by Spain. The Spanish minister had declined to word his declaration so as to include the "dependencies" of the place. Subsequent to the declaration the British ministry had made it clear that evacuation was regarded by them as leaving the question of right in *status quo ante.* It was their view that when Port Egmont was restored it affected in no way the question of right except in so far as the restitution of possession as a matter of fact restored the parties to the situation prior to the attack of Madariaga in June, 1770.

There seems reason to doubt the legal validity of the British position. While it is true that the physical situation of the parties after September 15, 1771, was identical with that in June, 1770, the restitution of Port Egmont had been

[1] There is some material on the Spanish administration of the colony to be found in *Documentos para la Historia Argentina* (1913), vol. I, pp. 16, 19, 20, 285, 287, 288, 313, 314, 315 and 333; vol. 2, pp. 7, 16, 19, 21; vol. 5, p. 314; vol. 7, pp. 7, 20, 24, 26; and *Documentos para la Historia del Virreinato del Río de la Plata*, vol. 1, p. 1; vol. 3, pp. 5, 37.

agreed to conditional upon evacuation. The moment this evacuation was effected the rights of the British to the territory were reduced to the extent that no longer having possession, their claims of sovereignty were correspondingly imperfect. We have considered hitherto the importance of possession in relation to the acquisition of sovereignty, and we are accordingly led to inquire into the importance of possession in respect to the loss of sovereignty.

The cases of abandonment of territory in international law have been relatively few, and prior to 1774 there is only one case—that of the island of Santa Lucia—from which the position of the European states on this question can be surmised.[2] The text writers up to this time had dealt with the matter, but what they have to say is of no great help in ascertaining what was the practice of states. In respect to occupation we have seen that the international customs were well fixed by the time the attention of text writers was drawn to the subject; what they had to say, therefore, was primarily in confirmation of existing rules of practice. The writers, having applied the principles of the Roman law to the acquisition of sovereignty, naturally enough turned to the *Corpus Juris Civilis* for their rules regarding abandonment. In this matter their work was of more consequence than it had been in fixing the rules of occupation, primarily because there had been no cases of abandonment, and with the growing popularity of international law as a special branch of jurisprudence it was natural that the views of text writers would be treated with deference.

The principles of the Roman law upon which the international law theories of abandonment are based have been the subject of much debate.[3] The first principle was that *res derelictæ* (abandoned objects) were objects of occupation, for when ownership was relinquished the territory reverted

[2] *Vide supra,* chapter V.

[3] The best discussion is in Czylharz, *op. cit.,* p. 88 *et seq. Cf.* Wolff, *Über Dereliktion von Recht und Besitz* (1888).

to its previous status of a *res nullius*. Abandonment consisted in the intention to abandon (*animus derelinquendi*),[4]
plus the actual execution of this intent. The proof of intent
to abandon is not easy to ferret out. Ordinarily a person
who abandons an object is consciously directing his will
only to the act of abandonment without reference to the legal effect—*i.e.*, no longer wanting an object he abandons it
without thinking of whether or not he is giving up his legal
rights. It is this hiatus in the mental processes of the person
abandoning which the law endeavors to supply by stating
that the *animus derelinquendi* embraces the waiver of right
because anyone who divests himself of all control over an
object must be presumed to do so in law as well as in fact.[5]
In the absence, therefore, of positive declaration of intent
to yield legal rights, this intent can only be deduced from
the surrounding circumstances.

The execution of the intent to abandon is a no less essential element to the legal act than the animus. It can be effected in a variety of ways. In relation to movables[6] it is of
course easier to designate acts of abandonment, and although the Roman law drew no distinction in this matter
between movables and immovables the proof in the latter
instance was uniformly more difficult. It is a rare occur-
rence that realty is abandoned, and as a rule the circumstances that induce it, war or economic pressure, are such
that abandonment cannot be forthwith presumed. It was because of this fact that during the decline of the Roman Empire special statutes were enacted to protect occupants of
farms abandoned because of war and taxes.[7]

The Romans appear to have entertained some doubt
whether abandonment could be effected by anyone except

[4] Inst. 2, 1, l. 47; D. 41, 7 (*pro derelicto*).
[5] D. 45, 3, l. 36.
[6] Czylharz, op. cit., p. 90.
[7] *Ibid.*, p. 95.

an owner in possession;[8] on the one hand, because owner-ship is presumed, and on the other hand, because the relin-quishment of possession is essential to fix the legal quality of the act. A person who is not the owner divesting himself of control over an object is said to have merely the *animus non possidendi*, for, having only possession or custody, he yields no more than he has. Furthermore, as title is in an-other person, the animus of the person in possession cannot, even by construction, be made the animus of the title holder. Conversely, the latter, when not in possession even though he may have the *animus derelinquendi*, not being so situated that he can perform the necessary relinquishment of pos-session, cannot be said to abandon. The acquisition of rights as against him can only be by usucapion or prescrip-tion, *i.e.*, adverse possession by lapse of time.

An object once abandoned can be occupied by another, ir-respective of *bona fides*, and in this process the rules of occupation already examined apply.[9] Abandonment and oc-cupation have no further relation to each other than that abandonment produces the circumstances (*i.e.*, the aban-doned object becomes a *nullius*) under which the rules of occupation can become operative. The case, however, is otherwise when a prescriptive right is claimed. In this event, the person claiming title by adverse possession must show *bona fides*, in other words, that he acquired and con-tinued to hold the property,[10] as abandoned property. In this case both the fact of abandonment (the only matter of importance in fixing a title by subsequent occupation) and *bona fide* belief that the object was abandoned form the ba-sis of claim.

In this connection the implications contained in the aban-donment of possession are of great importance, for here,

---

[8] Inst. 2, 1, l. 47, and D. 41, 7, l. 2.

[9] Czylharz, *op. cit.*, p. 150 *et seq.*

[10] *Ibid.*, p. 160; Buckland, *A Textbook of Roman Law* (1921), p. 242 *et seq.*, esp. p. 247.

indeed, rests the only claim of the holder by adverse possession to *bona fides*. It is not necessary to deal here with the much disputed question whether or not the possession can be surrendered *animo* and not also in fact.[11] We are concerned only with the converse proposition of what the effects of a relinquishment of possession really are. Irrespective of whether or not abandonment of physical control can be held to establish intent to abandon *title*, there can be no doubt but that such an act fixes the intent to relinquish *possession*. The Savignian theory[12] that possession is not surrendered by a mere act as long as the possibility remains for the erstwhile possessor to regain the object, has given way to the theory advanced by Jhering[13] that the essence of the Roman law rule is that possession once abandoned the right of possession is *eo ipso* relinquished. If this act is combined with intent to abandon then the title itself is thereby lost. Jhering bases his view upon the underlying principle of the economic utility of the particular object. Where continued physical possession is not the essential element in the use of the object, as where a fisherman leaves his nets in the water, no loss of possession or of ownership can be deduced. But where the contrary is the case, the implication is clear that not only the possession but the ownership are relinquished.

There can be no question but that the theory of economic use which underlies all rules of property is a factor which must be taken into account, particularly where there has been a long and uninterrupted abandonment of possession. Whether or not it is of sufficient legal consequence to outweigh declarations that an intent to abandon does not exist, is difficult to say. Certainly the very spirit of the law would be violated if a mere declaration could suffice to exclude others from the enjoyment of property until such time as

---

[11] Wolff, *op. cit.*, p. 20.

[12] Savigny, *Das Recht des Besitzes* (7th ed.), p. 339 *et seq.*

[13] Jhering, *Über den Grund des Besitzschutzes* (2d ed.), p. 160 *et seq.*

the original owner might choose to exercise his dormant rights. It was precisely to curb any such pernicious tendencies that the rules of prescription were designed, but with this doctrine we are not concerned, as it does not enter into account in our case.

The preceding statement of the Roman law rules regarding abandonment no doubt is colored by the study of modern civilian studies in interpretation. The picture of the Roman law in 1625 when its principles were first systematically applied to international law is indeed difficult to reproduce, and yet we can gain some idea of the theories with which Grotius was familiar if we next examine his application of the Roman law doctrine to the new science of international law.

In the fourth chapter of his second book Grotius[14] deals in detail with abandonment and prescription and the distinction between the two concepts. Citing at the outset the notion of Vasquez that as between sovereigns there is no statute of limitations, Grotius gives as his reason for denying such a view the tendency it would have to breed war, and the texts which he quotes in support are based in the main on the notion of economic use later advanced by Jhering. Having mentioned the effect of words as evidence of abandonment he goes on to say:[15]

A derelict thing may be indicated by the fact; thus if something is thrown away it is held to be derelict unless there be circumstances which oblige us to regard it as merely temporarily relinquished with the intent of recaption. . . . Thus one assumes that the owner has given up his right if he knowingly makes a contract with the mere possessor, as if the latter were owner. There is no reason why this should not obtain between Kings and free people.

Throughout this chapter Grotius has mixed theories of abandonment and prescription in such a manner that his

[14] Grotius, *De jure belli ac pacis*, lib. 2, c. 4.
[15] *Ibid.*

ideas are not easily disassociated. Obviously he has in mind a concrete problem which he does not state, to wit, whether when territory has been abandoned another state can acquire rights in respect to it by prescription. He states that when a person knows that another has taken possession and the former owner preserves a long silence, this silence can only be interpreted as conveying the intent that the former owner no longer regards the thing as his own. He then proceeds, ''to establish a presumption of the abandonment by silence two things are necessary that the silence be knowing and based upon the free will, for the inaction of a party which is in ignorance has no effect and when there is another cause known which influences the will conjecture as to what it is ceases.'' Finally, in chapter VI, he states:

> From what we have said it appears that both a King as against a King and a free people as against a free people, may acquire a right not only by express consent but by tacit abandonment and by possession following this or taking a new force from it.

It is not easy to separate the notions which these passages conceal. Briefly summarized, Grotius' doctrine is simply this, that abandonment may exist in fact unless some circumstance rebuts such an assumption. It may also be deduced from words, and from a failure to speak if the silence is a free one and not the silence of ignorance.[16]

There is reason to doubt whether Grotius' theory that a mere failure to speak could constitute a *res derelicta* was supported by antecedent legal authority. He is clearly assuming that possession by the original holder has been relinquished. Hence his case is really one of abandonment of possession under circumstances where there is not a *prima facie* dereliction. The fact that Grotius feels it necessary to add that continued silence plus possession by the other party

[16] *Cf.* Grotius, *Inleiding tot de Hollandsche Rechtsgeleerdheit* (1767), on abandonment, bk. I, c. 1, sec. 50; c. 2, sec. 12; on prescription, bk. I, c. 7.

gave title, shows that what he had in mind was really acquisition of title by adverse possession where the intent to abandon was absent. This, as we have seen, was something different from occupation following abandonment, for in that case two distinct legal acts were involved which in no way overlapped. In the situation supposed by Grotius the acts overlap, and to acquire title it is necessary to have a long-continued silence by the original owner, plus time, plus possession, to fix the rights of the second claimant. Such a case is obviously one of *usucapio pro derelicto* which arises where there is a mistaken belief that the object is a *res nullius,* and not of abandonment[17] where the new occupant enters without regard to *bona fides,* or *scienter* of the antecedent owner.

Pufendorf is somewhat more precise on the same point. He states:[18]

We likewise acquire by occupancy things in which the Dominion to which they previously were subject is extinct. This takes place if a person openly throws away an object with sufficient indications that he no longer desires it to be his but should be exposed free for the first occupant, and without any intent thereby of benefitting any one else. Or if having lost possession first against his will, he later gives the thing over, either because he despairs of recovering it or because its recovery is not important. For otherwise a man though he loses the actual possession yet never forfeits the dominion over a thing (unless it be taken from him by way of punishment or by war), but he still keeps a right of recaption till such time as he is no longer disposed to recover it or may be presumed to have ceased. Hence the dominion of such things as these cannot be acquired by occupancy so long as the right of the former owner still subsists. But since to make a thing completely abandoned or forsaken, two points are necessary, first that the person refuse to own it for the future, and secondly, that he divest himself of the posses-

---

[17] The doubtful view that *bona fides* is not an element in international prescription is traceable to Grotius' confusion here. *Cf.* Moore, *Digest,* § 88.

[18] Pufendorf, *op. cit.,* bk. IV, c. 6, sec. 12.

sion, by leaving the thing or casting it away; if either of these conditions be wanting the property is not evacuated. . . .

There is little precise information to be gleaned from these passages, further than the fact that the Roman law rules of dereliction were carried over into international law. Neither Grotius nor Pufendorf elaborated the principles[19] beyond the implications already mentioned and for this reason we are cast upon the Roman law itself for their understanding. We have already remarked that the circumstances for which these rules were designed are usually extremely equivocal and that both act and intent are usually by no means subject to a single interpretation. In private law the legal solution of these situations is difficult enough —the complexity of our international problem is of course enhanced by the fact that the issue is always over the sovereignty and that rules regulating title in private law are not necessarily designed in all respects to govern the acquisition and loss of sovereignty.

The Roman law rule that occupation could be effected only by possession in fact had become firmly entrenched in international practice at the time Grotius wrote. The mere marking of regions with the national flag or the royal arms had never been countenanced as the equivalent of possession in fact. While it is true that Spain had not effectively occupied all of the territory claimed by her, yet she had so distributed her settlements that she could rely upon the principle of territorial continuity or propinquity as a means of excluding intruders—at least as far as the mainland was concerned. This principle was based upon the fact of possession and was in reality a rule complementary of the rule of occupation.

The fact that nations insisted upon possession as the sole

---

[19] Wolff, *Institutions,* sec. 219, since an abandoned object no longer belongs to anyone it naturally belongs to the first occupier, but if one has already made use of the right of the first occupier it can be acquired only by the one who has this right.

act by which sovereign rights could be acquired and that discovery or merely formal acts of taking possession were completely discredited has an important bearing on the problem of abandonment. If possession alone could give rights, the continuance of possession alone could preserve them. Mere constructive possession being inadmissible for original acquisition, *a fortiori* it could not be admitted to perpetuate rights. In other words, the implications of an abandonment of possession necessarily were even clearer in international law than in private law, for, in the absence of a theory of constructive possession, a presumption of dereliction was established by the mere relinquishment of control.

This theory was of course a stranger to the common law.[20] Just as occupation of a *res nullius* was, as respects land, a concept for which an English lawyer had no possible use, so the notion of dereliction by which an object once occupied reverted to its previous state of *nullius* was equally unthinkable. The legal consequences of *seisin,* which lay at the bottom of the English law of property, were such as to preclude any absolute loss of rights—an idea implicit in the Roman law theories of abandonment to which the penalties incident upon a disseisin were in no wise comparable, at least from the procedural point of view. This was due to the fact that the essence of the English property law was the assurance of personal service to the immediate feudal su-

[20] *Cf.* sec. 218. Pollock and Wright, *An Essay on Possession in the Common Law* (1888), at p. 44, gives abandonment as a means of losing possession, but p. 45 states that occupation of land is "not now" possible in England, thus excluding the possibility of abandonment of land.

There is evidence of the emergence of a theory of abandonment in English real property law in relation to colonial practice. *Cf.* Chalmers, *Opinions of Eminent Lawyers on Various Points of English Jurisprudence* (1814), vol. 2, p. 44 (1723). The failure to maintain continued possession was regarded as sufficient to permit forfeiture of title by legislative act. On the importance of possession in relation to title in the colonies, *cf.* Penn *v.* Lord Baltimore, 1 *Ves. Sen.* 444, at p. 447 (1750).

perior, whereas the Roman law was designed to assure the economic use of the property itself.

It is not strange that the English, unfamiliar with the conception of abandonment and cleaving to their own fictions of possession (*i.e.*, seisin), should regard such a doctrine with suspicion. In the dispute with the French over the island of Santa Lucia, to which we have already adverted,[21] the issue was whether or not the British, having withdrawn their settlement on account of an Indian attack, could be considered as having abandoned it. It is interesting that the British commissaries in their brief of 1751 cited the passages in Grotius dealing on the one hand with dereliction and on the other with *usucapio pro derelicto*. Pufendorf was likewise called upon as supporting their position. The gist of their argument was that there had been no abandonment in law, as the withdrawal had been due to necessity —that ancient refuge of the hard-driven apologist. Furthermore, they contended that the few months which had elapsed before French occupation did not suffice to make the island a *res derelicta* so that France would have the right to acquire it by occupation. It will be observed that the British commissaries dealt rather ignorantly with the question of law. Having chosen to use Grotius as their chief prop, in their insular ignorance of the Roman law they inevitably confused occupation upon dereliction with occupation by adverse possession. If the abandonment of Santa Lucia had been a dereliction, it made no difference how soon the French seized it, or how long they held it. If there was no dereliction, the question of time was of the essence of the situation, provided the French were acting in good faith.[22]

The discussion over Santa Lucia was not an arbitration, and the memoranda exchanged by the commissioners, therefore, established no precedent. The incident is cited simply

---

[21] *Cf.* above, chapter V.

[22] Phillimore, *International Law* (2d ed.), vol. I, p. 308.

because it is some indication of the state of British opinion
on the law at that moment, and because it shows the practical difficulties of attempting to prove an *animus redeundi*
(intent to return) or, for that matter, an *animus derelinquendi*. The reasons, therefore, which urge a conclusive presumption from the fact of relinquishment of possession of
hitherto unoccupied territory seem to be very cogent, particularly if we believe with Jhering that the economic use
and the physical situation of the property are factors to be
considered in establishing such a presumption.

If we regard the evacuation of the Falklands in the light
of the rules hitherto discussed, and assume the British
claim to the islands had in the first place any validity, we
are led to the conclusion that at the moment it was consummated the abandonment was intended only as an abandonment in fact and not in law. The views expressed by Lord
Rochford after the signing of the declaration indicate that
the British were not necessarily evacuating *sine animo redeundi*—in other words, that they may not have intended
to make the *Gran Malvina* derelict land. On the other hand,
that possession itself was abandoned there can be no doubt.
The leaden plate left by Lieutenant Clayton announcing to
the world that Port Egmont was the sole property of his
king and was left as a "mark of possession," important
though it may have been as evidence of a *spes redeundi*, had
no more effect upon the fact of possession than if it had
never been left there. It had been agreed that the possession
would be surrendered, and, the agreement having been executed, the possession could not be constructively retained.
The status, therefore, of the *Gran Malvina* was at least that
of territory in fact abandoned, and assuming the British to
have been *sine animo derelinquendi*, the latter retained at
least a legal claim to the island.

It was stated above that time was not of the essence in
the matter of dereliction. There can be no doubt, however,

that as a matter of proof of an intent to abandon, particularly if there are intervening acts by an adverse claimant either admitted or acquiesced in, time is of great consequence. It is particularly so where the circumstances are such that the adverse claimant cannot show the *bona fides* necessary to establish a prescriptive right. An agreement entered into between the two claimants on the subject matter subsequent to the relinquishment of possession, might operate as a conclusive proof of an intent to abandon or as a sort of quitclaim. On the other hand, the situation might be such that a prescriptive right could be acquired. In such case the dereliction would be of importance only as a matter of fact, and not as a matter of law—*i.e.*, the adverse claimant's title would be perfected only at the end of the period of limitation and not at once, as in the case of occupation upon dereliction in law.

In this connection it is necessary to recapitulate briefly the specific acts of the Spanish upon which any claim to a title by prescription might be founded, or which would establish an intent on the part of the British to abandon. We have seen that upon receiving notice of the British design to evacuate, orders were dispatched to the governor of Soledad, instructing him to observe that the abandonment was fully and completely effected. Apparently no steps were taken to occupy the *Gran Malvina* itself, but the Spanish undoubtedly continued their supervision over the island in order that no new colonies might be placed upon it.

In 1776 Buenos Aires was constituted a viceroyalty,[23] and the Falklands were included in the region governed by the viceroy.[24] Port Egmont at this time appears to have been used by vagrant British and American ships, and as it was desired to avoid any new complications, orders were

[23] Moses, *Spain's Declining Power in South America* (1919), p. 153 *et seq.*

[24] Quesada to Bayard, May 4, 1887, in Quesada, *op. cit.*, p. 246.

issued to destroy the buildings still standing. This instruction was issued in 1777,[25] and was carried out. A report was sent in April 8, 1780, and was approved by a royal order of February 8, 1781.[26]

During all these years governors[27] were appointed to rule the Falklands and the Spanish government took every measure necessary for the preservation of its sovereignty. In 1783,[28] the viceroy of Buenos Aires, Juan José de Vertiz, appalled at the expense entailed by the preservation of settlements on the Falklands, proposed to his government that these establishments be abandoned. To this suggestion, however, the crown turned a deaf ear, and Vertiz was instructed[29] that such a step would be regarded as dangerous and prejudicial, as the British would then be justified in treating the islands as derelict and subject to occupation. It was suggested thereupon that a small force be kept to sustain possession, either at Soledad or Port Egmont so that foreign ships could be warned off and that the English could form no settlement.[30]

What has been said thus far of the legal claims of Great Britain to the Falklands after their abandonment has been *solely on the assumption that these claims had some validity in the first place.* We have seen, however, that neither under the rules of occupation nor under the existing Euro-

[25] *Ibid.*, p. 248.

[26] *Ibid.*, p. 249.

[27] These were Francisco Gil (1774-1777), Ramón Caraza (1777-1781), Augustin Figueroa (1781-1784), Ramón Clairac (1784-1790), Juan José Elizade (1790-1793), Pedro Pablo Sanguineto (1793-1799), Ramón Villgas (1799-1805), Juan Crisóstomo Martinez (1805-1811?). *Cf.* Boysen, *The Falkland Islands* (1924), p. 189.

[28] Quesada to Bayard, May 4, 1887, in Quesada, *op. cit.*, p. 246.

[29] Text in *ibid.*, p. 246 *et seq.*

[30] The treaty of peace with Great Britain, signed at Versailles, January 20, 1783, Cantillo, *op. cit.*, p. 574, contains nothing bearing on the Falklands.

pean treaties could these claims have validity as against the Spaniards. The declaration of 1771 did not alter this situation. Indeed, the existence of the treaties and the fact that they were not expressly repudiated is important proof of the view that the abandonment of Port Egmont was an abandonment in law as well as in fact. The declaration fixed no rights of the parties. We are compelled, therefore, to turn to the principles of international law and to such instruments as the Treaty of Utrecht between England and Spain to determine what these rights were. Measured by the provisions of this instrument, under international law as it was then understood, the action of the British in abandoning their colony particularly as it was in fulfilment of an antecedent promise was an act in compliance with the terms of the treaty. This fact seems to the writer to strip the British claim to the island after abandonment of all legal quality. Any merit that their claim may have had depended upon their ability to show prior occupation as well as a right to enter under the Treaty of Utrecht, and as the restoration of their colony was expressly stated to be no more than an act of satisfaction for an injury to the British crown, this restoration did not supply legal validity to a claim which had from the first lacked foundation.

If we take the view outlined above, the abandonment of Port Egmont really disposed of any shadow of right which the British may have had. Under the existing public law a right as against Spain could be maintained only by adverse possession. Once this possession was surrendered the claim itself would lapse.

In 1790 occurred an event which profoundly affected the legal position of the Falklands; this was the conclusion by England with Spain of the celebrated Nootka Sound Convention (October 25, 1790).[31] The events which led to the conclusion of this treaty are in many respects curiously like

[31] Cantillo, *op. cit.*, p. 623.

those which precipitated the earlier conflict of England and Spain over the Falklands.[32] Both states had sought, in 1789, to establish a colony on Nootka Sound, an inlet on the western shore of Vancouver Island. The Spanish expedition arrived before the British and when the latter appeared on the scene the Spanish commander seized the vessels and crews and sent them to Mexico. An earlier visit by an English trader had resulted in no permanent establishment, but the British government believed it to be enough to give England a better right than Spain.

When the matter was reported in Europe the same feverish preparations for war, the same interminable exchanges of view and the same stubborn refusal to surrender ensued as had taken place some twenty years before. The situation was so far different that Charles III was no longer king, and the events in France had made clear the fact that the revolution spelled the end of the Family Compact. The issue in the earlier Turks Island, Falkland and Crab Island disputes was again the real essence of the conflict between England and Spain: were the treaties which buttressed Spain's colonial system to be observed with continued respect, and were the restrictions on the navigation of the Pacific to be enforced to the exclusion of all new non-Spanish settlements?

It is beyond our purpose to dwell on the details of the controversy. The Spanish foreign minister, Floridablanca, took the view that the British had acted in derogation of the treaties and had violated Spanish sovereignty.[33] The British were equally insistent that the acts of the Spanish commander were a hostile attack in time of peace and consequently a breach of international law,[34] and denied in vig-

---

[32] Manning, *The Nootka Sound Controversy* (in *Reports of the American Historical Association,* 1904), p. 283.

[33] *Ibid.,* p. 374.

[34] *Ibid.,* p. 370.

orous language the claim of Spain to exclusive sovereignty in the Pacific.[35]

The diplomatic situation in Europe was at the moment so much more unfavorable than in 1770, that Spain, eventually, had no alternative except to submit to the British. On July 24, 1790, a declaration and counter-declaration were signed at Madrid, in the same form as the Falkland Declaration, by which Charles IV agreed to make reparation, the question of right, however, being reserved by both parties.[36]

The discussions over the question of right dragged on through the ensuing months. In October the British served a ten-day ultimatum insisting that their demands in regard to occupation and navigation were to be acceded to or war was to result. At stake was the whole fabric of the Spanish colonial system, the carefully executed policy of isolated settlements so scattered as to ensure claims over intervening territory, and the whole North American coast line which only exclusive navigation of the Pacific could save for future Spanish dominion. The firmness of the British government and the weakness of Spain were such that Floridablanca saw the necessity of surrendering the northern Pacific coasts in order to save the vast regions of South and Central America which were more effectively under Spanish control. Accordingly he summoned a special *junta* of the principal ministers and submitted to them the British proposals. The *junta* decided for war, but while they were debating Floridablanca was able to secure a partial amelioration of the British terms and on October 25, 1790, a convention was signed.

The Nootka Sound Convention provided for the restoration of the British holdings on Nootka Sound, and for the restoration of any property taken by either side since April, 1789, on the northwest coast of North America. By

[35] *Ibid.*, p. 377.
[36] Text in *ibid.*, p. 405.

the third article freedom of navigation and fishery in the Pacific or the South Seas and of landing to trade or settle in unoccupied regions was reciprocally agreed upon, subject to three qualifications. By the first of these (Art. IV) the British king engaged to prevent the navigation and fishery of his subjects in the Pacific or South Seas from being made a pretext for illicit trade with Spanish settlements, and expressly stipulated that the British should not navigate or fish within the distance of ten maritime leagues "from any part of the coast already occupied by Spain." Secondly, in the places restored in and off the northwest coast of North America and wherever settlements had been made since April, 1789, or might be made in the future the subjects of each power should have free access and the right to carry on commerce. The third limitation being the most vital, we shall cite it textually.[37]

It is further agreed with respect to the eastern and western coasts of South America and the islands adjacent, that the respective subjects shall not form in the future any establishment on the parts of the coast situated to the south of the parts of the same coast and of the islands adjacent already occupied by Spain; it being understood that the said respective subjects shall retain the liberty of landing on the coasts and islands so situated for objects connected with their fishing and of erecting thereon huts and other temporary structures serving only those objects.

This article was further limited in its duration by a secret provision[38] that it was to have force only as long as no establishment was formed by some other power.

The language in which this treaty was couched is by no means felicitous. It would perhaps be going too far to assert that the lack of verbal precision was due to design, and yet Floridablanca's defense of the instrument to the *junta*[39] was based upon the vagueness and elasticity of the text, the

[37] Cantillo, *op. cit.*, p. 624.
[38] Manning, *op. cit.*, p. 458.
[39] *Ibid.*, p. 454.

efficacy of which he made clear would depend chiefly upon the interpretation. What the treaty in effect accomplished, however, was to bring to an end the Spanish claims of an exclusive right to navigate the Pacific, and, by conceding the right of fishery off the eastern and western coasts of South America, to terminate also the claim to closed seas in these regions. In other words, the network of treaties by which the Spanish colonial system had been sustained was with one stroke relegated to the limbo of scraps of paper.

Although the Spanish were compelled to make an extraordinary and epoch-making concession, the surrender was not as sweeping as one might judge. The British right to colonize was recognized only as far as the northwest coast of North America was concerned. As to the other parts of the Spanish empire, the right merely to navigate for the purpose of fishing was admitted. There was a definite pledge by both parties not to establish new colonies in the South Pacific and South Atlantic. What was already occupied was to remain in *statu quo,* provided no third party attempted to settle in regions not already occupied.

This view of the effect of the treaty was taken by the British government itself in another relation. During the discussions with Mr. Gallatin, the United States minister, over the northwestern boundary, in December, 1826, the British commissioners, Huskisson and Addington, presented their government's view of the Nootka Sound Convention in the following language :[40]

But before the British plenipotentiaries proceed to compare the relative claims of Great Britain and the United States in this respect, it will be advisable to dispose of the two other grounds of right put forward by the United States.

The second ground of claim advanced by the United States is the cession made by Spain to the United States by the treaty of Florida in 1819.

If the conflicting claims of Great Britain and Spain, in respect

[40] *American State Papers, Foreign Relations,* vol. 6, p. 663.

to all that part of the coast of North America, had not been finally adjusted by the convention of Nootka in the year 1790, and if all the arguments and pretensions, whether resting upon priority of discovery, or derived from any other consideration, had not been definitively set at rest by the signature of that convention, nothing would be more easy than to demonstrate that the claims of Great Britain to that country, as opposed to those of Spain, were so far from visionary or arbitrarily assumed, that they established more than a parity of title to the possession of the country in question, either as against Spain or any other nation.

Whatever that title may have been, however, either on the part of Great Britain or on the part of Spain, prior to the convention of 1790, it was from thenceforward no longer to be traced in vague narratives of discoveries, several of them admitted to be apochryphal, but in the text and stipulations of the convention itself.

By that convention it was agreed that all parts of the Northwest Coast of America not already occupied at that time by either of the contracting parties should thenceforward be equally open to the subjects of both for all purposes of commerce and settlement, the sovereignty remaining in abeyance.

In this stipulation, as it has been already stated, all tracts of country claimed by Spain and Great Britain, or accruing to either in whatever manner, were included.

The rights of Spain on that coast were, by the treaty of Florida in 1819, conveyed by Spain to the United States. With these rights, the United States necessarily succeeded to the limitations by which they were defined, and the obligations under which they were to be exercised. From those obligations and limitations, as contracted towards Great Britain, Great Britain cannot be expected gratuitously to release those countries merely because the rights of the party originally bound have been transferred to a third Power.

While this language was used with reference to other sections of the treaty than those involved here, it is equally applicable to the arrangements regarding the South Atlantic. Hence this guarantee of the *status quo* in the Nootka Sound Convention, with its reiteration of the principle of *uti possidetis,* had a significant bearing upon the legal status of the Falklands at that time. The British had now in a solemn treaty recognized the *status quo;* the *de facto* occupation of the whole Falkland group was admitted by them to be an occupation in the legal sense. This seems to be the fair interpretation to put upon the treaty. In any event, the British by agreeing not to establish colonies to the south of regions *already occupied* by the Spanish, by implication recognized the sovereignty of Spain to all regions in fact occupied. This was the *quid pro quo* which Spain secured for her surrender of the privilege of exclusive navigation and fishery.

The practical effect of this convention was to open the seas to the British only for purposes of navigation. The islands surrounding Tierra del Fuego and further south, such as South Georgia, were the only places, however, where the British were allowed to land, and this temporarily. *The terms of the sixth article by inference forbade any landing at the Falklands as they were a place already occupied by Spain.* Consequently, even if we could assume that the British had up to this time kept alive their claim to the group, it was extinguished by this instrument, which precluded any possible perfection of the claim by actual possession. It was only by possession that the British could transmute their claim into a right, and, the means having been formally renounced, the claim itself lapsed.

The Spanish themselves adopted this point of view and took steps to keep all fishermen from their coasts and the British without the stipulated ten-league zone.[41] In the region of the Falklands the task was at once difficult and important. The climatic conditions, and the conformation of the group made effective police measures almost impossible, and yet whaling and sealing were too valuable economic resources to be handed over to aliens when the trade with the colonies themselves was forbidden. As the mainland ports were closed to the fishermen, operations in the South Atlantic were exceedingly hazardous unless a port of call

[41] Quesada to Bayard, May 4, 1887, in Quesada, *op. cit.,* p. 250.

could be found. For this reason the Falklands assumed a new economic significance, and the Spanish became all the more zealous in trying to maintain their rule of non-intercourse.[42]

From what has been said it will have been observed that subsequent to the British abandonment of Port Egmont in 1774, the Spanish exercised the fullest sovereignty over the whole group of islands, not limiting their acts of government and control to the islands themselves, but extending their powers over the surrounding seas in an effort to prohibit or at least make more difficult fishing activities of other nations in the South Seas. These acts appear at no time to have been disputed. The British acquiesced in them and through the Nootka Sound Convention gave their formal consent by recognizing the *status quo* in the southern half of South America.

The vicissitudes of Spain during the wars growing out of the French Revolution and the Napoleonic wars affected the colony on the Falklands but slightly. In June, 1806, the then governor of the islands, Juan Crisóstomo Martinez, having heard that Buenos Aires had been captured by the English under Lord Beresford, abandoned his post.[43] This news was premature, for Beresford's success took place in July, and was but short-lived, as the Spanish recaptured the place five weeks later.[44] Nevertheless, it does not appear that another governor was sent out, although the colony remained on the islands.

In 1810 occurred the opening struggles of the viceroyalty of Buenos Aires to break loose from the home govern-

[42] Even to the extent of starting a competing whaling company.

[43] Quesada, *op. cit.,* p. 256. Martinez was also the Commandante of Puerto Deseado. When the news reached him he was at that place and he decided to abandon the settlement rather than run the risk of a complete destruction. *Cf.* his report in Angelis, *Memoria sobre los Derechos,* doc. 42.

[44] On the plate of Lieutenant Clayton and its removal from Buenos Aires by the British *cf.* Groussac, *op. cit.,* p. 522.

ment.[45] In its inception this revolution was nothing more than the legitimist revolt against the rule of the Buonaparte family. Not until 1816, after the Congress of Vienna had restored the Bourbons to Spain, did the movement in what is now the Argentine Republic assume the character of a struggle for independence from the Spanish crown. In that year, on July 9, the provinces which had constituted the old viceroyalty declared their independence as the United Provinces of the Rio de la Plata.[46]

The revolt against the Buonaparte régime had as a direct consequence the withdrawal of the colonists on the Falklands. On January 8, 1811,[47] it was determined by the governing *junta* that the colony should be discontinued, and to this end the governor of Montevideo ordered the removal of the remaining colonists and proposed the evacuation of the settlements on the lower Patagonian coast. These facts were reported to the king by the viceroy, Don Xavier Elío, on March 18, 1811.[48] And thus the islands were once again abandoned to the elements.

The struggle through which the La Plata states passed in the ensuing years precluded for the time any notion of the revival of the Malvinas project. The attention of the country was absorbed in matters of more vital interest and importance. During this period, however, no attempt was made by any other nation to acquire control of the islands. They were visited with some frequency,[49] particularly by whalers,[50] who found them a convenient place to secure wa-

---

[45] On the Revolution *cf*. Otero, *La Revolution Argentine* (1917).

[46] The declaration is in *British and Foreign State Papers*, vol. 5, p. 804.

[47] Torres Lanzas, *Independencia de América* (1912), vol. 2, p. 485, no. 2932.

[48] *Ibid.*

[49] They appear very frequently in log books of the times.

[50] On the Falklands as a refuge during this time *cf*. Barnard, *A Narrative of the Sufferings and Adventures of Captain Charles H. Barnard* (1829).

ter and game. But these visits were of no consequence from the point of view of international law.

Meantime the war of independence had progressed with such success that in 1820 the new government of the United Provinces, anxious to secure all of the territory previously controlled by the viceroyalty, dispatched a frigate, the *Heroina,* to the Falklands for the purpose of taking possession. The frigate, in command of Colonel Daniel Jewitt, arrived in November, 1820, and on the sixth day of that month formal possession was taken of the group.[51] Jewitt found as many as fifty vessels of different nationality in the various harbors, most of them sealers or whalers. He notified the masters of these vessels of the fact of taking possession by the new republic. He also gave notice that the laws of the new state forbade all fishing and hunting on the islands, and that offenders would be sent to Buenos Aires for trial.[52]

The act of possession was soon followed by other steps to secure the sovereignty over the islands and to promote a successful colony. In 1823 Don Pablo Aregusti was appointed governor of the islands and during the three preceding years the claim of the United Provinces to the right to regulate the fisheries is said to have been respected by foreign vessels.[53] In any event, in the same year that a governor was appointed a concession was given by the confederation to Don Jorge Pacheco and Louis Vernet consisting of land on the East Falkland Island and the use of the fisheries and cattle. An expedition of three vessels was

[51] Jewitt to Orme, November 6, 1820 (*British and Foreign State Papers,* vol. 20, p. 422) (hereafter cited *Br. and For. St. Pap.*).

[52] *Cf.* Weddell, *A Voyage toward the South Pole* (1825), p. 80 *et seq.;* Freycinet, *Voyage autour du Monde* (*Historique,* vol. 2, pt. 3) (1839), p. 1237, esp. p. 1279. *Cf. Br. and For. St. Pap.,* vol. 20, p. 419. The *Heroina* was later convicted of piracy. *Cf.* enclosure, Baylies to Livingston, September 26, 1832 (*State Department, Manuscript Despatches, Argentine,* IV; hereafter cited *MS. Desp., Arg.*).

[53] Report of the Political and Military Commandant of the Malvinas, August 10, 1832 (*Br. and For. St. Pap.,* vol. 20, p. 369 *et seq.*).

fitted out under the direction of one Robert Schofield, but the establishment formed by him was abandoned in the following year.

The concessionaires were not discouraged by this failure. Louis Vernet immediately prepared a second expedition, which sailed in January, 1826, and by his personal energy and courage he was finally able to place his establishment on a footing of some security.

Regarding Vernet, a word is here in place, as he looms large as the villain of the piece, and he is still embalmed in the amber of the United States' official documents as a scoundrel and pirate. Vernet was of French origin, but as he had resided for a long time in Hamburg he was generally spoken of as a German.[54] He was a man of character and by no means the uncultivated barbarian that he was pictured in the American diplomatic correspondence. Captain Fitzroy in his *Narrative*[55] speaks of the kindnesses shown a brother officer by Vernet when his ship stopped at the Falklands, and he mentions the significant circumstance of finding books and a pianoforte in the residence of his host.

Vernet, judging by his correspondence, was well read and he enjoyed the unique capacity of translating his knowledge into action. In his report to the government at Buenos Aires,[56] he outlines his colonial schemes with no little vision:

Fully aware [said he] of the great advantages which the republic would derive from establishments in the South, and some experiments which I had made in agriculture being attended with success, I resolved to employ all my resources and avail myself of all my connections in order to undertake a formal colonization which should secure those advantages and lay the foundation of a national

[54] On the later fate of Vernet, cf. *Memoirs and Services of Three Generations* (1909), p. 31. This is a memoir of the Cilley family.

[55] Fitzroy, *Narrative of the Surveying Voyages of H. M. S. Adventurer and Beagle* (1839), vol. 2, pp. 266-267.

[56] *Supra,* note 53.

Fishery which has been at all times and in all countries the origin and nursery of the Navy and the Mercantile Marine.

With this notion in view, at a moment when the United Provinces were still wracked with civil strife, Vernet applied to the government for an exclusive grant to the fisheries, for the benefit of his colony. There was every reason why such a request should be granted. Almost at the outset of its existence the new state had taken measures for the conservation of fisheries, so as to exclude foreigners and promote their use by citizens. This policy, moreover, appears to have been aimed directly at the rights conceded to the British by the Nootka Sound Convention. On October 22, 1821, a decree had issued regulating fishery on the Patagonian coast[57]—the region where the British had by the 1790 convention the right to erect huts. By this decree foreigners were compelled to pay six dollars per ton reckoned on the "whole measurement or tonnage of the vessel whether her cargo be complete or not." When foreigners settled with families they were to be given free grants of land and they were to pay a lesser duty. Those aliens who erected buildings for the extraction of oil and preparing skins of amphibious animals were to pay an intermediate rate.

Vernet's application received favorable consideration and on January 28, 1828,[58] a decree was issued by which were conceded the island of Staatenland and all the lands off the island of Soledad (East Falkland) excepting those ceded previously to Pacheco and a strip of ten square leagues on the Bay of San Carlos, which the government reserved to itself, on condition that a colony should be established within three years, and the government be notified of the fact. The colony was declared free of all contributions excepting what might be necessary for the mainte-

[57] Text in *Br. and For. St. Pap.*, vol. 20, p. 421.
[58] Text in *ibid.*, p. 420.

nance of the local authorities for a period of twenty years. The fishery free of duty in all the islands and on the coast of the continent south of Rio Negro was granted for the same period. It is interesting that in the preamble of this law the government based its action upon its desire to promote the fishery and to secure a safe base for the operations of its privateers.

The new colony was so far successful that in the following year a decree[59] was issued by the government of Buenos Aires stating that when the revolution of May 25, 1810, had occurred, Spain held the Malvinas and the islands of Tierra del Fuego, a possession which was justified by the right of prior occupation, the consent of the chief maritime powers of Europe and by the proximity of the islands to the continent which formed the viceroyalty of Buenos Aires. The government of the republic having succeeded to all the rights previously exercised by the mother country had continued to exercise acts of dominion over the islands. As a measure of precaution and to secure the advantages offered by the islands it was decreed that the islands of the Malvinas and those adjacent to Cape Horn on the Atlantic be placed under the command of a "Military and Political Governor" to be named at once. The governor was to reside on Soledad (East Falkland), on which a battery should be erected flying the flag of the republic. The governor was empowered to enforce the law of the republic and provide for the due performance of the regulations respecting seal fishery on the coast. Pursuant to this decree Vernet was appointed political and military governor.[60]

Vernet was now placed in a position where he was no longer a mere private adventurer, but an official of the new republic charged with the duty of enforcing its laws. That the proper observance of the fishery decree was of interest

[59] Text in *ibid.*, p. 314. Issued June 10, 1829.
[60] *Ibid.*, p. 423.

to him as sole concessionaire[61] in no way detracted from his official status. Indeed, the fact that the warnings conveyed by Jewitt in 1820 had not been regarded in recent years rendered a step of this sort imperative, particularly as the right to seal or fish in territorial waters, in the absence of treaty provisions to the contrary, was, as it now is, a matter subject to the control of the sovereign.

The depredations of alien sealers upon the stock of seals gradually assumed serious proportions, and Vernet faced the possibility of having the most lucrative part of his concession wiped out. He had requested a war vessel from the government to enable him to end these conditions, but the most the government could do was to pass the decree already mentioned. As soon as he was formally installed as governor, therefore, on August 30, 1829, Vernet notified the masters of the fishing vessels of the new régime and requested them to cease operations under penalty of being sent to Buenos Aires for trial.

Apparently Vernet's warnings were regarded with scorn by the sealers. In any event, although previously warned in 1829, one of the ships, an American schooner, the *Harriet*, returned and was seized by Vernet July 30, 1831, together with two other American ships, the *Superior* and the *Breakwater*.[62] There is much dispute over the facts surrounding the seizure. The Americans claimed that it had been done with violence, and that Vernet had caused the *Harriet* to be plundered.[63] The governor, on his part, asserted that the seizure had been according to due process of law and without any unnecessary violence.

The *Breakwater* having escaped detention, the disposition of the *Harriet* and the *Superior* was discussed for some

[61] Vernet brought out Pacheco, his partner.

[62] *Cf.* Vernet's "Report," p. 386.

[63] Captain Davison's deposition enclosed in *MS. Desp., Arg.,* IV, Slacum to Livingston, December 9, 1831. The MSS. so cited are in the Department of State at Washington, D. C.

weeks, and finally an arrangement was made by which the *Superior* was allowed to proceed to a new sealing ground after giving security for reappearance, while the *Harriet* was to be sent to Buenos Aires with all the necessary documents to stand trial for the violation of the decrees. This arrangement was embraced in a contract[64] signed by Vernet and the masters of the *Harriet* and *Superior,* respectively.[65] As soon as this arrangement was completed the *Harriet* sailed for Buenos Aires with Vernet on board, arriving at that port on November 19, 1831.

At this time the United States had no diplomatic representative at Buenos Aires. The republic had been recognized in 1823, and Cæsar Rodney, who had been a member of the first commission to investigate the political conditions of South America in 1818,[66] had been appointed the first United States minister. Rodney had died shortly after his arrival, and thereafter the United States had been represented by the able and intelligent John M. Forbes.[67] Forbes was thoroughly conversant with South American social and political conditions and seems to have enjoyed the confidence of the government to which he was accredited. It was a dire calamity that he should have passed away just before the trouble over sealing arose,[68] and that the interests of the United States were handled by the consul George W. Slacum, a person of no diplomatic experience and utterly without tact or judgment.

The news of Vernet's seizures arrived at a moment when the government at Buenos Aires was engaged in an acrimonious dispute[69] with various foreign governments over

[64] *Br. and For. St. Pap.,* vol. 20, p. 373.

[65] Vernet was to get a share of the profits.

[66] *American State Papers, Foreign Relations,* vol. 4, p. 217 *et seq.*

[67] His correspondence is in *MS. Desp., Arg.,* vols. II-IV. Forbes was an extraordinarily able man whose services to his country are now almost forgotten.

[68] Slacum to Livingston, no. 1 (*MS. Desp., Arg.,* IV).

[69] Forbes to Livingston, Nov. 29, 1830 (*ibid.*), for origin of dispute.

the liability of aliens for military service. The whole confederation, moreover, was agitated with political strife and rumors of revolution; with Brazil trouble had been threatening over the newly established republic of Uruguay.[70] As regarded the United States the state of sentiment in the capital was none too favorable, for when Forbes had died some officious persons had taken it upon themselves to search his papers, an incident which had occasioned an exchange of sharp words between Slacum and the government[71] of Buenos Aires which was charged with the conduct of foreign affairs for the United Provinces.[72]

The arrival of the *Harriet* and the news conveyed by Davison, her master, of Vernet's actions stirred Slacum to a great pitch of indignation. He forthwith reported the matter to the Department of State,[73] and to Don Tomas de Anchorena, minister of foreign affairs, he addressed a note stating that he could not conceive on what grounds an American vessel engaged in lawful trade should be captured, and inquiring whether the government intended to avow the capture.[74] Four days later Anchorena replied that the case was before the ministry of war and marine, and would be laid before the governor in due course.[75]

This answer did not satisfy Slacum. Acting entirely without instructions, he at once advised Anchorena that he regarded the latter's note as an avowal of Vernet's act and his right to regulate the fisheries. This right, he said, he denied was vested in the government of Buenos Aires,

[70] Forbes to Van Buren, April 22, 1830; May 18, 1830; July 30, 1830 (*ibid*).

[71] Slacum to Livingston, nos. 1-3 (*ibid.*).

[72] Varela, *Historia Constitucional de la República Argentina* (1910), vol. 3, p. 433.

[73] Slacum to Livingston, November 23, 1831 (*MS. Desp., Arg.,* IV).

[74] Slacum to Anchorena, November 21, 1831 (*Br. and For. St. Pap.,* vol. 20, p. 313).

[75] Anchorena to Slacum, November 25, 1831 (*ibid.,* p. 314).

and he remonstrated against the decree of June 10, 1829, and all other acts past or future by which the Buenos Aires government might seek to impose restraints on the citizens of the United States engaged in fishing, or to impair their undoubted right to the freest use of the fisheries. This note he requested the ministry to receive as a formal protest against the seizures of Vernet.[76] Anchorena replied very coolly[77] that an inquiry was under way, but that he declined to admit Slacum's letter as a formal protest because it did not appear that he was specially authorized for the purpose, as he was merely a consul, and because the United States had obviously no rights, such as he claimed, upon which to found a protest. He added that he was willing to suppose Slacum was actuated by upright motives and that he trusted the case could be amicably settled.

Nothing could have been more calculated to create difficulties than Slacum's intemperate tone, and the rather insulting conclusion of Anchorena's reply. In the heated atmosphere so recklessly kindled, appeared the *deus ex machina* in the form of the U.S.S. *Lexington,* Commander Silas Duncan commanding. Slacum unbosomed himself to Duncan,[78] who replied that he regarded it his duty to proceed to the Falklands to protect American citizens.[79] This letter was communicated to the Buenos Aires government. As the reaction which Slacum hoped for did not occur, he again addressed Anchorena, informing him that Duncan's departure would be postponed until December 9 in order to await the receipt of a reply, "having reference to the immediate suspension of the right of capture of vessels of the United States," and ordering the restoration of property

[76] Slacum to Anchorena, November 26, 1831 (*ibid*).

[77] Anchorena to Slacum, December 3, 1831 (*ibid.,* p. 316).

[78] Slacum to Duncan, enclosed in Slacum to Livingston, December 9, 1831 (*MS. Desp., Arg.,* IV).

[79] Duncan to Slacum, December 1, 1831 (*Br. and For. St. Pap.,* vol. 20, p. 317).

taken. Slacum in conclusion insisted upon his right to protest.[80]

The dispatch of this ultimatum was the peak of Slacum's
indiscretion. His coadjutor, Duncan, true to the traditions
of navy diplomacy, on the next day entered upon his own
career as a diplomatic iconoclast by demanding the instant
surrender of Vernet for trial as a pirate and robber, or that
he be tried and punished by the laws of Buenos Aires.

It is very probable that Slacum's bold front and truculent
behavior was instigated by Woodbine Parish, the British
consul general. Shortly after the decree of June 10, 1829,
had been issued, the British consul had filed with the Buenos Aires foreign office a solemn protest against the occupation of the Falklands.[81] In this document he stated that
the Argentine Republic was assuming an authority incompatible with the rights of sovereignty of his Britannic Majesty over the Falkland Islands. These rights, he stated, had
not been invalidated by the withdrawal of his Majesty's
forces in 1774, as this measure had been taken in pursuance
of a system of retrenchment, and when withdrawal had been
effected marks of possession had been left, and all the formalities observed which indicated rights of ownership as
well as an intention to resume the occupation. The note
ended with a formal protest against the pretensions set up
by the government of Buenos Aires and any acts done to
the prejudice of the British rights of sovereignty.

Parish had received no more than a formal acknowledgment of his protest and for two years nothing further had
occurred. The present dispute between the United States
and Buenos Aires he no doubt saw as an opportunity to
turn things to his advantage. In any event, Parish informed
Slacum that the United Provinces had no legitimate claim
to the islands and coasts, and that Great Britain had never

[80] Slacum to Anchorena, December 6, 1831 (*ibid.,* p. 318).

[81] Parish to Guido, November 19, 1831 (*ibid.,* p. 346). On Parish *cf.*
Shuttleworth, *A Life of Sir Woodbine Parish* (1910), esp. p. 359.

given up her rights.[82] Of course, this information had the effect of stiffening Slacum's resistance to the "pretensions" of the Argentine government. At the same time as he hastened to report the matter to Washington, he supplied justification for his actions.

Anchorena did not reply to Slacum's ultimatum until after Duncan had sailed for the Falklands. The contents of his note, however, would scarcely have persuaded Duncan to remain in Buenos Aires.[83] Slacum was requested not to interfere in a matter which the government regarded as a private litigation. He was further notified that if the commander of the *Lexington* or any other person dependent on the United States government should commit any acts "tending to set at naught" the rights of the republic to the Falklands and the coasts adjacent to Cape Horn, a formal protest would be addressed to the United States government, and every means would be used to assert its rights and cause them to be respected.[84]

Duncan having departed, the United States consul turned to his British colleagues for comfort. The British minister, Fox, and Parish, the consul general, exhibited to Slacum the protest delivered two years before and advised him that they had filed this simply to keep alive a dormant right of which they intended to avail themselves when convenient. In reporting this interview to his government,[85] Slacum disclosed for the first time a sense of disquiet over what the English might possibly do. At the same time, he had gone too far in his protests to the Buenos Aires government to support in any way the right of the latter to the islands, and

[82] Slacum to Livingston, December 9, 1831 (*MS. Desp., Arg.,* IV).

[83] Anchorena to Slacum, December 9, 1831 (*Br. and For. St. Pap.,* vol. 20, p. 320).

[84] Anchorena also notified Slacum very sharply that he was not accredited as a chargé d'affaires, and requested that he therefore limit himself to his proper functions.

[85] Slacum to Livingston, December 20, 1831 (*MS. Desp., Arg.,* IV).

so he painted for his government a gloomy picture of what would happen to American trade if the Falklands remained in Argentine hands.[86]

In the meantime the *Lexington* had arrived off Puerto Soledad, and entered the harbor on December 28, 1831, under the French flag.[87] Before landing, Commander Duncan invited Vernet's lieutenants, Matthew Brisbane and Henry Metcalf, on board, holding prisoner the former but releasing the latter. Thereafter Duncan went ashore in force, spiked all the guns on the island, seized all weapons and burned all the powder. Not satisfied with this, he then sacked the habitations, seized some sealskins,[88] and put nearly all the inhabitants under arrest. He finally declared the island free of all government and sailed away with Brisbane and six Argentinians in irons.

It is curious that there is no notice of any of these transactions in the log book of the *Lexington*. Perhaps Duncan was a little ashamed of what he had done, or perhaps he feared the effect his actions would have upon his government. Nor was he too sure of the reactions of the United Provinces, for he anchored off Montevideo, the capital of the new state of Uruguay, and from there notified Slacum that he would liberate his prisoners if the government would

[86] Slacum to Anchorena, December 15, 1831 (*Br. and For. St. Pap.*, vol. 20, p. 322).

[87] *Apéndice á los documentos oficiales publicados sobre el asunto de Malvinas* (1832), for depositions on the conduct of Duncan.

[88] Davison *v.* Seal-skins, 2 *Paine* 324, where an action was brought to recover salvage on sealskins originally seized by Vernet and recaptured by Duncan, *held:* that an officer of the United States had no right in the absence of instructions forcibly to enter the jurisdiction of a friendly power and seize property. As it was proved Vernet was acting under authority of his government and Duncan's seizure was unlawful, a claim for salvage could not be sustained. However, in Williams *v.* Suffolk Insurance Company, 13 *Pet.* 415, in an action to recover a loss on the *Harriet* and her cargo incurred by the defendants, it was *held:* that the actions of the political department of the government in a matter which concerned it were conclusive, and could not be inquired into by the courts.

give assurances that they had been acting under its authority.[89] This assurance was given.[90]

The temper of the Buenos Aires government when the outrage on the Falklands became known can well be imagined. On February 14, 1832,[91] a public proclamation was issued apprising the people of what had happened, and the government pledged itself to secure satisfaction. Simultaneously Slacum was notified[92] that in view of the "aberration of ideas and irregularity of language in his official notes, and in view of the recent outrage, the government had judged it expedient to suspend all official communication with him, and requested he appoint a substitute." Slacum expressed[93] his surprise at these charges, and declined to appoint a successor on the ground that he had no authority. Had he hoped, however, to continue his functions, he was disappointed, for the government persisted in its refusal to deal with him.

The notice of the seizure of the *Harriet* and the other sealers had reached the United States some months before.[94] In his annual message of December 6, 1831,[95] President Jackson adverted to the incident, of which he could have known only the account brought by the escaped *Breakwater*. Jackson stated that the name of the republic of Buenos Aires had been used to cover with a show of authority acts

[89] The writer was privileged to examine the log of the *Lexington* in the Library of the Navy Department. See Duncan to Slacum, February 2, 1832, enclosed in Slacum to Livingston, February 25, 1832 (*MS. Desp., Arg.,* IV).

[90] Duncan to Slacum, February 11, 1832, and Garcia to Slacum, February 15, 1832, in *Br. and For. St. Pap.,* vol. 20, p. 328.

[91] Text in *ibid.,* p. 327.

[92] Garcia to Slacum, February 14, 1832 (*ibid.,* p. 326).

[93] Slacum to Garcia, February 16, 1832 (*ibid.,* p. 329).

[94] The notice was published in the Boston *Columbian Centinel,* September 25, 1832.

[95] Richardson, *Messages and Papers of the Presidents* (1896), vol. 2, p. 553.

injurious to American commerce. An American vessel, said he, engaged in a trade always enjoyed without molestation, had been captured by a band acting, "as they pretend," under the authority of the Buenos Aires government. He added that he had sent an armed vessel to the seas in question and would send a minister to inquire into the matter as well as into the claim, if any, set up by Buenos Aires to the islands. Meanwhile he submitted the matter to Congress in order that he might be clothed with means to provide a force adequate to the complete protection of American citizens fishing and trading in those seas.

It is strange that Jackson should have seen fit to address Congress on the subject before he had received Slacum's report and on the strength only of the story brought in by the *Breakwater*. His action, however, was characteristic of the man and of the tradition of blackguard diplomacy in South America initiated by his administration, and supplanting the aristocratic tradition of the Federalists and the Jeffersonian Democracy.[96] More than any other man, perhaps, Jackson was responsible for substituting an atmosphere of suspicion and ill will for the previous feelings of friendship and good will fostered by the American government. The person chosen by him to act as chargé d'affaires at Buenos Aires, a Massachusetts lawyer, Francis Baylies, was qualified to carry out the ideas of his superior, but he was temperamentally unsuited to a negotiation as delicate as the Falkland affair.

The instructions[97] given to Baylies regarding the seizures by Vernet were drawn by Edward Livingston, secretary of state. Copies of the Buenos Airean decree of June 10, 1829, had been forwarded to the Department of State by Vernet's

[96] The writer has been through all the correspondence of our representatives to the Hispanic-American states up to the year 1850, and has been convinced of the correctness of this view.

[97] Livingston to Baylies, January 26, 1832 (*MS. Insts. American States*, vol. 14, p. 235).

agent in Philadelphia, and yet the secretary of state did not hesitate at the very outset of his instruction to characterize the acts of Vernet as lawless and piratical. The proof that authority was lacking lay in the supposition that no government would authorize acts of this sort, and in the fact that Forbes had not reported the decree, which, said Livingston, had been issued during a civil war by a governor delegate who was shortly supplanted by revolution. At the time the decree was issued, wrote Livingston, the United States was on friendly terms with Buenos Aires and "it was known there that from the earliest period of our political existence our citizens engaged in the fisheries had resorted to the Falkland Islands for shelter, for such necessaries as it afforded, and for the purpose of carrying on their business on its shores. . . ." Believing the decree a mere pretense for piratical acts, the president had ordered the secretary of the navy to send all the force he could command to these regions to protect American citizens.[98]

All of this Baylies was directed to convey to the Buenos Airean government, and after explaining the attitude of the United States government, disavowal of Vernet, restoration of property and indemnity were to be demanded. The latter he was to require on the ground, first, that the United States had been in the actual use of the islands as a fishery for over fifty years. In consequence of this, capital had been invested and the United States had reasons to believe that it would be advised of any conflicting claim, particularly as the Buenos Airean government had permitted the use of the islands, and to make the first notice a seizure was in the nature of an hostile act. Furthermore, the reasoning supporting this was stronger if the matter were regarded as an action by an individual for his own benefit.

Livingston entered at some length into the question of notice, claiming that the decree had not been published[99]

---

[98] This sounded much fiercer than it actually turned out to be.
[99] It had been published. Livingston was wrong.

and even if it had been that the circumstances were such
that a special notice was necessary in view of the long use
of the Falklands. He added that even if publication were regarded as sufficient notice the decree was too vague in reference to what the regulations regarding fishing were, and to
whom these rules applied.

Following a discourse on the right of fishery and a
lengthy denial that any sovereignty had been exercised by
Spain over the Patagonian and Fuegian coasts to which the
new republic could be said to have been heir, Baylies was
ordered to press:

1. The perfect right of the United States to the free use of the
fishery—on the ocean, in every part of it, and on the bays, arms
of the sea, gulfs and other inlets which are incapable of being fortified. 2. To the same perfect right on the ocean within a marine
league of the shore, when the approach cannot be injurious to the
sovereign of the country as it can not be on the shores which are
possessed by savage tribes, or are totally deserted, as they are to
the south of the Rio Negro. 3. To the same use of the shores when
in the situation above described. 4. That even where a settlement is
made and other circumstances would deprive us of the right, a constant and uninterrupted use will give it to us.

Livingston added that the United States had always had
the use of the seal and whale fishery with the knowledge of
Spain, and, it was believed, particularly as regarded the
Falklands. Baylies was authorized to make a treaty on the
subject, to demand restitution of the seized vessels and, if
Vernet was disavowed, to order the commander of the
United States squadron to proceed to the Falklands to
break up the settlement and bring Vernet to Buenos Aires
for trial.

There can be no doubt that Livingston's claims regarding fisheries were colored largely by the state of that question between Great Britain and the United States.[100] The

[100] For a recent discussion *cf.* Balch, *Legal and Political Questions between Nations* (1924), p. 111.

Anglo-American fisheries question was, however, a matter that rested upon historical and legal antecedents which had absolutely no application to the fisheries of South America. It was idle to claim that any general rule could be deduced from the provisions of the Treaty of Utrecht regarding the Canadian fisheries. On the contrary, such provisions were special regulations affecting only the regions specified. In relation to South America, the evidence all pointed to a denial of the right as well as the use. As recently as 1803 Spain had made representations[101] regarding fishing of amphibia on the Spanish-American coasts and Madison had admitted the right of Spain to make regulations regarding the matter so long as the use of the seas and right of navigation were not interfered with. Furthermore, the Nootka Sound Convention had in no way extended general rights to all nations, but had limited the extension of right to Great Britain alone. Finally, we need only advert to the measures taken by Spain to enforce the convention in the Falklands and Patagonia to prove beyond a peradventure that neither the use of, nor the right to, fisheries in these regions had ever been conceded to the United States, nor admitted as a matter of law. Livingston's instruction was deliberately misrepresenting, not only in its statement of fact, but also in its delineation of the legal aspects of the matter. That it would not contribute essentially to the settlement of the dispute was a foregone conclusion.

Baylies reached Buenos Aires in June, 1832.[102] As soon as he was accredited as chargé d'affaires he dispatched to Don Manuel V. de Maza, the acting minister of foreign affairs, a note dealing with the Falkland affair.[103] In this document Baylies launched into a long account of the adventures of the American sealers recently captured and

---

[101] Moore, *Digest of International Law*, vol. 1, p. 875.

[102] Baylies to Livingston, June 20, 1832 (*MS. Desp., Arg.*, IV).

[103] Baylies to de Maza, June 20, 1832 (*Br. and For. St. Pap.*, vol. 20, p. 330).

specified with language surprisingly vigorous the whole catalogue of Vernet's sins. The most heinous of these appeared to him the arrangement by which Vernet had gotten the master of the *Superior* to join him in a sealing adventure, an act which Baylies characterized as a seduction of American seamen from their own flag. Some men of the *Superior* had been left on Staten Island before this contract was made and it was regarded as a particularly offensive act that Vernet had not allowed the vessel to go to their rescue. Baylies charged that Vernet had singled out the United States as his special victim, and had, on the other hand, favored the British. "A government," thundered the chargé d'affaires, "which justifies an officer who thus favors and spares one when both are in *pari delictu* must be considered as avowing a preference injurious and hostile to the nation which suffers."[104]

The decree under which Vernet had acted, continued Baylies, remained a dead letter until July, 1831, when the news of Forbes' demise reached the Falklands and depredations commenced—the implication of bad faith being obvious. The right of the United States to protest was clear, even if the acts had been within the limits of authority; he consequently demanded restitution of the property and reparation and indemnity both for the direct and the consequential injuries.

The fiery chargé had even a word to say for Slacum, in whose conduct he found nothing to justify his suspension. He therefore suggested that the consul be permitted to resume his functions.

To this violent communication, breathing fire and flame, de Maza[105] amiably replied that the charges made were so serious that they had been laid before the governor of the

---

[104] Groussac, *op. cit.*, p. 422, remarks ironically that Baylies was the "Old Hickory" type of envoy.

[105] De Maza to Baylies, June 25, 1832 (*Br. and For. St. Pap.*, vol. 20, p. 336).

province and that Vernet had been asked to give explanations of his public conduct. He promised that the governor
of Buenos Aires would discharge his duty without impair-
ment of the rights of United States citizens or without sacrificing to exorbitant pretensions the rights of Vernet, or
the public ones which by the law of nations belonged to the
Argentine Republic as a sovereign and independent state.

Perhaps this coolness irritated Baylies, for on the next
day he wrote de Maza that no explanations from Vernet
were needed. The injury was admitted and there remained
only the task of determining its magnitude. As for Argentine rights, these were not questioned, but the government
of the United States wished to know distinctly whether that
government claimed the right to molest or interrupt the
vessels of citizens of the United States fishing off the Falklands.

Two weeks passed and no reply was received. Baylies
thereupon decided to assist the deliberative processes of the
government by preparing a long note, dated July 10,[106]
which contained the gist of his instructions from Livingston, and a long and inaccurate excursus into the history of
the Falklands by which he sought to prove that the United
Provinces had no right to the islands. On the same day
(July 10) a note was dispatched by de Maza in which Baylies was told that the governor was trying to settle the matter equitably and therefore wished to have both sides of the
question. Upon receipt of this letter Baylies dispatched his
note of July 10.[107]

No reply having been forthcoming, Baylies addressed a
note to de Maza on August 6,[108] demanding an answer to his
question regarding the claim to the South Atlantic fisheries.
Two days later a note was dispatched by de Maza addressed

[106] Baylies to de Maza, July 10, 1832 (*ibid.*, p. 338).
[107] De Maza to Baylies, July 10, 1832 (*ibid.*, p. 355).
[108] Baylies to de Maza, August 6, 1832 (*ibid.*, p. 356).

452 THE STRUGGLE FOR THE FALKLANDS

to the secretary of state of the United States[109] which, although it dealt ostensibly only with the question of Slacum's conduct, was inferentially a defense of the Argentine position. The seizure and trial of the *Harriet*, wrote de Maza, was an internal question, and the right of the Argentine government to treat it as such arose from the fact of its absolute jurisdiction over the regions formerly a part of the viceroyalty of Buenos Aires. This note was followed by a communication dated August 14, 1832, addressed to Baylies,[110] announcing that Governor Rosas had examined the documents of the case and had reached a decision. Baylies was then told that his question regarding the claim to fishery rights was looked upon as an attempt to sidestep the main issue, which was the outrage of Commander Duncan on the Falkland colony. Characterizing Duncan's conduct as barbarous and ferocious, de Maza declared roundly that even if Vernet's acts had been unauthorized they were not an offense against international law, and in no case justified the violence used against the colony. In view of the utterly illegal character of the raid of the *Lexington*, de Maza demanded prompt and ample satisfaction, reparation and indemnity for all losses and damages, and he declined to discuss any of the other points raised by Baylies until this demand was granted.

Accompanying de Maza's note was a long and detailed report by Vernet,[111] which disclosed a knowledge of history and international law unusual for the time, particularly in a man who made no pretense of being a scholar. This document was forthwith returned by Baylies, and at the same time the chargé demanded his passports.

No sooner had Baylies made this demand than he addressed Livingston, advising him of what had happened[112]

[109] De Maza to Livingston, August 8, 1832 (*ibid.*, p. 358).
[110] De Maza to Baylies, August 14, 1832 (*ibid.*, p. 364).
[111] *Ibid.*, p. 369.
[112] Baylies to Livingston, August 13, 1832 (*MS. Desp., Arg.*, IV).

and explaining in a private letter[113] that the report of Vernet had been returned because he did not wish to place the United States in the position of a litigating party as against Vernet before the Argentine tribunals. He further advised Livingston that he believed the government desired war as a means of uniting the country.

Shortly after his demand for passports had been made Baylies was invited to an interview with the minister of foreign affairs.[114] This took place on August 27. De Maza opened the conference[115] by stating that he had invited Baylies because he desired to clear up points of misunderstanding, the first of which was the return of Vernet's report. Baylies explained his position, and the foreign minister indignantly denied he had had any idea of making the United States a private litigant, and that the enclosure of the report made it a part of the official note. Baylies insisted upon his own view and added that, as reparation had been asked for Duncan's attack before other matters would be discussed and as he was uninstructed on the subject, he deemed his further stay unnecessary and hence was obliged to demand passports. De Maza thereupon observed that Baylies had declared himself fully authorized and hence he could see no reason for breaking off the negotiation. He pursued his argument with great force of reasoning and he suggested that Baylies get new instructions. Thereafter if the matter could not be concluded de Maza would send a minister to the United States. As a final resort a third power could be called in.

Baylies asked whom he had in mind, to which de Maza replied that he merely made the suggestion to show that the

[113] Baylies to Livingston, August 19, 1832 (private letter) (*MS. Desp., Arg.*, IV).

[114] Baylies to Livingston, September 5, 1832 (*MS. Desp., Arg.*, IV).

[115] The Argentine minute is in *Br. and For. St. Pap.*, vol. 20, p. 437. The United States minute is enclosed in Baylies to Livingston, September 5, 1832 (*MS. Desp., Arg.*, IV). It was made by a United States citizen, J. D. Mendenhall.

negotiation was not yet in a state where passports need be demanded. There were, he said, two questions at issue— one of fact and one of right, the first related to Duncan's action, and this had to be settled before the question of right could be discussed. The conference ended at this juncture, as Baylies stubbornly insisted upon his passports.[116] All further efforts to renew conferences were likewise rejected by the chargé d'affaires.[117]

Baylies embarked for the United States the latter part of September, 1832.[118] He was undoubtedly convinced that further negotiation would be fruitless. He reported to Livingston that the assumption of a right to capture American fishermen precluded all candid discussion and left the United States "no hope of redress and no option but humiliation."

Before leaving Buenos Aires, Baylies had a conference with Mr. Fox, the British minister. He advised the latter that the United States laid no claim to the regions in dispute except as to the right of fishery, which would be maintained against the British as well as the Argentine government. He then asked Fox whether Great Britain, after giving notice to the United States of her sovereign right to the Falklands, would justify her countenancing a horde of pirates on the islands for the purpose of annoying American commerce. If this were so the United States would have cause to complain of unfriendly treatment. Fox replied that he had prepared a remonstrance against the occupation of the islands; and as the Argentine government had sent a frigate to the Falklands Baylies assumed that Great Britain would take action.

[116] *Ibid.*

[117] Slacum, who was being sought by the local police, found asylum in the chargé's house and was made private secretary to the American mission, this giving him immunity and the chance to return to the United States. *Br. and For. St. Pap.*, vol. 20, pp. 440-444.

[118] Baylies to Livingston, September 26, 1832 (*MS. Desp., Arg.*, IV).

Whether or not Baylies' indiscreet admissions to Fox on the attitude of the United States had any effect upon British policy it is difficult to say. Baylies' withdrawal had indicated the greatest coolness between the two American republics, and the message of the government to the legislature of the provinces transmitting the correspondence confirmed this impression.[119] The situation was such that any diplomatic support of the Argentine Republic by the United States was unlikely.

The posture of affairs being thus favorable to British designs, two warships, the *Clio* and the *Tyne,* were dispatched to the Falklands. The *Clio* first put in at Port Egmont, arriving on December 20, 1832. Commander Onslow attempted to repair the ruins of the old fort, affixed a notice of possession, and on January 2, 1833, appeared at Port Luis (formerly Puerto Soledad). Here was anchored the *Sarandi,* an armed schooner of the Argentine Republic which had brought to the islands Don Juan Esteban Mestivier,[120] the new governor. The *Sarandi* was commanded by Don José Maria Pinedo, who had just succeeded in putting down a revolt of the colonists which had resulted in the murder of the governor. Onslow called upon Pinedo and explained to him that he had come to take possession in the name of his Britannic Majesty. That same day he served on Pinedo a written notice that he had been ordered to exercise the rights of sovereignty over the islands, and that he would the next morning raise the British flag. He requested Pinedo to lower the Argentine flag and depart.

Pinedo at once waited upon Onslow, uttering vain protests against the outrage. He declared roundly he would never lower the Argentine flag. The next morning, however, a force was landed, the British flag was raised, the Argen-

[119] Text in *Br. and For. St. Pap.,* vol. 20, p. 311.
[120] The revolt appears to have been among the soldiers of the garrison. Mestivier was a Frenchman.

tine ensign was struck and subsequently delivered to the *Sarandi*.

Dismay greeted the arrival of this intelligence in Buenos Aires.[121] De Maza at once addressed the British chargé, Mr. Philip G. Gore, stating that the act of Onslow compromised the honor and dignity of the Argentine Republic and demanding explanations.[122] Gore replied next day that he was uninstructed.[123] De Maza thereupon filed a formal protest against the British occupation and the insult to his flag, and requested that the communication be forwarded to the British government.[124] Two days later a full account of the affair was submitted to the legislature, together with a promise to obtain an acknowledgment from Great Britain of the Argentine right to the Falklands and full reparation for the injury.

To Don Manuel Moreno, minister plenipotentiary to the Court of St. James, was entrusted the task of securing satisfaction. On April 24, 1833,[125] he addressed Lord Palmerston, inquiring whether orders had been actually given by the British government to expel the Buenos Airean garrison, and whether the declaration of possession made by Onslow was authorized. Palmerston replied on April 27 that this was correct.

After a delay of some weeks Moreno transmitted his protest.[126] In the main it relied upon Vernet's "Report" for its historical facts. The rights of Spain, to which the Argentine government was said to have succeeded, were, he asserted, based upon prior occupation and purchase from France, and by the abandonment of England. The discovery

[121] Message of the government to the House of Representatives, January 24, 1833 (*Br. and For. St. Pap.*, vol. 20, p. 1194).

[122] De Maza to Gore, January 16, 1833 (*ibid.*, p. 1197).

[123] Gore to de Maza, January 17, 1833 (*ibid.*, p. 1198).

[124] De Maza to Gore, January 22, 1833 (*ibid.*).

[125] Groussac, *op. cit.*, p. 444.

[126] Moreno to Palmerston, June 17, 1833 (*Br. and For. St. Pap.*, vol. 23, p. 1366).

of the islands was too much in doubt to form the basis of any title. Moreno entered into a long discussion of the incident of 1770-1771, and insisted that the abandonment of the British was in pursuance of a secret promise, and hence an abandonment *animo derelinquendi*. But, alas, in support of this he could cite only secondary works and the vaguest of rumors. His argument that the abandonment in fact must raise a presumption of abandonment in law was weighted with good reasoning, but the protest with which he concluded his note was the empty wail of one who knows he has lost.

Such, indeed, was the case. Nearly six months elapsed before the British foreign minister replied.[127] He pointed out coldly that Parish's protest of 1829 had been ignored by the Argentine Republic, and that there was consequently no reason to expect that the British government would silently submit to the continued usurpation of sovereignty over the Falklands by the Argentine Republic. The claim of Great Britain to sovereignty, said Palmerston, had been unequivocally asserted and maintained in the discussions with Spain in 1770 and 1771, and Spain had ended the discussions by restoring the British to the places from which the British had been expelled; "the Government of the United Provinces could not reasonably have anticipated that the British Government would permit any other state to exercise a right as derived from Spain which Great Britain had denied to Spain itself."

This fact, the note went on to state, was enough to justify the British government in refraining from any explanations on a question decisively determined over a half century ago. Nevertheless, as Moreno's charge, supported by unauthentic publications[128] not entitled to weight, involved an imputation against the good faith of Great Britain, the

---

[127] Palmerston to Moreno, January 8, 1834 (*ibid.*, p. 1384).

[128] He relied chiefly on *Anecdotes of William Pitt, Earl of Chatham*, vol. 3, chapter 39.

whole official correspondence of the period had been tran-
scribed and was forwarded. These papers, said Palmerston
in conclusion, contained no allusion to any secret understanding, but on the contrary afforded a conclusive inference that no such secret understanding could have existed.
Consequently, it was trusted, Moreno would see that his
note was prompted by an erroneous impression. The Argentine government would without doubt, when the true circumstances of the case were called to its attention, no
longer call in question the right of sovereignty exercised
by his Britannic Majesty as undoubtedly belonging to the
crown.

It is scarcely necessary to point out the obvious errors of
Palmerston's note. Shelburne's policy of having no embar-
rassing papers in the archives was at length fully justified,
and the British government could continue to hold the Falklands with a clear conscience; for who would charge Lord
Palmerston with knowledge of something his predecessors
had taken pains he should never know? The Argentine government, poor and wracked with civil war, had neither the
means to establish its claim nor the power. It is true that
Moreno, on December 29, 1834,[129] attempted to reopen the
question and finally, some seven years later, renewed his
claim, asserting that the statements of Palmerston were incorrect and that no proof had been adduced that the island
of Soledad (East Falkland) had ever belonged to Great
Britain, but that on the contrary this island had been in the
undisputed possession of Spain for a half century.[130] But
even this feeble attempt to save at least a single island
failed, for Lord Aberdeen, after acknowledging receipt of
the note, advised the Argentine envoy that the British government did not recognize that the United Provinces had

[129] Argentine Republic, Ministerio de Relaciones Exteriores, *Memoria,*
1888, p. 76.
[130] Moreno to Aberdeen, December 18, 1841 (*Br. and For. St. Pap.,* vol.
31, p. 1003).

any right to alter an agreement concluded between England and Spain forty years before their emancipation. As far as her sovereignty over the Falklands was concerned Great Britain regarded this arrangement as definitive and, as she was about to arrange the permanent colonization of the group, Moreno was advised that her determination did not permit any infraction of her incontestable rights.[131] Moreno had one more unsuccessful conference with Lord Aberdeen, and as a final gesture deposited a passionate note of protest against the British acts. But the British government regarded the matter as closed, and so the Falklands have to this day remained a British possession, and the patriotic Argentine, heedless of their bleakness and desolation, bemoans them as some unforgettable *terra irredenta*.

[131] Aberdeen to Moreno, December 29, 1841, *ibid.,* p. 1005. For Aberdeen's final reply of March 5, 1842, *cf.* Argentine Republic, Ministerio de Relaciones Exteriores, *Memoria,* 1888, p. 143. Moreno's reply was dated March 8, 1842.

CONCLUSION

WHEN Lord Palmerston, with his inimitable air of indignant self-righteousness, denied the charges of bad faith and rejected the Argentine claim, he sounded the death knell of the demands for indemnity on account of the raid of the *Lexington*. After Baylies' return to Washington the news of Onslow's expedition and the seizure of the Falklands reached the ears of the United States government. There was, however, nothing said of a violation of the Monroe Doctrine. It was convenient that the Falklands should be regarded as a pre-Revolutionary possession of Great Britain to which the doctrine naturally had no application. The Jackson administration, it is true, addressed an inquiry to the Spanish government to ascertain whether the Falklands had been a part of the viceroyalty of Buenos Aires and whether there was any evidence of a secret treaty by which the British had surrendered their claims to the Falklands. This inquiry was submitted to the historian Navarrete,[1] who replied that the Falklands had appertained to the viceroyalty of Buenos Aires, but as far as a secret agreement was concerned, he had not seen one; if it really existed it must be in the archives of the secretariat of state. This answer was sufficiently non-committal to have excited the interest of the United States government in further investigation. But this did not occur, although a slight attempt at conciliation with the Argentines was undertaken.

John Forsyth, Jackson's new secretary of state, on the occasion of sending a new consul to Buenos Aires addressed the Buenos Airean minister of foreign affairs on July 29, 1834,[2] expressing his regret that no minister had been ap-

---

[1] Cited in Quesada, *op. cit.*, p. 200.

[2] Forsyth to Buenos Aires Minister of Foreign Affairs, July 29, 1834, enclosed in Dorr to Forsyth, November 27, 1834 (*State Dept., MS. Consular Letters, Buenos Ayres*, IV).

pointed by the confederation and stating that the president was willing to listen to any communication from the Argentine government in a spirit of conciliation. To this the minister of foreign affairs replied that unexpected delays had intervened to prevent the appointment of a minister, but Dorr, the new consul, advised the Department of State that the outcome of negotiations with Great Britain was holding up the appointment. He likewise reported the inexpediency of attempting to appoint a diplomatic representative under the existing conditions.[3]

Manuel Moreno was finally appointed minister to the United States,[4] but as he declined the appointment General Alvear was named in his stead.[5] Alvear delayed his departure for some months, as the political situation of the confederation was most parlous. General Rosas,[6] who, some years before, had been made dictator, had at this moment decided to declare war on Peru and Bolivia.[7] The exigencies of national defense had led to an attempt to compel domiciled aliens to perform military service, a decision which brought the Argentine government into collision with the French, who, in March, 1838, blockaded the La Plata. These circumstances probably dictated the necessity of an accommodation with the United States, and Alvear accordingly left on his mission in the middle of the year.

Alvear forthwith presented the claim of his government[8] for the losses sustained by the raid of the *Lexington*. He

[3] Dorr to Forsyth, January 17, 1835 (*ibid.*).

[4] Dorr to Forsyth, November 21, 1835 (*ibid.*) ; and March 14, 1836 (*MS. Consular Letters, Buenos Ayres,* V).

[5] Dorr to Forsyth, June 5, 1836 (*ibid.*) ; June 30, 1837 (*ibid.*).

[6] Rosas was one of the extraordinary figures of the time. He is described by Watterson as "a real General Jackson of a fellow." Watterson to Secretary of State, April 27, 1844 (*MS. Desp., Arg.,* V).

[7] Dorr to Forsyth, May 19, 1837, enclosing the manifesto (*MS. Consular Letters, Buenos Ayres,* V).

[8] As stated in 1884, the basic amount of the claim was for Vernet's losses, figured at 207,728 *pesos fuertes* (*i.e.,* metallic currency).

was advised by Daniel Webster, secretary of state, on December 4, 1841,[9] that the right of the Argentine government to jurisdiction over the Falklands being contested by another power upon grounds of claim long antecedent to the acts of Captain Duncan, it was conceived that the United States ought not to give a final answer until the controversy was settled, as such an answer would, under the circumstances, involve a departure from what had hitherto been considered as the cardinal policy of the United States government.[10]

It will be observed that just as the dispute over Vernet's acts and the withdrawal of Baylies had furnished Great Britain an excellent opportunity to carry out her seizure of the Falklands without interference by the United States, so the British acts supplied a convenient excuse for the United States government to avoid the disagreeable pecuniary consequences of Commander Duncan's exploit. There was no need to disavow the latter and there was no need to protest against the British occupation.[11] The affair of the *Lexington* could remain suspended in mid-air, like the coffin of the Prophet, until the Anglo-Argentine dispute had been finally determined.

This policy has been consistently maintained by the

---

[9] Webster to Alvear, December 4, 1841, in Webster, *Writings and Speeches* (National ed., 1903), vol. 14, p. 371. Also in Moore, *Digest of International Law.*

[10] He had reference to the policy of non-intervention.

[11] In 1853 the British government notified the United States of its intention to send a force to the Falklands to prevent depredations. A warning was consequently issued by the Department of State to all vessels. Subsequently an American vessel was seized and then released. The Department of State complained of the seizure and intimated it did not regard the question of sovereignty as settled. To this the British government expressed great surprise and stated it did and would continue to exercise acts of sovereignty over the islands. A claim for damages was prepared but never presented. *Cf. Sen. Exec. Doc.* 19, 42d Congress, 2d session. Also Moore, *Digest of International Law,* vol. 1, p. 888.

United States. When a few years later an effort was made to settle outstanding claims between the two countries, the Argentine government was notified that the Falkland claims[12] would be excluded on the ground that the question of the jurisdiction was still undetermined.

The same stand was taken in 1884,[13] after the claim had been renewed by Sr. Luis L. Dominguez, the Argentine minister. President Cleveland adverted to the claim in his annual message (December, 1885) as follows:[14]

The Argentine Government has revived the long dormant question of the Falkland Islands by claiming from the United States indemnity for their loss attributed to the action of the commander of the sloop of war *Lexington* in breaking up a piratical colony on those islands in 1831 and their subsequent occupation by Great Britain. In view of the ample justification for the act of the *Lexington* and the derelict condition of the islands before and after their alleged occupation by Argentine colonials this Government considers the claim as wholly groundless.

Cleveland had been badly advised when he drew up this remarkable statement of fact. Dominguez' successor, Dr. Vincente G. Quesada, did not hesitate to inform the Department of State very tactfully to this effect.[15] In the reply of Mr. Bayard, secretary of state, dated March 18, 1886,[16] the view previously taken was reiterated, *i.e.*, that the question of the liability of the United States for Commander Duncan's acts was so closely related to the question of the sovereignty over the Falklands, that the decision of the former would inevitably be interpreted as an expression of opinion

[12] Brent to Calhoun, January 28, 1845 (*MS. Desp., Arg.*, V).

[13] *Cf.* Argentine Republic, Ministerio de Relaciones Exteriores, *Memoria*, 1885, p. 126 *et seq.; ibid.*, 1886, p. 48 *et seq.; ibid.*, 1887, p. 193 *et seq.* The notes referred to below are also to be found here.

[14] Richardson, *op. cit.*, vol. 8, p. 325.

[15] Quesada to Bayard, December 9, 1885, in Quesada, *op. cit.*, p. 207.

[16] Bayard to Quesada, March 18, 1886, in Moore, *Digest of International Law*, vol. 1, p. 889.

on the merits of the latter question. This the United States desired to avoid. Furthermore, the Monroe Doctrine did not apply, as its terms expressly excluded any retroactive operation, and even if it had applied to the case the government of the United States would not regard its failure to assert the doctrine as constituting a basis of liability for injuries sustained by another power in consequence of the omission. In conclusion Mr. Bayard asserted that even if it could be shown that the Argentine government possessed sovereignty over the islands there were ample grounds on which Duncan's conduct could be defended.

Enough has been said to indicate that the latter portion of Bayard's note was scarcely the result of an impartial examination of the record. That Duncan's acts were in themselves cruel and indefensible cannot be denied, particularly as at the moment the Argentine Confederation was unquestionably exercising sovereignty over the islands. It is difficult to understand upon what grounds the raid of the *Lexington* can be justified unless Mr. Bayard meant to hint that he regarded the Argentine claim of sovereignty as baseless in law. With the main point of Bayard's note, however, there can be no quarrel. The settlement of the Argentine claim against the United States depended upon the question of sovereignty, for in the last analysis the justification of Vernet depended upon the official quality of his acts, lacking which Duncan could properly treat his colony as beyond the pale of law.

In a long and able reply to Bayard Quesada reviewed at length the history of the islands and the claims of the Argentine government. In the main his historical relation was drawn from the earlier note of Moreno to Palmerston, and Vernet's "Report." As far as it went it was accurate, but it left out entirely the essential portions of the Anglo-Spanish negotiations related in the last chapters. Needless to say his animadversions were without effect.

About the same time the diplomatic exchange just narrated took place,[17] the Argentine government, on the occasion of a discussion over an alleged official map of the Patagonian region, renewed its representations to Great Britain over the continued occupation of the Falklands. But even this belated protest found no sympathetic response—each side continued to assert its rights, but the stronger power continued to hold the islands.

It is proper at this juncture briefly to summarize the legal merits of the claims of both sides. The British claim, based originally upon the so-called right of discovery and subsequent occupation, now rests, as a result of Lord Aberdeen's note of December, 1841, upon the declaration and counter-declaration of 1771, which, it is alleged, was a definite determination of the rights of both parties. Regarding the basis of the prior claim of right enough has been said to establish that discovery up to the year 1764 never had been regarded as furnishing the least ground on which a right to territory could be asserted, and, even if it had, the whole hierarchy of European treaties from 1667 to 1763 excluded the British from asserting such a right in the region under discussion. The only ground on which title could be based was the *de facto* occupation of the discovered territory, and in the present instance this had been effected by France, through whom Spain claimed by virtue of the surrender of France's rights. As between Spain and Great Britain, therefore, the equities lay with the former power.

The effect of the declaration of 1771, had it not been accompanied by the verbal promise to withdraw, would have been to throw the question of right into the *status quo ante* June 10, 1770, when Port Egmont was seized. In other words, it would have been governed by the existing European treaties and the principles of occupation at that time applied in international practice. The promise to evacuate, however, once it was executed, raised a presumption that

[17] The correspondence is in Argentine Republic, Ministerio de Relaciones Exteriores, *Memoria,* 1885, p. 233 *et seq.; ibid.,* 1888, p. 29 *et seq.*

the abandonment was *animo derelinquendi,* a presumption strengthened by the fact that Spain without protest from England exercised acts of sovereignty for years to come not only over the island of Soledad, but also over the *Gran Malvina,* on which the British colony had been. This *prima facie* presumption of abandonment became a definite presumption of law when the Nootka Sound Convention was signed and Great Britain recognized the existing Spanish occupations and agreed not to plant colonies to the south of them unless some third state should attempt so to do. The Spanish right to the Falklands became absolute at this moment, if, indeed, it had not been so before.

For Aberdeen to assert that the declaration of 1771 fixed the rights of the parties gave the lie to the very provisions of the instrument itself, for it confessedly was only an act of satisfaction which left the question of right untouched. The transactions surrounding the conclusion of the arrangement all testify to the correctness of this view. But even if the propriety of Lord Aberdeen's view were admitted and the declaration were regarded as fixing the rights of the parties, there was nothing in the instrument which would in any way derogate from the right of Spain to the island of Soledad. In other words, if the rights were actually fixed by this declaration then the British were given a right only to Port Egmont and the Spanish claim to Soledad was impliedly recognized. Every reason which would support the argument of Lord Aberdeen supports as well the claim of Spain to the eastern island.

There remains to be considered the question of the Argentine succession to Spanish rights and claims. The fundamental principle of territorial arrangements in South America is the so-called *uti possidetis* of 1810.[18] By this principle is understood the claim of the several republics carved out of the Spanish colonial empire to the regions

---

[18] Quesada, *Derecho Internacional Latino-Americano* (1918), p. 95 *et seq.*

embraced in the former Spanish administrative units. Thus the limits of the captaincy general of Chile were the boundaries of the new republic of Chile, and the limits of the Buenos Aires viceroyalty were taken as those of the Argentine Confederation. That the Falklands formed a part of this viceroyalty there can be no doubt; the mere fact that they were ultimately put under the same governorship with the South Patagonian settlements is sufficient proof of the fact. This principle would sustain a claim of sovereignty as against all other South American states. It is immaterial whether or not it would sustain a claim as against Great Britain, for in this connection the Argentine claim is supported by the practice of nations in matters that have been generally called questions of state succession.[19]

Briefly stated, the prevailing doctrine of state succession is that where a new state is formed of preëxisting body politic, either by secession or by the union of formerly sovereign states, the new state succeeds in certain instances to the rights and obligations of the mother state. In the case of violent secession, the accepted theory is that the new state, being an independent organism and having achieved its status by force of arms, does not succeed *eo ipso* to all the obligations or rights of the parent state. Treaties are not necessarily assumed, and failing special arrangement the financial obligations of the parent state do not pass to the new entity. In the matter of territory the sovereignty of the new state extends to those regions which in fact it controls successfully against the parent state. If this is not settled by treaty, the *de facto* exercise of sovereignty is the decisive factor. The question of succession to territory is therefore merely a question of power as between the new state and the parent state.[20]

That the passage of control of territory from the old to

[19] Schönborn, *Staatensukzession* (1913); Huber, *Die Staatensuccession* (1898).

[20] Schönborn, *op. cit.*, p. 80 *et seq.*

the new state involves what we may, for want of a better term, call the collateral equities, goes without saying. The new state takes the territory subject to all claims by third parties and in respect to the defense of its own rights it stands in the shoes of the former holder. No principle of law is better settled. It has been applied in many instances, and no one today would seriously question the doctrine.[21]

If we apply this principle to the case of the Falklands, it is obvious that the British notion that the Argentine Confederation could not have an interest in a cause settled between England and Spain is totally without legal foundation. The right of the Argentine nation to stand in the place of Spain with reference to the sovereignty over the Falklands was established by the successful revolution, and by the assertion and maintenance of sovereignty over the Falklands as against Spain. When Great Britain seized the islands in the year 1833 the legal consequences were the same as if the islands had never passed out of the hands of the Spanish crown.

There is a certain futility in interposing the lean and ascetic visage of the law in a situation which first and last is merely a question of power. Nevertheless, the present masters of the Falklands have called upon the law to testify to the justice of their acts, and it is but proper, therefore, that what this law is should be fairly set forth and understood. This it has been sought to do in the preceding pages, not with the anticipation that the facts narrated will necessarily alter the situation, or that a wrong will be righted, but because the law which states have so painstakingly wrought to govern their relations is too precious a heritage to be suborned to cover the imperialistic designs of any nation.

[21] A striking example of this is to be found in the arbitration of the *Misiones* dispute between Argentine and Brazil.

List of Manuscript Abbreviations

England

R. O. State Papers, Spain   Public Record Office, London, State
R. O. State Papers, France   Papers; listed by countries.
Addit. MSS.   British Museum, Additional manuscripts.

France

Aff. Etr., Espagne   Archives of the French Ministry of
Aff. Etr., Angleterre   Foreign Affairs; listed by countries.

Aff. Etr. Mém. et Doc.   Archives of the French Ministry of Foreign Affairs, Mémoirs et Documents.

Spain

Arch. Gen. Sim. Est.   Archivo General, Simancas (Spain), Estado; state papers listed by bundle and folio.

Archivo Histórico Nacional   National historical archives at Madrid.

United States

L. C. MSS.   Manuscripts in the Library of Congress, Manuscripts Division, at Washington, D. C.

MS. Desp., Arg.   Manuscript diplomatic despatches (here, from United States' representatives in the Argentine) in the Department of State at Washington, D. C.; listed by countries.

MS. Insts., American States   Manuscript Instructions to diplomatic representatives, in the Department of State; listed by geographic divisions.

MS. Consular Letters   Manuscript letters from U. S. consuls abroad, in the Department of State; listed by consulates.

INDEX